A NATION WITHIN

In *A Nation Within*, Ezra Rosser explores the connection between land-use patterns and development in the Navajo Nation. Roughly the size of Ireland or West Virginia, the Navajo reservation has seen successive waves of natural resource-based development over the last century: grazing and over-grazing, oil and gas, uranium, and coal; yet Navajos continue to suffer from high levels of unemployment and poverty. Rosser shows the connection between the exploitation of these resources and the growth of the tribal government before turning to contemporary land use and development challenges. He argues that, in addition to the political challenges associated with any significant change, external pressures and internal corruption have made it difficult for the tribe to implement land reforms that could help provide space for economic development that would benefit the Navajo Nation and Navajo tribal members.

Ezra Rosser is Professor of Law at American University Washington College of Law where he teaches Fedcral Indian Law, Property Law, Land Use, and Poverty Law. A graduate of Yale, Harvard, and the University of Cambridge, Ezra is a non-Indian who grew up, in part, on the Navajo Nation.

A Nation Within

NAVAJO LAND AND ECONOMIC DEVELOPMENT

EZRA ROSSER

American University

CAMBRIDGE
UNIVERSITY PRESS

CAMBRIDGE
UNIVERSITY PRESS

University Printing House, Cambridge CB2 8BS, United Kingdom

One Liberty Plaza, 20th Floor, New York, NY 10006, USA

477 Williamstown Road, Port Melbourne, VIC 3207, Australia

314–321, 3rd Floor, Plot 3, Splendor Forum, Jasola District Centre,
New Delhi – 110025, India

103 Penang Road, #05–06/07, Visioncrest Commercial, Singapore 238467

Cambridge University Press is part of the University of Cambridge.

It furthers the University's mission by disseminating knowledge in the pursuit of
education, learning, and research at the highest international levels of excellence.

www.cambridge.org
Information on this title: www.cambridge.org/9781108833936
DOI: 10.1017/9781108987585

© Ezra Rosser 2021

First published 2021

A catalogue record for this publication is available from the British Library.

Library of Congress Cataloging-in-Publication Data
NAMES: Rosser, Ezra, author.
TITLE: A nation within : Navajo land and economic development / Ezra Rosser, American
University, Washington DC.
DESCRIPTION: Cambridge, United Kingdom ; New York, NY : Cambridge University Press,
2021. | Includes index.
IDENTIFIERS: LCCN 2021012266 (print) | LCCN 2021012267 (ebook) | ISBN 9781108833936
(hardback) | ISBN 9781108987585 (ebook)
SUBJECTS: LCSH: Law and economic development – Navajo Nation, Arizona, New Mexico
& Utah. | Navajo Nation, Arizona, New Mexico & Utah – Economic conditions. | Navajo
Indians – Economic conditions.
CLASSIFICATION: LCC KIK1074 . R67 2021 (print) | LCC KIK1074 (ebook) | DDC 343.791/
3070899726–dc23
LC record available at https://lccn.loc.gov/2021012266
LC ebook record available at https://lccn.loc.gov/2021012267

ISBN 978-1-108-83393-6 Hardback
ISBN 978-1-108-98744-8 Paperback

To my mother, Norma Cady
&
To my father, James Rosser, and his wife, Zelma King

Contents

Contents

Illustrations

Preface

The translation my stepmother gives for the Navajo word "Bilagáana" is "white people, the other, or the enemy." Navajo-English dictionaries tend to use a more neutral definition. But I have always felt that the more pointed definition given by my dad's second wife, Zelma King, who for years taught written and spoken Navajo, was more accurate. At the very least, it better captures my experiences as an outsider who grew up in small part on the Navajo Nation. Tellingly, the Navajo word for themselves, Diné, means "the people" and is a term that does not include Bilagáanas.

I love the Navajo Nation, but my love is that of an outsider. It has its limits and frustrations. My wife likes to remind me that her love for our sons is unconditional but her love for me is without limits but conditional. The same can be said of my affection for the reservation. I both love and get annoyed by the vastness of the land, the long distances one can drive between towns and between grocery stores. I stand in awe at both the strength of some of the tribal leaders and the transparent selfishness of others. Perhaps more than anything else, my outsider status manifests itself in my conflicting desires: when I am away from the reservation, I often feel that I should return to it and that I don't belong in the privileged white world where I work, and when I am on the reservation, I often feel that I should escape it because the reservation is a place I visit but has never truly been my home.

Being an outsider undoubtedly influences my understanding of the Navajo Nation and the arguments found in this book.[1] In perhaps the single greatest book on Indian issues, *Custer Died for Your Sins: An Indian Manifesto*, Vine Deloria, Jr. dedicated an entire chapter to "Anthropologists and Other Friends." In a scathing, and quite funny, critique, Deloria skewered the often well-meaning scholarly outsiders who descend onto Indian reservations to conduct research. Deloria began, "Into each life, it is said, some rain must fall. . . . But Indians have been cursed above all other people in history. Indians have anthropologists."[2] He went on to explain that the researchers who invade every summer come with conclusions already formed and are indifferent to the practical consequences of their research.[3] Scholarship about Indians not only created false narratives regarding the nature of Indians, but Deloria wrote, "Academia, and its by-products, continues to become more irrelevant to the needs of the people."[4] Deloria argued that Indians "should not be objects of observation for those who do nothing to help us."[5] He ends by urging researchers "to get down from their thrones of authority and pure research and begin helping Indian tribes instead of preying on them."[6]

I first read *Custer Died for Your Sins* in graduate school in England, as far removed from the reservation as I had ever been, and I remember simultaneously laughing aloud in the library and being deeply troubled about what his insights meant for me personally. It was not until I met Professor Robert A. Williams, Jr., an Indian law scholar and member of the Lumbee Tribe, that I decided to become an Indian law scholar myself. As a non-Indian, but someone committed to working to improve the lives of people living on the Navajo reservation, it can be very difficult to figure out the best role to assume and career to pursue. I was all too aware of the challenges of being a Bilagáana on the reservation.

When Diné introduce themselves, they traditionally start by telling others the clans to which they belong. These fairly long introductions serve to place the speaker in the Diné social world and to establish connections between the people talking. If I was a member of the Navajo tribe, it might be enough for me to note my tribal membership. But given that my outsider status is so important, it is worth describing fully the extent and limits of my connection to the Navajo Nation. I was born in Fairplay, Colorado and by the time I was eight, my parents had lived in Colorado, Missouri, and Iowa. Following their divorce and a final custody determination just before I started fourth grade, my mother moved to Durango, Colorado to be a bus driver and my father moved to the nearest town where he could find work as a teacher, Kayenta, Arizona. For the next three years, I went to school in Durango, a somewhat distant removed border town, and my brother and I were shuttled the three-hour drive to Kayenta, a town well within the Navajo Nation, for weekend and summer stays with my father. Then in seventh grade, my brother and I lived with my father and his new Navajo wife in Kayenta while my mother got situated in her new job, working as an environmental planner for the tribe. She lived in Gallup, New Mexico in a tiny apartment on a hill overlooking the town and worked in Window Rock, the capital of the Navajo Nation. In eighth grade, my brother and I lived just outside of Window Rock in a partially-completed house before my mother bought a modular home across the street from the main government complex.

I left the reservation to go to boarding school in ninth grade. I did not suffer particular animosity in middle school on account of my race. If anything, there were frequent reminders – such as the assumption that white students should be in the high track classes – that I was relatively privileged. But the school system left a great deal to be desired. Most of my Bilagáana peers from middle school would go on to get in trouble with the law for everything from drug dealing to vehicular homicide associated with drunk driving. And neither the Kayenta nor Window Rock high schools offered advanced classes. So I left for boarding school, then college, then graduate school, and finally work as a law professor, returning to the reservation only to see my parents. My younger brother, Saul, suffered through one additional, particularly hard year on the reservation before he too left to follow a similar path. Non-Indians make up between 2 and 3 percent of the population of the reservation and Saul ended up needing school security officers to escort him on the bus to and from school to protect him from racially motivated attacks. (Saul stood out more than I did, not only because he has bright blonde hair, but also because his survival technique was to fight back when bullied whereas mine was to let it be known that I would tell on whoever picked on me.) After I left for boarding school, my mother, Norma Cady, continued to work as an environmental planner for the tribe in Window Rock and Tuba City, Arizona for another twenty years. My father, James Rosser, and his wife, Zelma King, built a house on her family's traditional lands near Red Valley, Arizona.

Given my childhood experiences on the reservation, it was a challenge to figure out the roles I could and should play, as well as those I should not. Committed to the idea that Diné should decide the direction of the tribe and that the most important jobs that impact the Navajo Nation should be filled by Diné – whether those jobs are located on the Navajo Nation or in Washington, DC – it was hard to see a way to support the tribe while being mindful of the fact that I am a Bilagáana. Having seen the valuable contributions Robert Williams, Jr. made to Indian country, when he suggested that I consider becoming an Indian law professor, it was as if light was suddenly shone on a path that would enable me to work on the issue I cared about, reservation poverty, without taking on roles best assumed by Diné. *Custer Died for Your Sins* resonated not only because I understood the pain and humor it expressed, but also because it forced me to once again question my place and work. There are two basic options after recognizing one's outsider status: to abandon the field or to acknowledge that status and move forward with as much humility as possible.[7] Though at various times I have stepped back a bit to work in the comfortable academic space of pure theory, my first and deepest commitment is to doing what I can to improve the welfare of Diné living on the reservation. The goal of this preface, accordingly, is to acknowledge my outsider status in the hopes that the book itself reads as authentic and fair to those most familiar with the Navajo Nation: Diné who grew up and spend their lives between the four sacred mountains.

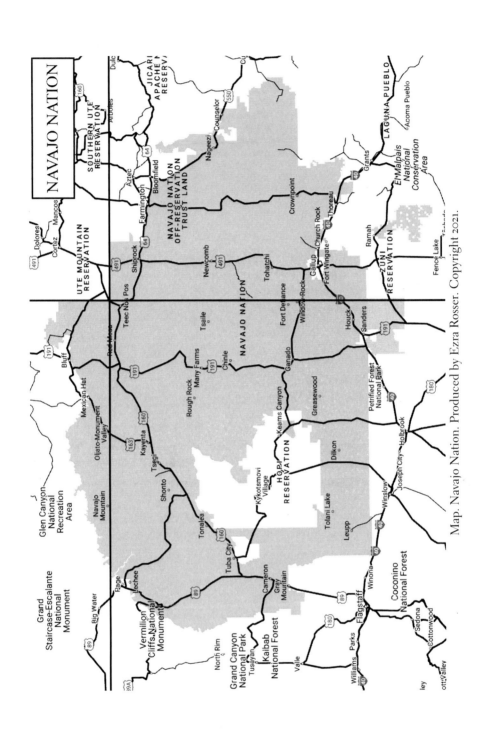

Map. Navajo Nation. Produced by Ezra Rosser. Copyright 2021.

1

Introduction

The Navajo people survived. They did so despite innumerable attacks and invasions by first Spanish, then Mexican, and finally American forces. They continue to survive. Since well before 1705, when "Maestre de Campo and principal military leader Rogue Madrid" recorded in his journal that he was ordered to "go forth to make war by fire and sword on the Apache Navajo enemy nation,"[1] Navajos have been under almost constant pressure from outsiders.[2] It wasn't until Kit Carson's campaign of 1863–4, in the midst of the Civil War, that the US Army ultimately defeated the Navajo tribe militarily. "Forces led by Kit Carson waged a scorched earth campaign against peach trees and goats, horses and squash, largely starving out the Navajos" until the Navajos had no choice but to surrender.[3] Thousands of Navajos were led on a forced march to Fort Sumner, where they were involuntarily held.[4] Yet, despite such genocidal energy directed against them, Navajos survived as a people and as a tribe.

On June 1, 1868, the United States government signed the Treaty of Bosque Redondo with the Navajo tribe.[5] The Treaty was a hard-fought victory for the Navajo people who had been interned at Fort Sumner for more than four years. General William Tecumseh Sherman was in charge of the negotiations on the American side, the same general who, just a few years before, played a pivotal role in bringing the South to its knees by marching his army across Georgia. Despite being seated across from such an imposing figure, the Navajo were unbending during the negotiations: they demanded that they be allowed to return to their homeland. Speaking directly to Sherman on May 27, 1868, Barboncito – a key Navajo leader involved in the negotiations – said, "It appears to me that the General commands the whole thing as a god. I hope therefore he will do all he can for my people . . . I am speaking to you now as if I was speaking to a spirit, and wish you to tell me when you are going to take us to our own country."[6] The treaty signed was far from perfect. The reservation envisioned by the treaty was too small to meet the needs of the Navajo people, did not account for their future growth, and would need to be supplemented by additional land set-asides. Navajos would continue to face hurdles and challenges, some from Washington and some decidedly more local. But despite such hardships, the Treaty of Bosque Redondo was an impressive victory. The Treaty not only recognized the right of the Navajo people to return to Dinétah, their homeland, it also paved the way for the modern Navajo Nation.

In some parts of the United States, it is easy to forget that the entire country once belonged to the Indians. But reminders are everywhere. Iowa and Kansas are named after tribes and the Mississippi River derives its name from a Choctaw word meaning "Great Water." Mohawk ironworkers helped build many of New York's iconic skyscrapers and numerous tribes work to protect the fish and water quality of the Great Lakes.[7] Paintings and carved depictions of Indians – including Pocahontas saving John Smith, Natives greeting settlers at Plymouth Rock, and the Lenape Indians signing a treaty with William Penn – adorn nearly every major room of the US Capitol building. And on reservation land across the United States, Indian nations continue to exercise tribal sovereignty, as they have since before the formation of the country.

From contact until the late 1800s, the Indian question was at the forefront of American politics. Competing powers – the British and the French, the British and the Colonists, the Spanish and the Mexican, the North and the South – actively sought alliances with Indian tribes in the many wars for control of what is now the continental United States. And though the popular mythology of the nation's expansion (both at the time and today) is often based on some version of manifest destiny, all along there were those who recognized the humanity of Indians and called for fairer treatment of Indigenous peoples. Villages and church groups across the country, some far removed from Georgia, sent memorials to Congress protesting Cherokee removal. Even policies such as allotment – an imposition of fee simple ownership of land on tribes and the sale of any "surplus" land to non-Indians – that proved disastrous for Indian tribes reflected both non-Indian desire for Indian land and a belief that Indians would benefit from such policies. To treat the conquest of the continent as an expression of a single racist ideology is to selectively forget that Indian policy was infused in and inseparable from politics. For much of American history, issues involving Indians were matters of intense public debate.

But once the Indian wars were over and Indians were confined to reservations, the Indian question receded, relegated by geopolitics and economic growth. Sure, there were occasional reminders that Indians were not entirely exterminated, but, by the twentieth century, Indian issues were of secondary importance throughout much of the country. Periodic flare-ups, such as the Alcatraz and Wounded Knee occupations, forced Americans to briefly take note of the continued existence of Indian tribes, but they did not return Indian issues to the front burner. That may be changing. During the 1990s, Indians regained a bit of the popular spotlight through the combined might of Hollywood, in the form of a white soldier (Kevin Costner) who goes native in the Oscar award-winning *Dances with Wolves*, and the almighty dollar, in the form of Indian casinos sprouting up in California, New York,

Connecticut, Florida, and elsewhere. But that could just be a taste of what is to come. Despite the relative neglect of all things Indian throughout the past century, the Standing Rock protests of 2016–17 suggest that Indian issues are poised to assume greater national importance.

Though legal battles remain, the Dakota Access Pipeline is now fully constructed;[8] by that measure, the Standing Rock protests failed. In August 2016, members of the Standing Rock Sioux tribe blocked further construction of a portion of the pipeline that was to run under the Missouri River, one half mile from their reservation. They described themselves as "water protectors," not protesters, and were quickly joined by Native Americans of other tribes who arrived in droves from across the country. The protest became front-page news, lasting into the winter, with the protest camps taking on the characteristics of entire towns. A temporary victory occurred when the federal government, under President Obama, temporarily halted construction of the pipeline, but that position was quickly reversed by President Trump, as discussed in Chapter 5. By late February 2017, authorities employed heavy equipment and their power to arrest resisters to force the last of the water protectors to leave Oceti Sakowin camp.[9] On the one hand, even with an unprecedented level of collective energy – perhaps even higher than the days of the American Indian Movement and the occupation of Wounded Knee – directed against the pipeline, Indians still lost. On the other hand, the protests showed that it will be hard for the country to ignore matters that are important to Indians moving forward. Given the right circumstances, Indian voices can and will help drive and push the national political and social conversation.[10]

Whether the larger society wants to engage Indians or not, there is likely to be a rise in non-Indian and Indian negotiations, agreements, *and* conflicts. In a 1970 Special Message to Congress on Indian Affairs, President Richard Nixon announced a change in the federal approach to Indian tribes.[11] Explicitly rejecting the preceding policy of terminating tribal authority, Nixon argued that "[t]he time has come to break decisively with the past and to create the conditions for a new era in which the Indian future is determined by Indian acts and Indian decisions." Nixon's speech ushered in the self-determination era, a period in which most tribes have assumed control over nearly all aspects of tribal governance. For the past half-century, "self-determination" and "sovereignty" have been the words on the lips of tribal and federal officials alike. Moreover, the idea that Indian nations should be in charge of setting their own course continues to be the primary operating principle of federal Indian law and policy. Many tribes today are flexing their muscles: opening off-reservation casinos, purchasing property to expand their land bases, and demonstrating in politics and in business that they must be taken seriously as peoples and as nations.

Popular views of white-Indian relations have changed over time but continue to deny Indian peoples an active role in shaping the country. The "good cowboys versus bad Indians" version of history has been partially replaced by popular acceptance of

"Indians as victims" in the settlement of the continent, but both accounts gloss over Indian decision-making and agency. The United States is "a nation built on land stolen, or skillfully traded (to put it in the best light), from the original inhabitants."[12] Indians lost much of the continent to whites militarily, but negotiated agreements – often formally memorialized through treaties – are as important in that story as the military defeats. Through these agreements, Indian tribes typically gave up land, often a significant amount, in return for recognition of their remaining land rights as well as for a variety of other guarantees, including peace, annuity payments, and protection from "bad men among the whites."[13] Treaties that conveyed vast tracts of land to the United States also recognized the right of Indian tribes to reservation lands and to valuable water, hunting, and fishing rights.

The country's history is replete with examples of Indians being pushed from their land because whites wanted it for farming, industry, and even national parks. Ironically, the undesirable land that Indians were often left with turned out to be quite valuable land.[14] Today, Indians reservations contain 56 million acres, or 2.3 percent of the total land area within the United States.[15] Significantly, "Indian lands contain about 30 percent of the coal found west of the Mississippi, up to 50 percent of potential uranium reserves, and as much as 20 percent of known natural gas and oil reserves."[16] Additionally, reservation lands have "substantial reserves of minerals such as gold, silver, copper, bauxite, and others."[17] Even when it comes to renewable resources, Indian reservations include some of the best sites for locating wind and solar electrical generation facilities.[18] As the Supreme Court has recognized, tribes enjoy significant water rights even if those water rights were not explicitly provided for in treaties.[19] The two major rivers that flow through the Navajo reservation, the Colorado and the San Juan, for example, "carry a big share of all water used in seven western states and northwestern Mexico."[20] These resources, coupled with recent enhancements in the political power and autonomy of the tribes, places relations with surrounding society on a knife's edge. Non-Indians have always wanted Indian resources, especially control or access to Indian land, and, going forward, conflict over resources could expose new fissures in the relationship between tribes and non-Indians.

When considering these potential challenges, it is worth highlighting that Native peoples and Indian nations survived the country's best efforts to eradicate them, to sweep them out of the way in the name of manifest destiny and development.[21] In many respects, the odds were long. Disease, conquest, confinement, and forced assimilation exacted a terrible toll on tribal communities.[22] And the legacy of what has been appropriately called a genocide[23] can still be seen in the hardships endured by many Native Americans today. Survival under such circumstances is itself a form of success, but many tribes are doing more: signs of a rebound can be seen across Indian country. Indian nations have taken over many of the programs formerly run by the federal government, population numbers are dramatically rising, and a sense of hope can be felt on many reservations.

The emerging power of tribes challenges some of the earliest lessons taught to American schoolchildren. Rather than two types of sovereigns in the United States, there are three: the federal government, state governments, and Indian nations.[24] More fundamentally, the importance of Indians in the national story can no longer be relegated to brief mentions beginning with discovery and contact and ending with westward expansion. Tribal assertions of their right to shape the direction of their economic development and to control their natural resources show that the existence and role of Indian nations cannot be relegated to the dustbin of history.[25] Instead, the decisions made by tribal governments can have tremendous and immediate significance to non-Indians living in neighboring and even distant communities.

This is not to say that tribes do not face significant challenges. President Nixon began his 1970 Special Message to Congress by stating, "The first Americans – the Indians – are the most deprived and most isolated minority group in our nation. On virtually every scale of measurement – employment, income, education, health – the condition of the Indian people ranks at the bottom."[26] Sadly, though the self-determination era ushered in a period marked by tremendous improvements in the power tribes have to determine their own fate, for many tribal communities Nixon's observations about the relative hardships faced by Indians remain true to this day.[27] According to the Census Bureau, 21.6 percent of all families, 29.8 percent of families with children, and 47.9 percent of single female-headed households of those identifying as "American Indian and Alaska Native" lived in poverty in 2015.[28] The same 2015 survey also reported that when viewed at the individual level, 26.6 percent of all people, and 33.8 percent of all Native children lived in poverty.[29] By way of comparison, the national poverty rate for 2015 was 13.5 percent.[30] On the Navajo Nation, the official 2015 unemployment rate was 21.5 percent compared to just 5.0 percent nationally;[31] the median household income nationwide, $56,516, was more than double that of the Navajo Nation, which was only $26,203.[32] Compared to the general population, Alaska Natives and American Indians live in worse housing: they are more than six times as likely to live in housing with inadequate plumbing (1 percent compared with 6 percent), six times as likely to have heating deficiencies (2 percent compared with 12 percent), and nine times as likely to live in overcrowded homes (2 percent compared with 18 percent).[33] Their life expectancy is 4.4 years lower than the nation's overall life expectancy, and they "continue to die at higher rates than other Americans in many categories, including chronic liver disease and cirrhosis, diabetes mellitus, unintentional injuries, assault/homicide, intentional self-harm/suicide, and chronic lower respiratory diseases."[34] They are more than twice as likely to be the victim of a homicide and are seventy percent more likely to commit suicide.[35] As President Obama observed in an op-ed published by *Indian Country Today*: "Native Americans face poverty rates far higher than the national average – nearly 60 percent in some places. And the dropout rate of Native American students is nearly twice the national rate. These numbers are a moral call to action."[36]

Sadly, Indians are too often seen by the larger society as either destitute wards, who depend on federal assistance, or as wealthy capitalists, who manipulate tribal sovereignty in order to operate casinos. The truth is that these extremes neither define the Indian experience nationwide nor the situation of any particular tribe. There are tribes that have gotten rich from Indian gaming; their success has allowed them greater independence from federal agencies and provided them freedom to diversify their economies. There are also tribes that continue to struggle with the debilitating effects of subjugation and land loss, a struggle that manifests itself in the form of chronic unemployment, limited educational achievement, and alcohol and drug abuse. With 574 federally recognized tribes, generalizations are impossible and carry the danger of characterizing Indian communities based on stereotypes rather than according to the nature of their lifeways.[37] The outsiders' gaze is impossible to entirely ignore or discount, but the best way to understand Indian life is to start with an examination of particular Indian communities. The struggles and challenges facing Indians look different from the ground up than they do from the standard perspective, which is narrowly focused on how Washington has treated tribes over time.[38] When the perspective on tribal economic development is based on reservation experiences, there is more space to recognize Indian independent action and to entertain cautious optimism.

Visitors to the Navajo Nation often marvel at the wide-open spaces, the brilliance of the stars at night, and the dramatic mesas and rock outcroppings found across the reservation. One can drive for miles without seeing a house, and along some roads it is rare to see another car. But just out of sight are many different environments and ways of living.[39] The word "Navajo" has been attributed to residents of Tewas Pueblo who encountered the tribe and "called them '*navahu'u*,' meaning 'farm fields in the valley.'"[40] The Navajo word for themselves is "Diné," which means "the people." In this book, the two terms will be used somewhat interchangeably, with a preference for Diné when referring to the people and for Navajo when discussing the tribal government. The Diné word for whites is "Bilagáana," which translates as "white, the other, or the enemy,"[41] and captures both the "us-them" dynamic at work compared to the word "Diné" and the difficult history of Diné-Bilagáana relations. Similarly, Navajo Nation and Navajo tribe, or "the tribe," are used interchangeably. Even though Navajo Nation is a better term when it comes to emphasizing the tribe's sovereign status, in practice "tribe" and "tribal government" are used frequently on the reservation and in writing about the Navajo Nation. Group names have been a challenge for the indigenous peoples of the Americas ever since Christopher Columbus thought he arrived in India.[42] These days, some people, particularly non-Indians, bristle at use of the term "Indian," preferring instead "Native American" or "Indigenous." But "Indian" is the term that continues to dominate writing on the subject and often is preferred on the reservation. For both reasons, this book will also not drop the term "Indian" even though it originated out of a mistake.

Diné believe that they are now in the fifth world, having emerged from four previous worlds,[43] and that their homeland was defined in this period of emergence. When First Man brought soil from the fourth world into the fifth world – the Glittering World – and used that soil to create the four sacred mountains:

> In the east he put Sisnaajinii, or Blanca Peak, Colorado, placed it in white shell, covered it with daylight and dawn, fastened it to the ground with lightening, and assigned it the symbolic color of white. To the south went Tsoodzil, Mount Taylor, in which he placed turquoise; he then covered it with blue sky, fastened it with a great stone knife, and gave it the color blue as its symbol. Dook'o'oosłííd, or the San Francisco Peaks, is the mountain of the west. Securing it to the ground with a sunbeam, First Man put abalone inside and covered it with yellow clouds and evening twilight, yellow being its color. Black is the color of Dibé Ntsaa, or Hesperus Peak in Colorado, the mountain of the north. It is fastened by a rainbow, impregnated with jet, and covered with darkness.[44]

The four sacred peaks mark the traditional boundaries of Diné territory and are central to Diné identity.[45] Depictions of them can be seen on the Navajo Nation seal and flag.

The Diné Glittering World has many layers that go unseen by tourists rushing to catch the sunrise at Monument Valley or stopping for a bite to eat at Cameron Trading Post on their way to the Grand Canyon. The Navajo Nation is larger than the state of West Virginia, with more than 27,000 square miles spread across significant parts of Arizona, New Mexico, and southern Utah. As a report by the US Commission on Civil Rights highlighted, "The reservation contains . . . some of the most visually magnificent landscapes in America."[46] The reservation includes everything from the sand swept expanses west of Kayenta to the forests and lakes of the Chuska Mountains above Cove. In Window Rock, graduates from some of the best universities in the United States are working to defend the sovereignty of the Navajo Nation using cutting edge tools. At the same time, just a few miles away, families herd sheep, much as their ancestors did following the return from Bosque Redondo. There are children who grow up on the reservation who never learn to speak Diné, but there are also children, especially in rural areas or those cared for by grandparents, who arrive at kindergarten speaking fluent Diné and few words of English. For many Diné, and some non-Indians with deep ties to the reservation, the area can exert a strong pull, making it hard to imagine living off-reservation.[47] After birth, Navajos traditionally bury the umbilical cord of their babies near their home, and returning to where their umbilical cord was buried remains a driving force for many tribal members throughout their lives.[48]

Such a strong connection to place may seem strange given the opportunities and experiences available off-reservation. A number of explanations exist to explain the strength of the Diné connection to their land and to their reservation. In academic literature, even as writers about Indians tend to criticize stereotypes, they argue that

Indians in general have a deeper relationship to the land than non-Indians. This position takes a variety of forms, including notions that Indians' lives are more tied to the land, that indigenous peoples tend to be more place-based, and that tribal peoples have a greater commitment to protecting the Earth. Even though this position is itself a stereotype, there is some truth behind it, at least when it comes to Navajos. Diné live where they were formed as a people according to their creation story and where all their stories are set: it was within the four sacred mountains that Changing Woman taught Diné about the stages of life and where the Hero Twins defeated the monsters.[49] The natural beauty of the area coupled with the fact that families are often very tight, with several generations living together, fortify the close ties many Diné have to their homeland. As a 1975 report about conflicts between Indians and non-Indians in border towns noted, "The Native American, unlike the white man, is not a stranger to this area. Indeed, the Navajo considers this land to be sacred."[50]

Land provides the basis for the independent sovereignty of the Navajo Nation and creates the space necessary for Diné families to live distinct lifeways.[51] Since contact, the relationship between colonizing non-Indians and the indigenous groups they encountered has been driven by two competing impulses: integration and separation. Indian policy swings between these two extremes, non-Indians alternatively hoping Indians will simply assimilate into the larger society or hoping Indians will remain removed from it. Reservations sprung out of the impulse to isolate Indian communities. Many were later opened up to non-Indian settlement when the integration impulse and desire for Indian resources once again came to dominate federal policy. But, importantly, the reservation lands that remain today provide the critical "center to resist the historical pressures created by the dominant society."[52] It is on reservations that words like "self-determination" and "sovereignty" assume concrete form. It is on reservations where Indian nations behave like nations, regulating life and providing governance services to their members. The Navajo Nation is a nation in part because it has a territory to govern. Such territory also allows greater opportunity for Indian families to live life on their own terms and on the terms of their ancestors. This is both a matter of separation from the heavy influence of American society off-reservation and a matter of belonging. While Indians are now ironically "outsiders" in much of America, Navajos belong and non-Indians fairly obviously do not "belong" on the Navajo reservation.[53] Even Bilagáanas who have spent considerable time living on the reservation remain "outsiders" in many public spaces – whether at the grocery store or at religious ceremonies – within the Navajo Nation. For Diné living on reservation, the land provides an immense sense of freedom and of home that is not available elsewhere. A place to be Diné among other Diné.

The long-term success or failure of the Navajo Nation implicates more than just a single tribe, it helps answer the question of whether the United States is better than its founding. The United States is built upon land that belonged to Indians; the country's existence owes itself in part to the fiction that the land was *terra nullius*, unoccupied, and therefore properly subject to European claims.[54] Though slavery is often referred to as America's original sin, the racist dismissal of tribal land rights as inferior to those of the US government is also a significant part of the country's ignoble foundation. Upon arrival, European immigrants had to confront a number of difficult questions, including: "Are Indians people?" and "what rights do Indians have?" In one of the first Indian law cases heard by the US Supreme Court, Chief Justice John Marshall started an answer to these questions by describing tribes as "domestic dependent nations."[55] Ever since then, courts, tribes, states, and the federal government have been trying to figure out what that means. At times, the non-Indian answer, as expressed through everything from indifference to assimilationist and even genocidal policies, has been that the content of "domestic dependent nations" is thin and easily wiped away in favor of the country's development.[56] Students at all levels, from elementary school through graduate school, are typically taught that there are only two types of sovereigns – the states and the federal government – in the United States, ignoring the sovereignty of the peoples who predate European settlement.[57]

The best description of the powers of tribes probably comes from the first treatise on Indian law, Felix Cohen's *The Indian Law Handbook*, published in 1941. Cohen explains: "From the earliest years of the Republic the Indian tribes have been recognized as 'distinct, independent, and political communities,' and, as such, qualified to exercise powers of self-government, not by any delegation of powers from the Federal Government, but rather by reason of their original tribal sovereignty."[58] What makes Indian nations unique is that they enjoy a legally enshrined right to differ from the surrounding society. States enjoy similar rights – Maryland can adopt a different definition of armed robbery than Virginia, for example – but the amount of state variation is limited by the Constitution. By contrast, Indian nations can adopt laws for their members that depart, sometimes sharply, from off-reservation norms.[59] Indians are not simply another racial group because, unlike other groups, they enjoy collective, sovereign rights that operate independent of their rights as US citizens. There are detractors who argue that collective rights have no place in America today, that Indian rights should be limited to the rights of ordinary Americans. This argument is but a modern manifestation of the same genocidal impulse that supported manifest destiny. Put differently, the continued ability of tribes to carve out separate space within the larger United States is remarkable given the tremendous efforts that have been put into making Indians and Indian nations disappear.

Although subject to certain limitations, especially when it comes to the exercise of authority over non-Indians on reservation land, Indian nations continue to have the power to set their own course. Tribes can, for example, determine membership rules, establish tribe-specific marriage, divorce, and inheritance laws, and enforce their development preferences through zoning and leasing.[60] For small tribes surrounded by non-Indian communities, such pockets of difference at times stand out. The Salt River Reservation, because of its relative lack of development, is a notable break from the ever-expanding blob that is Phoenix. At other times, such small tribes blend in almost imperceptibly with the surrounding non-Indian community. Aside from tribal members and some local non-Indians, people who regularly visit the area may not even know that there is Indian land nearby. For tribes with few tribal members and a small land base, not only is it hard to keep outside society from inserting itself into daily life, but a small population also means there are too few tribal members to independently staff a small government. Such tribes have little choice but to either depend on, or partner with, neighboring non-Indian governments. Part of what makes the Navajo Nation unique, even among recognized tribes, is that it is big.

The Navajo Nation has both the largest land base of any Indian tribe (including Alaska Native communities) and the largest population living on reservation.[61] According to the 2010 US Census, the total population of the Navajo Reservation, including off-reservation trust land, was 173,667.[62] And most people living on reservation were either "American Indian and Alaska Native Alone," or "American Indian and Alaska Native in combination" (166,321 and 2,497, respectively).[63] Only slightly more than 2 percent of the population, 4,346 people, were "Not American Indian and Alaska Native alone or in combination."[64] This means that the Navajo Nation is remarkably, for lack of a better word, "Navajo." Non-Indians living on the reservation are the exception. (Navajos are not the largest tribe in the United States; that honor goes to the Cherokee Nation, which employs a lineal descent rule for tribal membership instead of the Navajo Nation's one-quarter blood quantum requirement.) The Navajo Nation's large population means that the tribe has the ability to fill most government positions with tribal members. Additionally, the Navajo Nation governs a large territory, equivalent in size to the Republic of Ireland, populated almost entirely by tribal members. Finally, in part because "the 27,000-square-mile Navajo Nation boasts some of the most abundant energy resources on tribal lands in the United States, including fossil fuels and the potential for using wind and sun," the Navajo Nation has a wealth of natural resources.[65] Because of its population, size, and resources, the Navajo Nation is arguably better suited than any other tribe to provide meaningful content to the idea of "tribal sovereignty" and to test whether the United States is truly committed to treating Indians better today than they were in the past.

By exploring in detail the Navajo Nation, its history, development path, and future possibilities, this book illuminates the challenges facing Indian communities and the relationship between tribes and non-Indians. Others have written about various aspects of the Diné world prior to the establishment of the reservation, including their traditional beliefs[66] and their unique connection to elements of the natural world.[67] But *A Nation Within* largely leaves such matters to one side, focusing instead on the rise of the Navajo Nation following the signing of the Treaty of Bosque Redondo, and especially the period following the formation of the Tribal Council in 1923. While the Navajo Nation is neither a state of the United States nor a foreign nation,[68] Diné have created a large administrative state – complete with an active court system, numerous departments that deliver and regulate social services, and a three branch system of government – that in many respects mirrors that of other states and nations. For the Navajo Nation to become the nation that it is today and for it to fully assume these many roles and powers, it had to first change from a people to a nation. That change was not easy, in part because of the heavy hand that the United States played and continues to plays in limiting and shaping the options available to the tribe. Especially when it comes to use of the land, the federal government has an outsized role in directing the nature of reservation development and resource exploitation. The Navajo Business Council, the precursor to the Navajo Tribal Council, was created in 1923 in order to facilitate oil leases on the reservation for the benefit of off-reservation corporations. Most reservation land is held in joint trust by the tribe and the federal government, which means that tribes are still required to obtain federal permission for a wide variety of development decisions, from large scale projects to minor land use changes. Over time, Diné leaders have created more space for independence from federal oversight by select-ively pushing back against federal direction and by advocating for their rights to self-determination. The notable emergence of a robust version of tribal sovereignty on the Navajo Nation is a major theme of this book, even as the tribe's nation-building work continues today.

Not all the development challenges facing the Navajo Nation can be attributed to outsiders or to the colonial legacy. Despite how tempting it is for Diné leaders and well-meaning progressives to blame everything on whites or on the federal govern-ment, Diné have not always had the best leadership nor have the Navajo Nation's administrative agencies always put the best interests of the people first. Internal issues or failings within an Indian tribe are harder to write about or discuss than problems that can be attributed to non-Indians. As Raymond Orr notes in his path-breaking book on tribal politics, "Acts of Congress, decisions of the Supreme Court, and public depictions of American Indians receive greater critical attention in political science than the polities themselves."[69] One Indian law scholar joked to me at a conference that Indian law professors have never written anything negative about a tribe, while Indian studies scholars only write about the bad things tribal governments have done. The reluctance among Indian law advocates to criticize Indian nations comes out of a justifiable fear that anti-tribal forces will use any frank discussion of tribal government weaknesses as a weapon to further attack tribal sovereignty.[70] Left unacknowledged in the reluctance and fear that surrounds discussions of tribal governance failures is an appreciation of the fact that *all* governments are imperfect. The fact that greed, corruption, scandal, selfishness, and ugly politics can be found in tribal government should not be surprising – after all, politics in Washington and in state houses all too often can be described by the exact same words. A *Nation Within* focuses on tribal land and development, topics that cannot be covered without turning a critical eye not only towards the federal government but towards the Navajo Nation government as well. Orr observes, "It is believed, and mistakenly so, that tribes and American Indians are so fragile that to explore the disagreements within tribes would damage political units and communities that have survived cultural, social, biological, and spiritual catastrophes during five hundred years of colonization."[71] This book shares Orr's belief that scholarship should engage in the messiness of life and politics on Indian reservations.[72]

A frequent explanation given on the reservation for why something does not work – why a project failed, why a permit was stuck in process, why someone is referred to office after office without getting meaningful help – is that "it is the tribe." That such an explanation is accepted as normal reflects the fact that there remains a lot of space for tribal governance to improve. The history of the tribe includes its fair share of leadership challenges but also many moments when Diné leaders stepped up for the good of the people and the Navajo Nation evolved to better serve tribal members. Another major theme of the book is that the institutional development and capacity of the Navajo Nation government matters and is central to understanding the tribe and its future. If the Navajo Nation is to effectively chart a development course and earn the buy-in of those living on reservation, it will have to hold leaders accountable when wrongdoing is discovered, improve its institutional effectiveness, and learn from past experiences.

One lesson that Diné do not need to learn is that land use decisions shape reservation life. For outsiders, the Navajo reservation can appear as a vast emptiness, with little evidence of human habitation, much less development.[73] Through such a lens, it seems a trifling matter to permit a school to be built, to allow a new commercial development, or to approve a new coal mine. After all, there appears to be plenty of land that is not being used. But Diné know better. They know that it is hard to find any part of the reservation that is not subject to an ownership or use right claim. Rather than being unclaimed, land parcels – even land that appears to be of little use for either farming or herding – are often subject to multiple overlapping and conflicting claims. Since contact, non-Indians have justified the dispossession of Indians in part by arguing that Indians were not using the land adequately – that they were leaving the land "a wilderness."[74] Tribes on the East Coast were continually pushed west by Europeans who were convinced that they could get more value out of the land. Diné are not so different. Wave after wave of non-Indian experts and powerful corporations, convinced they know better than the tribe, have heavy-handedly imposed their understanding of how tribal land should be used upon the Navajo people. The New Deal stock reduction program, which wiped out much of the wealth of the tribe in the name of erosion control, is the most significant episode of direct federal domination, but is hardly an outlier. Senior federal officials have, at various points, bent to corporate lobbying to undercut the Navajo Nation's bargaining position when negotiating large-scale extractive industry leases; blocked development projects after the tribe had already obtained the necessary permits; and thwarted the ordinary growth of commercial enterprises through systematic inaction.[75] But it is a mistake to attribute reservation underdevelopment solely to federal land use priorities and practices. The tribal government has also struggled to establish a workable system for managing change and for dealing with alternative development views within the tribe. Not only has de facto tribal control of use of rangeland since the end of World War II failed to reverse the loss of usable reservation land, but the tribal bureaucracy dampens tribal entrepreneurship. Further limiting the role of the federal government in tribal land use decisions is a good first step, but the Navajo Nation must also improve the tribe's institutional capacity to facilitate locally appropriate development. If the Diné economic situation is to improve, if fewer children on the reservation are to be raised in poverty, then the federal government and the Navajo Nation must recognize the critical importance of establishing a fair, transparent, and responsive land use system.

One of the challenges when exploring tribal land use rights is that for centuries it has been convenient for whites to assert that Indians do not understand nor recognize private property rights, especially over land. The assumption that Indians, as tribes and as individuals, simply moved over the land and did not have ownership rights over the land has a long lineage. This narrative offered Europeans another excuse, besides religion, for dispossessing the continent: if Indians do not recognize property rights, non-Indians can treat Indian property rights casually. Like most stereotypes, the idea that Indians did not believe in ownership may have contained slivers of truth, but it worked more for the benefit of those doing the stereotyping than for those victimized by the stereotype. As Professor Robert Miller observes, "throughout history Euro-American settlers and government officials downgraded, ignored, and actually lied about how Indians and tribes supported themselves, defined property rights, and operated their economies."[76] As Miller explains, "It was perhaps a purposeful strategy in which Euro-Americans chose to ignore Indian property rights and economic abilities because they wanted to justify taking those rights and assets for themselves."[77] In truth, Indians had different understandings of property rights than the understanding of property rights imported into the New World, but that does not mean that property rights were not important to them. That it was hard for non-Indians to recognize the extent of Indian land claims or where the territory controlled by one tribe ended and that of another tribe began does not mean such boundaries did not exist. Accustomed to a particular form of enclosed farming and more intense forms of land use that did not characterize the New World, Anglo-Europeans adopted a dismissive attitude towards Indian property rights. That attitude persists into the present.

However much it found popular acceptance and contributed to the mistreatment of Indians historically, the belief that Indians do not believe in private property is mistaken. One of the foremost experts on Indian land, Professor Jessica Shoemaker, provides a great summary of Indian property rights:

The nuances of indigenous property law institutions varied by tribe, and they were necessarily informed by both the unique landscape in which each tribe was located and basic differences in social structures, such as whether a given tribe engaged primarily in settled farming or more nomadic hunting. Generally speaking, most of these indigenous property law institutions included at least some allocations of individual use rights. Although sometimes generalized in collective understanding as a historic communal or commons-ownership regime, in fact most original (pre-European contact) tribal land tenure systems consisted of indigenous institutions for the allocation of individual use and occupancy rights to tribal members based on an individual's actual, continuous use of a particular piece of land. Thus, indigenous tenure was based not on an idealized version of the commons but instead on systems of individual use and occupancy rights, with individual Indians enjoying specific rights in land as perfected by actual use. These individual use and occupancy rights, generally, would revert back to the tribe upon abandonment by the individual property holder.[78]

Although Indian land rights are wrongly equated with rights to the commons, in fact, as Shoemaker highlights, tribes had sophisticated systems of private property largely tied to use. Property rights extended beyond land; tribes traditionally recognized private rights over everything from personal property, such as cooking utensils and trade goods, to horses and other animals.[79] The fact that some Indian cultures emphasize sharing to a greater extent than the larger society does not mean that property rights are not important.[80] Just as a gift from parents to their children does not negate the idea of private property within the family, or, between the family and the rest of the world, so too, private property rights exist and matter even if customarily members of some Indian tribes have a wider circle of concern.

Unlearning much of what is "known" about Indians involves more than just rejecting harmful beliefs, it also requires questioning even positive stereotypes. The notion that Indians do not believe in property rights is not far removed from the "positive" stereotype that that Indians are earth-loving environmentalists. These views serve to make Indians "other" and fail to recognize that Indians participate in the same complexity, humanity, and dualities as non-Indians. Non-Indian stereotypes "that either romanticize Native peoples as pre-industrial, primitive peoples living in harmony with nature without the benefits of civilization or technology (the 'noble savage') or vilify Native peoples as rapacious commercial entrepreneurs" must be rejected.[81] The idealization of Indian life prior to contact, of Indian commitment to the environment, and of Indian spiritual knowledge threatens to reduce Indians to a two-dimensional romantic caricature.[82] Imagining that Indians are only Indian if they fit in a particular, externally created box, provides fodder for those who would like to curtail tribal sovereignty. Spaghetti westerns left an indelible mark on the American psyche. Indians were only Indians if they looked like Sioux warriors, lived in tipis, and hunted buffalo. But most Indians were never thus and Navajos in particular do not fit that mold. Diné have a living, constantly changing culture that defies non-Indian stereotypes about what Indians are or how they should live.

Diné survived as a people and as a culture in part through selective incorporation of ideas and elements from the other groups they encountered. Much of what is considered traditional in Diné society today reflects the influence of neighboring groups. Diné got sheep and horses from the Spanish, aspects of their family life from Pueblo tribes, and everything from automobiles to basketball from Americans.[83] Despite not originating in the tribe, these and many other elements incorporated from other cultures have become integral to reservation life.[84] Yet, despite incorporation being a constant in their history, Navajo culture remains distinct.[85] Kids living on the reservation may play video games, speak English at school, watch the same shows on television as kids do in Iowa, and even be brought up in non-Navajo religions,[86] but all around there are reminders that a distinct cultural understanding of what it means to be Diné continues to exist. The same can be said about the Navajo government. It is easy to identify moments at which the tribe, often but not always with the strong encouragement of the federal government, adopted institutional practices or structures that replicate something found off-reservation. But the Navajo Nation government remains distinctly Navajo, in part because the tribe makes incorporated elements its own, infusing institutions that appear identical to their off-reservation counterparts with Diné values.[87] It is rather remarkable when one considers the various invasions the tribe has faced, from military to pop culture, that the Navajo "have thrived in spite of forces that, upon surface examination, might have seemed overwhelming."[88]

The first action Roque Madrid took upon invading Navajo Country in 1705, according to his own campaign journal, was to seize two Indian women, without provocation, one with a child, that he came across and "put[] them to torture so that they would tell me where they were from, what they were doing there, or where their camps were."[89] Madrid reported that the torture didn't work, and later noted that all of Navajo country "did not want to fight but to be our friends."[90] This was true despite the fact that Navajos would have been well within their rights to make the same demands of the invading force. The Navajo desire for peace was not enough: "In a campaign of only twenty days, Mre. de campo Rogue Madrid led approximately four hundred soldiers, citizen militia, and Pueblo Indian auxiliaries through little-known country in northwestern New Mexico, fought three battles with the Navajos, and suffered only five men wounded and one killed. A later historian stated that between forty and fifty Navajos had been killed."[91]

Roque Madrid's invasion, and others like it, became the model not only for Kit Carson's 1863 scorched earth campaign but also for the more subtle attacks on Diné life and independence that continue to this day. For some non-Indians, the current Indian renaissance is something to fear and it is almost inconceivable that tribes should be able to exercise authority over their territory. As one anti-Indian journalist recently wrote, "As you enter reservations across the country, you'll find ominous signs warning that you're subject to the laws of the tribe and the territory."[92] Such signs also are found whenever one drives across state lines, but in this reactive political environment, forces opposed to Indians see "ominous signs" whenever tribes assert their sovereign authority. Rather than fear the fact that Indian tribes are arguably better positioned today than they have been since conquest to establish tribe-specific and culturally appropriate land and development frameworks for life on the reservation, non-Indians should welcome Indian nations and recognize their unique place.

The story of the Navajo Nation told in *A Nation Within* unfolds in three parts: past, present, and future. Chapters 2–4 focus on the past. Though it is the size of West Virginia, the Navajo Nation is relatively unknown to non-Indians except the few who live there. Chapter 2, "The Navajo Nation," presents a portrait of the reservation, covering everything from the ubiquitous poverty and unemployment to the structure of Navajo extended families. The chapter also launches the reader into a brief history of the tribe, moving from the Navajo creation story to the Navajo long walk and internment to the establishment of the reservation with the signing of the 1868 Treaty with the United States. This part of the Diné story is full of highs and lows. On the one hand, the US Army's scorched earth campaign succeeded in forcing Diné to leave their homeland at gun point. The cruelty of the long walk and of the tribe's subsequent four year internment at Fort Sumner is a cultural trauma still felt today. On the other hand, tribal leaders succeeded in negotiating the tribe's return to their land. Not only were Diné able to return home, but also they were able to push for additional territory to be added to the Navajo reservation at a time when most tribes were experiencing continued land loss.

Chapters 3 and 4 highlight the close connection between land use demands, including the interests of non-Indians in reservation resources, and the evolution of tribal governance. As Chapter 3, "A New and Old Deal for Navajos: Oil and Sheep," shows, the modern Navajo Nation government was founded in large part so that oil leases on the reservation could be approved. But the Navajo Nation government did not act as mere rubber stamp for non-Indian interests. Though it did permit oil leasing, the tribe went on to reject the signature piece of New Deal policy directed at Indians, the Indian Reorganization Act. After presenting this foundational period of the Navajo Nation government, the chapter then presents one of the most tragic events in the collective memory of the Navajo people, federally imposed livestock reduction, which continues to shape tribal land use patterns as well as federal-tribal relations. Chapter 4, "War Production and Growing Pains: Uranium and Coal," focuses on the problematic nature of Navajo uranium and coal development following the end of World War II. By not revealing the dangers involved and holding back information on the value of the resources, the US government facilitated particularly destructive forms of development while failing to ensure the tribe received fair compensation. The half century reliance of the Navajo Nation on extractive industries for jobs and government revenue can be traced, in part, to the inequities in bargaining position and legal authority over the land that surround the mining agreements approved by the tribe in the early part of the self-determination period.

Having described the growth of the reservation, the formation of the Navajo Nation government, and the land use and resource challenges, *A Nation Within* switches gears to the present. Chapters 5–7 set up some of the more controversial questions – should the tribe pursue environmentally destructive forms of development? What should be done when tribe leaders are corrupt? Can economic or governance theories improve reservation life? – that animate the rest of the book. Chapter 5, "Alternative Environmental Paths," uses the pan-Indian 2016 anti-pipeline protests at Standing Rock as a jumping off point for discussing the complicated relationship between Indians and the environment. It shows why stereotypes about Indians as environmental stewards are misleading while also affirming the special connection that Indians often have to their land. As the chapter shows, tribal sovereignty provides a way of dealing with both tribal environmental justice concerns and tribal decisions to pursue development that harms the environment.

In many ways, Chapters 6 and 7 are the most difficult parts of the book. Chapter 6 because it tackles a difficult subject and Chapter 7 because it is more theoretical than the other chapters. Arguably the most controversial chapter of the book, Chapter 6, "Golf Balls and Discretionary Funds," focuses on corruption by tribal officials. Tribal sovereignty advocates and non-Indian scholars are often reluctant to talk about tribal governance failures, but this chapter highlights the significance of corruption and the need for improvement within the tribal government. It uses the stories of Tribal Chairman Peter MacDonald's corruption in the 1980s as well as the more recent controversies involving the Tribal Council's use of discretionary funds for personal benefit to show how corruption impacts tribal economic development and tribal land policies. Chapter 7, "Improving Tribal Governance," uses economic theory and tribal-centered writings to explore ways that the Navajo Nation might improve its governance practices. A section on the dominant form of economic theory off the reservation, neo-classical economics, provides a grounding on approaches that have been dictated to tribes by outside experts. The subsequent section on tribal economic development theory, highlights the importance of cultural match and good governance when it comes to reservation development. Although the ideas discussed in Chapter 7 are useful when considering the land use and governance challenges presented in the chapters that follow, readers whose interests are less theoretical and more grounded in the Navajo experience can skip this chapter without losing too much.

Building on the previous sections, *A Nation Within* in Chapters 8–11 considers the future direction of the Navajo Nation. These chapters highlight existing land use challenges as well as efforts by the Navajo Nation to assert authority over land on the reservation as well as over resources located beyond the reservation border. Chapter 8, "Locally Grounded Development," focuses on how governance changes and allowance for greater local autonomy might create space for economic development. The Navajo Nation has 110 chapters, each with a separate governance role and each with unique challenges. Just as American politicians routinely advocate for local control under the banner of federalism, so too many Diné feel that the tribe would be better with some form of Navajo federalism. Chapter 8 looks at whether rebalancing the division of authority between the centralized bureaucracy in Window Rock and local chapter houses could help cut through the red tape that currently undermines efforts to build community at the local level.

Chapters 9 and 10 relate closely to Chapter 8. Despite the Navajo Nation's size and relative lack of development, tribal members often find it nearly impossible to get permission to use land. Chapter 9, "Reclaiming the Land," focuses on homesite leases and, revisiting a topic first introduced in Chapter 3, grazing regulations. Both areas are ones in which the tribal government and tribal leaders recognize contribute to stunted growth on the reservation. The chapter argues that returning to a use-dependent understanding of property rights offers a way to free up land for those who want to make a life on the reservation. Chapter 10, "Creating Space for Experimentation," continues along a similar line, exploring business site leasing and public housing on the reservation. It highlights the dynamic potential of local experimentation, coupled with an allowance for localities to capture some of the benefits of experimentation, to facilitate development. Both public housing and business site leasing offer lessons from past successes and past failures, but, as the chapter explains, local empowerment could help spur deeper capital investment in parts of the reservation that are currently neglected.

The final substantive chapter, Chapter 11, "Sovereign Assertions," looks at ways the Navajo Nation is pushing its sovereignty beyond the reservation border. This chapter discusses three areas where the Navajo Nation must push the physical and legal boundaries of sovereignty in order to protect tribal interests. When it comes to water rights, off-reservation environmental destruction such as uranium mining, and protection of sacred sites, the Navajo Nation has played an active role asserting its interests and lobbying neighboring non-Indian governments. This chapter celebrates such efforts and emphasizes the ways Navajo interests are interconnected with surrounding off-reservation communities.

The conclusion, Chapter 12, observes that while the Navajo Nation faces serious challenges, it is up to the task and should be allowed the freedom to pursue its own path. Connecting the grassroots Diné response to the COVID19 crisis to the response by tribal leaders to previous crisis moments, the conclusion argues that the Navajo Nation must be allowed moments of failure and face consequences when it makes bad calls if it is to succeed. The Navajo Nation is uniquely situated to push for a more full version of sovereignty. It is time for Diné and non-Indians alike to recognize the power of the Navajo nation to move forward with a form of sovereignty that is wrapped in fewer federally-imposed guard rails.

The hope is that this book, by drawing out the history, law, and forces that impact tribal lands and tribal economic development, contributes to the independence and strength of the Navajo Nation and of other Indigenous peoples. The place of Indian nations within the United States cannot be understood through a purely theoretical lens. Exploring the history and institutional development of the Navajo Nation opens a window on the practical significance of tribal sovereignty today, highlighting the central role of the tribal land base in the continued vitality of Indian society and peoples. In 1848, one of the great Navajo leaders, Manuelito, argued for an attack on Fort Defiance. "We will make war and drive these blue-eyed ones from Navajoland."[93] The attack failed, and blue-eyed ones still have their outposts across the reservation. But the reverse is also true: on the reservation, Navajos, much more than the few non-Indians in their midst, not only still exist, but also have created a living, distinctly Navajo culture.[94] Undoubtedly, Diné will continue to survive and thrive in their own ways.[95]

PART I

Past

2

The Navajo Nation

The Navajo Nation's existence, ironically, owes a great deal to the demands colonial powers placed on the Diné tribe. Beginning with the Spanish and Mexican governments, non-Indians looked for a centralized Navajo political structure with whom to establish relationships.[1] Diné had the advantage of being slightly removed from Spanish settlements in New Mexico and Pueblo Indians absorbed some of the Spanish attention that might otherwise have been directed towards (or against) Diné. The Pueblo Revolt of 1680 successfully pushed the Spanish out of Santa Fe, but following their successful return a dozen years later, they were never again directly challenged.[2] Fleeing the Spanish (and later other hostile tribes), some Pueblo peoples joined Diné, bringing with them some of their farming and housing techniques.[3] Today, one-third of the sixty Navajo clans are tied to Pueblo peoples.[4] Prior to conquest and internment by the US Army, shared culture and language united Diné, but the tribe was not a singular entity.[5] Instead, it was organized around family groups, clusters of which formed "natural communities," defined largely by spatial proximity.[6] Diné leaders (Naat'áaniis) would occasionally come together in larger regional gatherings (nááchid) that were presided over by the peace leaders in years of peace and war leaders in years of war.[7] Leadership was based on persuasive ability, not force or the threat of force.[8] Neighboring powers, namely the Spanish and the Americans, found the tribe's lack of a strong central government that could speak for, and control, tribal members troublesome.

According to Peter Iverson, author of *Diné: A History of the Navajos*, it wasn't until around the 1400s that "distinctive Navajo culture began to emerge."[9] For tribes already in the area at the time, Diné were a relatively new and disruptive group. Given the ways in which tribal creation stories are often place-based and tied to local geography, it is not surprising that questions involving how and when Indian groups populated the Americas are some of the more controversial areas of study involving Indians as peoples. Tension surrounding such questions has only increased with the availability of DNA sequencing.[10] Without getting mired in the debates surrounding when Navajo ancestors might have crossed a land bridge between Asia and Alaska,[11] it is enough to observe that by the time of Roque Madrid's invasion on behalf of the Spanish Crown, Navajos were understood to be a distinct group and that they have been treated as such ever since.

Across today's reservation there are reminders that the Navajos were not the first inhabitants of the region: "Between 5000 B.C. and A.D. 1400, the Colorado Plateau supported the dynamic Anasazi Culture. The Navajos provided that name, meaning 'ancient ones,' for the early basket-maker and pueblo people who inhabited the enormous rocky province that stretches across northern Arizona, Utah, New Mexico, and southern Colorado."[12] A number of explanations, including hostility with neighboring tribes and environmental pressures, have been offered for why the Anasazi culture died out, but today all that remains are the ruins – most notably Betatakin, Chaco Canyon, and Mesa Verde – of that once great society.[13] From the 1500s to the 1700s, Diné lived primarily in an area known as Dinétah, the traditional Navajo homeland and "cradle of Navajo civilization," to the east of the modern-day city of Farmington, New Mexico.[14] Diné took over land formerly occupied by the Anasazi as well as land claimed by groups who were already in the area, which Diné justified by adopting a use-based understanding of land rights rather than a first-in-time theory.[15] This was a pragmatic choice for an expanding tribe, but a choice that invited conflict with surrounding tribes at risk of displacement.

Neither Diné nor their neighbors did much to win allies or establish good relations. Diné raided Spanish, Mexican, and American settlers to build up their stock holdings, with raiding a largely accepted and normalized way for poor Navajos to get a leg up. And settlers and colonial governments, for their part, similarly raided Navajo country to recover animals, and, in an underappreciated part of the history of the west, to take Navajo children as slaves. According to one estimate, Navajo and Apache raiders "took over 450,000 Spanish sheep" between 1846 and 1850.[16] This is not to say that efforts – including multiple treaties – were not made to establish peace between the Spanish Crown, and later the Mexican government, and the Navajos,[17] but such efforts were generally short-lived. Diné did not have a European-style strong central government, which meant that "Spanish and Mexican authorities sought in vain for an overall political leader of the Navajo people with whom they could negotiate peace."[18] Even when an agreement was reached, neither party had sufficient control over their respective population to prevent smaller groups from engaging in independent raids and participating in cycles of retribution.[19]

Spanish colonial rule came to an end with Mexican independence, and the United States assumed control of New Mexico and Arizona following victory in the Mexican-American War of 1846–8. Diné had retained their land and independence, outlasting Spanish and Mexican colonial efforts in the region. Adopting a utilitarian approach to conversion efforts, there was "a common pattern of Navajo acquiescence to missionary overtures until they obtained the material inducements which were promised them."[20] After getting such goods, Navajos withdrew, returning to their homelands and to their social and religious system.

By the time the United States government reached the Southwest, Navajos had made sheep and horses part of their lifestyle, but their culture remained distinct. Unfortunately for Diné, the United States was better able and more inclined to bring greater military might to bear against them.[21]

Following the Mexican-American War, the United States wasted little time asserting its authority and ambitions in the area. In 1849, US forces killed Narbona, one of the most important leaders of Diné at the time, in the Chuska Mountains, along with at least seven other Navajos.[22] Fort Defiance was established and manned in 1851,[23] providing a home base for US military invasions of the Diné homeland.[24] Like those before them, the United States hoped to stop Navajo raiding and viewed Diné as a "'hostile' and 'savage' threat to US control of the New Mexico Territory."[25] Diné, however, had their own grievances with their neighbors:

> Between 1860 and 1868, citizen expeditions of up to four hundred participants, plus Puebloans and Utes as well, were encouraged to raid the Navajos, and they took many Navajo women and children as slaves. Witnesses before the 1865 government commission to determine the causes of the Navajo wars stated that even colonist families of modest means kept a Navajo slave or two.[26]

By this point in time, Navajos were living in the mountains and plateaus north of Fort Defiance, further west than they had originally been when the tribe was concentrated in Dinétah.[27] Following the creation of Fort Defiance, it would take more than a decade for the US military to conquer the Diné tribe. Partly, this can be attributed to the large upheavals rocking the country leading up to the Civil War, but expense might have been a factor as well: an estimate at the time was that it cost the United States one million dollars to kill a single Indian.[28]

Ultimately, Diné were defeated by the US military under the leadership of Kit Carson who drove them to surrender through a scorched earth campaign deep into the heart of Navajo country.[29] Starting in the summer of 1863 and continuing through the fall, Carson's forces "ravaged the Navajo countryside ... They killed as many sheep, goats, horses, and cattle as possible; they cut and uprooted standing corn, squash and melons; they burned harvested crops and chopped down peach orchards."[30] The attack was not an attack on Navajo warriors so much as it was an attack meant to crush the Diné tribe.[31] The attack also involved contaminating local water supplies.[32] The defensive heart of Navajo land at that time was Canyon de Chelly, whose curves and high, steep sides offered Navajos protection and the possibility of escape. In January 1864, Kit Carson rode into Canyon de Chelly expecting resistance. Instead, Diné surrendered in such large numbers that Carson had no way to handle the scores of prisoners and had to tell Navajos to delay their surrender until March.[33] The January 1864 foray into Canyon de Chelly marked the end of full Diné independence.[34]

It is worth quoting at length the conclusion of a 1968 article about the Carson campaign: "But the lesson had been finally grasped: the Navajo was tamed. Never

FIGURE 2.1 Canyon de Chelly, where Diné were forced to surrender in droves as a result of Kit Carson's scorched earth campaign. Photo by Ezra Rosser. Copyright 2010.

again did the Dineh sweep out of the mountains to pillage and plunder. Instead, they turned their face from war to the peaceful artistic and agrarian pursuits about which General Carleton [Carson's boss] had dreamily written, and which Colonel Kit Carson had made a reality."[35] What is remarkable about such a summary is the extent to which it inverts culpability and denies Carson's cruelty. According to this imagined history, it was the Navajo who needed to turn away from war towards agrarian pursuits, and it was Carson who made this happen. Never mind that it was the US Army, not the Navajos, who were invading, and that Carson achieved victory by applying slash and burn tactics. According to this whitewashed narrative, any means that would tame the Navajos were justified. To hammer home the Army's determination to crush the Navajos, even after the majority of Diné in Canyon de Chelly surrendered, the scorched earth campaign resumed in March when a force of soldiers "felled a remarkable 4,150 fruit-bearing peach trees" in the Canyon.[36] Not long afterward, soldiers once more invaded the Canyon in order to destroy an additional 1,000 trees.[37] The destruction of the peach orchards shows that Carson's war against Navajo agriculture was not simply about starving Diné out of hiding. As inhumane as that would be, Carson went further: he wanted to make it difficult for Diné to ever rebuild.

Following their defeat, Diné were led on a forced march from their homeland to a distant reservation, Bosque Redondo, that the military established in the hope it would become a new permanent home. Bosque Redondo was anchored by Fort Sumner. The march to Bosque Redondo and Fort Sumner came to be known as the Long Walk and is often described as the Navajo Trail of Tears. Diné who fell ill during the march died along the path or were shot by the troops escorting them, such that the "route of the Long Walk was marked by the frozen corpses of Indians."[38] Things were not much better when Diné arrived at Bosque Redondo, or Hwéeldi (which means "people suffering") as it was called in Navajo.[39] The goal of Bosque Redondo was in keeping with a goal of much of Indian policy since contact: to turn Diné into yeoman farmers.[40] But the site chosen for such an attempt was a poor one – a fact which was known to Army officials well in advance of when Diné were interned there.[41] The ground was infertile and the water was brackish and unfit for human consumption.[42] Diné would be held there for four years and the experience lingered with them long after they left. As one scholar observes, "[t]he Bosque Redondo years (commonly referred to as the Fort Sumner years after the fort near the reservation) are the central terror of Navajo secular myth."[43] An estimated 2,000 people died during internment or roughly one-quarter of those forced to live at Bosque Redondo.[44]

The problems faced by Diné at Bosque Redondo also drew the attention of American officials and non-Indians living nearby. "The plight of the Navajos at Bosque Redondo could no longer be ignored. Try as it might, the army could not hide the fact that this reservation was little more than a concentration camp."[45] Faced with starvation, Navajos were escaping the reservation, both to return secretly to their homeland and to raid neighboring ranchers and tribes.[46] Navajos and non-Navajos urged the US government to do something to improve the situation and to come up with a lasting solution.[47] Additionally, the government was "at a heavy expense to support them," according to the Commissioner of Indian Affairs.[48] In addition to the expense of a constant security presence, drought and crop failures necessitated that the government provide the interned Diné with costly rations on an ongoing basis.[49] Though some estimates are considerably lower,[50] the Commissioner reported in 1867 that the Bosque Redondo experiment had cost the government ten million dollars.[51] In January 1868, the Peace Commission released a report to the President proposing that a treaty be made with the Navajos, observing that "[t]he Navajo Indians in New Mexico were for several years held as prisoners of war at the Bosque Redondo, at a very great expense to the government. They have now been turned over to the Interior Department, and must be subsisted as long as they remain there."[52] Clearly something needed to be done.

The man chosen to right the situation was Civil War hero General William Tecumseh Sherman. In a letter to Ulysses S. Grant, Sherman wrote, "I found the

FIGURE 2.2 "Fort Sumner, New Mexico. Guadeloupe County at the Bosque Redondo on Pecos River. Counting Indians." War Department, Records of the Chief Signal Officer. National Archives (111-SC-87964)

Bosque a mere spot of green grass in the midst of a wild desert and that the Navajos had sunk into a condition of absolute poverty and despair."[53] The negotiations were challenging and time-consuming, in part because Sherman's words had to be translated not from English to Navajo or Navajo to English, but from English to Spanish by one translator and then from Spanish to Navajo by a different translator, and translated in the opposite order when the speaker was one of the assembled Diné leaders.[54] But the time was ripe to restart US-Navajo relations: Kit Carson had died just before Sherman arrived at Bosque Redondo.[55] On the Navajo side, there was not a single leader who spoke for the tribe, despite an 1858 armistice including as one of the terms that the Navajos "were to select a principal chief to whom must be given strict obedience."[56] But Diné were united behind a single goal of being allowed to return to their homeland. Barboncito told Sherman:

> When the Navajos were first created, four mountains and four rivers were appointed for us, inside of which we should live, that was to be our country, and was given us by the first woman of the Navajo tribe. It was told to us by our forefathers, that we were never to move east of the Rio Grande or west of the San Juan rivers and I think that our coming here has been the cause of so much death among us and our animals . . . Outside my own country we cannot raise a crop, but in it we can raise a crop almost anywhere; our families and stock there increase, here they decrease; we know this land does not like us, neither does the water.[57]

The US government's starting position was that the Diné tribe should relocate to a different reservation that might accommodate them and people from other tribes. It was a plan similar to the strategy used in the removals of Indians from across the country and the concentration of many different tribes in Oklahoma. But as Andrew Curley notes,

> It was the Navajo people themselves who voiced opposition to these plans and pleaded with US authorities to let them go back to their homeland on the Colorado plateau. The US government eventually relented and decided to allow the Navajo people to return to their homes. This was the biggest accomplishment for those headmen who were negotiating on behalf of the Navajos, and perhaps the most significant diplomatic event in Navajo history.[58]

The Navajos had won the right of return.

The treaty was signed on June 1, 1868 and ratified by Congress on July 25, 1868. It established a reservation that straddled the Arizona-New Mexico border, extending approximately thirty miles into each state, and running north from Fort Defiance to the southern border of Utah and Colorado.[59] All told, the 1868 treaty set aside three and a half million acres of land.[60] This was much less land than Sherman had promised during negotiations and notably did not include parts of Canyon de Chelly.[61] It also did not extend further south because the US government was interested in protecting land for a developing transcontinental railroad line that would eventually pass through Gallup, New Mexico.[62] Sherman also promised that "any Navajos who severed tribal relations to live as white men could settle anywhere on vacant public domain."[63] As two leading historians on the treaty argue, Sherman's statement could easily be interpreted by the Navajos as granting them the basic permission needed to establish home sites beyond the reservation's boundaries.[64] The treaty was far from perfect. It reserved less land per capita than any other treaty signed in the same period, and, given the nature of the terrain and climate, was inadequate to meet the tribe's subsistence needs even at the moment it was signed.[65] But, despite these failings, it did the one thing Diné wanted most, it allowed them to return to their homeland and begin to recover from their four-year Hwéeldi internment.[66]

Today the treaty – or the *Old Paper* in Navajo[67] – is treated as perhaps the most significant document in Navajo history; June 1 is tellingly celebrated annually as "Treaty Day." Such celebration by the tribal government is warranted. Prior to conquest and internment, Diné were only loosely connected politically, but through the treaty "a category of people called 'the Navajo' was given legal and political weight in the eyes of US governing officials."[68] According to this view, the treaty did not create Diné culture or identity, but it played a foundational role with respect to the Navajo Nation. The tribal leadership structure would continue to evolve; centralized authority would not truly exist until the formation of the Navajo Business Council in 1922, but the Treaty of Bosque Redondo simultaneously recognized and created the tribe as a separate administrative group.[69] Other tribes were not so lucky. Many continue to exist as amalgamations of various tribes stuck together by happenstance and the US government. One of the challenges when it comes to indigenous sovereignty is that it is hard not to impose western constructs of statehood. Prior to conquest and the 1868 Treaty, the Diné tribe was sovereign and independent, but it is hard to fit its loose affiliation of family clusters with periodic larger gatherings into western notions of sovereignty.[70] After internment at Bosque Redondo and the signing of the 1868 treaty, however, Diné could not be dismissed as merely a people.[71] By acknowledging the need of the US government to reach a binding agreement on a nation-to-nation basis,[72] the treaty also planted the seeds of the Navajo Nation.[73]

Almost immediately after signing the treaty, Diné began their long exodus from captivity back to their homeland. Diné called the reservation Diné Bikéyah, which means Navajoland.[74] "Escorted by troops under the command of Major Charles J. Whiting, the procession of approximately 7,300 Navajos stretched for ten miles."[75] Upon their return, some families headed straight for their old homesteads and lands, while others remained around Fort Defiance to wait for promised rations. Those returning home encountered not only reminders of Carson's deadly campaign – "[t]he peach trees in Canyon de Chelly had been burned to stumps"[76] – but also found that many of the best lands were already claimed by those Navajos who had managed to hide long enough to avoid having to go to the Bosque Redondo reservation.[77] The Navajos had been "sent home because the government did not know [what] else to do with them," but rebuilding would take time.[78] Navajo country was considered "a sprawling wasteland described in 1868 by William Tecumseh Sherman ... as 'utterly unfit for white civilization.'"[79] In the decades that followed, Diné would show what they could do with the land.

The post-treaty period was marked by tremendous growth. Livestock, particularly sheep, became an even more integral part of Diné identity, and Diné demonstrated their ability to use sheep as the basis for strengthening their welfare. More than a year after the treaty was signed,

> [t]he promised livestock finally arrived. Purchased in La Cueva, New Mexico, the animals had been driven to Fort Defiance and were a little thin, but the sheep were tough, little Spanish *churros* who managed to survive and multiply under the extreme care provided by their new owners. The distribution of the animals, 2 per person, took five days, and 8,121 people appeared for the distribution of 14,000 sheep and 1,000 goats.[80]

Together with stock already in their possession, this distribution provided a launching point for economic growth. Over the next fifteen years, the US government would continue to distribute annuity goods, including more livestock as well as farming equipment.[81] Despite the "ecological fragility" of the reservation[82] and its "harsh and unforgiving character,"[83] Diné families, by carefully protecting younger ewes and those sheep still capable of mating, increased their herd sizes dramatically.[84] As best as they could, Diné butchered only the oldest sheep; the fact that Navajos tend to eat mutton and not lamb probably traces, at least in part, to such husbandry practices. Sheep were a way to store and transport wealth.[85] They also provided protection against hard times and wool to use in weaving.

The Santa Fe railroad arrived to the area in 1881, and, just as it had done for the country as a whole, the railroad transformed the Navajo economy.[86] Klara Kelley, whose work focuses on labor history, labels the period from 1881 until the New Deal as the "railroad era" and argues that the introduction of cheap transport opened up the Navajo economy but also left many Diné families vulnerable. The railroad linked Navajos to imported commercial products and provided an outlet for Navajo handicrafts, most notably Navajo rugs and silverwork.[87] A proliferation of trading posts, which first began in 1870,[88] facilitated these exchanges, selling goods on credit and accepting rugs and livestock as payment. Traders were not all scrupulous; many paid in their own chips or other forms of local currency that could only be used at their store for goods from Navajo families.[89] But for most tribal members, traders were the non-Indians with whom they had the greatest contact, making them perhaps the most important cultural and economic intermediaries on the reservation at the time.[90]

The opening up of the Navajo economy brought with it increased inequality, as some families thrived and others became more vulnerable. The wealthiest Diné were as wealthy as the wealthiest whites of the area:

> Narbona of Sheep Springs, on the east side of the Chuskas, perhaps epitomized the *rico*. He had three wives and presided over a sprawling menage in which his first wife's mother cared for almost a dozen children. The family owned 2000 sheep, 200 goats, 50 heads of cattle, and 200 horses . . . Narbona's own homesite consisted of a Hogan for each of his wives, one for his mother-in-law, one for a married daughter, and one for his aunt, as well as a corral built against a sheltering cliff and two sweathouses (small bathing chambers that people heated with rocks and then entered to bathe by sweating), one for women and one for men, dug into the bank of any arroyo nearby.[91]

Wealth was measured in various ways, but herd-size counted for a lot. Even as some Diné grew wealthy, inequality abounded. For some Diné families, the 1880s were difficult years marked by starvation caused by the inadequacy of their land holdings.[92]

Notwithstanding the rise in inequality and the struggling of some families, this was a relatively good period for Diné. Within twenty years of returning from Bosque Redondo, "many families had over a thousand sheep and cattle" and "[f]orty years later Navajo herds were over a million head."[93] This era of renewal was not limited to livestock: "upon returning to Diné Bikéyah, the Navajos of Canyon de Chelly masterfully regrew their orchards and, by the 1880s, were harvesting peaches once more."[94] Indeed, the 1880s have been called a "golden age" for Navajos; one scholar estimates that Navajos were among the wealthiest tribes in the country at the time.[95] Friction with Bilagáanas, in the form of US agents in Fort Defiance and ranchers moving westward from Santa Fe, did not stop during this period, but much of the focus was inward. Agents interacted with the tribe through various headmen, but leadership was a negotiated process more than a decree. The federal presence was sufficiently thin that the United States needed Navajo cooperation, and Navajo leadership was not so centralized that orders could be issued and compliance expected. Put differently, while outside society was putting demands on the tribe, those demands were not nearly as unilateral as they were during internment, nor as heavy-handed as they would be during the New Deal. When Manuelito, one of the most important Navajo leaders of the period, returned from a trip to Washington in 1875, he "simply said that he was happy to be home in the mountains and on the plains, where the air was 'free.' He had been fascinated by the East but concluded that it was far too crowded."[96] As Manuelito's perspective shows, Navajo freedom in some respects required the separation and space only partially provided for by the Treaty of Bosque Redondo.

Diné during this period had space, but only because they ignored the reservation boundaries established by the 1868 treaty. Poorer Navajos looking for land upon which to graze their sheep or hoping to establish their own homesteads ventured to more marginal lands west of the reservation border.[97] Navajos also went east of the 1868 reservation but faced greater competition in that direction from non-Indian ranchers. Diné moves beyond the original reservation boundaries were not centrally planned but were but one example of the ways Diné resisted the limitations of the treaty and of colonial rule.[98] The expansion of Diné Bikéyah was accomplished as much by a thousand small actions as it was by the series of federal acts acknowledging that the original reservation did not capture the full extent of tribe's land. Although federal Indian policy during this period was driven by the disastrous allotment policy, through which reservations were carved into smaller individual plots and "surplus" lands made available to non-Indians, the Navajo land base expanded over the same period. Indeed, the Dawes Act, the legal basis for the allotment of other reservations, would be used to expand the size of the Navajo reservation.[99]

The federal government ostensibly passed the Dawes Act with the hope that it would not have to continually give aid to tribes if the reservations were broken up and individually owned land was given to Indians and their families.[100] Like much of Indian policy, allotment was a reaction against the failures, real and perceived, of the preceding policy of isolating Indians on reservations.[101] The reservation system was meant to contain Indians, putting an outer bound on Indian land claims to help clear the way for further non-Indian settlement. Reservations were part of the larger colonizing project, albeit a form of control administered by Indian agents, not army officers. As an extended study of the Indian Affairs department notes,

> In the end, reservations effectively achieved their primary goals: containing, weakening, and subjugating native populations. While other missions – education,

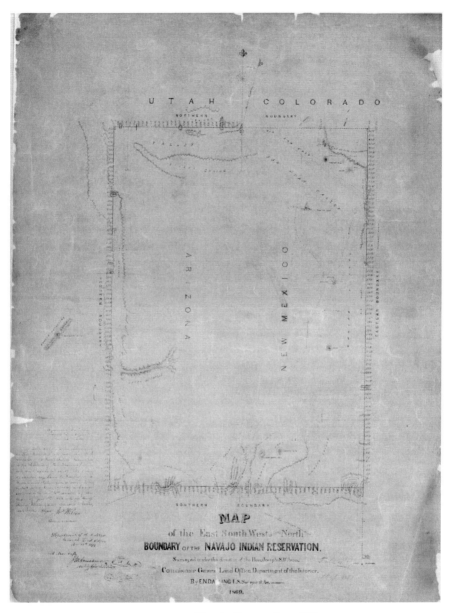

FIGURE 2.3 Navajo Reservation 1868

civilization, job training, and economic development, for example – interested various administrators at different times, as in prior years these goals ran second to the purpose of reservations in supporting and promoting managed expansion and conquest of the continent by administrative means.[102]

But the social ills plaguing many reservations in the late 1870s and 1880s –
especially poverty and dependence – could not be entirely ignored, nor could non-
Indian desire for more land.

Allotment was to be the solution to two problems. First, non-Indian advocates
hoped that Indian families could become yeoman farmers, the independent small
farmers romantically considered central to the country's mythology, who would
achieve self-sufficiency through hard work and the magic of private property.[103] As
Jessica Shoemaker writes, "The idea was that by formalizing individual title to
parcels of land – rather than allocating individual use rights, if at all, through tribal
tenure systems – the federal government could promote more individualistic behavior by Indians, and in turn, greater exploitation of Indian resources by the Indians
themselves."[104] Second, by opening surplus reservations to settlement by non-
Indians despite the promises of various treaties, allotment could address the seemingly insatiable demand of non-Indians for tribal land. Ultimately, allotment only
accomplished the second of these two goals. Indians lost approximately two-thirds of
the land allotted and the amount of land held in trust for Indians went from
137 million acres in 1887 to 52 million acres in 1934.[105] Parceling out the reservation
was not successful in lifting tribal members out of poverty. It also provided no space
for tribal population growth: after the first generation received farmsteads and
surplus land was sold off to non-Indians, there was no land available to accommodate population growth generation-to-generation. Fortunately for Diné, the Navajo
reservation was generally spared the devastation of allotment, because federal officials knew that it would be impossible for people to survive on small, individual
parcels given the limited rainfall and nature of the land.[106]

In 1871, Congress passed an appropriations rider that ended the practice of US-
Indian treaties. The decision to stop making treaties with Indians was a result of a fight
over power between the Senate, which has the sole power to ratify treaties, and the
House, which had to provide funds to Indian tribes after treaties were ratified.[107] After
1871, modifications to the relationship between the United States and particular tribes
would be made by agreements, executive orders, and Congressional acts, but not
through treaties. Though it is questionable whether this change was constitutional, it
created a distinction between treaty-tribes, such as the Navajo, and tribes whose
relationship with the United States was formalized after 1871. Most of the time this
distinction is immaterial, but treaty-protected land rights have slightly greater protections against federal policy reversals that diminish tribal land rights. Yet, despite the
rhetorical force of describing Navajo rights as treaty-based, for land claims beyond the
original 1868 reservation boundaries, such an assertion is inaccurate.

The first expansion of the reservation came in 1878 after a visit by General
Sherman to Fort Defiance. His visit was a notable act for a man known for his cold-
hearted approach to both war and Indians. "Sherman had come because he had
promised the Navajos a visit ten years earlier at the treaty negotiations."[108] As
William Haas Moore reports in his detailed history of US-Navajo relations from

the treaty until the arrival of the railroad, Sherman "informed the Navajos that he would help them get the rest of the Canyon de Chelly region because, accidentally, it had not been included in the treaty description of the reservation. He recommended in his report that an executive order be issued to adjust the boundaries to include the entire Chinle Valley."[109] Sherman's recommendation fell on receptive ears and land was added to the original reservation in 1878.[110] Remarkably, additional land was added to the reservation at ten different points between 1880 and 1934.[111] This growth is less dramatic than successfully negotiating the Treaty of Bosque Redondo, but it is equally impressive, because it came at a time when Indian tribes elsewhere witnessed their reservations carved up and sold off to non-Indians.[112]

The willingness of the US government to expand the Navajo land base over this period can be attributed to number of factors, including the limited non-Indian demand for the land and the practical reality that Diné needed and were already occupying the land. As Traci Brynne Voyles highlights, "[b]y the 1880s, more than half of all Diné were living outside of the reservation boundaries."[113] The United States had few options but to ratify through executive action the de facto expansion of Diné Bikéyah. To do otherwise would have required forcibly rounding up the Navajos once more and confining them to a reservation, which the US government and sympathetic neighboring non-Indians acknowledged was too small to begin with.[114] Fortunately for Diné, non-Indians had largely bypassed the high desert west of the original reservation, which is marked by extended periods with little rain and long stretches without much vegetation.[115] Though land would be added to the north and east of the original reservation as well, non-Indian demand was greater in those directions, making it comparatively easy for tribal members to move west and the US government to eventually recognize such claims. The westward spread of Diné eventually did butt against Hopi villages, but Diné ultimately established their presence around, and in some cases upon, these Hopi mesas. As one Diné scholar explains, "Because we simply put our feet on the ground and claimed it, on more than one occasion we gained possession of our lands."[116] Navajos were aided by Father Anselm Weber of St. Michaels Mission, which had been founded by Franciscans in 1898. Father Weber was a tireless advocate of Navajo interests and regularly petitioned the government to add land to the reservation.[117] He was joined by agents stationed at Fort Defiance who likewise saw the need to expand the reservation. All told, land additions would take the Navajo land base from 3.5 million acres in 1868 to nearly 12 million acres by 1930.[118] After 1934, the Navajo Nation's land holdings continued to grow incrementally – most notably through the controversial Navajo Nation purchase of the half million acre Big Boquillas Ranch in 1987. Today the Navajo Nation has an area of approximately 17.5 million acres or 27,000 square miles, a much larger territory than initially agreed upon at Fort Sumner. That being said, even with this impressive expansion over the last century and a half, the reservation still does not include the four sacred mountains that defined the Diné world prior to conquest.

3

A New and Old Deal for Navajos

Oil and Sheep

If the Treaty of Bosque Redondo solidified the Navajo position as a distinct group in the eyes of the US government, it was oil and sheep that forged the Navajo Nation government. Oil discoveries led the United States to create the Navajo Tribal Council; the Council's independence and voice emerged in battles over sheep stock reduction. Tribes across the country struggled economically well before the onset of the Great Depression. After the depression hit, the Roosevelt administration sought to improve life on reservations by introducing radical changes to US-Indian relations. Federal policy switched from allotment to formal support of a cookie-cutter version of tribal sovereignty, provided through the Indian Reorganization Act of 1934. For Diné, the period from the early 1920s until the end of World War II was a trying but formative time. External pressures not only limited their ability to continue growing through federal land transfers, they also sought to tap on-reservation tribal resources. Even more traumatic for the Diné, New Deal scientists and government officials, concerned about overgrazing and determined to cut the size of Navajo herds, attacked the Diné way of life.

The Navajo Business Council was created to approve leases with oil companies. In 1921, oil companies approached the Secretary of the Interior about leasing Navajo land.[1] They knew there was oil on the Navajo reservation, but, unfortunately for outside companies, there was no established mechanism for them to acquire permission to establish operations on the reservation. On the Navajo reservation, oil companies could not take advantage of allotment era excesses – such as rampant leasing of tribal lands and issuance of fee patents to tribal members that were then sold off to non-Indians – that worked on other reservations. Though other tribes had seen their land base broken up through such processes, the Navajo reservation was largely intact, except for a few areas to the south and east of the reservation near the railroad line. In 1849, as part of Grant's Peace Policy, administration of Indian affairs had been moved from the War Department to the Interior Department. And the Secretary of the Interior's position that Indian leases had to be approved by Indian tribes themselves meant that outsiders could not simply get the Secretary to sign off on such leases; Indians had to be involved.

Although the negotiations leading to the Treaty of Bosque Redondo showed one way oil companies could reach agreements with the tribe, it would hardly be practical to require the convening and gathering of headmen to negotiate every lease. Such a process would be prohibitively time consuming and would invite questions of legitimacy. The solution was the Navajo Business Council.

The Navajo Business Council began modestly in 1922 with only six delegates and a quite limited charge. The Council was created by the US government, and initially, the Secretary of the Interior reserved the right to remove any member of the Council "for cause," but by 1923 this Secretarial prerogative was withdrawn.[2] The Council's first Chairman was Henry Chee Dodge, the largest Navajo stock owner at the time, who, with his wife, "owned five thousand head of sheep, controlled 131,000 acres of reservation land, and possessed the largest private bank account in nearby Gallup."[3] The Council convened for the first time on July 7, 1923,[4] but met only infrequently after that for the next six years. The Council's work was largely limited to approving leases presented to them after oil companies and the Bureau of Indian Affairs (BIA) negotiated the terms.[5] As critical commentators have noted, the original Navajo Business Council arguably acted as a rubber stamp for outside interests seeking to access tribal resources.[6] The Council did push for further land transfers and other forms of support for the tribe, but to a large extent it acted more as agent for the US government and private oil and gas companies than as an independent body.[7] It is no wonder that, according to Jacob Morgan, an influential Navajo politician in the 1930s, "The original council has always been known as the 'men who are boss over the oil.'"[8]

Despite its limited purview and role, the Navajo Business Council did make its mark on the Navajo Nation. The United States wanted the Diné to be represented by a centralized government and formed the Council in the hope that it could perform that role. And though the Navajo Nation today is governed by three branches – the Navajo Nation Council, the Navajo Nation President, and the Navajo Nation Supreme Court – the centralization project began with the Navajo Business Council. Even though "the history of the Council indicates that for about ten or twelve years the majority of the Navajo either ignored or were unaware of the existence of the new tribal-wide political structure,"[9] centralization survived.[10] The Council replaced the informal governance structure of local family clusters and informally accepted headmen who had previously negotiated on behalf of the tribe with Indian Affairs officials on the reservation and in Washington, DC.[11] Diné society flourished after the Treaty of Bosque Redondo using essentially the same loose governance model as existed prior to conquest. Shared beliefs, values, and familial norms, such as the clan system, provided the basis for Diné interactions with colonial authorities until the formation of the Council. The decentralized nature of these practices made it difficult for non-Indians to recognize them as legitimate forms of governance; nonetheless, Diné were in fact exercising sovereignty and governance continuously.[12] But by replacing informal, ad hoc Diné leadership with a formal body that could speak for the tribe, the formation of the Council centralized and consolidated Navajo power.[13] The Council also crucially provided the institutional space needed for the tribe to better push for Navajo interests.

The Navajo Business Council made three especially significant and lasting decisions. First, tribal members living in the six administrative regions selected their delegate to the Council through a popular election. Because Diné did not previously have a central government, this structural choice did not run afoul of tribal traditions, though by moving some authority from local family units to the Council, it arguably did reposition various Diné actors. In particular, the expectation on the part of the US Government as well as the pre-existing gender-based division of responsibility served to elevate male leadership at the expense of women. Scholars have argued that Europeans brought with them not just Christianity, but misogynistic gender norms that were imposed on the tribes they encountered. Traditionally, Diné women had more power than Anglo-American women, a fact which debatably remained the case through this period. Diné society is matrilineal and matrilocal, meaning that property is owned and inherited through women, and upon marriage, couples live with the wife's family not the husband's. Matriarchs have tremendous power in assigning roles and rights within the extended household. But the larger non-Indian society was not prepared for women in leadership roles and expected Indians to send men to the negotiating table and to tribal government positions. The Council, insofar as it prioritized men's voices and came with an expectation that delegates would be men, diminished the power of Diné women in ways that have yet to be fully undone.[14] But turning away from the gendered impact of centralization, the decision – imposed by the US Government – to have Council delegates selected democratically has become fundamental to Navajo governance.

Second, the Council decided to collect oil and gas revenues at a national, not local, level. Even though oil and gas wells were being placed in particular tribal communities, the Council decided that associated revenues belonged to the entire tribe. The Council chose not to distribute such lease revenue on a per capita basis nor to target the regions that happened to have such natural resources.[15] This decision had tremendous impact on the tribe, on the power of the central government, and on the incentives for leasing land to energy companies. Had tribal revenues from leases been retained by local communities, some areas would have gotten quite wealthy while other parts of the reservation would have seen little advantage in approving extractive energy leases. Positioning the Council as the entity that collects and distributes lease payments strengthened the Council's authority and power. Ensuring that such revenues from different parts of the reservation were pooled also meant that the newly established central government had a degree of economic might that off-reservation parties had to acknowledge. Finally, treating revenues as national funds meant that local communities bore the negative environmental impacts of particular projects while the central government and tribal members collectively received the benefits. Even in cases where a local community might object to a proposed project, leases were still likely to be approved because revenue flowed to the Council. This imbalance, whereby local communities deal with the downside of hosting projects while lease revenue flows to the central government has led to moments of crisis and divisions within the tribe. But without continued adherence to this early decision of the Tribal Business Council, the Navajo Nation government would be considerably smaller and weaker.

Third, the Council opened up the reservation to private oil and gas companies. Since the Council was formed purposefully to accomplish as much, the fact that it did in fact approve oil and gas leases is not surprising.[16] However, the Council was empowered to say yes or no, making the fact that it said yes, again and again, notable. At its very first meeting, the Council approved a fast track oil leasing arrangement.[17] Opening up the reservation to energy companies would have far-reaching consequences, not only because the tribe would discover that leases, once approved, were hard to rescind, but also because the tribal government, which had expanded as a result of lease revenue, became dependent on extractive industry. As early as 1933, when the Council "passed a resolution to cancel all oil or gas leases, even those extended by council in 1926 and renewed in 1931," the durability of leases generated buyer's remorse.[18] But the die had been cast.

Though the tribe received less for its resources than it should have, the tribe's oil leasing revenues contributed significantly to the rise of the Navajo Nation government. The early leases were auctioned off at a time of high production nationwide, which served to depress tribal gains.[19] Subsequent leases similarly had notably low returns, in part because the federal government had little interest in maximizing tribal benefits.[20] Despite the trust relationship that exists on paper between the United States and Indian tribes, Washington's interests seem to have aligned more closely with those of private companies, such as Standard Oil, than with the Navajo Nation. Between 1880 and 1970, "royalties actually paid were less than one-eighth (or one-sixth) of the assessed value of the oil produced" on Indian land.[21] Indeed, by 1978, while "well over $2 billion in crude oil had been exported from the Navajo Reservation," the tribe had only "received about $300 million in royalties."[22] As Michael Joseph Francisconi noted in his 1998 book on the Navajo economy, the tribe "receives lower royalties from its oil than most third world countries."[23]

Told in this way, the story of Navajo oil is a story of exploitation. After all, the tribal government was formed to approve of oil leases yet the tribe received only a fraction of what non-Indian land owners would have been paid for their oil. Certainly there is some truth to this version of the story. In 1955, the comparatively large Aneth oil field was discovered, located on the small part of the reservation that extends over the Arizona border into Utah.[24] The Aneth field would produce for decades, but revenues peaked in 1957.[25] In 1977, Navajos in the Aneth, Utah area of the Navajo Nation set up roadblocks and "shut down operations" at the Aneth oil field.[26] The occupiers complained that "the underground wealth of their land has not meant a better or easier life."[27] Led by the Coalition for Navajo Liberation, the "occupying force" eventually "swelled to one thousand" people, and, according to the *Navajo Times,* residents threw rocks at oil representatives.[28] But besides showing local dissatisfaction, the occupation also shows that tribal members at times are at odds with the tribal government. Just as there are factions and policy splits off-reservation, the story of oil development can be told from a perspective different than that of the protestors and of those who emphasize the exploitative element of the oil leases. For all their faults, oil revenues – in the form of royalties, bonuses, and rents – fueled the rise of the tribal bureaucracy. Though oil would subsequently be supplanted in importance to the tribal budget by revenue associated with coal mining, tribal oil revenue was $27.7 million in 1958, which amounted to 90 percent of the entire tribal budget.[29] The original Council might have accurately been called the "men who are boss over the oil," but oil provided enough of an incentive for the United States to form a centralized Navajo government[30] and these revenues allowed Diné leaders to substantially expand the tribal government's role.[31]

Diné were not alone in witnessing their tribal government expand over this period. Federal Indian policy reversed course in the late 1920s and early 1930s, from its emphasis over the previous fifty years on breaking apart reservations through allotment to a focus on the right of tribes to govern themselves. This change in the direction of the wind coming out of Washington was aided by the publication in 1928 of a report, *The Problem of Indian Administration*, by the Institute for Government Research. The report, commonly known as the Meriam Report after its lead investigator, Lewis Meriam, was both comprehensive – it was nearly 850 pages long and involved sending senior researchers to reservations across the country – and damning.[32] The tone for the report was set in the Report's first sentence, which read, "An overwhelming majority of the Indians are poor, even extremely poor, and they are not adjusted to the economic and social system of the dominant white civilization."[33] Although the Meriam Report was about how the United States should deal with Indians moving forward and quite deliberately avoided talking about the wrongs done to Indians in the past, it repetitively highlighted the extreme poverty, poor health, and bad conditions experienced by Indians living on reservations. It acknowledged the arguments made by allotment advocates but came down in opposition to the "experiment" of regularly issuing fee patents to Indians.[34]

When it came to reservation poverty, the report oscillated between blaming Indians for their own situation and faulting the US government. Indians, the report argued, had grown accustomed to government-issued rations and consequently "developed a pauper point of view."[35] The report even cited race-based intelligence testing of the sort then in vogue that purported to show that Indians were not as smart as whites.[36] In language that today would be recognized as racist, the report stated, "[a] relatively small number of Indians make the transition from primitive to civilized life successfully; the great majority tend to shift from primitive ways to the ways of the poorest and least enterprising of the white population."[37] According to the report, Indian women were neither competent nor industrious, though, it added, "women of some tribes, notably the Hopis and the Navajos, know how to do many things and are usually found busy at their tasks."[38] But the report laid most of the blame for Indian poverty on the US government. Though laced with language that betrays a host of racist assumptions, the Report's summary of the causes of Indian poverty began, "The economic basis of the primitive culture of the Indians has been largely destroyed by the encroachment of white civilization. The Indians can no longer make a living as they did in the past by hunting, fishing, gathering wild products, and the extremely limited practice of primitive agriculture."[39] Not only did white civilization destroy their economies, but, according to the report, "it is doubtful whether a well-rounded program of economic advancement framed with due consideration of the natural resources of the reservation has anywhere been thoroughly tried out."[40] The report did not entirely neglect the efforts tribal members were making to improve their economic wellbeing, and even went so far as to label the Navajos the "largest body of self-supporting Indians in the United States."[41] But it described reservations as largely dependent on the United States: "As wards of the government the Indians find their economic affairs largely shaped and controlled by governmental policies and the acts of government officers."[42]

The Meriam Report did a tremendous job documenting the state of Indian reservations at the time and by so doing helped change US-Indian relations. But there were a number of possible paths forward in the wake of the report. One route, which finds some support in the report itself, especially when it comes to criminal jurisdiction, would be to incorporate Indians as much as possible into the states, converting the federal-Indian relationship into a state-Indian relationship. But there were reasons to pause before going down that path. As Justice Miller wrote in 1886, Indian communities "owe no allegiance to the States, and receive from them no protection. Because of the local ill feeling, the people of the States where they are found are often their deadliest enemies."[43] The Meriam Report's chapter on Indians who migrated to neighboring off-reservation towns showed that Indians there were often relegated to the edges of society. An alternative path would be for the United States to invest the resources necessary to attract skilled administrators and fully staff programs serving reservations. Besides highlighting Indian poverty, finding better ways to support tribes by revamping the Indian Service was the main thrust of the Meriam Report. The report went into considerable detail about improvements that could be made to Indian health care provision, educational training, and even family organization.

As important as the Meriam Report was, federal policy does not turn on a dime. A year and a half after its publication, Black Friday and the stock market collapse of 1929 plunged the country into the Great Depression. Franklin Delano Roosevelt was elected President in 1932, and Roosevelt appointed John Collier as Commissioner for the Bureau of Indian Affairs. The Meriam Report provided a launching point for radically reshaping Indian policy. Roosevelt and Collier could take for granted a general agreement that past policies had not worked and that something had to be done about the poverty on Indian reservations. What that something would be, however, was a more open question that was answered by the Indian Reorganization Act (IRA) of 1934. The Act officially ended allotment and established a mechanism for tribes to assume greater governance authority. Tribes who decided, through referendum, to become IRA tribes opted into adopting new tribal constitutions and tribal governments under the IRA model. Though debates rage about whether the IRA was a colonizing document or an enlightened way to support tribal sovereignty, the truth probably lies between those two extreme characterizations of the Act. Compared to the allotment era, the Indian New Deal was a tremendous step forward. Through it, tribes could form governments that would be recognized by the United States and were empowered to determine priorities for their nations. IRA governments could take a lead role in managing tribal lands and tribal natural resources. The IRA allowed tribes the possibility of exercising their tribal sovereignty. But negatively, the IRA was a one-size-fits-all, top-down, Washington-based plan; IRA governments were not tribally developed forms of governance. For some tribes, the IRA model worked. It fit with their prior governance traditions and became a powerful tool for tribal advancement. For others, the IRA did not work. It imposed a form of government that was foreign and ill-fitting. And the pendulum only swung so far: IRA left in place many of the structural features of continued federal control over reservations, most notably a requirement that the Secretary of the Interior sign off on major tribal decisions.

FIGURE 3.1 "The United States Indian Commissioner John Collier and Navajo Chief Chee Dodge meet in 1933. They stand for a portrait against a wall with the assistant commissioner Charles Collier, Collier's son, and Chairman of the Indian Council Tom Dodge, Dodge's son." (Photo by Bettmann Archive/Getty Images)

For Diné, the question of whether to approve or reject the IRA was bound up in their feelings about John Collier and his plan to reduce the number of sheep on the reservation. At first blush, Collier appeared the epitome of a nerdy, wonky bureaucrat. Not particularly tall and awkward looking in photos, Collier nevertheless wielded tremendous power over Indian tribes across the United States. Collier saw himself as a champion of tribal sovereignty who stood in opposition to the forced assimilation policies of the past.[44] But his actions present a more complicated picture.[45] As Donald Fixico explains, "[b]ehind the glasses of Collier's myopic eyes, if you were not for him, you were against him."[46] Collier was a frequent visitor to Window Rock, where he spoke at a number of Navajo Business Council meetings to urge the tribe to accept the IRA. According to Collier, should the Diné approve of an IRA government, they would be able to expand their government.[47] Collier sweetened the pot by saying the tribe would have access to a revolving loan fund, better educational programs, and a tribal court system. But tellingly, at a March 1934 meeting of the Council, Collier gave a standard stump speech for the IRA instead of speaking to Diné issues:

> Collier erred by explaining the program in excruciating detail, including pages of his address dedicated to allotment, a policy that barely affected Navajos. Details became more confusing when translated into Navajo for the 90 percent of the people in attendance who did not speak English. One attendee compared the presentation to a game where a "person hides the ball and others guess where it is."[48]

Navajos were not convinced, and by a razor-thin margin voted "no" on the IRA referendum.[49] Because of the large population and geographic size of the Navajo reservation relative to other tribes, it was a significant defeat for Collier. Rejection of the IRA was followed by a government reform project, this time Navajo-led, which established the basic structure of the Navajo Nation government from 1938 until 1989. Over two days in April 1937 a Navajo constitutional assembly met, and in October 1937, a new Navajo constitution was transmitted to the Secretary of the Interior for approval. But the Secretary rejected the proposed constitution and in July 1938, sent back a minimal set of by-laws that only provided for the election of the Navajo Tribal Council.[50] To this day, the Navajo Nation government continues to operate without a formal constitution, though it declared Navajo customary law, or "Navajo Fundamental Law," as the highest law of the land in 2002.[51] Even though the tribe rejected the IRA-defined parameters for establishing a tribal government that would be recognized by the United States, out of necessity or because there was little alternative, the Navajo Tribal Council formed in the wake of the rejected constitutional effort was immediately acknowledged as the legitimate political body of the tribe.

Indeed, the post–Meriam Report period witnessed the rise of another significant feature of Navajo governance, the creation and spread of the chapter house system across the reservation. Chapter houses, much like the Council before them, were not a Diné creation, though with time they became uniquely Navajo institutions. An Indian agent organized the first chapter because he sought a way to reach and hear from tribal members in his assigned area. Unlike the Tribal Council, this innovation sprang out of the needs of a local Indian agent, but it spread because it worked. At various times, the US government and the Tribal Council saw the utility of supporting this more grassroots form of governance.[52] Unlike the central tribal government, chapters more closely reflected the ways Diné traditionally made decisions and governed themselves.[53] With 110 chapters spread across the reservation, chapters could build on the tribe's loose governance model of local family clusters organized much as they were prior to the Treaty of Bosque Redondo. But the chapter system fits uncomfortably alongside the central Navajo Nation government. Because there is no Navajo constitution and the chapter system developed somewhat organically, the relationship between chapters and the central administration is unclear and subject to contestation. In theory, chapters could deal with local issues and the central government could focus on the relationship between Navajos and outsiders,[54] but in practice the central government's role came to dwarf that of local chapters. The tension between local and national governance will be discussed in greater detail in Chapter 8, but that tension was evident even during this formative period.

Diné faced many tough moments in the late 1920s and 1930s. But on the whole, Collier's efforts to establish an IRA government and the tribe's efforts to reform their government were minor headwinds compared to the crisis and hardship of stock reduction.[55] It is often hard for outsiders to understand the central role of sheep in Diné culture and the connection Diné have to their animals. Though the Spanish brought sheep to the New World, by the time Diné were interned at Bosque Redondo, sheep were a fundamental part of Diné identity.[56] In spite of living in a challenging environment with little rain or vegetation, sheep herds expanded dramatically from 1868 onwards under the skilled care of Diné shepherds. Until stock reduction, sheep and goats were the primary form of wealth for most Diné families.[57] Relative status in the community was connected to herd size, and herds were one of the main material gifts that parents gave children upon marriage and through inheritance. Wool was sold to traders, exchanged at trading posts for food or made into rugs, the sales of which were a significant source of income across the reservation. Animals also provided a source of food in lean times. Without their herds, many Diné faced a very real prospect of starvation.

So, when Collier insisted that Diné reduce the number of sheep, goats, and horses on the reservation, it wasn't just a minor administrative change, it was an existential threat to Diné livelihood, identity, and way of life.[58] The idea that Navajos had too many sheep originated in reports from experts who warned that the tribe faced catastrophic soil erosion. Engineers working on completing the engineering marvel then known as Boulder Dam, now called Hoover Dam, also feared that the dam's utility would be reduced if Navajo silt caused by overgrazing filled up behind the dam.[59] A US Geological Survey report called the Navajo reservation "practically

'Public Enemy No. 1' in causing the Colorado Silt problem."[60] Additionally, overgrazing was causing deep scars, arroyos, to form on the land, and was creating further desertification that threatened to erode the range-carrying capacity of much of the reservation. Experts used photos of the same areas taken at different times to show growth of these arroyos.[61] From the perspective of Washington scientists and policy-makers, something had to be done; experts felt they had to protect the tribe from itself, lest Navajos inadvertently ruin their own territory.[62] Many Diné saw things differently, of course. They had been through droughts and bad spells before but they believed that the hard years would give way to better conditions if they lived according to their traditional values.[63] Even if they agreed that something had to be done about overgrazing, many Diné leaders felt that solutions should come from the tribe, rather than be imposed by Washington.[64] But that is not what ultimately happened; the United States, with a thin veneer of tribal buy-in, forced stock reduction upon the reservation.

Federal officials raised stock reduction as an issue before the Council in 1928,[65] but livestock reduction was not implemented until the Roosevelt Administration. Told they had little choice, and that stock reduction would be accompanied by additional land transfers to the tribe accompanied by jobs to offset the pain of culling the herds, the Council voted to approve a federal plan of voluntary reductions in 1933.[66] Experts of all stripes descended on the reservation.[67] Parts of the reservation were fenced off as demonstration sites to show how the range could recover with proper care. Estimating that the reservation had double as much livestock as the range could support, agents began culling the herds.[68] In theory, agents told tribal members they had to reduce their herds and then agents paid for sheep turned over to them. But the first round of livestock reduction was not terribly successful. Diné families got rid of their least productive animals, keeping the younger sheep in order to rebuild their herds later. That is not to say that reduction was a voluntary program. After imposing a cap on the number of animals a family could have, those responsible for carrying out the reduction would force sales – by telling Navajos that they had no choice – at prices that were supposed to be fair but were below what Diné would have willingly accepted for their animals.[69] Subsequent rounds were more heavy-handed.

Livestock reduction struck the poorest Diné families the hardest.[70] The largest stock owners, such as Dodge and other elites, raised their stock to sell to outside markets, but those with smaller holdings lived with their animals, eking out a subsistence living. For the poor, each animal was part of their family, and they were living close enough to the edge to know that the loss of even a small part of their herd could have tragic consequences. The poor disproportionately owned goats, so when the federal government decided to target goats, it was also targeting the poor. Even across-the-board decisions, such as reducing every family's herd by five sheep, involved much greater relative hardship for poorer families with smaller herds.[71] A similar dynamic occurred when chapter officials implemented reduction according to pasture quality, making decisions about allowable herd sizes according to the carrying capacity of each family's traditional use area.[72] Because large stock owners controlled the best pasture land, tying reductions to land quality also tended to hurt the poor.[73] Collier was not blind to these equity issues, but efforts to put caps on herd size invited challenges based on different definitions of family and owner-ship. Simply declaring that no one could have a herd above 1,000 head did not solve the problem because many different members of a large extended family might in fact own sheep within a larger herd. An observable herd associated with a single Diné couple could include sheep owned – in reality or at least for the purpose of avoiding the demands of reduction – by various aunts, uncles, cousins, and children. Cutting through such family and cross-cultural minefields was naturally hard,[74] which, along with the political might of the largest stockowners, limited the ability and appetite of officials to use livestock reduction as a mechanism for advancing equity. Instead, those who could least afford to lose part of their herd bore the brunt of livestock reduction.[75]

Livestock reduction also exacted a heavy emotional and financial toll on the tribe. Rather than go to the expense of transporting animals to off-reservation slaughter-houses already overwhelmed by Navajo sheep, agents would sometimes kill the animals in front of families still grieving over having to surrender them.[76] Though livestock reduction took place in the midst of the Great Depression, some of the animals "were merely shot and left to rot" – a level of waste that Navajos "were incapable of understanding."[77] Navajos who resisted reduction by hiding or by not turning over their animals were imprisoned or faced other forms of judicial enforcement.[78] Diné intensely disliked stock reduction. In a letter written to John Collier in 1936, Chee Dodge reported, "the tribe is practically unanimous in their determination to turn [further reduction] down."[79] The vote of some members of the Council in 1937 in support of stock reduction inspired "[a] virtual storm of protest."[80] Most damaging, for a tribe that had been identified as "self-supporting" by the Meriam Report in 1928,[81] stock reduction threatened to make it impossible for many Diné families to earn enough money to care for themselves. In 1940, tribal members observed, "[f]rom a tribe self-sufficient and self-supporting, the Bureau is forcing us to become depend[e]nt upon charity for our subsistence. We only desire to be financially independent and make our own way."[82] And in the same year, a delegate argued before the Council, "What I mean is we cannot stand any more reduction. We are all going to fall into a big hungry lot."[83]

Ultimately, stock reduction succeeded in pushing down the number of sheep on the reservation, but it did so by undercutting tribal economic independence and the Diné way of life. Prior to stock reduction, Navajos had more than one million sheep; by 1946, that number was more than halved to 449,000 sheep on the reservation.[84] Prior to stock reduction, of course, Diné were connected to the larger society and to external markets. Off-reservation demand for wool and Navajo rugs, in part, drove the growth of Diné herds. But Diné families could meet such demand in ways that largely preserved their isolation from the Bilagáana world and continued traditional ways of life. Stock reduction threw a wrench in the engine of Diné economic growth and self-sufficiency. Collier promised the Council that new employment opportunities would fill the economic holes created by stock reduction, and many Diné did find jobs working for New Deal government programs such as the Civilian Conservation Corps and the Soil Conservation Corps.[85] But the promised jobs did not fully offset stock reduction losses,[86] nor did such jobs continue in the post-war period.

For Diné, stock reduction is remembered as a trauma approaching that of their earlier internment at Bosque Redondo.[87] Families living at near subsistence levels could ill afford stock reduction, and even those who were better off suffered dramatic wealth declines.[88] Collier's hope was that stock reduction would protect Diné self-sufficiency by preventing overgrazing from ruining the range, but ironically stock reduction forced the tribe into dependency.[89] As Kathleen Chamberlain notes in her fabulous history, Under Sacred Ground: A History of Navajo Oil, 1922–1982, "[m]any Navajos lost their livelihood altogether and were forced to accept government subsidies for the first time."[90] In a 1940 letter to Senator Dennis Chavez, Deshna Clah Cheschillige complained, "Many of our people are now poor and are forced to live on relief. We do not like relief and want to make our own living and we know we can do so if we are left alone."[91] While New Deal job programs protected some tribal members against the worst effects of reduction, when that sort of support disappeared in the post–World War II period, bad weather and a devastated economy left Diné not at risk of starving, but actually starving. Emergency relief came to the reservation after popular magazines published photo essays of the poor conditions on the reservation. And to this day, Diné receive welfare in a form that is not common among other places in the United States: commodities such as bread, cheese, and surplus canned goods. High poverty rates and welfare dependency cannot be attributed entirely or even primarily to stock reduction of course, but stock reduction had a devastating impact on tribal agency and independence. Backlash against stock reduction contributed to the Navajo vote against the proposed IRA form of government, but rather than celebrating this example of a tribe exercising independent judgment, something Collier claimed to support, Collier arguably hardened his resolve to carry out stock reduction.[92] Although Collier supported tribal governance rhetorically, for Diné, Collier was the worst sort of Bilagáana; he may not have burned down their peach orchards, but he took away their sheep.

The stock reduction program provided clear evidence to Diné that the United States was ultimately in charge of the reservation economy. From the time Diné returned from Bosque Redondo in 1868 until the stock reduction program, the Diné economy could be described as internally managed. Though there were of course external forces such as market demand for Diné products and pressure to not extend the reservation into areas with non-Indian ranching interests, Diné made independent choices regarding how to respond to those forces. As a people, they had done well even in the face of tremendous obstacles. Though the society beyond the reservation border assumed Diné would die off and that their culture would fade, they rebuilt their herds and their population. Stock reduction changed the narrative by substituting Diné priorities with Washington edicts.[93]

The Diné belief that the range would recover and that Diné should manage their own agriculture was pushed aside by New Deal bureaucrats confident that they knew better.[94] Diné knowledge of the land tied to the tribe's experience living between the four sacred mountains since before Spanish contact was brushed aside. The point is not that nothing should have been done to protect the reservation against overgrazing and desertification but that the stock reduction program, in part because it was externally imposed, crippled the tribe's ability to right itself. Similarly, the move to wage labor was already well underway – it was "clear by the 1930s that the Navajo could 'no longer live by sheep alone'" – before being pushed by Washington.[95] Navajos warned US officials that the livestock levels of the stock reduction program would impoverish tribal members,[96] yet the program went forward until the Navajo Tribal Council convinced the Bureau of Indian Affairs (BIA) to effectively end the stock reduction program at the end of World War II.[97] Tribal members correctly saw stock reduction as a threat to their way of life. Compounding the problems that could have come from any livestock reduction program, which would have been difficult enough on its own, is the heavy-handed way that the program was implemented by the federal government – a foreign, historically-hostile government.[98]

Since the end of the livestock reduction period, efforts to restore the range have been much less ambitious.[99] Grazing, while still important culturally and still part of tribal identity, became a matter of secondary importance with the rise of the wage economy after the war.[100] Spurred along in part by the termination era policy of encouraging tribal members to leave reservations under the Indian Relocation Act of 1956, many Diné found work off-reservation. The Navajo range is no longer able to provide a suitable livelihood for the entire tribe.[101]

4

War Production and Growing Pains

Uranium and Coal

In 2002, MGM released the blockbuster film, *Windtalkers*, starring Nicolas Cage and Adam Beach. John Woo's movie highlighted the role Navajo code talkers played in World War II. Though it was the white sergeant, played by Nicholas Cage, who was the central figure in *Windtalkers*, the movie brought popular attention to the part Navajo code talkers and the Diné language played in the war. It was the only unbroken code of the war. Congress and several presidents have recognized the code talkers as heroes.[1] Navajos, like Indians in general, marched off to fight in Europe and the Pacific in disproportionate numbers. But when veterans returned to the reservation, they faced many of the same problems of bigotry and poverty that existed prior to the war. In Arizona, it wasn't until 1948 that Diné were allowed to vote in off-reservation elections, and literacy tests kept the number of registered Diné voters artificially low until the Voting Rights Act of 1965 partially opened up the ballot box.[2] The period after the war was particularly challenging when it came to tribal sovereignty and economic development. The Navajo reservation, like the rest of the country, passed through the post-war recession, but unlike areas off-reservation, the tribe was largely denied the opportunity to find its footing. Instead, Washington's general antagonism to tribal sovereignty, coupled with demand for Navajo uranium and coal, severely undermined Navajo independence.

If the pendulum of federal Indian policy under President Roosevelt and the IRA supported tribal sovereignty, federal Indian policy swung hard in the opposite direction after the war. In 1949, the Hoover Commission's Report on Indian Affairs called for the "complete integration" of Indians as US citizens.[3] Integration was to be accomplished through assimilation and denial of collective rights, often in the form of attacking the reservation land base. The "Termination Period" lasted less than two decades, from 1945 to 1961, but for the unlucky tribes targeted, the results of termination were even more devastating than allotment. Terminated tribes lost both their land and federal recognition as tribes. State jurisdiction was extended over tribal members who lost federal recognition, and as a result, these tribes lost access to Indian-focused programs. Although tribal identity exists independent of federal recognition, termination made denial of that identity and of tribal sovereignty official federal policy. Whereas the US government had sought during the country's westward expansion to use military might to defeat and constrain Indian tribes to reservations, through termination it hoped to define tribal nations out of existence.

Just as had been the case with allotment, Navajos once again survived. They were not terminated and even succeeded in beating back an effort by Arizona to limit their sovereignty. The Navajos were one of the more fortunate tribes, but that does not mean there were not scars. Termination reminded tribes of the power of the US government to unilaterally strip their sovereignty. With termination as the overarching framework, it is perhaps not surprising that reservation economic development became a Washington-based, top-down endeavor. The Navajo government remained intact, but powerful external interests steered tribal land use decisions. By not revealing the dangers involved and by holding back information on the value of tribal resources, the US government facilitated particularly destructive forms of development, while at the same time it failed to ensure the tribe received fair compensation for its resources.

The Manhattan Project, centered in Las Cruces, New Mexico, and the subsequent dropping of bombs on Hiroshima and Nagasaki ushered in the Nuclear Age. Diné were blessed and cursed with large deposits of extractable uranium. With the Cold War heating up, national security demanded that the federal government and mining interests get access to this form of powdered gold; large and small operations were set up across the reservation. In pursuit of radioactive material, the US government treated Navajo workers and tribal lands indifferently, exposing both to long-term harm that has yet to be rectified. A similar, if less dramatic, dynamic played out with regard to Navajo coal deposits. Although national security was not at stake, Navajo coal was needed to fuel the growth of off-reservation southwestern cities. Energy interests, eyeing the expanding metropolises of Las Vegas, Los Angeles, and Phoenix, clamored for cheap coal far removed from areas that would object to such intense natural resource extraction. They found it on the Navajo reservation. And, despite the trust obligation, energy companies also found that the federal government was more aligned with their interests than with the best interests of the tribe. Though the harm from unfavorably long-term coal leases is less striking than abandoned uranium tailing piles and cancer-stricken workers, a belief that Navajo resources are available for the taking underlies the tribe's experience with both uranium and coal mining after World War II.

4.1 URANIUM

In 1939, Albert Einstein wrote a letter to President Roosevelt urging him to "speed up the experimental work" on nuclear chain reactions.[4] Einstein expected "that the element uranium may be turned into a new and important source of energy in the immediate future," and noted that from such material "extremely powerful bombs of a new type may thus be created." At the time he was writing, the Belgian Congo was "the most important source" of uranium and Germany had ominously decided to stop the sale of Czechoslovakian ore, which was then under its control. The Manhattan Project, which Roosevelt greenlighted, acquired most of its uranium from the Belgian Congo, though the United States also imported uranium from Canada and South Africa.[5] The world learned of the deadly power of nuclear energy when Colonel Paul Tibbet's Boeing B-29 Superfortress, the Enola Gay, dropped "Little Boy," an atomic bomb, on Hiroshima, Japan the morning of August 6, 1945. Three days later, the United States dropped a second atomic bomb on Japan, this time targeting the port city of Nagasaki. The Japanese surrendered less than a week later, on August 15, 1945, ending World War II. The embers of the war were still hot when the nuclear arms race took off in earnest. This time Diné contributions to the war effort came not in the form of an unbreakable code, but in the exploitation of their land and their health.

Although it is hard to imagine this today, initially uranium was the waste product surrounding minerals that were more valuable: radium and vanadium. "In 1917, when the global market for radium hit its pre-World War II peak and uranium's radioactivity was discovered, a white trader to the Navajo Nation named John Wetherill hauled some uranium-bearing carnotite ore to Flagstaff, Arizona to be sent to France for Marie Curie's radiological experiments."[6] Demand for domestic sources of uranium surged with the Manhattan Project, which recovered approximately 76,000 pounds worth from the tailings piles of vanadium mines on the reservation.[7] But the secrecy associated with the Project, as well as the availability of imported uranium, limited the exploitation of the reservation during the war itself. Afterward, the world knew about the bomb, so secrecy faded in importance. The government paid well for uranium as part of the nuclear arms race with the USSR, leading large non-Indian companies and small wildcat operations to scour the reservation, establishing thousands of mines between the late 1940s and late 1970s.[8]

The Navajo Tribal Council approved of uranium mining and companies paid the tribe to extract uranium from Navajo land, but Council approval did not prevent exploitation. Because of the intensity of mining operations, some parts of the reservation became pockmarked with exploratory mines and tailing piles.[9] Mining took place in some remote parts of the reservation, such as throughout the mountains near Cove, Arizona, but it was not geographically limited.[10] Shovels were sunk into Monument Valley, one of the reservation's most iconic areas,[11] and the riverbank of the San Juan River near one of the tribe's larger cities, Shiprock, New Mexico, became an industrial storage site. All one needs to locate these locations today is a Geiger counter or a trained set of eyes. The land has not been reclaimed and, at current funding levels, it will be decades or even centuries before many of these areas are made safe once again. Low levels of radiation are not harmful, but the mining process significantly raises the level of exposed uranium and radiation at former mining sites.

Uranium mining is dangerous work. To get uranium, ore with encased uranium must be broken into small particles and then extracted using a chemical leaching

FIGURE 4.1 "Navajo Indian mining uranium in United States, May 1951." (Photo by Loomis Dean/The LIFE Picture Collection via Getty Images)

process that results in a powder known as "yellowcake." The ore is broken up with dynamite, pick-axes, and shovels, then moved out of the mine by hand or pushcart. Leaching can be done at distant sites, but many of the operations on the reservation used in situ leaching, extracting the uranium at the mine itself. For miners, dangers are everywhere. When rock is exploded, particulate matter fills the air and radiation levels soar. Proper mine ventilation, the use of water to reduce the amount of airborne particulate matter, respirators or breathing masks, and shorter shifts per worker can reduce the risk associated with such mining. Incredibly, "rates of exposure in some mines were one thousand times the maximum level recommended by the Public Health Service and exceeded radiation doses from the atomic bombs in Japan."[12] But even though the dangers of uranium mining were understood, such practices were seldom required, and when they were, they were poorly enforced on the Navajo reservation. US government health specialists knew that men working in the mines would suffer an "epidemic of lung cancer" and sounded the alarm, but the Atomic Energy Commission neither protected nor warned workers of the dangers.[13] Charitably, the Commission deemed national security and, later, energy interests sufficiently important to warrant putting Navajo lives in danger.[14] Looking back, however, it seems the US government and mining companies considered Navajo miners expendable – unworthy of the added costs required to protect them.

Cancer and other respiratory diseases spiked, as expected, but miners were not the only ones impacted.[15] Diné families built homes using mine tailings as the gravel base for the concrete floors of their hogans, the traditional eight-sided Diné house. Children played on open tailing piles located next to trading posts and freely explored abandoned mines that were poorly marked and not sealed off. Leaching impacted neighboring wells, which tribal members continued to use unknowingly for decades. Recovery efforts remain sporadic, dependent on federal superfund priorities and funding. For many of the communities most impacted, the extreme poverty of the area complicates their view of past mining. Congress passed the Radiation Exposure Compensation Act in 1990, which provided compensation for workers who suffered or died as a result of leukemia, thyroid cancer, bone cancer or any other cancer identified by an advisory board on the health effects of radiation and uranium exposure connected to the Cold War nuclear arms race.[16] Applying for compensation required proving employment from decades prior, or, for widows, proving the legality of their marriage. These paperwork hurdles meant that victims had to climb high bureaucratic walls in order to get compensation.[17] However, for those who managed to get through the process, the payments often felt life changing. Six-figure compensation checks do not bring back loved ones, but do go a long way in areas where unemployment hovers around 50 percent. For some communities and workers, the uranium mining costs were staggering: "Of the 150 Navajo miners that worked at the Shiprock, New Mexico uranium mine until 1970, 133 had died of lung cancer or various forms of fibrosis by 1980."[18] No wonder then that when Red Valley, Arizona finally got a high school, ending the practice of transporting children on hour long rides from the state line to Shiprock, New Mexico, the community picked "The Miners" – complete with a depiction of a Navajo man wearing a hardhat with a lamp on top – as the school's mascot.

The tribal government treated uranium revenues in the same way as they had gas and oil leasing: receiving such payments in Window Rock and using the proceeds for the benefit of the central government. On the strength of booming oil and gas wells in the Four Corners and around Shiprock and Farmington, combined with uranium royalties, the tribal budget soared.[19] The tribal government was able to take on additional responsibilities, providing social services and "soon became among the largest employers" on the reservation.[20] As Andrew Needham notes, "Tribal budgets increased exponentially throughout the 1950s, from $1 million in 1954 to $13 million by 1958. By that time, 23 percent of wages earned on the reservation came directly from tribal government."[21] As the tribal government expanded, the Navajo Nation became more capable of expanding and defending its sovereignty.

One of the more significant tribal victories during the 1950s began relatively innocuously when an Indian trader seized twenty-eight sheep and four goats from Paul and Lorena Williams in 1952. The dispute over this seizure, made under the authority of the state of Arizona, ultimately reached the US Supreme Court. Bethany Berger's detailed histories of the case reveal the ways a seemingly simple dispute over household debt helped guarantee the tribe's right to govern the reservation.[22] The trader, Hugh Lee, had extended credit to the Williamses for purchases made at the Ganado Trading Post.[23] On October 21, 1952, Sherriff John Crosby of Apache County, Arizona took the Williamses' animals "indiscriminately, taking ewes from their lambs and lambs from their mothers," then brought them to the trading post.[24] The tribe, which recognized that this was an attack on both the centrality of sheep for Navajos and on the powers of the tribal government, immediately got involved, asserting that Arizona did not have jurisdiction over the dispute. The case wound its way up the state judicial system. The Williamses lost before the Arizona Supreme Court, but the US Supreme Court granted certiorari and held in favor of the tribe. The Court held that the tribe had authority over the dispute, not Arizona. Writing for the Court, Justice Black explained, "There can be no doubt that to allow the exercise of state jurisdiction here would undermine the authority of the tribal courts over Reservation affairs, and hence would infringe on the right of the Indians to govern themselves."[25] The Court's unanimous decision in 1959 protected the Navajo Nation from state interference and helped shore up the foundation of the Navajo judicial system.

Efforts on the part of the Navajo government were aided by federal efforts to improve the tribe's economic situation and to provide needed infrastructure to the reservation. In the wake of national attention to starving Navajos and the need for the US government to provide emergency assistance, Congress passed the Navajo-Hopi Long Range Rehabilitations Act of 1950.[26] The Act, modeled on the Marshall Plan, provided "$88 million for roads, communications, business enterprises, and other services."[27] The money, supplemented with funding from the Atomic Energy Commission, helped connect parts of the reservation that had previously required time-consuming and difficult journeys. It was during this period that roads were built connecting Kayenta with Tuba City, Monument Valley, and Teec Nos Pos.[28] Though few paved roads existed on the reservation in 1950,[29] by 1961 "nearly 300 miles of new paved highways and 360 miles of gravel roads were constructed across the reservation."[30] This infrastructure spending was in accord with the nationwide emphasis on road construction, including most notably the Eisenhower Interstate System. Reservation roads, such as the "Navajo Trail" between Tuba City and Kayenta, were "built not just to facilitate tourism, but also to improve access to oil, coal, and uranium deposits then being developed."[31]

Uranium mining on the reservation fits uncomfortably in the larger history of the post-war years. As the road improvements show, there were advances during this period and the tribal government matured, taking on additional roles and providing additional services to tribal members.[32] But the federal government continued to be in the driver's seat. For both financial and political reasons, it is hard to imagine that the tribe could have meaningfully resisted the establishment of mining operations on the reservation. In the 1950s and 1960s, Navajo children were still being compelled to study in distant boarding schools,[33] the Bureau of Indian Affairs pursued an assimilationist strategy of encouraging tribal members to move off-reservation through its urban relocation program,[34] and the threat of termination hung over tribal governments. The dangers of uranium mining extended beyond the health effects on workers and area families, which the tribe learned the hard way in 1979. The

United Nuclear Corporation and Kerr-McGee Corporation operated large mines in the Church Rock, New Mexico area, including the world's largest underground – as opposed to open pit – uranium mine.[35] Mill tailings were dumped in an evaporation pond formed behind a poorly maintained earthen dam.[36] When the dam broke on the morning of July 16, 1979, "it released 1,100 tons of milling waste and 94 million gallons of wastewater – all radioactive – into the Puerco [River], eventually contaminating 80 miles of streambed."[37] As a Government Accountability Office (GAO) report notes, it was and is "the largest release of radioactive materials in the United States."[38] This was not the first time that radioactive waste flowed downstream: "Before the mid-1970's, untreated water from the mines and the processing mill was discharged directly" to a tributary of the Puerco River.[39] The spill was bad, but "[a]t least 300 times more uranium and 6 times more total gross-alpha activity were released by day-to-day pumping from the underground mines than was released by the spill."[40]

The cleanup costs associated with uranium mining on the reservation are extraordinary. So far the federal government has not provided the funds necessary to aggressively attack the problem.[41] Compensation to individual employees in the mining industry "does not compensate the Navajo Nation for the harm that it suffered and continues to suffer from the contamination of tribal land and water resources."[42] In 2014, the GAO estimated "that EPA's costs to fund removal actions at just half of the highest priority mines, or 21 mines, could be a minimum of about $150 million," but acknowledged that that figure did not include the cost of transporting and disposing of the waste off-reservation.[43] Given that there are more than 500 abandoned mines with little plan to deal with most of them any time soon, the total cost of fully cleaning up these sites is staggering.[44] Treating uranium royalties as tribal property was not necessarily a bad choice, but it did ensure that those communities most impacted by the legacy of uranium mining did not experience a significant mining "bump." The mining areas remain mired in poverty even though many in the community paid for uranium mining with their health.

4.2 COAL

If the tribe's relationship with uranium is tragic, its relationship with coal is complicated but similarly exploitative. Rather than a relationship driven by national security interests, the development of Navajo coal owes itself to the demand by regional non-Indian cities for cheap, reliable, and largely invisible energy. Transmission lines connecting the Navajo Nation with Phoenix, Las Vegas, and Los Angeles powered a population and economic development boom in the Southwest. Open pit mines, together with wells pulling water from deep underground, provided a steady supply of low-sulfur coal to power plants scattered across areas surrounding the reservation. Royalties from coal provided a significant fraction of the overall Navajo government's budget, and tribal members with jobs at the mines were relatively well paid. These gains occurred despite the fact that many of contracts signed with mining companies wrongfully denied the tribe the full value of their coal. The US Supreme Court blocked a Navajo suit for damages, and the federal government failed to live up to its trust responsibility to the tribe when it came to coal leases on the reservation. Companies such as Peabody Coal gleaned enormous profits from their exploitation of Navajo natural resources, but Diné received only a small fraction of the overall gain. Perhaps most importantly, the tribe, and especially the tribal government, became dependent on coal. Environmental pressure associated with climate change and a reduction in the price of renewable energy technology are causing energy companies to abandon Navajo mines and coal-fired power plants. Unfortunately, the Navajo Nation has yet to figure out how to navigate this post-coal reality.

Coal development on what would become the Navajo Nation began modestly. Archeologists have found remnants of campsites that indicate that native peoples in the area burned coal one thousand years ago.[45] Between 1300 and 1600 AD production on Black Mesa "may have totaled 100,000 tons."[46] Non-Indian capital and technological improvements in the transmission of energy helped Navajo coal take off. In 1909, a "rapid reconnaissance was made by wagon" of the coal beds of Black Mesa by M. R. Campbell and H. E. Gregory.[47] While acknowledging the "fragmentary" nature of their data, they reported that "there is considerable coal in this field" and that it was of good quality.[48] They also reported that a small mine, producing 2,500 tons annually "to supply fuel for the Indian school," was already in operation at Keams Canyon.[49] The ability of turn-of-the-century explorers to locate the Black Mesa coal field owed itself in part to the relative shallowness of the "overburden," as little as six meters in depth, separating the buried coal from the surface.[50] Black Mesa is located in northern Arizona and includes contested portions of the Navajo and Hopi reservations. Later surveys confirmed the existence of a "considerable" amount – 400 million tons – of strippable coal at Black Mesa,[51] and helped make Black Mesa the site of the world's largest strip mine. Coal discoveries were not limited to Black Mesa. Gallup, New Mexico owes its existence to coal: "In 1881, coal mines to supply the railroad drew the first settlers to Gallup."[52] By the 1930s, small-scale, cottage-industry-type family truck mines, employing between seven and nine men, emerged across the Navajo Nation.[53] Together, these small operations "produced 3,300 tons of coal annually ... [and] provided ready cash of $6 a wagonload."[54]

Truck mines alone would not have transformed the reservation economy, but starting in the 1950s, Navajo coal caught the attention of outside capital and energy interests.[55] The first large lease, finalized in 1957, was between the Navajo tribe and Utah Construction and Mining Company for 24,320 acres in the eastern part of the reservation.[56] It was the first of many leases. Agreements signed in 1964 with Pittsburg & Midway Coal Company for 11,157 acres near Window Rock, and with Peabody Coal Company for 24,858 acres on Black Mesa, reflect the "unprecedented commercial interest" in Hopi and Navajo coal during the 1960s.[57] By 1971, Black Mesa alone was producing over one million tons of coal annually.[58] As the works of Andrew Needham and Judith Nies show, increasing exploitation of Navajo coal was a major factor contributing to the dramatic growth of Southwestern cities in the post–World War II period.[59] Between 1952 and 1962, Phoenix experienced a population boom of more than 400 percent.[60] Phoenix, Las Vegas, and Los Angeles offered amenities that few other parts of the country could: nearly 300 days of sunshine a year, ample space for expansion, relatively inexpensive housing, and the allure of the West. City and state leaders, however, knew that they could not sell the dream without the availability of cheap electricity to power both household electronics, especially air-conditioning, and industrial parks. The ordinary solution of building a local power generating station involves both local pollution and considerable transportation expenses in order to bring the fuel to the plant. But improvements in transmission line technology solved both problems. There is always energy loss when power is sent over transmission lines and the loss rate was high enough until the 1950s that it was unimaginable to locate a power plant hundreds of miles away from the intended consumers. Technological improvements reduced the amount of energy lost in transmission, changing the energy development calculus. It became possible for cities to rely on distant power plants built closer to industrial coal mines. Cities would still be powered by coal, but residents would be shielded from the unsightliness of such plants and from most of the associated air pollution. For people living in Phoenix, Las Vegas, and Los Angeles, the production process could be ignored. Transmission lines rendered power generation largely invisible to the beneficiaries and made electricity something people could take for granted.

Western coal was an attractive energy source for a number of reasons. As Andrew Needham relates, one of the largest parties in Los Angeles history occurred on October 9, 1936, after engineers flipped the switch that brought electricity from the recently completed Hoover Dam to the city. But by the mid-1960s, hydroelectric power had fallen out of favor with environmental groups. When Arizona and federal officials pushed for two additional dams on the Colorado River to provide energy for the Central Arizona Project, groups such as the Sierra Club pushed back. In its effort to protect the Colorado River, including areas near the Grand Canyon, the Sierra Club went along with the alternative plan of relying on Navajo coal to power the project.[61] Ironically, concerns about air pollution also moved the country towards western coal. Mining operations in the mountains of Appalachia dig out coal that is relatively high in sulfur compared to Navajo coal. The Clean Air Act of 1970, in particular, caused energy interests to look west as a way to solve their sulfur problem. Navajo coal was also attractive because strip mining is more efficient than shaft mining.[62] But while those living in distant cities can close their eyes to the harms of industrial strip mines and mega power plants, for those closer to the power plants, of course, it is harder to ignore their environmental and social impacts.

Before Martin Cruz Smith became famous for *Gorky Park*, a detective story set in Moscow, he wrote *Nightwing*, a dark tale of vampire bats and spirits on the Hopi reservation angered by Peabody's Black Mesa mine.[63] The Navajo and Hopi tribes share control of Black Mesa, and in 1966 both tribes signed leases with Peabody Coal for what would become the world's largest strip mine. The leases were controversial from the moment they were signed. The Kikmongwi – traditional Hopi village religious leaders – challenged the Hopi central government in federal court, questioning the government's power to enter into the Black Mesa lease. The Ninth Circuit Court of Appeals sided with the central government, slamming the door on the Kikmongwi challengers.[64] A non-Indian attorney, ostensibly representing the tribe, but who in fact had close, ongoing ties with Peabody, orchestrated the lease.[65] At the time, those ties and the lawyer's conflict of interest were not disclosed to the tribe; they only came to light through subsequent research by a law professor, Charles Wilkinson, writing a history of Black Mesa.

Unfortunately for the Hopi villages, which benefitted for centuries from the protection afforded by their location on top of the mesa, Peabody got more than just a right to mine coal, it also got water. In order to move coal from Black Mesa to the Mohave Generating Station in Laughlin, Nevada, Peabody constructed a 275-mile dedicated pipeline. Black Mesa coal was crushed into small enough chunks that, when mixed with water, could be pushed to Laughlin. Until the mine closed in 2005, this coal slurry pipeline used three million gallons of water a day that Peabody did not adequately pay for and which was pumped from an ancient aquifer that lies thousands of feet below the mesa.[66] By 2016, "close to 40 billion gallons of groundwater" had been pumped for use by the coal-slurry pipeline.[67] The aquifer, which formed over thousands of years, has a low replenishment rate and could not keep up with the demands placed on it by Peabody's coal slurry. Not surprisingly, springs on the mesa dried up and Hopi lifeways were adversely impacted.[68] Studies conducted after the coal slurry was built "showed that Black Mesa and its surrounding countryside were dying of thirst."[69] A second mine that opened on top of Black Mesa, the Kayenta Mine, used rail to deliver coal to the Navajo Generating Station, which sits on the banks of Lake Powell in Page, Arizona and which stopped operation in 2019. Three times daily, a cargo train carried the coal needed to feed the plant's furnace seventy-eight miles away. The significant infrastructure required to extract and exploit Black Mesa's coal is a testament to the power of the financial interests behind these leases.

Perhaps because of its location, far removed from Window Rock, there was minimal Navajo opposition to Black Mesa strip mining. In much the same way that the Council's mere agreement to sanction uranium mining did not guarantee fair dealing throughout that process, the negotiation of lease agreements for coal mines did not guarantee that Navajos participated as full partners once leases were signed. As the United States Commission on Civil Rights concluded in its 1975 report, *The Navajo Nation: An American Colony*, development at the time was "no more than exploitation, with profits flowing off the reservation."[70] The Commission also quoted former Navajo Nation President Peter MacDonald's take on the coal leases: "Well, we, the Navajos, did not have an opportunity to even discuss the pros and cons of strip mining when it was put to us, that we leased the coal to the companies and that they were going to mine it, surface mining or strip mining."[71] But Peabody Coal Company, as a major employer in the area, was largely spared Navajo anger. Instead, for Diné, the main issue connected to mining on Black Mesa was a long-simmering conflict with Hopis over territory. The Navajo-Hopi land dispute began when the United States government created an executive order reservation for the Hopi tribe in 1882 that included within its boundaries 300–600 Diné families.[72] By 1958, Navajo numbers far exceeded – roughly 8,800 Navajos to 3,200 Hopis – the Hopi population on the 1882 reservation.[73] The dispute, though, was not solely about population imbalance. Lawyers for the tribes and for the federal government, hoping to establish clear rights to the subsurface estate, worked to divide up Black Mesa. Congress intervened with a special act allowing the two tribes to sue each other so that that a court could determine the proper boundary. In 1962, a federal district court established a Joint Use Area to be shared by Navajo and Hopi residents of the area.[74] By disregarding the population imbalance, the creation of the Joint Use Area exacerbated the land dispute. Subsequent acts by Congress attempted to force negotiation, and when that failed, directed the court to partition the land. The final line in the desert forced approximately 100 Hopis to move and left between fifteen and seventeen thousand Navajos on the wrong side of the partition line.[75] Federal actions, most notably the Bennett Freeze – a prohibition on all new development, including repairs and renovations, by Navajos living within the Joint Use Area that lasted from 1966 until 2009 – only compounded the hardships associated with the land dispute.[76]

It is difficult to discern the degree to which the tribe independently approved coal leases. Officially, of course, coal leases during the 1960s and 1970s were the result of arms-length negotiations between the tribe and mining companies; it is presumed that the Navajo Nation freely entered into these long-term contracts. But it takes only a dash of realism to see beyond the thin veneer of tribal agency. The contracts entered into during this period lack even the most basic protections and locked in low royalty rates for decades. In a Special Message to Congress in 1970, President Nixon announced that the Indian policy would be to support tribal self-determination. Nixon renounced the prior, post–World War II policy of unilaterally terminating tribal existence. Termination had been a disaster for affected tribes, though, fortunately, Congress spared the Navajo reservation. Self-determination is rightly celebrated as a turning point in the relationship between tribes and the United States, for it not only allowed tribes to take over the provision of services which previously had been in federal hands. but also recognized the right of tribes to set their own course. Since President Nixon's announcement, self-determination has been widely supported by republicans and democrats.[77] But self-determination is more than a single speech, it is a process and a way of thinking. It is not realized by a single act of Congress, but through decades of hard work and frustration. The Navajo Nation has not fully emerged from the shadow of exploitative coal leases signed a half century ago, and the nation's efforts to dig itself out highlight the contextual nature of self-determination.

Coal is controversial. It enjoys a central place in the Navajo economy, and a sizeable portion of the tribal government's entire budget has been dependent on coal.[78] But perhaps in part because coal is so significant to the tribe, internal environmental groups – led by tribal advocates and supported by well-funded national environmental organizations – generally oppose any efforts to expand reservation coal mining or extend the operational life of coal-fired power plants. Inequities involved in some of the existing lease agreements – including undeniable breeches of trust ordinarily owed to the tribe by the federal government – make coal mining a point of contention in Navajo government-to-government dealings with state and federal officials as well. Ultimately, coal is controversial because although the Navajo Nation is nominally empowered to set its own development path, it is simultaneously subject to crippling legal and economic restrictions that narrow the tribe's range of options.

Notwithstanding ever-present federal limitations, there have been significant changes in the tribe's approach to coal. In particular, Peter MacDonald, during his time as Tribal Chairman, from 1970 to 1989, used the rhetoric of Navajo

FIGURE 4.2 "Strip mining with dragline equipment at the Navajo mine in Northern Arizona." Image courtesy National Archives, Arizona, 1973. (Photo by Smith Collection/ Gado/Getty Images)

nationalism to transition the tribe from passive recipient of coal royalties to an active participant in managing Navajo natural resources.[79] MacDonald is one of the most important, and polarizing, leaders in Navajo history. He, perhaps more than anyone else, changed the relationship between the tribe and outside energy companies. MacDonald emphasized sovereignty and self-determination, redirected the frustrations of tribal members, and flexed the tribe's muscles in provocative ways. By the late 1960s and early 1970s, divisions among Diné on energy projects made reservation politics particularly charged. A local protest movement succeeded in blocking plans to build a gas electrification plant near Burnham, New Mexico, which was remarkable not only because tribal members were acting against the development plans of the central government, but also because Burnham is a fairly remote part of the reservation. The ability of activists to shape tribal development was part of a wave of popular activism. Inspired by the Civil Rights movement, Indians occupied Alcatraz Island from 1969 to 1971 and Wounded Knee in 1973. On the Navajo Nation, protests erupted in 1974 after white teenagers beat and killed three Diné in Farmington, New Mexico, a town with a history of racism against Navajos.[80] In response to these murders and the inadequate response of Farmington officials – the only punishment for the white teenagers was for them to be sent to reform school – the United States Commission on Civil Rights investigated the situation on the reservation and in border towns. The Commission's 1975 report noted, "It is not that the Navajos are lagging behind. It is that the Navajos are being kept behind."[81] And Navajos knew it.

Although Diné activists and their elected leader, Peter MacDonald, differed on whether the tribe should pursue development through extractive industry, they shared a similar perspective on the roots of Navajo under-development. "[T]he rhetoric of [Navajo] activist groups began cohering in the late 1960s to form a shared view of Navajos as a colonized people and the Navajo Nation as a colony of the metropolitan Southwest."[82] As Andrew Needham highlights, the position that the editors of an alternative newspaper of the period, *Diné Baa-Hani*, took reflect this stance: "They say the Indians must join the market economy, but they force us into a colonial economy. This is not economic development. This is economic termination."[83] Similarly, Peter MacDonald argued that previously signed agreements undermined tribal agency. "Until quite recently, mineral development on Indian lands was by industry with the assistance of the federal government. Industry selected the area to be developed and the federal government dictated the terms, conditions and procedures of the proposed development. This arrangement left the Indians with little or no control."[84] As MacDonald told the Commission on Civil Rights, "the Navajos did not have an opportunity to even discuss the pros and cons of strip mining when it was put to us."[85]

There were real differences between Diné environmental activists, who "saw non-development as the key to preserving Navajo cultural identity,"[86] and MacDonald, who did not oppose energy development so long as the tribe saw more benefit from the deals reached with energy companies. But both Diné environmental activists and MacDonald were frustrated by the poor conditions on the reservation compared to the wealth generated by Navajo coal. In an op-ed published by *The Navajo Times*, MacDonald complained:

> It is obscene for energy to be produced on Indian lands and yet see our own people deprived of the very barest necessities of civilized life ... Think for a minute about how it feels to be a Navajo shivering through a cold winter on Black Mesa ... without electricity or gas or water, while at the same time you watch well-paid anglo workers assemble a ten or fifteen million dollar drag line only a few hundred yards from your front door.[87]

As this quote highlights, MacDonald was a force to be reckoned with. From fairly modest beginnings, MacDonald rose to be the dominant figure in Navajo politics for two decades. As Donald Fixico recounts, Peter MacDonald's parents named him "Peter" after "a trader had told his father about a famous person in the Bible named Peter," and he got his last name because a "teacher could not pronounce his last name, 'Hoshkaisith,' in the Navajo language, so he was called 'MacDonald' from the nursery rhyme 'Old MacDonald Had a Farm.'"[88] He went to serve as a code talker in World War II; after the war, he earned an electrical engineering degree and worked in the defense industry until he entered tribal politics in the early 1960s.[89]

After becoming Tribal Chairman in 1970, MacDonald sought to reset the relationship between energy companies and the tribe. Copying from the Organization of the Petroleum Exporting Countries (OPEC) handbook following the 1973 OPEC oil crisis, MacDonald co-founded the Council of Energy Resource Tribes (CERT) in 1975.[90] An umbrella group of the tribes with the largest energy holdings, CERT under MacDonald became a platform to enable tribes to negotiate with industry and the federal government from a position of strength.[91] MacDonald explained to *People Magazine* in 1979, "All we want is the fair market value for our resources ... We have been gouged by the raw deals we find ourselves in, thanks to the US government."[92] In his autobiography, published in 1993, MacDonald was more direct, describing the mid-1970s leases as forms of environmental and financial "rape" and linking these leases to the formation of CERT.[93] Peter MacDonald's political career ended in disgrace. He was thrown out of office and subsequently sent to federal prison after being convicted of bribery and corruption associated with the tribal purchase of Big Boquillas Ranch.[94] Chapter 6 discusses the case against MacDonald and the controversy surrounding his removal in greater detail, but it is undeniable that despite his downfall, MacDonald deserves credit for changing how the Navajo Nation managed its natural resources. During MacDonald's tenure as Tribal Chairman, the Council stopped being a "rubber stamp" for BIA supported energy projects.[95]

The relationship between outside energy interests and the Navajo Nation is similar to the workings of a powerful, slow-moving boat; it can take decades for policy changes to bear fruit or for course corrections to take effect. Given the long-time horizon of energy investments and coal leases, as well as the power of the interests – private companies and, at times, federal officials – intent on exploiting Navajo resources, it is no surprise that the tribe faced and continues to face obstacles in its quest to get a fair deal for its coal. The record and proceedings of two Supreme Court cases highlight the nearly impossible position the tribe is in when it comes to long-term coal leases. Despite clear evidence that the United States government failed to meet the most basic elements of its trust obligation to the tribe, the Supreme Court twice rejected the Navajo Nation's effort to hold the BIA accountable for undermining the tribe's negotiating position.[96] In 1964, the Navajo Nation and Sentry Royalty Company entered into a lease on Black Mesa, which the Secretary of the Interior approved. Peabody Coal subsequently acquired the rights from Sentry Royalty. The lease, which paid only 37.5 cents per ton, did not give the tribe "adequate recompense,"[97] but did provide that the terms would be renegotiated after twenty years. When the twenty year window expired in 1984, the tribe and Peabody entered into talks. The tribe asked the BIA for their technical conclusion regarding the appropriate royalty rate for the tribe's coal. BIA officials, on the basis of their own studies and those of the Bureau of Mines, were prepared to recommend that the royalty rate be raised to 20 percent, but the Secretary of the Interior, Dan Hodel, put the brakes on that recommendation. Peabody had paid Stan Hulett, a former aide and close personal friend of Secretary Hodel, $13,000 to visit the Secretary privately in order to quash the department's 20 percent recommendation.

After Hulett's visit, Secretary Hodel sent a letter telling the parties that the appeal decision was "not imminent" and that they should continue to try to resolve the royalty dispute "in a mutually agreeable fashion." This memorandum misled the Navajo government into thinking that the 20 percent was not an acceptable rate. Consequently, the Navajo Nation finalized a lease agreement with Peabody without knowing that the Government found the 20 percent rate appropriate. As Paul Frye, the Navajo Nation's lawyer in the first *Navajo Nation* case to reach the Supreme Court, noted during oral argument, considering how much Peabody's $13,000 bought, Stan Hulett was "underpaid for [this] bit of skullduggery." The Navajo Nation argued that the US government was guilty of "colluding with Peabody Coal Company to swindle the Navajo Nation." Even senior BIA employees recognized the objectionable nature of the events. Then Associate Solicitor for Indian Affairs Tim Vollmann sought to warn Hodel that if the Navajo Nation learned all the details, the tribe "would likely sue." Another BIA official, when presented with a memo he was to sign suggesting Secretarial approval, refused to because, in his own words, "I thought that I would be participating in a breach of trust."

Despite these clear violations, the Supreme Court, taking a narrow view of the trust responsibility owed Indian tribes, held against the tribe not once but twice. In *Navajo Nation I*, the Court rejected the tribe's $600 million damages claim, concluding that the Indian Mineral Leasing Act did not require the Secretary to reject an agreement simply because it did not maximize value for the tribe. The Court emphasized the independent agency and degree of control that the Navajo Nation had in the lease negotiations. It was a perfectly sensible outcome but for Secretary Hodel's actions, which the tribe was fortunate enough to discover and which were clearly in violation of the government's trust obligations to Indian nations. The federal relationship with Indian tribes supposedly involves "moral obligations of the highest responsibility and trust."[98] The trust doctrine generally requires that the US government act in support of tribes, not in opposition to them. Thus, lawyers for the government took the lead role in protecting tribal water rights in the 1908 precedent-setting case of *Winters* v. *United States*[99] and reservation land is not subject to taxation because it is held in joint trust by tribes and the US government. When *Navajo Nation* was sent back to the lower federal courts, they once more found that, in light of the web of federal statutes governing coal mining on reservation, the US government had breached its trust obligations to the Navajo Nation by signing off on an agreement that federal officials knew undercompensated the tribe. The Supreme Court, however, disagreed, and, in *Navajo Nation II*, the Court summarily dismissed the tribe's suit as well as the courageous, defiant holding of the lower court.[100] Notwithstanding the unanimous opinion of the Court, the actions of Secretary Hodel undeniably breached trust obligations owed to tribes, even if the Court decided that it could not award the Navajo Nation monetary damages. The episode illustrates the tremendous legacy costs of long-term leases. The only good stemming from the two cases is that they underscore the importance of tribal control over reservation resources and the dangers of trusting federal government agencies.

Today, the Navajo Nation and mining companies are wrestling with how to deal with the decline of coal. Environmental pressure linked to climate change and technological advances in renewable energy make further coal exploitation a marginal enterprise. Window Rock, backed by industrial capital, is resisting these market forces, but in the process is greenlighting projects with significant environmental and legacy costs. During President George W. Bush's second term, the Navajo Nation made a push for approval of a new coal-fired power plant, Desert Rock. More recently, in 2014, the tribe purchased the aging Navajo Mine, the mine that supplies the coal for New Mexico's Four Corners Power Plant. The tribe's efforts may be too little, too late. In the post-World War II boom, market forces and the desire of western developers drove capitalists to look for coal and energy in the far reaches of the Navajo Nation. In the period that followed, Navajo politicians grew dependent on coal royalties to fund the tribal government and provide on-reservation jobs. But today, environmental concerns and market forces, operating in tandem, are causing tribal coal revenues to dry up.

With the Four Corners Power Plant operating just south of the road between Shiprock and Farmington, New Mexico, the proposal to construct a second coal-fired power plant, Desert Rock, not much further south was odd. For environmental

FIGURE 4.3 View of the Four Corners Power Plant from Indian Route 36. Photo by Ezra Rosser, Copyright 2007.

activists, such close proximity was evidence of environmental injustice. An editorial cartoon by Jack Ahasteen published by the *Navajo Times* showed two plants side-by-side spewing out toxic smoke. Yet, the fact that the proposed Desert Rock Power Plant was a Navajo Nation-led initiative meant that it defied easy categorization.[101] It did not fit nicely into the stereotypes of Indians as environmental stewards and non-Indians as predatory capitalists.

Desert Rock's biggest champion was Joe Shirley, Jr., the president of the Navajo Nation from 2003 to 2011, who saw the plant as a way to bring relatively high paying jobs to the reservation and to generate additional government revenue. Formally, the plant was to be a joint project of the Navajo Nation and Sithe Global, a New York-based energy company. The project was promoted as a new sort of coal agreement, an arrangement between equals. Technically, there was some truth to this characterization: the agreement with Sithe Global provided the tribe a right to buy an ownership stake in the power plant. However, doing so required the tribe to put up so much money or pledge such a significant fraction of its associated coal royalties that that supposed benefit was substantively unattainable. Instead, the main financial incentive took the form of the Navajo Mine Extension Project, which would provide Desert Rock 6.25 million tons of coal per year every year for fifty years – the design life of the plant.[102] Had it been built, the plant would have been controlled and operated very much like existing power plants fueled by Navajo coal:

outside capital would pocket the returns on energy generation, while the tribe would sell its coal. But the Obama administration sided with environmentalists and blocked Desert Rock. Backers had gotten the green light from the EPA during the Bush administration, but that was rescinded following President Obama's inauguration, proving once again the significant impact of US politics on Navajo Nation economic development.[103] The EPA reopened the plant's environmental impact study, ultimately blocking the tribe's hoped-for power plant. The rejection ironically occurred on "Sovereignty Day."[104]

Sithe Global and the Navajo Nation tried to sell Desert Rock as having minimal impacts on the environment, but it was what it was: a coal-fired power plant. Promotional materials touted the possibility of building an experimental underground carbon capture facility at the plant, though neither partner was committed to actually constructing such a facility. Unlike the power plants fueled by Black Mesa coal, Desert Rock was to be a mine-mouth plant, which meant there would be no need for a dedicated train or slurry line to deliver the coal. Even without the slurry, the power plant would require ten to twenty new wells to supply a whopping 2,795 gallons of water per minute.[105] Finally, the mine and power plant site was well chosen – 592 leased acres on a remote, even by reservation standards, parcel of tribal trust land – to have minimal direct residential impacts. The Draft Environmental Impact Statement identified only one house within a half mile of the plant facing dislocation, and only 148 families within a half mile of new transmission lines, access roads, and water wells to be constructed in connection with the plant.[106] While the plant would increase local haze and adversely impact local air quality, the *Durango Herald* reported that "an air-quality expert with the federal Environmental Protection Agency's Region 9 [concluded] the Four Corners region has air so clean that it can absorb additional pollutants without harm."[107] In terms of siting, peripheral harms, and local pollution, the original Draft Environmental Impact Statement presented Desert Rock favorably.

Environmentalists on and off the reservation disagreed vehemently with this assessment. Desert Rock was opposed by national environmental groups, including the Center for Biological Diversity, the Environmental Defense Fund, the National Parks Conservation Association, the Natural Resources Defense Council, and the Sierra Club. Local off-reservation groups, such as Conservation Voters of New Mexico, the Grand Canyon Trust, New Mexico Conference of Churches, New Mexico Citizens Alliance for Responsible Energy and Sustainability, San Juan Citizens Alliance, and Western Resource Advocates joined in the opposition.[108] Diné Citizens Against Ruining our Environment (Diné CARE) and Doodá Desert Rock, which stands for "No Desert Rock," emerged as leaders of the local stand against Desert Rock. 1,500 Four Corners residents signed a Dooda Desert Rock petition opposing Desert Rock.[109]

Environmental activists approached the proposed plant from different positions. Off-reservation, the main issue was climate change and the appropriateness of any new coal-fired power plant. San Juan Citizens Alliance argued that the plant's Draft Environmental Impact Statement "completely fail[ed] to consider the impacts of 12.7 million [tons per year] of CO_2" on world resources and global warming.[110] Then New Mexico Governor, and 2008 presidential hopeful, Bill Richardson issued a statement in 2007 that said that he was "gravely concerned about the potential environmental impacts" of Desert Rock, adding that he believed the plant "would be a step in the wrong direction."[111] Richardson argued that the plant, which would raise the state's total CO_2 emissions by 15 percent, would make his "aggressive greenhouse gas reduction goals difficult – if not impossible – to meet."[112] A little over a month before the EPA issued the PSD permit, Governor Richardson and his Attorney General wrote the EPA with "serious concerns about the environmental impacts of constructing Desert Rock in a region already impaired by other large coal-fired power plants."[113] The concerns of the New Mexico Governor's office were shared by county and city governments in New Mexico and in other states.[114]

Doodá Desert Rock's focus was on the interests of the "most impacted people who still reside within close proximity of the proposed power plant site."[115] Powerful images of the faces and lives of those who would be displaced and those who would be most affected by the plant were captured by photographer Carlin Tapp, who had been invited to take the photographs by Doodá Desert Rock and whose work was later exhibited in Santa Fe.[116] In December 2006, protestors prevented surveyors from accessing the proposed site by blocking trucks and later occupying the site.[117] Plant developers obtained a temporary restraining order against the occupiers, but the parties agreed to coexist so long as the site work was allowed to go forward.[118] A permanent "resistance camp" built on January 20, 2007, and Diné people, along with representatives of other organizations, "sat vigil."[119] By July 2007, the vigil was down to "[a] handful of people, mostly Navajo women"[120] who had cause to celebrate when the EPA sided with them.[121] Following EPA's reversal in February 2009, Doodá Desert Rock President Elouise Brown triumphantly exclaimed, "the Desert Rock power plant is dead!"[122]

Desert Rock's demise has not prevented the tribe from aggressively investing in coal. In 2013, after coal sale negotiations between BHP and the operators of the Four Corners Power Plant broke down, the tribe created Navajo Transitional Energy Company (NTEC) to purchase Navajo Mine from BHP Billiton (BHP).[123] The tribe had a lot at stake in what happened to Navajo Mine; the tribe received more than $40 million from the mine in 2011.[124] Including the power plant, the overall tribal stake climbs above $100 million annually.[125] Navajo Mine is the sole source of fuel for the power plant, so failure to reach a sales agreement threatened not only to cut off coal royalties from the mine but also to shut down both the mine and the plant, both of which provide approximately 900 relatively high paying jobs, mostly to area Diné. NTEC's Board Chairman, Steve Gunderson, noted "If the mine and power plant were removed from the Navajo economy, the results, within a year, would have been devastating. We needed to preserve the business and income."[126] BHP's lease with the tribe expired in 2016; the company felt it could no longer make a profit running the mine. In order to prevent the mine shut down, the Navajo Nation agreed to accept a lower payment for its coal, and, crucially, agreed to release BHP from "past, present, and future" damages connected to the mine.[127] Considering the many adverse environmental impacts of strip-mining an area for five decades,[128] the liability waiver is a remarkably large concession from the tribe. The liability waiver, together with a decision to channel future disputes connected to NTEC's management to state, not tribal, arbitration, made the tribe's offer of $85 million quite attractive to BHP.

But not all Diné shared the tribal government's enthusiasm for the purchase. On one hand, the tribe got what it wanted: the mine and the plant were able to continue operating without interruption. The tribe also got much greater control over its natural resources than it had under standard arrangements. On the other hand, environmental advocates argued that the tribe gave up too much for a marginally viable mine that the tribe was set to reacquire in three years anyway. As Winona LaDuke wrote in an op-ed about the mine purchase published by *Indian Country Today*, "A war is raging between traditional Diné people seeking to maintain their way of life ... and the relentless economics of fossil fuels."[129] In 2012, Four Corners Power Plant was the nation's "biggest emitter of nitrogen oxides (NO_2), a greenhouse gas" and contributed to the haze problem in northern New Mexico and Arizona.[130] Though Diné Care protested outside the Tribal Council, holding signs such as one that read "Dying coal mine equals bad deal," their efforts were unsuccessful.[131] After purchasing the mine, NTEC and Four Corners Power Plant signed an agreement guaranteeing that the tribe will provide coal to the plant through 2031.[132] The power plant's lease with the tribe extends through 2041.[133]

A similar dynamic played out on the western part of the reservation. Energy companies, led by the Salt River Project, which has a long history of operating the Navajo Generating Station – the coal-fired power plant located near Page, Arizona that receives its coal from a dedicated train line connecting it to Black Mesa Mine – voted to close the plant at the end of 2019.[134] Navajo Generating Station is a notable feature of the western reservation. It sits just above Lake Powell and "the plant's three smokestacks, at 775 feet high ... are taller than any building in the entire American Southwest."[135] It also was the major employer in the area, providing good jobs: "each salary derived from [Navajo Generating Station] probably supports 20 to 30 people ... and at $141,500, on average, it is seven times greater than the median salary on the reservation."[136]

The plant was expected to operate for an additional twenty-five years, but environmental regulation and pressure, especially from California, altered the cost structure of coal-fired power plants. Coal used to be the cheap alternative. It is now relatively expensive and risky. Renewables have taken a small sliver of the market, but natural gas is the main driver of coal's relative decline.[137] As one industry analysis concluded,

The outlook for the Navajo Generating Station ... is bleak. Declining energy market prices and rising production costs have made the power produced by the plant more expensive than power sold in the larger energy market. NGS, in a word, is no longer competitive. These factors are not likely to change, leaving the plant's financial viability in doubt – regardless of who owns it. A substantial subsidy will be needed to keep the plant operational.[138]

Indeed, in December 2019, NGS shut down for the last time.

The operation of Navajo Generating Station had a large environmental footprint. Combined, the plant and mine "emit nearly 20 million metric tons of carbon dioxide, methane and other greenhouse gases" annually.[139] This represented 29 percent of Arizona's total emissions from energy production.[140] The plant is partly owned by the Bureau of Reclamation, which used its share of the power generated to move Colorado River water to Arizona cities.[141] The water was "lifted 3,000 vertical feet and carried 336 miles" by pumps powered by Navajo Generating Station, which "has enabled the cities of Phoenix and Tucson to rapidly expand."[142] Each year, the plant itself used 9 billion gallons, 28,000 acre feet, of water drawn from Lake Powell for steam generation and cooling purposes.[143] The Navajo Nation received $35 million annually from Salt River Project and from the operator of Black Mesa Mine, but the combined figure paid to the Hopi Nation, $13 million, was even more significant because it made up 85 percent of the entire Hopi budget.[144] The power plant owners, as well as the Navajo tribe, were keen to see new investors assume ownership of the plant so that it could continue operating beyond the 2019 deadline.[145] The closure of NGS was a result of both changing economics in the energy sector and local activism.

The Navajo Nation's age of coal is coming to a close; what remains to be seen is how much pain will be inflicted by the death throes of an industry that was critical to the tribe for so long. Just as the full impact of uranium mining was not fully appreciated until decades later, the scars from coal mining run deep and a full accounting of its costs will take time. Coal provided southern Arizona, southern Nevada, and southern California with both energy and water that was both reliable and cheap. It is no wonder that rural parts of the reservation sprouted large mines and power plants. Just because they were located in areas far removed from the consuming non-Indian public does not mean they were insignificant. Astronauts claim to have seen Navajo strip-mining operations from space,[146] and, more concretely, the Navajo Nation central government grew dependent on coal royalties to fund its operations.

Mining was central to the development of the Navajo Nation from the end of World War II until the present. Mining became intertwined in the history of the Navajo Nation and of the Diné. The early periods of uranium and coal extraction were undoubtedly exploitative, but with time, the Diné came to control reservation mining. Given the need to fund the tribal government through mining royalties, as well as the high poverty and low employment rates on the reservation, it is not surprising that tribal leaders signed leases with extractive industry interests and with energy companies to exploit the tribe's natural resources. Uranium mining companies' failure to protect tribal employees, as well as the artificially depressed prices that coal companies paid for Navajo coal, demonstrate that at least through the 1970s, mining interests abused the tribe's desperation and the tribe's dependent status. But, by the end of the 1980s, partly reflecting Peter MacDonald's strong will to wrest control of mining away from outside capitalists, Navajo choices to enter into or extend long-term coal leases were choices that "belonged" to the tribe. However much environmental activists might want to frame the tribe as a mere puppet to external forces, the Navajo Nation has assumed "ownership" over its leases.

Today, the Navajo Nation is in the driver's seat when it comes to development of extractive industries on the reservation. The tribe's past experiences with uranium and coal show the long tail of any decision. The tribe must still deal with the legacy of periods in which outside energy interests and the federal government dictated the nature of development, but times have changed. Royalties fueled an expansion of the tribal bureaucracy, and the tribe now has a deep bench of lawyers – both in-house and outside counsel – involved in vetting energy deals. As subsequent chapters highlight, tribal leaders have failed in many different and troubling ways, but it is simply inaccurate to cling to the image of Navajos as a downtrodden tribe being exploited by outsiders. Such a characterization is not only falsely ahistorical but fails to respect tribal agency and tribal sovereignty.

PART II

Present

5

Alternative Environmental Paths

On September 3, 2016, private security guards attacked Indian protesters at Standing Rock with dogs and pepper spray.[1] Six people, including a child, were bitten and images of the attack made national and international news.[2] The attack did not succeed in stopping the protests – if anything, it galvanized Native Americans from across the country who flew, drove, and even walked to the middle of North Dakota and the Standing Rock Indian Reservation to join the protest that was gaining steam.[3] The protests – which began when a small group of women from the Standing Rock Sioux Tribe (SRST), upset about the construction of an oil pipeline near their reservation, founded Sacred Stone Camp[4] – came to symbolize much more.

In 2016, Energy Transfer Partners (ETP) was building a 1,172 mile pipeline in order to move 470,000 barrels of Bakken Oil Field crude each day from western North Dakota to southern Illinois.[5] The company's original plan was to have the pipeline cross the Missouri River upstream and to the north of Bismark, North Dakota, but due to concerns about the effect oil spills at that location might have on the city of Bismark, ETP moved the crossing site further to the south.[6] The new pipeline path cut through land reserved to the Sioux under the 1851 Treaty of Fort Laramie, crossing the Missouri River less than a mile north of the Standing Rock Sioux Reservation.[7] Although not accepted as fair or just by the Sioux, the US government position is that the Sioux lost much of their 1851 treaty land through subsequent treaties,[8] which meant that, technically, the pipeline did not cross tribal land as it approached and crossed the Missouri River. Energy Transfer Partners had met with the SRST as they developed the plans for the pipeline, but tribal members and the tribal government, led by SRST Tribal Chairman David Archambault, Jr., felt that the level of consultation was inadequate.[9] The pipeline was to cross the river though a tunnel beneath Lake Oahe, a Missouri River dam-created lake, and ETP claimed that there was no downstream risk to SRST. Those opposed to the pipeline, who called themselves "water protectors" as opposed to "protestors," argued that pipeline leaks are commonplace and that a leak at the river would threaten the whole reservation. They also recognized the environmental injustice of protecting the largely white town of Bismark while siting a potential hazard at the very border of the SRST reservation.

What started out as a tribe-specific protest became an ever-expanding gathering of Indians and environmental activists from across the county. Oceti Sakowin Camp, which was formed to accommodate those arriving, had to deal with the logistics of feeding, housing, and caring for thousands of people.[10] As David Treuer notes, "While it lasted, it was the largest gathering of Indians in the United States since the same tribes (Lakota, Cheyanne, and Arapaho) formed the tribal armies that defeated the US Cavalry at the Little Bighorn, not far from the #NODAPL protest camp."[11] Water protectors faced continued hostility from company representatives, state police, and National Guard units that were called in to protect the company's property interests and put down the protests. Three days after attack dogs were used against protestors, the North Dakota governor sent more than 500 National Guard members to Standing Rock, not to protect water protectors but to better protect the pipeline.[12] Months later, in October and November 2016, in the below-freezing temperatures of North Dakota's winter, law enforcement used tear gas, fire hoses, and rubber bullets against protesters.[13] Tribes across the United States expressed their support for the SRST and for the water protestors. Navajo Nation President Russell Begaye and Vice President Jonathan Nez, in a letter sent to SRST Chairman Archambault in August 2016, wrote, "the Navajo Nation stands in solidarity with the Standing Rock Sioux tribe," and noted, "I am proud to see so many other tribes come to support your efforts because it is time tribes finally stand against these threats to our lands. We will be heard because we are one, not one as a tribal nation but one as Native people."[14] And indeed the water protectors were heard. President Obama, who struggled for several weeks to avoid questions about the pipeline, eventually caved, temporarily blocking further construction at the river.[15] The euphoria following Obama's course reversal, however, was short-lived.[16] Four days after being sworn in as president, Donald Trump "issued a memorandum declaring DAPL to be in the national interest and directing federal agencies to review and approve it."[17] Subsequently, Trump signed executive actions in support of the Dakota Access Pipeline as well as the Keystone XL Pipeline, and within weeks the US Army Corps of Engineers greenlighted the DAPL easement across the river.[18] Shortly thereafter, in late February 2017, Oceti Sakowin Camp was burned by retreating protesters,[19] then razed by government tractors,[20] and the few remaining protesters were arrested.[21] By June 2017, the $3.7 billion pipeline was in "full commercial use."[22] As of August 2019, the new pipeline had already suffered at least ten oil spills.[23]

There is no one right way to look at the Standing Rock protests.[24] It failed in its immediate objective: the pipeline was constructed exactly where ETP wanted it built. Though environmental groups continue to challenge the pipeline in court,[25] some protesters face the prospect of years in prison.[26] Not only are federal and state officials aggressively prosecuting protesters,[27] but, in the wake of Standing Rock, states also rushed to amend their laws to further criminalize energy-related protests.[28] The SRST reservation remains impoverished and faces a long list of socioeconomic difficulties.[29] But such a dark reading of the protests arguably misses the point. The demand that developers engage in meaningful consultation with tribes and the idea that environmental harms to tribes must be taken seriously echoed across Indian country and across the United States as a whole.[30] The protests brought attention to the struggles of tribes and their continued relevance in the American republic in a way that few other events have since the occupations of Alcatraz and Wounded Knee.[31] Standing Rock was more than an isolated protest by a single tribe, it was a gathering of nations, a call for the rest of the country to take tribal environmental justice seriously, and a sign of the growing political power of tribes.

Things are a lot simpler when Indians can easily and rightly be identified as the good guys and whites as the bad guys on environmental issues. That was largely the case in the Standing Rock protests, with "corporate greed" partially taking the place of the generic evil white actor. It is still the case, I believe, that the mental shortcut of Indian as good and non-Indian as bad works for many issues, from poverty to land rights to recognition of sovereignty, but it is becoming more complicated with regard to the environment. To explain why that is so, it is worth thinking about the broad trends that have defined the relationship between environmental destruction and Indian nations. For much of American history, the relationship was an oppressive one. Whites – whether in the form of the US government, companies, or as individuals – simply took natural resources from Indian tribes or, by subordinating Indian agency, simultaneously exploited both Indian land and tribal members. Later, recognition that tribes should at least formally play a role in approving natural resource use and extraction changed the relationship from oppressive to inequitable. Tribes were compensated for their environmental goods, but Indians received less and lost more than they should have. Bad faith in the form of the failure of the United States to live up to its trust obligations or a mere pro forma role for tribal leaders in decisions with an environmental impact, led to inequitable compensation for Indian tribes. The relationship between tribes and environmental destruction is now entering the modern period, one in which the terms of such destruction are often tribally accepted even if the relationship is not entirely tribally defined.

For better or worse, environmental degradation occurring on Indian reservations cannot be simply chalked up to oppression of tribes.[32] While Indians are sometimes positioned, as they were in the Standing Rock protests, as defenders of the environment, that is not always the place Indians find themselves. Especially when the environmentally destructive project is sited on trust land where tribes have greater say than projects off-reservation, Indian nations cannot necessarily be described as victims. Some tribes have begun, through their sovereign governments, deliberately seeking out the exploitation of their land and natural resources. By choosing to prioritize economic development over the environment, Indian nations are challenging the instinctive "love" that progressives have for all things Indian.[33] Forced to choose between attacking the decisions of Indian nations on the one hand and turning a blind eye to harmful environmental policies on the other, progressives are faced with a classic apples and oranges dilemma. For their part, Indian governments pursuing economic development through environmental destruction have to grapple not only with non-Indian opponents – a familiar role for tribal governments – but also with tribal members less willing to make such a trade-off or adversely impacted by particular proposed projects. Besides challenging romantic notions of Indians as the first environmentalists, tribal activities that harm the environment undermine the position of some Indian advocates that Indian policies should not be subject to critique or limitation because of the inherent sovereignty of Indian nations.

5.1 STEREOTYPES AND TRIBAL CHOICE

Natural resource exploitation on reservations is antithetical to the stereotype of Indians as environmental stewards. With the publication, in print and as a public service television commercial in 1971–2 of a stoic Indian crying because of pollution, "Indian and environmental concern became synonymous, and public discussion turned to whether America might somehow tap native wisdom in solving the environmental problems facing Mother Earth."[34] The notion that Indians are by definition also environmentalists pervades popular culture and is thought by many academics to have explanatory power when considering reservation development. This mental shortcut raises the challenge of any other stereotype: namely that though the romantic notion of tribes as environmental stewards does not hold for all tribes or for all points in time, the stereotype nevertheless is grounded in some element of truth.[35]

Frank Pommersheim's aptly titled *The Reservation as Place* illustrates the challenge of simultaneously accepting *and* rejecting the stereotypes of Indians as environmentalists.[36] In it, Pommersheim first unequivocally states: "Land is inherent to Indian people; they often cannot conceive of life without it. They are part of it and it is part of them; it is their Mother. Nor is this just a romantic commonplace."[37] But, after saying that the relationship that many have with reservation land has changed, Pommersheim cautions against the "disturbing utopic visions that endlessly romanticize the people and the land."[38] Similarly, Armstrong Wiggins, a lawyer with the Indian Law Resource Center, argues that "sustainable development is part of the cultural and religious heritage of most Indian peoples," but adds that it is "a mistake, however, to take too romantic a view."[39] Robert Laurence goes further, arguing that "romanticizing 'Indianness' can come very close to condescension and insult."[40]

What is the stereotype? Born out of the idea that Indians are somehow different, less civilized, the stereotype is at once a description of Indians and also, by contrast, of non-Indians. In the early 1970s, Indians were popularly thought of "as the continent's first conservationists."[41] This romantic conception of Indians preceded the birth of the environmental movement; as early as the 1830s Indians were thought of romantically as "children of Nature," unburdened by the troubles of civilized society.[42] In *American Indians and National Parks*, Robert H. Keller and Michael F. Turek provide a nice summary of the stereotype, namely that "Indians had always lived in harmony with nature, revered Mother Earth as sacred, and offered a special wisdom to non-Indians."[43] More subtle versions of the stereotype assume for example that Indians will necessarily reach better decisions than non-Indians or will always favor preserving the environment over economic development.[44]

There is *some* truth to the stereotype. As Donald Fixico observes, "the 'Mother Earth' concept is one of the few universal concepts among American Indians."[45] The "Indian 'heritage' of 'environmental sensitivity'" positively has facilitated tribal takeover of environmental protection responsibilities, while also legitimizing arguably racist US environmental policies.[46] Simply rejecting the stereotype risks ignoring the truths it contains. "The continuing link between the tribal communities and their holy lands," Jeanette Wolfley writes, "is critical to Native people's continuing political and social wellbeing, cultural identity, and tribal sovereignty."[47] Rebecca Tsosie argues that the "cultural connections between Native peoples and the land" should not be dismissed "as a 'romanticized' notion that is of limited utility in a modern era."[48] And studies confirming or making note of the central place of nature and land in Indian belief and value systems are ubiquitous.[49] What is required is to reject the stereotypes and the "environmental myths" surrounding Indians without "suppressing their historical associations with the land."[50]

Given that the stereotype on its face seems a positive one, why must it be rejected? The answer is that the stereotype is too readily accepted as truth both when it is deployed to explain environmentally protective decisions *and* when it is used to block a tribe's decision to participate in or cause environmental harms. The stereotype confines Indians to an ahistorical moment, and potentially deprives tribes of their sovereignty. It is ahistorical because while it is surely true that some tribes balanced concerns for the environment with economic development differently than non-Indians, it is impossible to reduce the history of every, or even any, tribe so neatly in this way.[51] As Jace Weaver notes, "In reality, modern Natives and their ancestors are neither saints nor sinners in environmental matters. They are human beings."[52] It is also ahistorical because in order to accept the stereotype, the pretension that Indian societies are static and have not always changed with time must also be accepted.[53] The stereotype is "dehumanizing" and "masks cultural diversity."[54] It operates independent of reality, such that a "romantic conception of what 'Indians' should be is frequently inconsistent with what 'Indians' actually are today."[55] The stereotype of Indians as nature's protectors should be corrected, according to Robert Cooter and Wolfgang Fikentscher, because it is "misleading."[56]

With regard to development, "misleading" is an understatement. The stereotype is not neutral with regard to the tradeoffs between the environment and industry; as a consequence, the construction "Indian = environmentalist" lends itself to manipulation.[57] Those who want to derail particular environmentally destructive development on reservations embrace the stereotype and claim that what is being proposed is not keeping with tribal values. It is worth quoting at length Nancy B. Collins and Andrea Hall's powerful rejection of such use of the stereotype in their article, *Nuclear Waste in Indian Country*:

> Environmentalists, in pursuit of "Indian's best interests" may engage in stereotyp-ical thinking, characterized by romanticism, which effectively deprives Native Americans of the right to make their own decisions about accepting waste on their lands. It is important to break down this malignant romanticism into its major component stereotypes so that we recognize them and strip them from our law and policy. Some of these stereotypes include viewing "real Indians" as histor-ical, primitive, unsophisticated, and rapidly on their way to extinction; essentializ-ing the hundreds of Indian tribes into one group; assigning Indians the role of guardian of our environment as well as theirs; failing to recognize Native American tribes as modern, twentieth century sovereign nations within the United States; and viewing Indians as dependent and in need of our protection and guidance.[58]

Though Collins and Hall focus on tribal acceptance of waste products, the above critique holds for other tribally accepted and environmentally destructive choices. The challenge such choices present is that they do not necessarily fit within the *Indian-as-victim* paradigm. Separating good from bad, right from wrong is easy when tribes are suffering from either the policies or the practices of non-Indians, without tribal involvement, that reflect environmental racism or environmental injustice.[59] It is much harder to know if environmental racism or injustice is involved when a tribe itself makes "an affirmative and informed decision to undertake an environ-mentally controversial project."[60] But the full meaning of sovereignty is such that it cannot be the case that tribal decisions depend on "satisfying the emotional needs of a romantic tradition."[61]

5.2 ENVIRONMENTAL JUSTICE

The environmental justice movement provides some perspective on how harms suffered by and caused by tribes should be viewed.[62] Reports documenting the disproportionate environmental risks suffered by minority groups as a result of siting choices that concentrated industrial, waste, and other harmful activities in minority communities led to recognition of environmental justice issues.[63] With race, for example, being "the most important variable associated with the siting of hazardous waste facilities nationwide," there was a need to address the problem.[64] In 1991, at the First National People of Color Environmental Leadership Summit, a broad concept of social justice that recognized "both public health and economic opportunity as indispensible aspects of the quality of life" emerged.[65] Those at the Summit concluded that "people should not be faced with choosing between an unsafe livelihood and unemployment."[66] In 1994, President Clinton put the imprimatur of the President on the movement when he signed Executive Order 12898 which required that federal agencies "make achieving environmental justice" part of their mission.[67]

The primary goal of the environmental justice movement has been to ensure that disadvantaged populations, whether defined along racial or socioeconomic lines, are not "shouldering an unequal share of the burdens of hazardous waste" and other harmful activities.[68] The term "environmental racism" conjures up images of whites deliberately targeting minority communities, but siting decisions can have a disparate impact even where overt racism is hard to identify or prove.[69] Though one may not find a Bull Connor equivalent in the site decisions of environmentally harmful activities, "[w]ell-meaning environmentalists and worried citizens of affluent communities" opposed to facilities in their communities may have a similar effect: the concentration of harmful activities in minority communities.[70] Lack of political power and limited ability to effectively participate in decision-making processes may explain in part disadvantaged populations' excess exposure to nearby hazardous facilities.[71] Cheap land can play a role, as can the hope among members of the affected community that any new facility would also mean new job opportunities.[72] Ultimately, as Alice Kaswan argues, "unequal distributions are of concern regardless of whether they were determined by discriminatory processes or ostensibly neutral market forces."[73]

Wholesale application of the environmental justice paradigm when considering Indian experiences, even if capturing tribal distributional burdens, fails to take sovereignty into account. As Sarah Krakoff noted about environmental activism and Indigenous peoples in the wake of the Standing Rock protests, "standing with tribes means supporting tribal sovereignty."[74] Scholars often describe the history, including recent history, of Indian-white relations as one characterized by "exploitation of Indian peoples and their lands."[75] Such a history would seem to lend itself to an environmental justice approach. But Indian environmental issues receive only passing asides in articles on environmental justice[76] and, by treating Indians as equivalent to any other minority group when looking at environmental racism, their unique sovereign rights are largely ignored.[77] The marginal place of Indians in the environmental movement generally[78] thus far has largely carried over to the environmental justice approach.[79] "Indian values and belief systems are not reflected in or accepted by our environmental law," Robert A. Williams, Jr. explains, "in Indian visions of environmental justice, all land is sacred, but that does not mean that tribal lands should never be used by the people."[80]

Environmental paternalism might be appropriate – and has been called for – when distributional justice is taken to be the sum total of environmental justice. Accepting the need for environmental paternalism requires that the group being "protected" be seen as unable to protect themselves.[81] Only when it is accepted that tribes are doing something "wrong" when they decide to prioritize economic growth or that tribes are powerless to resist the interest of harmful industries can a case for paternalism be made.[82] Consider for example the following quotes from leading scholars:

> Examples of outsiders to be opposed might be the corporate disposers of nuclear and other toxic waste who want to dump in South Dakota and Indian country . . .[83]

> Unfortunately, the cultural meaning of Mother Earth to many tribes becomes less important as their people seek sufficient education, well-paying jobs, modern health services, updated housing, and adequate food supplies.[84]

The first quote assumes that Indian tribes should never agree to accept nuclear or toxic waste in return for payments that would alleviate reservation poverty. There is nothing wrong with that position, but its paternalism is self-evident.[85] The same is true of the second quote: "unfortunately" only makes sense if well-paying jobs and adequate food supplies are not thought of as rightly being significant enough to alter the cultural meaning of Mother Earth.

Avoiding environmental paternalism requires expanding the understanding of environmental justice to include respect for sovereignty when it comes to Indians.[86] Doing so will not be easy. Indians have not "fully participated in or embraced environmental justice."[87] And, according to Williams, environmentalists find it "difficult" to deal with tribal governments who are willing to entertain environmentally harmful siting proposals.[88] Yet there is some agreement among scholars and government officials that "addressing environmental justice in Indian country require[s] creative solutions utilizing tribes' governmental status."[89] Once tribal sovereignty is acknowledged to play a role in environmental justice, things get a lot more complicated: Indians must be distinguished from all other disadvantaged groups facing environmental injustice,[90] Indian rights to self-(re)definition must be respected,[91] and, arguably, Indian environmental perspectives should be incorporated to a greater extent into general environmental law.[92] This is not to suggest that the tensions between environmental justice as distributional justice and a broader understanding of environmental justice simply disappear. In the preface to his book on environmental justice in Indian country, James Grijalva writes that "[o]ne of the main premises of this book is that tribes' absence from the national dialogue and implementation of federal environmental programs is largely responsible for creating environmental injustice in Indian country, the concept that some minority communities suffer disproportionately higher environmental risks than many white communities."[93] Grijalva's premise challenges tribal and environmental advocates because it asserts that tribes should play an expanded role while seeming to accept that results should be judged based on whether Indians bear a disproportionate burden. The potential conflict between distributional justice and tribally-embraced harms to the environment makes it hard to describe what an Indian-centered approach to environmental justice looks like. When it comes to environmental justice in Indian country, should standard, racially-defined concerns about distribution of environmental harms dominate or should respect for tribal sovereignty?

A new book by Dina Gilio-Whitaker, *As Long as Grass Grows: The Indigenous Fight for Environmental Justice, from Colonization to Standing Rock*, starts to address just this question, laying out a vision of Indigenous environmental justice. The book highlights how the environmental justice movement has done a poor job incorporating indigenous perspectives and concerns. Gilio-Whitaker argues that the environmental injustice confronting tribes is a continuation of the colonial relationship Indians have with non-Indians, connecting the genocide following contact with the exploitation of Native land through the present. *As Long as Grass Grows* emphasizes that Indigenous peoples have a stronger connection to place and spatial orientation than non-Indians.[94] In part because environmentalists prefer to imagine America pre-contact and America's national parks as pristine wildernesses rather than land with a long history of Indian use, Gilio-Whitaker shows that the relationship between Indians and the environmental movement is complicated and, at times, contentious.[95] The majority of *As Long as Grass Grows* focuses on environmental harms done to tribes, but Gilio-Whitaker acknowledges, "things get ethically complicated when Native nation governments willingly choose to engage in resource extraction – especially fossil fuels – given the harm they cause, both in the extracting and in the production of climate-changing greenhouse gases."[96] That Gilio-Whitaker quickly retreats from this "realm of difficult choices," is understandable;[97] after all, given the long history of colonial exploitation, wrongs done to Indians necessarily weigh more heavily than environmental harms done by Indian nations. The solutions offered by Gilio-Whitaker to these difficult choices is a return to tradition and grassroots activism serving as a check on tribal governments.[98] As the first book dedicated to exploring the relationship between Indigenous rights and environmental justice, *As Long as Grass Grows* does a great job showing the ways in which the environmental movement must change if it is going to better take into account tribal sovereignty and indigenous knowledge. Gilio-Whitaker leaves for others further consideration of the "realm of difficult choices," such as when sovereignty should give way to environmental concerns and whether tribes are ever truly capable of independent choice when they embrace environmentally harmful forms of development.

Should tribal contracts or lease agreements with environmentally harmful industries be considered contracts of adhesion, as is true of Indian treaties? Or when a tribe decides to accept a payment, whether in the form of royalties, taxes, or jobs, in return for suffering environmental harm does it do so "freely" and out of its own powers of self-determination? On the one hand, without having an adequate amount of freedom to walk away from environmentally harmful projects, the "choice" to accept such projects is arguably merely the illusion of choice and the formal acceptance through contract hides the true tribal position. On the other hand, the presence of constraints or tribal needs should not automatically taint all such agreements as adhesionary.

Treaties between Indians and the United States have been likened to contracts of adhesion and have been interpreted in that way by the Supreme Court.[99] Recognizing the "power disparity" between Indians and the US Government in drafting treaties, the Court, starting with Chief Justice John Marshall, has consistently viewed treaties as agreements "in which the negotiation process had not been one of arm's length bargaining between equal adversaries."[100] In order to partially offset the adhesionary aspects of the treaty negotiation process, the Court created a set of rules or "canons of construction," liberally favoring Indians, to be used when interpreting treaty ambiguities.[101] Importantly, the canons of construction inform treaty interpretation, but do not invalidate treaty terms – a recognition that whatever the failings or imbalances in the negotiations, the treaties are still valid instruments. The United States stopped making treaties with Indians in 1871 and since then what used to be accomplished through treaty has been in part accomplished by agreement and contract between Indian tribes and non-Indian governments.[102]

Power disparities between Indians and non-Indian interests did not go away with the end of treatymaking; what changed was the form of the relationship and, to some degree, the contracting parties. The contracts of adhesion interpretative lens used for treaties fits imperfectly with contracts for environmentally hazardous or destructive activities – whether for the storage of nuclear waste or the mining of coal – between tribes and companies and/or non-Indian governments. Dramatic proof of formal contracts still being little more than adhesion contracts can be seen in a 1948 Associated Press photograph which showed Fort Berthold Chairman George Gillette weeping as the Interior Secretary signed a contract to build a dam and flood much of the reservation.[103] The resulting dam had "devastating effects" on the tribes affected and "almost totally destroyed" their way of life.[104] This was accomplished by a government-to-government *contract* not by treaty, yet unequal bargaining positions makes this supposed agreement akin to an adhesion contract.

Some of the commentary on reservation mineral leases blurs the line between non-Indian governments and non-Indian corporate interests, between power and economics, treating them alike as powers that disadvantaged tribes are forced to accept. Donald Fixico's thesis in *The Invasion of Indian Country in the Twentieth Century: American Capitalism and Tribal Natural Resources* is that the continued exploitation of tribal natural resources by American capitalism has forced Indian leaders "to adopt modern corporate strategies to ensure the survival of their nations and people."[105] Similarly, Nancy Collins and Andrea Hall write, "the federal government may force tribes, by the power of law *or economics*, to accept nuclear waste."[106] According to this perspective, the subordinate position of tribes forces acceptance of environmental costs in return for compensation. Compensation, while it may "ameliorat[e] the unfair consequences of siting," also "can be seen as deliberately exploiting the special status of these land-rich, economically poor, and isolated sovereigns in order to secure a dumping ground where the community is in a poor position to object to the infusion of economic incentives."[107] Viewed this way, the role of businesses with undesirable characteristics is to seek out "vulnerable" communities that have little choice but to accept payments for environmental harms.[108]

The problem with this perspective is that it denies the agency of affected communities and tribes, falsely equating economic need with deterministic outcomes. Considering the pro-business orientation of the United States government and its failures to live up to its trust duty to tribes, it may be fair to blur the line between government and corporate contracts with Indian nations. But simply because a community is hurting economically does not mean that when it agrees to allow harmful projects it does so "unwillingly," as one commentator has suggested.[109] Why is this important? Large multinational corporations bring to negotiations not only their own resources but knowledge of the tribal position. Tribal governments are heavily dependent upon both royalty receipts and US government assistance.[110] And for the Navajo Nation, "chronic unemployment and an extremely low per capita income level would seem to make the people of this area receptive to any form of industrialization, including mining."[111] In his study of Diné attitudes towards coal mining, Andrew Curley found that "indigenous attitudes toward 'development' and extractive industries are complicated and are not always sites of resistance against extractive industries."[112] Mining, Curley explained, not only "enables Navajo people to stay in the reservation on their traditional lands," but it also paid well: "the children of coal workers were the ones who had new shoes and nice backpacks."[113] Companies engaged in harm-causing activities thus enter into negotiations from a position of strength, but acknowledging that economic conditions may favor accepting compensation for environmental harms does not mean that tribes are powerless to resist corporate interests or that they will never reject harm-causing proposals.[114] As Joe Shirley, Jr. explained while he was the President of the Navajo Nation: "The Navajo Nation is part of the modern economy. We do not oppose creating jobs, but there are lines we do not cross in order to make money."[115]

5.3 ACCEPTANCE AND DEVELOPMENT

The city of San Diego had a problem, too much trash, and a solution, the Campo Band of Indians was willing to accept the trash. The Band, in partnership with Mid-American Waste Systems, Inc., wanted to open a large solid waste landfill on the remote reservation.[116] The tribe's revenue from the 28-million-ton capacity landfill was estimated to be $1.6 million a year.[117] EPA approved the landfill in 1995, but a year later the United States Court of Appeals for the District of Columbia reversed, holding that the EPA did not have authority to issue the approval.[118]

The attorney for the tribe at the time was Kevin Gover, who would go on to become the Assistant Secretary of the Interior for Indian Affairs from 1997 to 2001, a law professor, and later the director of the Smithsonian's National Museum of the American Indian. A law review article by Jana Walker and Kevin Gover on the proposed landfill unapologetically supports the Campo Band.[119] They argue:

> Under certain circumstances, a solid or hazardous waste disposal project is a viable and appropriate form of industrial development for some Indian tribes. Waste disposal projects are not only extremely profitable, but also require little up-front cash. Moreover, waste disposal projects can provide job opportunities to reduce significant involuntary tribal unemployment. The drawback is, of course, the potential environmental problems.[120]

Potential environmental problems are treated in both the above quote and in the article as being of secondary importance and as something that only the Campo Band should concern itself with.[121] Walker and Gover assert that reservation wealth and job creation should be important elements to consider regarding the viability of disposal projects.[122] Stuttering economic development provided the impetus for this form of growth,[123] and, according to Walker and Gover, writing in 1993, the proposal "instilled a sense of pride and purpose in the Indian community . . . the Band has changed from a pocket of poverty and hopelessness to a community of Indian people united by a determination to succeed."[124] But the court decision in 1996 blocked the tribe from reaping the expected improvements in education, housing, economic self-sufficiency, and government facilities planned in connection with the landfill.[125]

Campo Band's decision to convert part of the tribe's reservation into a receptacle for San Diego's trash powerfully illustrates the challenge of such a path towards economic development. It goes beyond the scope of this chapter to go into the full details of the Campo Band's proposed landfill controversy,[126] but at least according to Walker and Gover's account the Campo Band "choose this form of development" freely and knowingly.[127] As a choice it is not entirely novel: Indian – non-Indian relations have historically been defined by exchanges of land for money or promises.[128] Given the poverty and economic development challenges of many tribes, the basic decision of the Campo Band – acceptance of environmental harm in return for financial reward – is likely to be repeated, with local variation, by other tribes.

Popular stereotypes of gaming tribes aside, most tribes are still struggling economically. "Despite abundant natural resources of land, timber, wildlife, and energy, Indian reservations remain among the most impoverished areas in the United States."[129] The success of Foxwoods and Mohegan Sun, along with media coverage of the large per capita payments made by some tribes, obscure the "overall depressed state of Native American economic development."[130] Reservation unemployment and underemployment has long been common.[131] For many reasons, some of which affect all tribes and some which differ across tribes, poverty is a fact of reservation life.[132] It is now unfair to say, as one author has, that "[t]he reservation economy *is* the welfare state," but some reservations can seem that way, especially to outsiders.[133] And importantly, "Indians do not want to be poor anymore."[134]

The economic and social payoff for tribes whose environmentally destructive projects go forward can be significant. Successful projects allow tribes to invest in things such as education and government services.[135] Additionally, tribes may need a "viable economic base" in order to defend their sovereignty before the US government.[136] Recognizing that poverty can threaten tribal survival, tribal governments do not merely react to outside economic interests.[137] While Fixico writes that growing natural resource demand "forced tribal leaders into two arenas – economics and law," such language fails to appreciate the motivating power of poverty.[138] Just like non-Indians, Indian tribes feel the conflict between protecting the environment and economic growth, but when they decide to pursue growth with some sacrifice, that choice should not be dismissed as "capitalist greed."[139] As Sam Deloria argues: "we cannot help but create confusion in American society if we blame the system for Indian poverty and then denounce opportunities for Indians to get themselves out of poverty."[140] Despite Fixico's concern about "law and economics," while most scholars talk about Indian poverty, there is little focus on economics.[141] Tribes have begun improving their economic situation by pursuing opportunities created by "the resource problems of the industrialized, affluent societies" that surround them.[142] Partly this pursuit reflects limited options,[143] but success also reflects advantages that tribes have when pursuing such opportunities.[144]

The Navajo Nation is no different. In *Red Capitalism: An Analysis of the Navajo Economy*, written in 1973, Kent Gilbreath argued that Navajos do not want "to isolate themselves from the surrounding society," rather "Navajos hope that self-determination will free them to pursue in an individualistic manner their own economic improvement while maintaining their cultural values."[145] The problem is that hope has not turned into reality. In a 1981 introduction focused on Navajo economic development, Al Henderson highlighted the role energy resource development could play in eliminating reservation poverty.[146] But the goal he articulated, "achieving substantial reductions in the social and economic disparities between the Navajo and the rest of the United States," has not been achieved.[147] Instead, decades later many of the same debates about energy development continue to animate Navajo politics even as coal mining on the reservation winds down.[148]

In 2019, Navajo Transitional Energy Company (NTEC) attempted to buy Navajo Generating Station, located next to Page, Arizona, as a way to keep the plant open and keep the trains of coal from Kayenta Mine running. But that effort was shot down by a close vote in the Navajo Nation Council, which ultimately agreed with opponents of the deal that the purchase, which would have released the utility company consortium that owned the plant from all future liabilities, was not a good idea.[149] As a consequence, Kayenta Mine closed in August 2019 and Navajo Generating Station closed just before Christmas in 2019, after it burned off the last of the coal stockpiled near the plant.[150] NTEC still had big ambitions, however, and later the same year bought three large coal mines in Wyoming from the bankrupt Cloud Peak Energy.[151] A scathing report on NTEC's move by the Institute for Energy Economics and Financial Analysis concluded, "NTEC is seeking to buy a company that few companies or investors want. If it were to complete the transaction, it would be putting hundreds of millions of tribal dollars at risk."[152] As a related op-ed by the report's main author noted, "A push by a Navajo Nation-owned company to purchase the Montana and Wyoming assets of bankrupt Cloud Peak Energy comes at the worst possible time to buy into the US coal industry – a sector that is sinking fast."[153] NTEC, which is a Navajo Nation-owned company, purchased the three mines for $75.7 million, without first telling the Navajo Nation President, Navajo Nation Council, or Navajo Nation Department of Justice, which is supposed to review any agreement that purports to waive tribal sovereign immunity, about the purchase.[154] As NTEC's press release declared, the purchase made NTEC "the third largest coal producer in the United States."[155] The irony of NTEC's purchase should not be lost: a Navajo-owned company with "Transitional Energy" in its title has doubled down on coal at precisely the moment when the Navajo Nation is going through an overdue transition away from coal.

5.4 FAINT GLIMMERS OF CHANGE

The Navajo Nation has begun building up the reservation's alternative energy portfolio. The row after row of elevated solar panels that make up the Kayenta Solar Project, a Navajo Tribal Utility Authority (NTUA) project that began in 2016, show that alternative energy projects are feasible on the reservation.[156] The two phased project, Kayenta I and Kayenta II, is located on land near the Agathla Peak, also known as El Capitan, just outside of Kayenta, Arizona. NTUA took the lead on the project but it also is supported by Salt River Project, which agreed to purchase renewable energy credits associated with the solar field, as well as by the US Department of Agriculture, which gave the tribe a $94 million loan to complete the second phase of the project and to assist with expanding the electrical grid.[157] Combined Kayenta I and II generate 55.1 megawatts of electricity, enough to power 36,000 reservation homes.[158] A project of this scale is not cheap, the first half of the project, Kayenta I, required mounting 120,000 solar panels and cost $64 million.[159] The combined Kayenta I and II project uses 365 acres of land.[160] Despite these expenses, the Navajo Nation is bullish about solar, looking to increase its total solar power plant capacity nearly tenfold, to 500 megawatts, by 2028.[161]

It will not be easy. The Navajo Nation's high desert environment means that the reservation has abundant solar resources compared to much of the rest of the United States.[162] The move away from coal has led to "a growing number of proposals for solar and wind power development on tribal lands."[163] Indeed, a 2018 count of all forms of solar generation on the reservation, which includes small, off-the-grid panel

FIGURE 5.1 Kayenta Solar Project, Navajo Nation. Photo Courtesy of Navajo Tribal Utility Authority.

systems but would not have included Kayenta II, which came online later, found that the total Navajo solar capacity at the time was 462,886 megawatts.[164] Similar to solar power, the Navajo Nation has significant untapped wind energy production potential, with the same 2018 study reporting that the reservation has an installed capacity of 162,427 megawatts compared to a net generation potential of 329,108,277 megawatts.[165] In an op-ed about the transition from coal to solar, Chris Deschene, a former candidate for the Office of Navajo Nation President and later the general counsel for Navajo Power, a private solar company, described the Navajo Nation as "a sleeping energy giant" that is well positioned to get massive capital infusions from the energy sector.[166] But "potential" wind and solar energy is not the same as installed capacity. The Kayenta Solar Project could only be built after a Diné grandmother, Mary Toadcheenee, donated part of the land covered by her grazing permit for the project.[167] Though the Kayenta project was able to go forward, "One of the strongest perceived barriers to developing utility-scale solar energy is grazing permittees with *or without* livestock."[168]

Taking a broader perspective, the value of newly constructed solar projects depends on much more than the ease of construction. As Andrew Curley notes, "[t]he underlying problem is not what kind of energy is produced but the terms under which it is produced. The problem is the Navajo Nation's relationship to resource colonialism, whether that's wind, solar, or coal, and Navajo leaders must resolve this structural inequality."[169] A massive stored energy project proposed for the site of the former Navajo Generating Station next to Lake Powell illustrates the complications that can arise even with renewable energy facilities. Daybreak Power submitted preliminary paperwork for construction of a $3.6 billion energy storage project that would use water pumped from, and then slowly released back into, Lake Powell as a way to provide power "to Los Angeles, Las Vegas, and Phoenix for 10 hours, lasting from peak daytime hours and into the night."[170] The Navajo Energy Storage Station (NESS) would take advantage of the existing infrastructure – principally the transmission lines – associated with the now-closed Navajo Generating Station.[171] NESS would take advantage of the relative abundance of solar and wind energy on the reservation during the day to pump water to an upper reservoir and the water would be released as needed during the night to drive hydroelectric turbines. The Daybreak Power press release explained that their proposal is essentially to build "a gigantic battery," which would have more storage and a longer working life than alternative lithium-ion battery systems.[172]

The NESS proposal is not the only proposal being floated that seeks to couple solar energy, pumps, and hydroelectric power in the area on or near the northwest region of the Navajo Nation.[173] It is too early to know which, if any, project will actually be constructed. But likely something will be built. When Navajo Generating Station was decommissioned, the Navajo Nation received the right to transmit 500 megawatt-hours of electricity along the plant's existing transmission line,[174] which, as one Diné activist, Percy Deal, argued in a 2018 interview, represents a significant "economic opportunity" for the tribe.[175] For their part, the major western cities that formerly depended on the reservation's coal-fired power plants see the value in the existing infrastructure as well as the solar potential located on or near the Navajo reservation. Navajo Nation President Jonathan Nez spoke before the Los Angeles City Council, for example, in February 2020,[176] and the city council directed the Los Angeles Department of Water and Power "to meet with representatives of the Navajo Nation to explore the feasibility of partnering on tribal solar projects to supply power to the city."[177] According to the city council's motion, a new partnership with the Navajo Nation would allow the city to "obtain cost-effective clean energy while ensuring environmental justice and economic equity to tribal members."[178]

It is too early to know the nature of the relationship that will emerge between the Navajo Nation and neighboring non-Indian cities interested in energy produced on the reservation. The details – especially the contract terms, ownership forms, built-in renegotiation options, and project externalities – matter a lot. The Kayenta Solar Project, which is owned by the Navajo Nation and generates power which is consumed on the reservation, offers a glimmer of hope, a suggestion of a path forward for the tribe as it transitions away from dependence on coal. Notably, after doubling down on coal in 2019, in 2020 NTEC put forward a proposal for a 200 megawatt utility-scale solar power facility on reclaimed land at Navajo Mine.[179] A new era is arguably dawning.

5.5 THE BIG PICTURE AND TRIBAL ENVIRONMENTAL POLICIES

The world is in the midst of an environmental crisis that will have far-reaching and global impacts. Environmental organizations and indigenous peoples worldwide will both be called upon to deal with the challenges associated with climate change, resource depletion, and sustainable development. Tribes must be careful not to replicate the development and consumption practices that are responsible for global warming and for other forms of environmental degradation that threaten life on Earth.[180] The development of alternative energy sources is required and Indian tribes have an important role to play in how the United States powers itself and consumes resources.[181]

Indigenous peoples, globally and in the United States, are "among the most vulnerable" to the effects of climate change.[182] In 2007, the Natural Resources Law Center at the University of Colorado Law School published a report entitled *Native Communities and Climate Change* that captures the big picture regarding Indians and their environment.[183] The report goes region by region, exploring how climate change will threaten Indian life ways and in the process covers everything from treaty-based fishing rights to water rights.[184] The report's focus is outward, that is to say it is largely about how Indians are affected by climate change. Thus, the report notes that tribes "are among the most vulnerable to impact from climate change caused in large part by conventional fossil-fuel-based energy development."[185] The outward focus of this report is shared by nearly all writing on indigenous peoples and climate change and is easily justified. As the UN Permanent Forum on Indigenous Issues website states, indigenous peoples "have been among the first to face the direct consequences of climate change."[186] The meeting report from the 2008 Copenhagen Conference on Indigenous Peoples and Climate Change explains further that "while indigenous peoples bear the brunt of the catastrophe of climate change, they have minimal access to resources to cope with the changes."[187] The "survival of indigenous communities worldwide" is threatened by climate change, "even through indigenous peoples contribute the least to greenhouse emissions."[188]

Given these facts, it is no wonder that the *Native Communities and Climate Change* report looked outward, which is where most of the action is and where most of the blame – for lack of a better word – can be found. Picking off the low-hanging fruit first makes sense and is likely not going to be controversial among Indian advocates. Non-indigenous peoples and governments *do* make for good bad guys. The report, however, does include brief acknowledgment that "[c]limate change will require tribes to confront the long-term unsustainability of natural resource extraction."[189] Rhetorically and factually an outward-looking analysis makes sense, but there is also the need to engage with Indian complicity in what could be described as the current US indifference to both climate change and intergenerational equity.[190] As Shepard Krech III explains in *The Ecological Indian: Myth and History*:

> critics who excoriate the larger society as they absolve Indians of all blame sacrifice evidence that in recent years Indian people have had a mixed relationship to the

environment. They victimize Indians when they strip them off all agency in their lives except when their actions fit the image of the Ecological Indian.[191]

The "easy" cases that seem to call for scholarly analysis and anger are those that involve sympathetic tribes suffering as a result of non-Indian actions; the "hard" cases involve tribes imposing harmful externalities on others. A Native Alaskan village "in imminent danger of falling into the sea" because protective sea ice is melting as a result of global warming that decides to sue ExxonMobil is an easy case.[192] As the complaint makes clear, climate change could well force the villagers into environmental exile even though they "have contributed little or nothing to global warming."[193] Standing Rock is an easy case. The Navajo Nation's dogged pursuit of coal, even when the market has moved away from coal, is a hard case. When the tribe was debating construction of a new coal-fired power plant, a nineteen-year-old, Orion Yazzie, noted at a public hearing: "Navajo sovereignty is a lot of times brought up during this debate on the power plant – but it is a terrible paradox that us Navajo people would be responsible for upsetting numerous other indigenous people's life ways by contributing to global warming."[194]

6

Golf Balls and Discretionary Funds

Hearings before the Senate Committee on Indian Affairs are ordinarily rather dull. However, in February 1989, the Committee heard riveting testimony describing corruption at the highest level of the Navajo Nation. The testimony ultimately brought down Navajo Nation Chairman Peter MacDonald, Sr., who eventually served time in prison, but not before two MacDonald supporters were killed in riots that broke out in Window Rock. The MacDonald episode exposed rifts among Diné factions as well as the distance between tribal leaders and tribal members – fractures that still animate tribal politics today. In 2009, twenty years after MacDonald's corruption aired before the Senate committee, the *Navajo Times* uncovered systematic abuse and corruption of tribal discretionary funds by nearly every member of the Tribal Council. Although discretionary funds were meant to help those in need, Council delegates were instead funneling money to family members of other delegates and to relatives of the legislative staff. The depth and extent of corruption is troubling, even to those fervently committed to the ideas of sovereignty and tribal independence advanced by MacDonald and the Tribal Council during this period. Unlike Fort Sumner and stock reduction, these corruption crises were not externally driven, in spite of cries to the contrary by the guilty; they were significant and telling tribal governance failures.

Business is never far removed from politics on the Navajo Nation. This closeness limits the transformative potential of traditional resource driven development because of corruption with a capital "C" and with a lower case "c." Just as individual tribal leaders have become dependent on revenues tied to extractive industries, the structure and scale of the tribal government, too, is built on oil, uranium, and coal royalties. Power remains centralized in part because lease revenues flow to Window Rock which also exercises direct and indirect control over major businesses operating on the reservation. For tribal elites and even ordinary tribal members, it can be hard to imagine alternative economic and social structures, even though many tribal members view the land as sacred and Diné had a decentralized governance structure prior to conquest. Regardless, alternative models do exist.[1] Tribal economic development challenges have not escaped the attention of scholars. While there are differences in approach and terminology, there is general agreement that tribes do better when they protect the reservation business decisions from ordinary political interference. This is not to say that tribes should simply adopt a laissez-faire approach to business regulation; there is still ample space for tribes to set a development path based on tribal values. But too close a relationship between businesses and politicians – in terms of daily operations, subjective decision-making, and mutual dependence – leads to missed opportunities and invites corruption.

Corruption on the Navajo Nation is but a symptom of continuing structural governance problems. Before describing the details of the MacDonald and discretionary fund incidents, it is worth acknowledging the difficulties involved in discussing tribal corruption and government failures. It is always delicate for tribal rights advocates, especially outsiders, to criticize tribes and tribal leaders. Given the extent to which non-Indian governments have historically used accusations of corruption and intra-tribal schisms to weaken and exploit tribes,[2] it is not surprising that advocates are reluctant to say anything negative about tribal governments. A friend once told me that Indian law scholars never write about what tribes do wrong, only what they do right. As leading scholars have noted, the US Supreme Court and other non-Indian institutions often utilize minor criticisms of tribes, contained in works largely supportive of sovereignty, to justify placing further limitations on tribal sovereignty. More generally, the genocidal treatment of Indians historically and the continued denial of the sovereign rights of tribes is based in part on the racist belief that Indian nations were, and are, not entitled to the same respect as European nations. Scholarship that highlights tribal corruption or other tribal governance problems can play into the narrative that tribes cannot be trusted with meaningful sovereignty.

Faulting tribal leaders or tribal policies is a particularly fraught exercise for non-Indians. No matter the depth of their connection to the reservation or to members of the tribe, non-Indians are permanent outsiders. Non-Indians may have access to writings about traditional beliefs, may even have Native friends and family members, but there will always be a limit to their cultural understanding and to the authority of their voice within the tribe. This is a fact that some non-Indians have a hard time internalizing. While Bilagáanas tend to pass through the reservation as tourists or as workers who move off-reservation quickly, typically within two to five years, some remain on the reservation for decades. Whether because they marry into the tribe or simply fall in love with the land and people, many non-Indians develop strong connections to the reservation. Even so, it is important for all non-Indians, including those with significant ties to the Navajo Nation, to tread lightly when writing about internal tribal politics. Though this chapter explores corruption among Navajo leaders, it aims to do so with a significant measure of humility.

It would be possible to write a book about Navajo land and economic development that glosses over past corruption and governance challenges facing the tribe.

Such a choice is certainly understandable: it is easier to adapt an "Indians as good guys" stance publically than it is to see and describe the Navajo Nation as a full nation, as a government with flaws that is more than the institutional equivalent of the noble savage. It is worth keeping in mind throughout this chapter that there is nothing unique about tribal governance failures, fights among political factions, or corruption by elected officials. On a daily basis, the *Washington Post* and the *New York Times* describe harrowing examples of political paralysis in Washington, DC, pervasive conflicts-of-interest involving elected officials, and political corruption. It is possible to write books about the United States that focus only on the good things, on the promise of "all men are created equal," but such celebratory works tell only part of the story. Just as the history of the United States is both incomplete and inaccurate if it does not include coverage of the genocidal mistreatment of Indian tribes, scholarship that ignores internal tribal political challenges and failures tells only part of the story. As Raymond Orr notes in his work on tribal politics, "[w]ithout a willingness to engage in unflattering aspects of community, a full discussion of politics is not possible."[3] The Navajo Nation's purchase of Big Boquillas Ranch only makes sense when a full account is made of Peter MacDonald's corruption; similarly, the reluctance of Navajo leaders to step away from coal is partly explained by pervasive graft involving tribal discretionary funds. There are good reasons to be cautious when it comes to airing tribal dirty laundry. But scholarship about the Navajo Nation that leaves tribal leadership failures unexplored neglects powerful forces driving tribal politics and tribal development decisions. More importantly, the Navajo Nation, like all nations, is a work-in-progress that is capable of improvement. An honest accounting of past struggles as a part of the larger study of tribal land and development may help Diné activists and political leaders improve the tribe's governance institutions. While scholars working in Indian law tend to focus on the failure of the US government to live up to its obligations to tribes, improving the institutions and political accountability of Indian nations should be a priority for those concerned about bettering life on reservations.

This chapter focuses on recent corruption charges and does not explore governance before the 1980s. It starts with the most traumatic corruption case for Diné, that of Peter MacDonald, then shifts to explain the discretionary fund abuse scandal. The chapter's goal is not to rehash divisive political moments, but to connect those moments with the larger narrative of tribal development policies and to examine possible corrective paths forward. The revenue generated through environmentally adverse land use policies is closely connected to the problem of corruption in Navajo politics.

6.1 GOLF BALLS

Peter MacDonald, Sr. was elected to his fourth term as Navajo Nation Chairman in 1986, returning to power after his loss four years before to Peterson Zah. It was a tight race: though there were more than 60,000 votes cast, MacDonald won by less than 600 votes.[4] MacDonald had the support of powerful backers, who, in the hope of doing business with the tribe, supported his campaign. His thin margin of victory highlights what a controversial figure he was among Diné. A US Senate Select Committee on Indian Affairs investigation into corruption related to the Navajo Nation's purchase of Big Boquillas Ranch "revealed the full scope of MacDonald's corruption" and led to his downfall in 1989.[5] More broadly, the investigation exposed the pervasive nature of political and administrative corruption on the reservation.

Though the Big Boquillas Ranch purchase rightly occupies the central place in any telling of the corruption case against MacDonald, the February 1989 hearings before the Senate Select Committee also offer a rich and detailed portrait of more routine, and normalized, corruption. The Navajo Nation revised its government structure after ousting MacDonald, creating the office of the Navajo Nation President, thus splitting executive and legislative authority. But in 1987, MacDonald was not President of the Navajo Nation, he was Chairman of the Tribal Council, and as such he made committee assignments and generally allocated power throughout the government.[6] The MacDonald episode is rightly difficult for many Diné. Navajo corruption was the focus of an inquiry by the United States Senate, and the political consequences of MacDonald's actions are still felt on the reservation. MacDonald continues to have the support of many tribal members. While there is a tendency among advocates, whether they are Diné or Bilagáana, to minimize corruption's significance, it is worth lingering a bit on what was revealed by the Senate investigation.

The first person to testify on February 2, 1989 was John Paddock, a contractor who set up a fake Indian preference company with his foreman (who was Navajo) and who offered MacDonald use of his personal plane during the campaign against Zah.[7] After being granted immunity in return for his testimony, Paddock told the Committee that MacDonald made approximately thirty-five trips on Paddock's plane with an estimated market value of roughly $60,000.[8] The trips included an all-expenses-paid trip to Las Vegas to watch a major rodeo competition.[9] A subsequent Vegas trip for MacDonald, his family, and some staff was paid for by Bud Brown, a crucial figure in the Big Boquillas Ranch purchase.[10] In December 1987, MacDonald asked Paddock for a one year, $35,000 loan at 10.5 percent interest, but then made no payments.[11] Neither MacDonald nor Paddock ever discussed the loan again, though MacDonald did say "thank you" when it was given.[12] Paddock was also asked to help MacDonald's daughter, Hope MacDonald, get a rental truck, but when the rental company would not give her a car, Paddock loaned his truck to her for a month and paid the $400 phone bill tied to her use of the phone in the truck.[13] The requests continued. Paddock was asked to contribute to the costs of a birthday party for MacDonald's wife, Wanda MacDonald, which he agreed to, but when no one else contributed, he was stuck paying for half of the costs of the party, between $1,200 and $1,300.[14] Paddock testified that the total amount given to MacDonald, including the value of the flights, was $110,795.57.[15]

Pat Chee Miller, a Navajo contractor who entered into a sham Native Preference agreement with a non-Indian bonded contractor, was the second person on the stand that Thursday. Miller testified that MacDonald requested $1000 from him for the 1986 campaign.[16] Miller noted that after MacDonald won the election, MacDonald asked Miller for another $4,000, though Miller only gave him $3,000.[17] Senator McCain asked Miller whether bribes were "the price of doing business" on the reservation, and Miller answered in the affirmative.[18]

Another vendor, Larry Byron Ward, who managed a tribal insurance program under MacDonald but not during the Zah administration, testified that after MacDonald asked about housing, he offered MacDonald his double-wide trailer in St. Michaels, Arizona.[19] Not only did MacDonald accept the offer, he requested improvements (construction of a large master bedroom and installation of a Jacuzzi) to the property.[20] The contractor who made the improvements, Johnny Donaldson, was not paid by either MacDonald or Ward, and instead did it as a way to curry favor with MacDonald.[21] MacDonald subsequently asked for an additional improvement, an extension to the family room, and the contractor again did the work based on the expectation that he would be awarded work from the tribe.[22] That is exactly what happened. MacDonald's staff members gave Donaldson part of the work remodeling the tribal headquarters.[23] (All told, MacDonald spent $650,000 sprucing up the Chairman's office suite.[24]) Ward admitted that operating on the reservation in prior administrations involved paying bribes to Division of Finance officials.[25] Doing business on the reservation, Ward testified, required paying "a high volume of minimum expense items" in order to grease the wheels of the bureaucracy.[26] Donaldson, near the end of his testimony, stated, "There is no economic development program going on out there [across the reservation]. There is nothing going on on the Navajo Reservation. This place is going backward."[27] Donaldson also complained, "One administration signs a contract, the next administration comes in and wants to void it. Who's going to invest millions of dollars with something like that?"[28] And with that, the first day's testimony concluded.

The Senate Committee hearing resumed on Monday, February 6, and began with the testimony of Drex Hansen, President of American West Aircraft Corp., a company based in Texas that was approached about selling a charter jet to the tribe. Hanson testified that MacDonald took seven or eight charter trips, including several to visit the Chairman's daughter who was graduating from Harvard.[29] The tribe had agreed to pay for these flights.[30] For his return to the Navajo Nation from that graduation, MacDonald, flying home alone, declined a much cheaper option that the company arranged – a first-class ticket to Denver with a Lear jet shuttle connection between Denver and Window Rock – because MacDonald wanted "something that was more meaningful to his demeanor or stature – a Lear jet all the way."[31] Hansen presented the $50,000 bill for the commencement flights to the tribe numerous times.[32] But as of his testimony, there was an outstanding balance for flight services of $89,269.48 for those and other flights.[33] Hansen was also asked to give $45,000 in cash to an "undescribed person" as an "advance kickback," if he wanted to sell planes to the tribe.[34] After Hansen refused, the tribe purchased the exact same planes from a different broker and paid half a million more for the planes than they would have had to pay Hansen.[35] Subsequently, the Navajo Nation paid the outstanding balance, discounted by $25,000, after Hansen threatened to tell the FBI about the kickback attempt.[36]

The main thrust of the Senate Committee's investigation did not concern unpaid charter flights, housing improvements, or campaign contributions made under the table; instead, it focused on the corruption that led the Navajo Nation to overpay for a large off-reservation property, Big Boquillas Ranch. The ranch is located south of the Grand Canyon and, at the time of purchase, it included 729,000 acres, with 491,000 for sale; the remainder were state lease lands.[37] The Committee sought the testimony of Peter MacDonald himself, but MacDonald wrote the Committee stating that if called he would invoke his Fifth Amendment privilege against self-incrimination.[38] He did not end up testifying.[39] But enough major participants did talk, after being granted immunity, that it is fairly easy to piece together what happened.

The owner of Big Boquillas Ranch would have accepted $18 million for the property in 1985.[40] In 1986, two buyers entered into deals to buy it for $25 million, only to pull out later.[41] In 1987, an independent expert gave the ranch a maximum appraised value of $25 million.[42] On February 16, 1987, a non-Indian company, Tracy Oil and Gas, posted $100,000 to put the property into escrow based on a $25 million purchase price.[43] Immediately afterward, Tom Tracy wrote to the Navajo Nation to offer the ranch to the tribe for more than $33 million.[44] The offer arrived on stationary bearing the company name "Big Boquillas Cattle Company," a company Tracy created to facilitate the sale and conceal the fact that he was flipping the ranch.[45] An employee of the Navajo Nation tasked with looking into the property initially valued it well below $33 million but subsequently was "pressure[d] to inflate his appraisal" by the director of the tribe's land administration office.[46] Two BIA officials also wrote to MacDonald on July 2, 1987 that the value of the ranch was only $25 million.[47] The same letter expressed concern that Bud Brown, who was Tracy's partner on the deal, was MacDonald's friend and "advised that there was no way Tracy Oil and Gas could have consummated that deal if, in fact, the Navajos were not buying it on the back end. Which meant that if the Navajos had been patient, they could have backed out of that deal and secured that property directly from Tenneco for $25 million."[48] Navajo Attorney General Mike Upshaw argued that the tribe should delay signing onto the deal for two weeks so it could be further investigated.[49] In a June 26, 1987 memo to MacDonald, Upshaw wrote, "I think we could have some problems on this one in the future because the price seems to me to be too high."[50] Although the paperwork made it appear as if Tracy Oil and Gas was to receive the profits from flipping the property to the tribe, in fact, Tracy and Brown had agreed that Brown would receive two-thirds of the profit.[51] In the end, after a modification to their agreement, "Bud Brown received close to $5 million out of the deal and Tom Tracy received close to $3 million."[52] Tracy had put up the earnest money so he had money at risk, but Bud Brown "brought the most essential element and that was Mr. Peter MacDonald."[53] Brown estimated that he would end up paying MacDonald between $500,000 and $750,000 after the ranch deal closed.[54] He also testified that he made $5,000 installment payments to MacDonald to avoid scrutiny.[55] Brown and MacDonald agreed "that every time he [MacDonald, Sr.] needed money, we'd put $6,000 in an envelope, [and] meet him wherever."[56] In total, Brown claimed to have given $50,000 to MacDonald in this way.[57]

Bud Brown had a close relationship with MacDonald and he used that relationship to lay the groundwork for the Big Boquillas deal. In November 2016, Brown paid for a Hawaiian vacation, including flights, hotel, and golfing, for MacDonald, MacDonald's wife, and MacDonald's daughter, Hope MacDonald.[58] MacDonald had told Brown that he would like to go someplace warm.[59] The trip took place days after MacDonald's election as Chairman in 1986.[60] During the trip, Brown brought the idea of purchasing Big Boquillas to MacDonald and, after returning from Hawaii, Brown did more research before meeting with MacDonald the week before his inauguration.[61] At that meeting, Brown told MacDonald that he was interested in purchasing the ranch to flip it to the tribe for a profit.[62] According to Brown, MacDonald "smiled and said, 'I assume I'll be taken care of.'"[63] As a court would later find, "The conspirators also agreed that MacDonald Sr.'s interest in the transaction and the payments made to him would be kept secret."[64]

Brown partially lived up to his promise to MacDonald, though the investigation complicated their arrangement. Brown agreed with Tracy to take care of MacDonald out of Brown's two-thirds cut of the land deal's profit.[65] Brown told Tracy that MacDonald would get one-third of the profits.[66] After MacDonald requested it, Tracy, through one of his companies, wired MacDonald $25,000 just four days after Tracy offered the ranch to the tribe.[67] The instruction line on the wire transfer stated that it was money from Bud Brown to MacDonald, meant to be put towards paying down an outstanding loan MacDonald had with the receiving bank.[68] Brown also arranged for a BMW dealership to deliver a leased 1986 BMW 735i ("a very expensive car") to MacDonald that Brown paid for; Brown then flew the deliveryman back from Window Rock in Tracy's private plane.[69] MacDonald was unhappy about the car because he had requested a 1987 model, not a 1986.[70] Brown also gave MacDonald's son, Peter ("Rocky") MacDonald, Jr., a $25,000 loan as well as "an unusual consulting agreement" stating that "the services to be supplied [by Rocky] are very unique."[71] Rocky was to be paid $5,000 per month for twelve months for his consulting services.[72] Brown acknowledged in his testimony that Rocky had not actually provided any consulting services.[73]

Unrelated to the Big Boquillas transaction, but reflective of the general atmosphere of corruption, Rocky testified that he had obtained valuable consulting arrangements with other companies. Although those contracts were not inherently problematic, for someone who was just starting a career, they were remarkable. Rocky acted as a consultant for both High Tech Recycling, which was paying him $6,000 a month for work on a lease for a waste disposal facility in a small reservation city, and Thriftway, which was paying him $5,000 a month to keep the company informed of changes to tribal law that could impact the company.[74] These jobs are themselves unusual, as was Rocky's solicitation of a $36,000 loan from the owner of High Tech Recycling.[75] Rocky was given the loan money, which was used to pay the boarding school tuition for MacDonald, Sr.'s daughters, though Rocky had not repaid the loan at the time of his testimony.[76]

Ultimately, Brown turned on his old friend, agreeing to wear a wire to meetings with MacDonald. In return for betraying his friend and business partner, Brown was not prosecuted and got to keep his profits from the sale of the ranch.[77] MacDonald got no such offer. As MacDonald explained in a taped conversation with Brown on November 22, 1988, MacDonald hoped to convince investigators that the $25,000 Brown wired to MacDonald "had nothing to do with his father, and his father had no part in this transaction, and Rocky had no part in Big Bo."[78] Although Rocky once referred to the three conspirators – Rocky, his father, and Brown – as "The Three Musketeers shoulder to shoulder,"[79] ultimately both Rocky and Brown testified against MacDonald, Sr., in return for immunity. Brown, on a phone call with Rocky that he taped for the government, ironically noted, "usually what happens [is], somebody cracks."[80] MacDonald agreed with Brown during a subsequent taped conversation that the cover story was "bullshit."[81]

Tracy Oil and Gas closed on the ranch on July 6 and "sometime before July 8," the Navajo Nation closed on the purchase.[82] For six or seven months, Brown had "practically lived at Window Rock," and arranged buses to take interested council members out to see the ranch.[83] Brown also testified that Attorney General Upshaw requested $18,000 from Brown to pay for an IRS problem, but MacDonald told Brown not to pay Upshaw.[84] In a written response to the Senate committee, Upshaw "unequivocally" denied Brown's allegations.[85] The investigator noted, "My conclusion is this was a major fraud on the Navajo people."[86] After invoking his right to remain silent and receiving immunity, Rocky testified before the committee as well. He agreed that Bud Brown was his father's close friend,[87] and admitted that his father and Brown met to "plan a false story" that Rocky, and not his father, had asked Brown for the money in order to explain the $25,000 previously wired to MacDonald.[88] Rocky confirmed that the three co-conspirators then fabricated both the $25,000 promissory note and the consulting agreement.[89] They also agreed to pretend as if the BMW was intended for Rocky all along.[90] Rocky stated that he agreed to participate in the cover up "[b]ecause I love my father."[91]

Perhaps the most memorable part of the hearing occurred when Rocky explained how his father requested additional cash from Brown. According to Rocky, his father used the code words "golf balls" whenever he wanted more money. Every "golf ball" he requested equaled $1,000.[92] They used code words because MacDonald believed his phones were being tapped.[93] Brown even recorded a meeting on January 7, 1989 with MacDonald and Rocky in which MacDonald, already fully aware of an ongoing investigation against him, asked Brown if he can "get some of those funny golf balls" and even went on to say, "Know what I mean?"[94]

Years later in his autobiography, MacDonald tried to explain away the "golf balls" corruption, arguing that "golf balls" meant simply a meeting and not a cash payment.[95] He blamed his son for making "golf balls" mean more than they were supposed to: "Rocky had to be 'cute,' so he and his wife referred to the money as 'golf balls,' an idea he 'cleverly' got from what he, Bud, and I were saying as our code for 'meetings.' Under Rocky's code each golf ball represented $1,000. Thus he might transfer seven and a half golf balls to his wife, or deposit five golf balls in his own account, or whatever."[96] MacDonald's memoir acknowledges that "being forced to speak against a member of his family was emotionally shattering" for Rocky,[97] but goes on to call Rocky "a weak, naïve young man" who was unable to handle the pressure the government put upon him.[98] Read in light of the taped recordings, MacDonald's deflections strain credibility.

FIGURE 6.1 Peter MacDonald and Wanda MacDonald walking away from a hearing with Navajo Police on either side of them. 1988/1989. Photo by Paul Natonabah. Photo Courtesy of the Navajo Times.

After the Senate hearings, the Navajo Nation descended into a period known as "the turmoil," during which MacDonald supporters and opponents battled for control of the tribe.[99] On February 17, 1989, less than two weeks after the damning hearings in Washington, the Navajo Tribal Council stripped MacDonald of his powers and placed him on paid leave.[100] MacDonald challenged the Council's action and Kayenta District Court Judge Harry Brown, who was MacDonald's brother-in-law, issued a restraining order against the Council, which the Navajo Supreme Court reversed.[101] As researcher Eric Lemont observes, the Navajo court system deserves much of the credit for the eventual resolution of the crisis connected to MacDonald's corruption.[102] Even after the Senate revelations, MacDonald enjoyed the support of a large faction of the Council, as well as of the police, and he mobilized them to contest his removal.[103] Council sessions devolved into shouting matches and eventually violence broke out in Window Rock.[104] In May, tribal police forced MacDonald and his supporters out of the Chairman's office, where they had been issuing orders in defiance of the Council.[105] Following a rally near the Arizona-New Mexico state line on July 20, 1989, MacDonald supporters, armed with clubs and two-by-fours, stormed into the tribal capital area.[106] As Peter Iverson reported, "A riot erupted. When it was over two people had been killed, three others shot, and six more injured."[107] A US District Court eventually sentenced MacDonald to more than fourteen years in prison for corruption and for his role instigating the riot.[108] MacDonald spent just over eight years in prison until President Clinton, on his last day in office, commuted MacDonald's sentence.[109]

In his autobiography, MacDonald presents himself as an innocent victim of federal overreach, targeted because he dared to stand up for Navajo interests. Arguing that "[b]ribery and implied (oral) contracts are a creation of the white world," MacDonald argues that he did nothing wrong.[110] According to him, Navajos traditionally could freely accept gifts without it being about corruption:

> For example, if a man came to your Hogan and wanted to give you a horse, you would take it. You might know that the man was trying to ingratiate himself with you, that he wanted some favor. But he was not asking for a favor. He was not asking for a promise. He gave you the horse. You took the horse. And then you did as you pleased, even when that went against the man's wishes . . . The Navajo consider gifts as expressions of love and respect, nothing more. There were no tribal laws governing the giving of gifts.[111]

MacDonald's "aw shucks" response to the serious charges leveled against him extended to the many benefits he received from his co-conspirators. MacDonald acknowledged that he was "comfortable being wooed, whether that meant being flown somewhere to see a facility, being taken to play golf, or even being given a gift," but insisted, "I was not being bribed. I was not selling out. I was not seducing anyone, nor was I being seduced."[112] MacDonald, "known as the most powerful Indian in America" prior to his downfall,[113] insisted that while he "enjoyed [his] life-style, [he] would have been content herding sheep all [his] life."[114] It is exactly the sort of statement – reaffirming traditional Diné values while deflecting attention from his corruption – that won MacDonald widespread support when speaking to elder Navajos, but that rhetoric rings hollow under the spotlight of the Senate investigation. MacDonald admitted that his friends "were involved in the deal, and there is no question that they made enormous profits," but he cannot bring himself to admit that he, too, benefitted from the land deal.[115] Regardless of how important the purchase of Big Boquillas might prove to be for the tribe,[116] or how likely it is that the tribe could have acquired the property without using a double escrow purchase,[117] it is undeniable that MacDonald abused his office and the trust of Diné. MacDonald complained that the federal government should never have been involved in prosecuting him, arguing that his "corruption, if it existed, was a Navajo problem to be settled in a Navajo tribunal," and that the Senate "had no legal mandate to attack a lawfully elected tribal leader."[118] There is some, but because of the trust responsibility, only some, truth to this complaint. Fortunately, the federal government was not the only entity to prosecute MacDonald: the Navajo Nation brought multiple charges of "criminal conduct relating to conspiracy, bribery, fraud, and violations of the Tribe's ethical code" against MacDonald.[119] In a ruling that undercut MacDonald's claims about a traditional allowance for corruption, a Navajo district court convicted MacDonald of thirteen counts of criminal misconduct.[120]

6.2 THE COUNCIL FLEXES ITS MUSCLES

In response to MacDonald's corruption, the tribe enacted sweeping changes to the structure of the Navajo Nation government and embarked on a lengthy period of government reform that continues to the present. The Council voted in December 1989 to transition from a quasi-parliamentary system in which the Tribal Chairman also controlled the Council to a system with a clear line between the executive and legislative branches.[121] The legislation created three new offices, Navajo Nation President, Navajo Nation Vice President, and Speaker of the Navajo Nation Council, striking a new balance between the branches as a way of curbing the excesses of the MacDonald era.[122] Since 1989, a battle has waged between the branches, with the newly independent Council on one side, and the Navajo President, generally supported by the Navajo Supreme Court, on the other. The battle has taken many forms, including multiple efforts to remove Navajo Nation presidents from office for corruption. Some attempts were successful, others were not. The 1989 governmental changes expanded the power of the legislative branch and perhaps shifted power too far in the direction of the Council. Efforts to check the Council through reduction in the Council's size and through exposure of rampant discretionary fund abuse revealed the extent to which the Council believed itself above the law. Whereas MacDonald was held accountable for his abuse of power and corruption as Chairman, the Council delegates have not been. Diné have suffered from rampant corruption and abuse of power at the hands of the Council.

Starting in 2008, Navajo Nation President Joe Shirley, Jr. began pushing to reduce the size of the Council from eighty-eight to twenty-four delegates.[123] The Navajo Nation Supreme Court had to step in three times to ensure that a vote took place. In the end, Diné "overwhelmingly approved" Shirley's proposal by a vote of 25,206 in support, to 16,166 opposed.[124] The Council did not accept the results gracefully.[125] Fearful that the Navajo Supreme Court would uphold the popular referendum, the Council passed legislation in 2010 declaring, "The courts of the Navajo Nation shall not hear any disputes nor render any decisions on the interpretation, application or validity of the Diné, Diné Law and Diné Government statute or its underlying core principles."[126] This legislation was a blatant power grab and effort to thwart the political will of tribal members.

In 2002, the Council amended the Navajo Nation Code to "[r]ecognize the Fundamental Laws of the Diné."[127] The 2002 legislation acknowledged that judges were already applying Fundamental Law, which are the set of beliefs and values that form the unique cultural and social system of the Diné. The Council, therefore, arguably codified something already accepted by Navajo courts, namely, that Navajo common law (or customary law) is the highest law of the tribe.[128] At least for a while, the Council agreed: the 2002 Act referred to Diné Fundamental Law as "immutable" and explained that these laws are the foundation of Diné sovereignty, government, and the rights of Diné as individuals.[129] But by 2010, the Council, in an effort to protect themselves from reduction, had a change of heart and attempted to strip Diné Fundamental Law of legal significance, declaring that Diné Fundamental Law should not be "heard or resolved in the courts of the Navajo Nation."[130] Fortunately, the Navajo Supreme Court courageously stood up to the Council.

On May 28, 2010, the Navajo Supreme Court issued rulings in two related cases, siding with President Shirley both on the impropriety of his suspension and on the legality of reducing the size of the Council.[131] In an unusual move emphasizing the importance of the cases, the Chief Justice of the Navajo Supreme Court, Herb Yazzie, read the Court's opinions aloud in Navajo and in English over public radio. The Court struck down the Council's amendments that purported to strip the judiciary of its ability to interpret Fundamental Law. The Court blamed the Council for having "become so intransigent in its position" in the ongoing dispute between the legislative and executive branches that it "purports to have authority to enact a new statute that would reduce the discretion of our courts to question the sources and complexion of our laws and governmental authority."[132] In a move reminiscent of *Marbury* v. *Madison*, the US Supreme Court case establishing the judicial review power of the federal courts,[133] the Navajo Supreme Court held that the Council cannot declare legislation to be outside the purview of judicial review.[134] Recognizing that the Council had attempted to "encroach upon the independence of the Judicial Branch," the Court declared the 2010 amendments invalid.[135]

As the Navajo Supreme Court opinions recognized, by attacking both separation of powers and the role of Diné Fundamental Law, the Council was trying to position itself as "the absolute source of governance for the Navajo People."[136] Connecting the position of the Council to the colonialism experienced by the Diné, the court emphasized the continuing indigenous aspects of the Navajo Nation government and unapologetically stated that it was "obligated to respond in blunt manner" to the assertions of the Council.[137] As the Court observed, the three-branch version of the Navajo Nation government was a result of the MacDonald era "turmoil," but the Court also argued that the post-1989 structure reflects the lesson that power should not be concentrated.[138] The Court drew not from the political history of the United States, but rather from a Diné emergence story, in which a question about who should lead the People was ultimately resolved by the decision that power should be shared among four leaders – a wolf, a bluebird, a mountain lion, and a hummingbird – each with its own unique contributions to the People.[139] When it came to reducing the size of the Council, the Supreme Court looked beyond formal limitations on the power of popular referenda, including the nearly impossible bar that all chapters must vote in favor of such proposals for them to become effective, and held that a simple majority was sufficient for an initiative to pass.[140] The Court based its holding on the importance of participatory democracy contained both in Diné Fundamental Law and in the post-1989 restructuring of the Navajo government.[141]

Together, these two opinions reflect the best of the Navajo Nation Supreme Court. The Council attempted to determine the outcome of cases involving the Council that were already on appeal, causing the Navajo Nation to pass through something akin to a constitutional, or in this case, an unwritten constitutional crisis. The Court faced another crisis moment in late 2014 and early 2015, when it was asked to rule on whether a popular candidate, Chris Deschene, should be allowed to run for the office of Navajo Nation President even though he did not speak Navajo. Deschene did well in the first election, but when it was discovered that he had lied by signing a form affirming Navajo fluency that was required for him to get on the ballot, he was barred before the run-off. The Navajo Supreme Court ruled that the language requirement was the law and therefore Deschene could not run for office. It was an unpopular and courageous decision that led tribal members and Council delegates to call for removing Chief Justice Yazzie from the Court.[142] A few months later, Yazzie decided to retire.[143] Referring in his retirement announcement to the Court's role reining in the Council, Yazzie noted his "steadfast hope that the Judicial Branch may continue to be the disciplinarian and gatekeeper without interference."[144] Given that Yazzie had suffered through years of interference directed against the Court as an institution and against Yazzie individually as the Chief Justice, Yazzie knew better than most that "continue" has a broad meaning and requires effort. After all, as Yazzie's retirement announcement highlighted, "there will always be people who will insist on behaving as if the function of government is to destroy itself."[45] Yazzie's retirement and his observations reflect the sad state of the Navajo Nation Council.

6.3 DISCRETIONARY FUNDS

Perhaps no episode since the Big Boquillas Ranch purchase highlights the problems of corruption and abuse of power more than the Council's use of tribal discretionary funds for the personal benefit of Council delegates and Council staff. Starting in late 2009, the *Navajo Times* published a series of articles detailing rampant corruption by nearly every member of the Navajo Nation Council. The tribe dedicated a considerable amount of money to the various discretionary funds. "The allocations absorb up to $10 million a year in tribal revenues and are subject to few rules and almost no oversight."[46] From 2005 to 2009, $35,811,495 of tribal money went into the discretionary slush funds of the Council, Speaker's Office, and President's office.[47] These discretional funds are designed to allow tribal leaders to respond to the needs, often pressing and meritorious, of tribal members. In theory, these funds enabled the government to be responsive and connected to constituents. In practice, things were messy. The funds were labeled "social assistance fund appropriations,"[48] but in reality, they were used to line the pockets of connected individuals and families.

As part of its effort to discredit President Joe Shirley, Jr. and stop his proposal to reduce the size of the Council, the Council hired Alan Balaran as Special Prosecutor to look into "alleged misconduct" by Shirley involving two failed business deals.[49] But Balaran, at the direction of the Navajo Nation Attorney General, also looked into abuses of the discretionary fund by Council delegates. What Balaran, and, through the *Navajo Times*, tribal members discovered was that corruption was widespread and egregious. Following an earlier discovery of abuse of the discretionary fund system, the tribe created a rule that prohibits tribal delegates from using the funds to directly support family members. So, as a way of working around this ethics rule, delegates would give to each other's families. The Pinon chapter delegate whose daughter needed to make a truck payment or pay for braces, might, for example, give several thousand to a family member of the Red Rock chapter delegate in return for a reciprocal payment.[50] Council delegates were not the only ones in on the scheme: family members of legislative staff members with financial oversight responsibilities also benefitted handsomely. *Indian Country Today* reported:

> According to court documents, defendants secured slush fund dollars in a variety of fraudulent ways: taking personal kickbacks, transferring financial assistance checks into personal bank accounts or falsifying requests for assistance and then pocketing the money. Some defendants personally authorized tens of thousands of dollars in

financial assistance to their own family members. Others conspired with colleagues to approve each other's requests for funds.[151]

This was not a case of a few bad apples; nearly everyone was caught with their hands in the people's till. Special Prosecutor Balaran's initial move was

the unprecedented filing of 259 criminal charges in the Window Rock District Court in a two-day period from October 20–21, 2010, all alleging that 78 delegates of the 20th and 21st Navajo Nation Council had committed theft, fraud, forgery, abuse of office, tampering with public records and conspiracy concerning millions of dollars of discretionary funds intended for the assistance of indigent members of the Navajo Nation public.[152]

In response to having countless requests for information about the use of discretionary funds denied by the President's office and the Speaker's office, the *Navajo Times* nominated Speaker Morgan and President Shirley for the 2009 "Brick Wall / Arpaio First Amendment Disservice Award," which is given by the Arizona Press Club for "the most deceptive government agency or politician in the state."[153] Shirley and Morgan won.

The list of delegates who faced criminal complaints was a who's who of Navajo politics.[154] Peter MacDonald's daughter, Hope MacDonald-Lonetree, a beneficiary of MacDonald's corruption decades before was on the list, accused of "theft [and] conspiracy involving $12,200 in discretionary funds."[155] Delegate David Tom's alleged corruption, however, rose to a different level: he was accused of "conspiracy, theft, fraud and forgery involving $279,175 in discretionary funds."[156] Amanda Teller, the stepdaughter of the legislative branch's financial advisor, senior financial adviser Laura Calvin, and daughter to Council Delegate Leonard Teller, received more support from Council delegates than any other Diné individual.[157] Over a six-year period, Teller received over $28,000 in assistance, but she was hardly the only relative of a legislative branch employee to receive special consideration.[158] According to the *Navajo Times*, "[t]wo close relatives of another legislative branch employee, secretary Eva Smiley, received over $43,000 since 2006."[159] While some delegates stole only small quantities, "18 defendants – including three who were previously sentenced – helped themselves to a total of $850,000 between 2005 and 2009."[160] As reported by the *Navajo Times*, "Neither Morgan nor the delegates could say how many other tribal members, particularly those without close ties to the council, have received similarly large amounts of aid."[161]

For a variety of reasons, including the scale of the corruption uncovered, Balaran withdrew the criminal complaints and brought civil cases instead. The cases were against "eighty-seven of the eighty-eight former Council delegates, former President Joe Shirley, former Attorney General Louise Denetsosie, current Attorney General Harrison Tsosie, Controller Mark Grant, and fifty anonymous individuals."[162] Unfortunately, this meant that most of those caught red-handed were allowed to

escape with little more than a slap on the wrist.[163] Balaran dropped charges against
Shirley after he agreed to support the corruption inquiry. In a telling editorial in the
Navajo Times, reporter Bill Donovan argued that there should be no prosecutions
connected to the discretionary fund corruption cases in part because "[s]tealing or
misusing tribal funds will not get you put in jail here. At the most you could lose your
job and get ordered to make restitution – which just means the tribe spends the next
few years begging you to pay back a portion of what you stole."[164] Donovan
explained, "Either be committed to press the charges all the way, or decide now to
save the cost of prosecution."[165]

Perhaps most troubling, not only did most delegates escape without consequence,
but Diné voters reelected them. *High Country News* noted,

> President Shirley's vice president, Ben Shelly, was also caught in Balaran's net – charged
> with the theft of $8,850 when he was a council delegate. Yet even while Shelly was
> under that cloud, Navajo voters elected him as the new tribal president. They also
> elected former delegate Rex Lee Jim, charged with conspiracy and the theft of $3,200, as
> the new vice president.[166]

The same was true of the now reduced Council of twenty-four delegates: "Of the
charged delegates, eleven were re-elected in November, 2010 and now serve as
delegates on the 22nd Council."[167] A *Navajo Times* article following the election
noted, "[w]hile some voters expressed indignation that their delegates had been
accused of funneling their slush funds toward each other's relatives, most didn't
seem too bothered by it."[168] The case against Ben Shelly was dismissed after Shelley
agreed to repay $8,250 through payroll deductions and to work to reform the
discretionary fund program.[169] Former Speaker of the Council, Lawrence
Morgan, pled guilty in 2014.[170] Even David Tom, the delegate who diverted
a whopping $279,175 for himself and his family, was reelected after he was
indicted.[171]

Being a Council delegate or Navajo government employee has long come with
certain perks, some explicitly allowed, and some decidedly less so. The Council and
other tribal institutions regularly hold tribal meetings and attend conferences in
Phoenix, Albuquerque, and Las Vegas. After payday, it is normal to see tribal
vehicles ("tribees") on the road to Gallup or Farmington. And some departments
routinely provide their entire staff with quality jackets and other forms of "swag." In
2007, for example, "a vast majority of delegates voted for a special amendment,
tacked on to a measure funding summer youth employment, to allocate $50,000 to
buy gold rings for all the delegates, to commemorate their service."[172] But even in the
context of such standard low-level corruption, the discretionary fund cases are
notable: "Over the course of five years, according to Balaran, delegates engaged in
shameless self-dealing – even siphoning money from a fund intended to buy
eyeglasses for poor Navajos, to fill the coffers of their families and friends."[173]
Whereas MacDonald got caught in part because co-conspirators revealed the

elaborate efforts he went to in order to conceal bribes, the Council did not even feel the need to do a cover up. As Balaran wrote, "Indeed, the directness with which the delegates and their staff stole millions of dollars earmarked specifically for the poor was notable not only for its brazenness but for its callous disregard of the needs of their indigent constituents."[174]

6.4 CORRUPTION AND THE LAND

All governments suffer from corruption. Politicians of all types and at all levels of government disappoint their constituents by abusing the power and position entrusted to them. Diné are no different and the Navajo Nation government is no better or worse than other governments in this respect. But that doesn't mean that such failures or episodes should be simply ignored or swept under the (Navajo) rug.

MacDonald's corrupt Big Boquillas Ranch purchase and the Council's abuse of the tribal discretionary fund system rest on the giant pile of money generated by permitting extractive industries to tear up the land. That Diné did not unite in complete opposition to MacDonald after the Senate hearing, instead they broke into two camps – with one camp defending him despite the overwhelming evidence of a conspiracy to defraud the tribe – reflects either MacDonald's skill as a politician or the low expectations tribal members have of their leaders.[175] (It is worth emphasizing, especially given the Trump-era, that this is not a uniquely Navajo issue.) The same can be said of the reelection of so many Council members following public exposure of both their corruption and their efforts to undermine the rule of law by attacking the Navajo Supreme Court. Abuse of power and corruption have become normalized; people expect Council delegates to be self-serving and to use their position to benefit friends and family. The split between the subset of the population that benefits from mining or administrative jobs funded by mining interests and the rest of the tribe, largely relegated to the informal economy, limits the ability of Diné to hold their leaders accountable. Revenues from mining provided a cushion for the bad behavior of tribal politicians, enabling them to provide limited goods to tribal members while also finding ways to enrich themselves.

Those in Window Rock can become detached from the struggles found across the reservation and it is important that everybody committed to a better future not pretend that all problems faced by the tribe are externally created. If a sizable fraction of the money collected by the central government is going to be used to line politicians' pockets, then it makes sense for tribal members to be skeptical about promised jobs or other benefits supposedly associated with permitting particular industries to operate on the reservation. Episodes of corruption that go unchallenged in a meaningful way, by officials or by voters, color how Diné view their government. Even efforts that might make sense on paper – for example, rationalizing land use and diversifying tribal revenues through a centralized permitting scheme – might face pushback because tribal members justifiably do not trust those in the central government. Put differently, corruption matters. It has an obvious direct impact on what the tribe is able to do with the money from the royalties of extractive industries but its negative impact on how Diné imagine improving the reservation and on the expectations Diné have of their leaders is arguably even greater.

7

Improving Tribal Governance

How can the Navajo Nation improve governance? How can the tribe better support reservation economic development? These are pressing questions, not only because of the ongoing challenges associated with corruption discussed in the last chapter, but also because poverty continues to limit the lives and aspirations of Diné. The unique size and importance of the Navajo Nation makes it also important to other tribes that Diné get things right. It is impossible to present a single list of things that would improve governance and lead to economic growth. As a "domestic dependent nation," the Navajo Nation is not the equivalent of the United States or other established nation-states especially when it comes to the tribe's power over land and over nonmembers. It also is not the same as a state or a local government, such as a city or county. And the Navajo Nation has its own history, culture, resources, and belief system that makes it different from other indigenous groups, including other federally recognized tribes. These differences make it hard to know where to look for answers. What can tribal leaders learn from economic theory and from scholarship on tribal economic development?

This chapter transitions A Nation Within from looking backward at the forces that shaped the reservation to exploring the future direction of the Navajo Nation. It addresses the tension between ideological openness on the one hand and the uniqueness of the Navajo Nation on the other. The chapter explores the governance and economic development prescriptions offered by economic theory and by tribal development scholars. To put the cart before the horse, economic theory highlights the importance of incentivizing economic actors, providing people with clear property rights, and making credit available, especially in connection with land. Experts on Indian economic development largely agree that tribes should follow a tribally defined development strategy, ensure judicial independence, and protect tribal business decisions from ordinary politics.[1] Although this chapter details outsider ideas about good governance, the application of those ideas to the Navajo Nation must be accompanied by a great deal of humility. There is certainly space for the Navajo Nation to improve – to provide citizens with better governance and to create more possibilities for economic growth – but the tribe has done a remarkable job surviving and adapting when necessary in the face of significant external pressure. Instead of insisting on external solutions or governance models, efforts to respond to Diné poverty and reservation underdevelopment must align with, and build upon, Diné wisdom.

There is no single right answer that economics can offer the Navajo Nation. Though economics is popularly presented as a monolithic discipline, with a well-formed and universally accepted view of the world, there are multiple economic approaches, and the field is rife with simplifying assumptions. In the United States, "economics" usually refers to neoclassical economics and is primarily concerned with understanding market forces. Europeans likewise appreciate the importance of microeconomics, but also tend to appreciate the role government and culture play in shaping markets. For those parts of the world either under communist rule or with greater tolerance for robust leftist ideology, such as parts of Latin America, intellectual views on markets are often based on Marxism, statism (such as is practiced in China), or other critical perspectives on economics. This section focuses primarily on the dominant form of economic thought in the United States, neoclassical supply and demand.[2] What emerges is not a prescriptive list, but rather a suggestion that Indian nations take greater account of incentives and property rights.

But before moving into a theoretical discussion anchored in non-Diné ways of thinking, it is worth acknowledging the limitations inherent in such an exploration. First, no matter what theory says, tribes have ample experiential knowledge that some economic magic boxes simply do not work. Therefore, though the chapter will cover the arguments in support of land privatization, ultimately it rejects land privatization as an experiment that has already been attempted and shown not to work. Put differently, just because something has theoretical support does not mean that it should be implemented if it amounts to a break with both community knowledge and Diné understandings of the nature of land. Second, this chapter is concerned primarily with the work of non-Diné academics and schools of thought. A lot of great work is being published as part of the emerging Navajo/Diné Studies field and this book looks to some of that work throughout the text.[3] But by its very nature, Diné Studies embraces a multiplicity of voices and perspectives.[4] It is not monolithic: different scholars push forward different prescriptions and models for everything from the nature of Diné leadership to the culturally appropriate response to economic or social challenges. That makes it hard to say with any precision, in contrast to neoclassical economics, for example, what the Diné studies response would be to a particular development challenge.

Equally significant, as noted previously, the author of this book is not Diné. As a Bilagáana, especially as a Bilagáana who does not speak Diné, I have limited access to or understanding of the origin stories and oral history of the tribe that are the basis for much of the wisdom contained in the Diné Studies literature. Even where there are published accounts in English, the stories are not mine and not part of who I am.

That matters. It limits my ability to fully engage with some Diné Studies work; additionally, some of the knowledge is not the sort that I feel should be disseminated publicly to a largely non-Navajo audience. Though there are Bilagáana academics who feel differently, who see themselves as conduits for sharing Diné knowledge and stories, that is not a role I am willing to assume. One of the great things about Diné Studies so far is that it is Diné-centered, with Diné academics in the driver's seat.[5] If those academics decide it is appropriate to share a particular story or that there is a single right way, a Diné way, of responding to current challenges facing the tribe, then I will read such works eagerly, but that should not be my role. Accordingly, this chapter, for better or for worse, focuses on academic insights provided by neoclassical economics and by tribal economic development experts.

7.1 NEOCLASSICAL ECONOMIC THEORY

The foundation of neoclassical economics (upon which the entire intellectual edifice is constructed) is the intersection of the supply and demand curves. Price is determined by that intersection and is responsive to changes in either supply or demand. A movie theater can charge four dollars for a soda because in that space there are no other suppliers, but in the food court right next door, vendors charge less because of competition. The market rewards economic actors who can satisfy consumer demand for a particular product or service; such rewards encourage individuals to behave entrepreneurially. The role of the state, in theory, is to define property rights, establish clear rules of participation, and enforce the expectations of market actors, but otherwise to get out of the way. Proponents of neoclassical economics believe that Adam Smith's "invisible hand" will lead to the best overall societal outcomes, paving the way for economic growth. According to this view, people are rational economic actors motivated by self-interest. The field has a rich literature, full of nuance and alternative models, of course, but at its core, neoclassical economics emphasizes this antiseptic view of individual agency.

Although economics has been called "the dismal science," its simplistic view of what motivates people is also its primary strength. The assumption that everyone behaves rationally and out of self-interest allows economists to ignore individual differences. Neoclassical economics proves its "value" (for lack of a better word) through its ability to make predictions about behavior and markets based on the observable power of supply and demand. Generally speaking, neoclassical economists, including law-and-economics professors, focus on how markets increase national income. They do not deny that distribution matters – indeed many of their models begin with the diminishing marginal utility of money – they just assert that concerns about inequality and distribution are best addressed through tax and transfer schemes, not through rules directed towards distributive goals.[6] Just because one person can only afford Taco Bell while another can pay for lunch at a nice hotel restaurant does not mean that the government should get involved. What matters is whether everyone has the same rights to participate in the market and whether the state allows for efficient transfers. Markets depend on the ability of participants to transfer property among themselves largely free from state intrusion. If I have ten dollars and want to eat at Blake's Lotaburger, the restaurant should be allowed to accept my money in return for their food. In much the same way, if a tribal member has an idea for how a particular parcel of reservation land should be used, the tribe should not place too many barriers in front of a voluntary transaction between that person and the person who has a use or ownership right in that parcel.

At an abstract level, neoclassical economics suggests that Diné would benefit from the establishment of clear rights to property and the creation of active markets. Clear property rights enable people to form expectations regarding their rights over particular objects of property and their relations with others.[7] Clear property rights permit people to interact easily without requiring a full accounting of all interests for all interactions. To use a famous example, when I park my car on the street, I do not need to tell everyone else that it is my car, nor do I need a contract relationship with everyone else setting forth our respective interests in the car. The nature of the object and background principles of law permit us to interact through default assumptions about ownership on everything from who has a right to a car, to the consequences of purchasing an object at a flea market. Some markets are relatively straightforward affairs: if you have a candy bar that I want, we can negotiate a price for the candy bar. But many markets are more complicated. If someone wants to build a store selling candy bars, he or she may need to purchase land, inspect the land records in the process, secure a mortgage, go through the local business permitting process, and follow acceptable accounting standards as required by those governments with oversight authority. In some circumstances, a market may not exist and the responsibility for creating the market rests with the state. According to neoclassical economics, markets lead to more efficient outcomes and largely solve the problem of allocation; therefore, to the extent possible, the state should create and support markets.

Navajo economic development is stunted, especially when it comes to land management. There is not a functioning land market. A neoclassical economist looking at the reservation land regime – non-alienable trust land with limited individual control subject to severe bureaucratic checks and costs – instinctively knows why development is limited: reservations have "no market for land."[8] A land market establishes clear user rights within the bounds of the property, promotes business development through loans guaranteed by the land, and allocates land to the most efficient, value-generating user. For empirical support, the neoclassical economist simply contrasts reservation poverty with off-reservation development. Many who unapologetically embrace neoclassical economics advocate for carving reservations into individually owned parcels, as was done in the allotment era. For those neoclassical economists who accept that reservation land will not be individually alienable, the solution is to establish tribal land regimes that come as close as possible to approximating a "normal" land market.

Applying neoclassical economics to the Navajo Nation is dangerous; it risks prescribing solutions that are overly defined. For example, although economists tend to write about property rights monolithically, with norms drawn from non-Indian society, neoclassical insights could inform tribal policy without requiring outright mimicry. Given the limits on the alienability of trust land, the Navajo Nation could provide tribal members with clearer user rights simply by affording them more individualized and complete delineations of their use rights and clarifying the extent to which those rights are protected. That Navajo trust land is not individually owned does not mean that lands do not have associated use rights, nor does it mean that the tribe does not recognize different priority rights in land.[9] Thus, a land regime that allows individuals with land use rights a larger scope of permissible activity might facilitate tribal entrepreneurship. Even if the tribe decides to closely regulate the use of individual parcels, clarifying use rights could help tribal members form reasonable expectations vis-à-vis their neighbors and the tribal government.

For a neoclassical economist, regulations that limit or define use rights are not necessarily inferior to expansion of such rights. Off-reservation plots are often zoned residential, commercial, or industrial; the state denies landowners the right to use land for certain activities and can even dictate less general parameters, such as the building set-back, the compliance with environmental, disability, safety, and other regulations; and the state holds the ultimate power to determine use through compensable takings. Given the advantages of clustered, similar land uses, full expansion of user rights over all land is not necessary in order to encourage a land market. It is important, however, that some subset of the land is available for economic activity. Thus, from a neoclassical perspective, zoning all land as residential, with variation only through permission from the tribal and US governments, would be suboptimal because such zoning substitutes political decision-making for market allocation.

In the same vein, improving the availability of information regarding land use rights and creating a system for recording such rights is a critical step in bringing the power of the market and capital to those who currently use the land but do not enjoy all of the benefits of their use right. Although Hernando de Soto's writings focus on land titling, his description of the benefits of land titling arguably applies to reservation land and fits with the neoclassical response to reservation poverty.[10] Land is not merely a physical space but also a means of leveraging capital; titled land allows land and resources tied to land to be transformed, through capital markets, into working capital. As de Soto explains: "Any asset whose economic and social aspects are not fixed in a formal property system is extremely hard to move in the market … Without such a system, any trade of an asset, say a piece of real estate, requires an enormous effort just to determine the basics of the transaction."[11] While use rights differ, when the tribe injects itself into the market in the form of a tribal enterprise and preempts local use rights, the necessity of conducting on-site investigations into use rights delays development and increases transaction costs.[12] When the actors are not tribal governments, the lack of an accessible land use registration system serves to tie up land, blocking the emergence of an internal tribal land market.

Cultural expectations surrounding land titling and use rights vary widely across tribes. For some tribes, making land use rights the personal property of individuals or families would be a cultural imposition, while a mere land registration scheme might not. For other tribes, the communal ownership of the land through the tribe is already tempered by strong support and defense of individual use rights. Strengthening land use rights that are personal to the holder moves tribes closer to creating a land market, especially if tribal members could transfer, or even sell, their use rights to others. The non-alienability constraint associated with the trust status of reservation land – the limits on the transfer of use rights in reservation land to non-Indians – provides an outer boundary on the degree to which Diné can hold transferable use rights.

Closely related to the issue of clear user rights is the fact that off-reservation banks and lending institutions do not accept reservation land as collateral on loans. If tribal land was freely alienable and used as the security interest in mortgage loans, then individual default by tribal members could serve to reduce the size of the reservation. The trust status of the land prevents such land loss but also limits the willingness of banks to offer loans to tribal members. A possible solution to this challenge, and one that aligns with neoclassical theory, is for the tribe or another entity to put up other assets to serve as substitute collateral. Loan guarantees could make tribal land functionally similar to off-reservation land for borrowing purposes. Earmarked federal funds could provide loans directly to tribes or be used to provide private lenders with alternative guarantees for on-reservation lending. Likewise, tribes with sufficient resources could pledge tribal resources for the same purpose. The Navajo Nation, for example, was able to secure development loans by pledging mining income as collateral. Bankers and tribes working to promote business development might tie loans to future profits or to the right to operate a particular franchise on the reservation. Such loans are tied to land development, but security comes not from the land but from associated development rights.

More radically, tribal trust status need not prevent tribes from establishing sufficiently clear user rights and transfer rights to allow lending to be tied to the ownership or use rights of particular tribal members. While the trust status of land protects against tribal land loss, tribes could individualize ownership among tribal members such that default on tribally issued or tribally secured loans would result in foreclosure. For tribes with a large enough population and high enough effective demand, a tribal lending institution with such devolved government power would be in a position to make loans in much the same fashion as off-reservation banks do off the reservation.

Such expansive powers in the hands of a banking institution, even a tribal banking institution, might be antithetical to other values such as the permanence of family claims across generations. For example, Diné families who could be forced off their ancestral land because of an ill-conceived business idea ending in foreclosure arguably stand to suffer too grave a loss, one that should not be tolerated in the attempt to ascertain and secure use rights. Thus, clear user rights and allowance for land transfer as part of a loan guarantee might be inappropriate for large parts of the Navajo Nation. As Demsetz notes, "[A]ccount [must] be taken of a community's preferences for private ownership."[13] Even within the same tribe there can be regional differences. Where wage labor is the norm, especially in the area around Window Rock, the costs of not having a tribal land market that can support lending are large enough that expanded use and transfer rights may be appropriate. In rural parts of the reservation, where work is more traditional and centered on land-based production, a system where a tribal bank makes land-tied lending decisions might do more harm than good. Even though such power is in line with neoclassical economic theory, tribal banks or other tribal institutions should not necessarily be granted the power to foreclose against tribal members. Yet, for segments of the Diné professional class, increasing access to capital could expand access to quality housing and allow for greater entrepreneurial activity, both of which could help the tribe as a whole.

From a neoclassical economics perspective, the principal problem of reservation land – even more important than the ways that the land's trust status limits credit – is the lack of a market to ensure that land goes to its highest and best use. Off-reservation, the market theoretically ensures that particular parcels move to those economic actors who can make the best, defined in terms of ability to pay, use of the land.[14] If I own undeveloped land near the center of a city experiencing economic growth, I am likely to either build on the land myself or sell to someone with a better idea on how to use that land. Through its tax authority, the city will encourage construction or sale of the property by raising the amount of tax due as the assessed value moves up. Consequently, except in the minority of cases where the landowner can afford to be irrational, the land will be sold eventually and predictably to the highest bidder, the person or entity best able to generate value from the land. From this perspective, the market allocates land efficiently. Alternative allocation schemes, such as relying on the tribal government to decide who gets to use land and how they can use those parcels, limit growth. The non-alienation rule means that the tribe or tribal members cannot alienate land from the tribe; however, a market could be created for rights that could be bought and sold amongst tribal members.

Given neoclassical economics' privileged place in the United States, it is not surprising that many of the pushes to improve tribal economic development flow from neo-classical thinking. Vine Deloria noted that "[a]mong the more surprising elements of Indian land tenure is the aspect of continual experimentation with property rights which has been visited upon the individual tribes by Congressional fiat."[15] Allotment and termination are extreme examples of federal control over tribal land, but ever since Indians were first confined to reservations, the United States has attempted to meet development goals by changing the rules surrounding reservation land use.[16] Sadly, such experimentation has not had a good track record.[17] There have been numerous attempts to deal with the crippling and costly land use bureaucracy. Yet, reservation land remains mired in red tape, and banks remain reticent about lending on reservations. Underfunding is partly to blame. The funds for loan guarantees or direct business development loans, for example, have been available only at a fraction of the tribal demand. But another explanation for the failure of these programs is that those models do not reflect the reality of reservation economies.

Neoclassical models start with the individual utility function and from that generate increasingly complex descriptions of the world. The problem is that the assumptions underlying these models often do not hold true for the majority of reservations with regard to both the nature of tribal economies and the motivations of tribal members. "Indians are suspicious of development projects which ignore the existing system of social relationships and ideas about land use."[18] The cultural argument is dangerous because it rejects neoclassical economics on the tenuous idea that the Indians are different from everyone else. After all, the defining characteristic of Indians might be the diversity of tribes, values, and experiences, making assumptions of this nature wholly inappropriate. However, the ineffectiveness of neoclassical economics might not be limited to tribal economics. Rather, it might be that while the neoclassical approach is good at describing and even predicting outcomes given a shared set of assumptions, the approach's utility is limited in situations with markedly different institutions and norms. Thus, it remains critical to examine what experts in tribal development have to say.

7.2 TRIBAL ECONOMIC DEVELOPMENT THEORY

Despite the number and diversity of tribes, tribal economic development experts largely agree on the basic building blocks required for tribal economic growth. Tribes that are deliberate in setting their own path, establishing an independent judiciary, aligning their work and culture, and separating politics from business, have better results than tribes that fail to do these things. Although federal and state constraints on the authority of tribes matter, how tribes exercise their sovereignty is far more important. That governance plays a significant role in the promotion of growth or the perpetuation of poverty is the central conclusion of the scholarly literature on tribal economies. This section presents the Harvard Project's nation-building approach, which is principally the result of decades of work by Stephen Cornell and Joseph Kalt, and then connects it to the work of two other leading scholars, Angela Riley and Robert Miller, who have written about good governance and tribal economic growth. These academics occupy an uncomfortable, seemingly inconsistent space; their work highlights things that work across tribes even as they decry a one-size-fits-all, top-down approach to economic and governmental tribal systems. This awkward positioning aside, what is clear after surveying their work is that they largely agree about what works. This section presents the rough consensus on what works and begins the task of pulling from that consensus those insights that can benefit the Navajo Nation.

As the most significant and sustained exploration of reservation economies, the Harvard Project on American Indian Economic Development has been uniquely influential, shaping the understanding of the connection between economic growth and tribal governance for the past several decades. In addition to the groundbreaking research of Cornell and Kalt, the Harvard Project provides an institutional and intellectual home for generations of Indian-focused scholars, both Native and non-Indian alike.[19] It is hard to overstate the Harvard Project's importance to those looking for ideas on how to improve tribal economies; their work is usually the first consulted and the Harvard Project's framework – presented in countless articles and reports – has become the standard against which other proposals regarding tribal institutional change are measured.

At its core, the Harvard Project's nation-building approach involves rejecting the sort of federally-led and grant-focused development path that tribes historically followed in favor of a tribally driven set of governance changes. In the first chapter of *Rebuilding Native Nations: Strategies for Governance and Development*, Cornell and Kalt contrast the standard approach with their nation-building approach.[20] Their presentation of what works and what does not when it comes to tribal governance and economic development begins by laying out the five characteristics of the standard approach: "(1) decision making is short term and nonstrategic; (2) persons or organizations other than the Native nation set the development agenda; (3) development is treated as primarily an economic problem; (4) Indigenous culture is viewed as an obstacle to development; and (5) elected leadership serves primarily as a distributor of resources."[21] Under the standard approach, tribal leaders look for the next big project or grant rather than thinking strategically about the direction the tribe should take. Thinking about the next big thing leads them to pursue new opportunities without nurturing existing businesses or programs; it also means the tribal operations are reactionary, driven by federal grant-making, not tribal needs. The emphasis is off as well: "In its focus on economic factors, the standard approach ignores institutional and political issues and thereby misses the key dynamic in economic development."[22] And in an explanation that hits home for Diné, under "the standard approach, tribal leadership is concerned much of the time with distributing resources: jobs, money, housing, services, favors, and so forth ... Tribal politicians often get more electoral support from the quick distribution of 'goodies' than they do from more prudent investment in long-term community success and security."[23] Cornell and Kalt conclude that while things can work out with this nonstrategic approach, "overall, the standard approach to economic development has served Indian Country badly. It is fatally flawed, it seldom works, and it should be abandoned."[24]

The Harvard Project's main goal is not to tear down the standard approach but rather to present better solutions. The Harvard Project annually gives Honoring Nations' awards to tribal offices, departments, and enterprises that are improving the lives of tribal members. Drawing from the Honoring Nations' examples as well as fieldwork with tribal nations, Cornell and Kalt describe their nation-building approach in terms of five governance characteristics: "(1) Native nations comprehensively assert decision-making power (practical sovereignty, or self-rule); (2) nations back up decision-making power with effective governing institutions; (3) their governing institutions match their own political cultures; (4) decision making is strategic; and (5) leaders serve as nation-builders and mobilizers."[25] In some respects, the move to self-determination as the official policy of the federal government provides the foundation for the nation-building characteristics identified by Cornell and Kalt. The self-determination policy allows tribes to take a more active role running formerly federal programs and to assume responsibility for the success or failure of those programs. The Harvard Project's emphasis on practical sovereignty mirrors the work of other scholars. Charles Wilkinson shows in *Blood Struggle: The Rise of Modern Indian Nations* the myriad ways tribes pushed against the boundaries of federal control in the twentieth century in order to exercise de facto sovereignty, not on a delegated basis but as a continuation of independent national identity.[26] Provocatively, Cornell and Kalt claim that there is not a single example of "sustained economic development in which an entity other than the Native nation is making the major decisions about development strategy, resource use, or internal organization ... [such that] practical sovereignty appears to be a *necessary* condition for a Native nation's economic development."[27]

Cornell and Kalt are quick to point out that practical sovereignty alone is not enough, Indian nations must also have effective institutions. The Harvard Project's account of what effective governance looks like chafes against the idea that the match between governing institutions and the political culture of the tribe is crucial. There is a potential conflict, in other words, between the second and third nation-building characteristics. Cornell and Kalt largely gloss over policy and instead present what works in terms of effective governance irrespective of any historical or cultural differences across tribes. Successful development, according to the Harvard Project, has four key features:

- Governing institutions must *be stable*. That is, the rules don't change frequently or easily, and when they do change, they change according to prescribed and reliable procedures.
- Governing institutions must *protect day-to-day business and program management from political interference*, keeping strategic decisions in the hands of

elected leadership and putting management decisions in the hands of managers.

- Governing institutions much *take the politics out of court decisions* and other methods of dispute resolution, sending a clear message to citizens and outsiders that their claims and their investments will be dealt with fairly.
- Governing institutions must *provide administration that can get things done* reliably and effectively.[28]

Cornell and Kalt situate these four key elements under the broader heading of effective governing institutions, which is only one of the five characteristics of the nation-building approach. For those with experience dealing with the Navajo Nation, it is easy to think of instances in which the tribal government has met and has failed to embody these traits. Nevertheless, it is noteworthy that these four features, while tailored to the tribal situation and the result of decades of research, are largely in line with the policy prescriptions a neoclassical economist might offer. Stability, separation of business from politics, judicial fairness and independence, and efficient bureaucracy are standard aspirations of those interested in improving the business environment of an area, regardless of whether that area is on-reservation or off-reservation.

Tribal differences come into play where cultural mismatch creates tensions. "Building legitimate institutions," Cornell and Kalt argue, "means tapping into Indigenous political cultures."[29] They explain,

> [t]he crucial issue is the degree of match or mismatch between formal governing institutions and *today's* Indigenous ideas – whether these are survivals from older traditions or products of the nation's contemporary experience – about the appropriate form and organization of political power. Where cultural match is high, economic development tends to be more successful. Where cultural match is low, the legitimacy of tribal government also tends to be low, governing institutions consequently are less effective, and economic development falters.[30]

It is when discussing cultural match that Cornell, Kalt, and the Harvard Project generally move away from a standard prescriptive plan and emphasize the importance of differences across tribes. IRA constitutions worked for some tribes and not for others, which Cornell and Kalt attribute to the degree of fit between the IRA's top-down, integrated model and each tribe's governance tradition. If there is a mismatch between the governance structure of the central tribal government and the cultural views of tribal members regarding leadership and decision-making, then the tribe is often unable to advance politically or economically.

Adopting a long-term, nation-building perspective on tribal priorities, governance, and tribal economic development is a crucial job of tribal leaders, but how to do that? Eric Lamont, who worked on tribal constitutional reform for the Harvard Project, argues that tribes seeking to reform their government should consider establishing a government reform committee, often separated by design from ordinary politics.[31] Lamont specifically notes that expanded civil education, attention by tribal colleges, and consideration of the experiences of other tribes, might help tribal governmental reform efforts.[32] Government reform is not necessarily easy. "Perhaps the thorniest issue faced by American Indian nations engaging in governmental and constitutional reform," Lamont explains, "is developing consensus and shared strategies for incorporating tribal traditions into new governing institutions."[33] In part because it can be difficult, a strategic and far-sighted approach to development and governance is important. By thinking strategically about tribal priorities rather than simply reacting to the latest federal grant or crisis, tribal leaders foster a governance environment that supports tribal economic development and, ultimately, improves the lives of tribal members.

The Harvard Project is without question the most important academic center focusing on tribal economic development, and its nation-building approach sits at the head of the table for those interested in tribal economic growth. Given its prominence, there are of course detractors, those concerned about how much the Harvard Project seems to "promote conditions leading to even more neoliberal-style policy in Indian Country."[34] Taking a broader picture, in light of the continued poverty and underdevelopment of many reservations, it is surprising how few scholars focus on tribal economic growth. There are, of course, scholars who have explored aspects of tribal economic development. Gavin Clarkson, for example, called attention to inequities in the way that the IRS treats tribal borrowing as compared to the more favorable treatment given municipal bonds.[35] From a broader perspective, quite a few scholars dedicate themselves to matters involving tribal natural resources and the environment. But the remainder of this section concentrates on the work of Angela Riley and Robert Miller, who have written extensively on the intersection of governance and growth.

In *Good (Native) Governance*, Riley argues that tribes should practice their own form of good governance and lays out what that means.[36] *Good (Native) Governance* was published in 2007, at the height of academic interest in good governance models, which emphasize participation, flexibility, and the role of nonstate actors.[37] Riley's article shows ways that good governance theorists could learn from the practices and governance efforts of Indian nations and presents an Indian nation version of good governance. Provocatively putting tribal difference front-and-center, Riley asks, "If tribes ought not to be remade in the image of the dominant society, how, as a normative matter, should tribal governments act? Or, in other words, to what extent can Native governance stray from that of a liberal democracy and nevertheless constitute good governance?"[38] Just as Cornell and Kalt found themselves on a tightrope between respecting tribal difference and describing universal best practices, so too Riley emphasizes the importance of governance "based on each tribe's tradition and contemporary tribal culture,"[39] while simultaneously presenting the "guiding principles" of good (Native) governance.[40]

Without good governance, people lose faith in their government,[41] avenues to create change narrow, and economic development suffers. According to Riley, the guiding principles of good Native governance are: (1) "that citizens are ensured the freedoms of exit (or opt-out rights) and dissent (or voice)," (2) that "tribal governments should be based on and guided by their own foundational governing principles and must also provide both members and outsiders with a fair forum for the resolution of disputes," and (3) "that every facet of tribal governance constitute a cultural match to the structure, religion, and value system of the particular tribe."[42] Just as the Harvard Project's Honoring Nations Awards shine a light on departments or tribal institutions that are doing good work, so too Riley argues that most tribes, despite the views of critics to the contrary, are well governed.[43] The primacy Riley gives "exit" and "voice" is relatively unique among Indian law scholars, but it is an idea with a lot of scholarly support elsewhere.[44] Given the often-heated nature of tribal politics, Riley's choice to emphasize the importance of Indian nations providing opportunities, even beyond democratic elections, for tribal members to express their views, including dissenting views, is important.

Riley's second guiding principle has two parts, one tied to tribe-specific "foundational principles" and the other a more general admonition that tribes should be just when resolving disputes. Tribal governance should be based on tribally identified foundational principles that "set the parameters for all aspects of the government and empower leaders and the polity alike to contemplate, examine, and, if need be, press the bounds of such foundational principles for change."[45] These foundational principles might be set out in a written constitution, but that is not a requirement.[46] What matters is that the tribe, not outsiders, identifies and agrees on the foundational principles and that these foundational principles provide the framework within which the tribal government and tribal leaders operate. Good Native governance also requires that tribes provide forums for tribal members and nonmembers that can fairly resolve disputes.[47] Indian nations do not have to copy off-reservation court systems, but good Native governance requires that they provide "judicial (or quasi-judicial) systems that are fair and nonpolitical."[48]

The third guiding principle of Riley's theory of good Native governance, echoing the work of the Harvard Project, is that cultural match matters. Riley explains, "'cultural matching' simply means there is a match between the 'governing institutions' of the particular tribe and its 'indigenous political culture.' In other words, a tribal community's ideas regarding the proper use and scope of authority must be reflected in the tribe's governing institutions."[49] Tribal institutions should "reflect each nation's particular history, values, and vision"[50] both because there is an independent value in such matching and because cultural match leads to better governance and economic development outcomes. Tribes should be permitted to set their own path, Riley argues, and "there ought not to be greater federal (or international) encroachment on the internal governance of tribal nations."[51] Interestingly though, Riley does see a greater role for human rights norms as a part of good Native governance. Tribal sovereignty can be used by tribes "to preserve their differentness – even when tribal laws are seemingly inapposite to American civil rights norms,"[52] but sovereignty "should not be used as a shield to justify the denial of basic rights and liberties."[53] Riley is entering challenging territory with this argument – albeit an area other scholars, most notably Wenona Singel, have explored – because elevating human rights law threatens to make it simply the latest iteration of the western legal system limiting tribal self-determination.[54] Riley defends elevating human rights laws by observing that indigenous peoples are calling on "international human rights systems to advance their own claims," and therefore, Indian nations "must contemplate the concomitant obligations they have, as sovereigns, to the Native polity."[55]

Whereas *Good (Native) Governance* focuses primarily on improving tribal governance, relegating the economic benefits derived from good governance to the background, the opposite is true in Robert Miller's *Reservation Capitalism: Economic Development in Indian Country.*[56] Miller suggests that economic development is necessary for good governance, rather than the other way around, and should be a priority for scholars. Miller writes, "Tribal governments and reservation communities desperately need to create functioning economies in Indian Country to increase economic activities and improve living conditions. The present-day development and the long-term existence and success of reservations and Indian communities and cultures are dependent on these factors."[57] Miller argues that economic development is the most important issue tribes and tribal members face; after all, "society simply cannot function with 20 to 80 percent unemployment. It is a recipe for disaster for community building and for preserving a nation and a culture."[58] *Reservation Capitalism* begins by tackling the idea that Indians historically did not understand or own property. This pernicious idea supported the country's westward expansion and the related denial of Indian land rights, but Miller shows that it is historically inaccurate.[59] Indians traditionally understood and respected property rights, managed their economic affairs, and developed extensive and important patterns of trade.[60] After marching through the different ways in which the United States (mis)treated Indians, Miller observes, "it is clear that the Euro-American impacts on Indian and tribal economies and their lands and assets have been a disaster for Indians … the majority of tribal assets are now in the hands of non-Indians, and Indian peoples are the poorest Americans."[61]

Reservation Capitalism presents a list of governance best practices that Miller argues will lead to greater commercial development and small-scale entrepreneurship on reservations. For many tribes, including the Navajo, jobs and economic development are closely tied to the central tribal government or to large industrial or natural resource projects. Missing from the reservation economy, Miller observes, are the sort of small-to-medium-scale formal businesses – restaurants, repair shops, box stores, clothing stores, et cetera – that play large roles in most off-reservation communities. Tribal members have the money to support such enterprises and they do, just in off-reservation border towns. The result is that money earned on reservation quickly flows off-reservation and tribes lose out on the multiplier effect that happens when earning circulates within the community. As Miller highlights, money will circulate longer and the multiplier effect of money earned on reservation will be higher if there are businesses and services available to meet tribal members' needs and desires.[62] Certainly, *Reservation Capitalism*'s presentation of the dynamics of reservation earnings fits the Navajo Nation where weekend trips to off-reservation border towns – Farmington, Gallup, and Flagstaff – are a routine part of reservation life.

Many, but not all, of the governance best practices that Miller argues will foster a better business environment are familiar. Crediting the Harvard Project at points, Miller argues that tribes should keep politics out of business as much as possible. Even when the tribe is the owner, tribal politics should be removed from daily business operations.[63] Miller agrees that separation of powers and an independent judiciary are important: "If tribal courts and governments are perceived as favoring the government or politically connected litigants, no investor is going to risk their time and money in such a jurisdiction."[64] Miller however goes further, arguing that tribes should actively nurture business expertise among tribal members[65] and should consider adopting business-friendly laws such as the Uniform Commercial Code (UCC).[66] *Reservation Capitalism*'s most novel idea, and one that makes a lot of sense, is that tribes should "buy Indian," meaning that tribes should prefer tribal suppliers when buying goods or services.[67] Miller identifies a wide-range of levers – everything from getting bank branches to open on reservation to minority business contracting – that tribes can pull to improve their economies. But the larger point of *Reservation Capitalism* is that strong, functioning, and diverse tribal economies matter. It is less "about making money" and instead "about building and sustaining tribal communities."[68] Reducing tribal poverty improves the lives of tribal members and reduces the pressure they feel to leave their community.

7.3 CONCLUSION

Academics whose work focuses on tribal economic development do not claim a single right answer in terms of institutional change. Certain governance traits seem to work, but solutions must be tribally driven and tribally appropriate. Cornell, Kalt, Riley, and Miller would likely differ on some of the details and they emphasize different things, but there is broad agreement on what works. The policy recommendations of these experts in tribal governance and economic development are a blend of the structural lessons of neoclassical economics and the situational perspective of new institutional economics (NIE). Although neoclassical economics has a virtual stranglehold on how economics is taught in the United States, NIE enjoys considerable support elsewhere. The central insight of NIE is that "institutions matter,"[69] and therefore, policies must take into account community particulars. NIE defines institutions as "the rules of the game of a society, or, more formally . . . the humanly devised constraints that structure human interaction. They are composed of formal rules (statute law, common law, regulations), informal constraints (conventions, norms of behaviour, and self-imposed codes of conduct), and the enforcement characteristics of both."[70] This definition is quite broad but captures the way in which NIE differs from neoclassical economics, which largely assumes away governance issues. By insisting on the importance of cultural match and that tribes set their own development agenda or strategy, tribal economic development experts seem to be blending some of the lessons of neoclassical economics, such as the importance of predictability and of neutral arbiters in order to protect market participants, with those of the NIE literature.[71]

Other scholars and activists have done work on tribal economic development and this chapter is not suggesting that only the covered authors or that only neoclassical economics and new institutional economics approaches matter. In the 1970s and 1980s, Marxist theory resonated with many left-leaning academics, who, though following a different intellectual tradition, similarly concluded that Indians should be in charge of setting the direction of tribal governance and of the reservation economy. Similarly, it is hard to observe the sustained success of China's mix of state-led growth and selective openness to capitalism over the last thirty years without wondering what tribes might learn from their model. What matters is less rigid adherence to a particular framework or model and more an appreciation of the importance of creating space for businesses to thrive on reservations. There does seem to be a consensus that some governance practices are better than others. The attacks on the judiciary discussed in the last chapter, for example, undermine both the rule of law and the business climate on the reservation. Adopting a long-term, strategic orientation instead of short-term, election cycle-driven economic plans would also benefit Diné. Regardless of the particular school-of-thought, what matters is that economic development is prioritized and progress is made. As Miller's provocative conclusion of *Reservation Capitalism* notes:

> Letting tribal and reservation communities strangle on poverty is not an option . . . Today, Indian Country remains poor. Indian people, communities, and tribal governments need economic development and operating economies. They need capitalism, socialism, free market entrepreneurship; whatever you want to call it, Indian Country needs it. And only Indian people and their governments and communities can make this happen.[72]

PART III

Future

8

Locally Grounded Development

Moving from theory to practice can be challenging, especially when it comes to reservation economic development. Institutions matter, cultural match matters, and collective determination to look for solutions matters as well. But what does all of that look like in practice? This chapter focuses on how governance changes and allowance for greater local autonomy can create space for economic development. The Navajo Nation has 110 chapters, each with a separate governance role and each with unique challenges.[1] Just as American politicians routinely advocate for local control under the banner of federalism, so too many Diné feel that the tribe would be better with some form of Navajo federalism. Rebalancing the division of authority between the centralized bureaucracy in Window Rock and local chapter houses could help cut through the red tape that currently undermines efforts to build community at the local level. This is not a novel idea. The Navajo Nation passed the Local Governance Act (LGA) in 1998 with the hope that local chapters could assume many of the responsibilities and powers long controlled by Window Rock. This chapter explores the history of the LGA and the roadblocks that limited its devolution of authority. But the LGA is not the only mechanism by which a locality can assume a greater role in determining how land is used and development occurs. The chapter also looks at the Kayenta Township model and the possibilities of empowering select municipalities.

Although expressed in different ways, often as a combination of anger and resignation, there is a significant level of dissatisfaction with the Navajo Nation's central government. The corruption scandals, covered in Chapter 6, are contributing factors, but such dissatisfaction has deeper roots, too. Diné did not traditionally have a permanent centralized government; instead, authority and governance were hyper local, built around family and clan units.[2] The formation of the Navajo Business Council in 1922 changed that by centralizing authority in Window Rock. This is not to say that the Navajo Nation government is somehow not "Diné," it is. Over the last hundred years, Diné have worked with, molded, and established their own unique form of governance that is now the modern Navajo Nation. Indeed,

FIGURE 8.1 Navajos gather outside the Navajo Tribal Council Building. Photograph by Milton Snow, 1939. Records of the BIA, RG75, National Archives at College Park, Md., RG75-Nav-104.

when it comes to setting the direction for the tribe, the central government in Window Rock is arguably the most significant Diné institution. But the mismatch between the current centralized structure and the way Diné traditionally governed themselves helps explain some of the dissatisfaction and suggests there are limits to a governance strategy that overly relies on a central bureaucracy. Pushing some authority back to the local level might help restore a better match between the cultural values of tribal members and their institutions of government.

Empowering local decision-making would also be a way for the tribe to deal with the scale and diversity of the Navajo Nation. For many of the same reasons that federalism enjoys popular support in the United States – including a preference for small-scale government, faith in local knowledge and experimentation, and distrust of central authority – localism resonates on many parts of the reservation. Chapters located a long way from Window Rock frequently complain that the central government does not understand their challenges nor respond to their needs in a timely fashion. The result is that chapter-supported proposals that would be community enhancing never take off, often because of bureaucratic delays in allocating land or in granting other permissions. As market forces push the Navajo Nation away from its reliance on extractive industries, local empowerment takes on even greater urgency. It was one thing for tribal members to acquiesce to the central bureaucracy when Window Rock provided employment opportunities and services. But the demise of coal, drawn out as it is, is going to place tremendous financial pressure on the Navajo Nation as royalties dry up. The Navajo Nation Trust Fund, set up in anticipation of the decline in extractive energy revenues, will help offset these losses, but losses will still be felt. Most likely, services that are not self-supporting will face cuts, along with the size of the central government. In that environment, calls to wrest authority from Window Rock in the name of economic development, and perhaps tradition as well, will likely grow more pronounced.

There are paths forward for the Navajo Nation, ways that the tribe can empower local communities and in the process create space for economic growth. Managing the relationship between the central government and local communities – "clos-[ing] the gap that has emerged between local governance and national governance" – will require that the Navajo Nation turn over additional authority to local actors without completely stepping away from its oversight role.[3] Devolution is likely to be a complex, iterative process with a steep learning curve. If done right, it will facilitate economic development without sacrificing Diné values. But there are multiple wrong turns, missteps that would harm the tribe, threaten the tribal land base, and undermine Diné lifeways. Though the focus of this chapter is on devolution to local institutions, chapter houses and local communities, another option is to privatize the reservation, relying on market forces to check the central administration. Chapter 7 raised privatization as a theoretical possibility and this chapter begins by considering whether the Navajo Nation should fully privatize the reservation. Land privatization, the chapter argues, is a wrong turn, the wrong way to break Window Rock's current hold over reservation development.[4] The notion that land privatization is the solution to Indian poverty and underdevelopment is not a new idea nor an idea worth spending too much time refuting. For that reason, after discussing privatization, the bulk of the chapter focuses on empowering local communities by changing the relationship between local communities and the central government.

8.1 THE BAD PATH: LAND PRIVATIZATION

Indians have long been told that their way of holding land was wrong, that they should own land in the same way that whites do. At various points, the federal government imposed such changes, forcibly divvying up land from collective tribal control to distribute to individual Indians. Today, however, there are very few champions of privatizing Indian reservations. The most notable academic is Terry Anderson, a researcher at Hoover Institution, who has spent several decades touting the advantages of converting reservation trust land into fee land.[5] New York Post columnist Naomi Schaefer Riley also called for land privatization in her recent book, *The New Trail of Tears*.[6] As Professor Matthew Fletcher noted in his review of *The New Trail of Tears*, "Riley's analysis relies upon non-Indian free-market advocates and anti-government think tanks. She uses this one-sided approach to develop a theory that the best thing for Indian people is to dismember their governments and liquidate their reservation and trust lands. Only then, she writes, will Indian people benefit from the 'magical force' of private property."[7] Fletcher's devastating review concludes, "anyone versed in actual tribal–federal relations, in what economically successful tribes are actually doing, or in the real, but nuanced challenges of governance in Indian country will see this book for what it is: a modern-day screed that promotes the very ideas that led to some of the most disastrous policies toward Indians in American history."[8] Looking at academic, journalistic, and political calls to privatize Indian reservations, Professors Angela Riley and Kristen Carpenter, similarly note, "there is healthy skepticism about whether the advocated free-market approach to tribal property is based on a genuine concern for Indians' wealth or well-being."[9] Their work highlights "the potentially dire consequences privatization poses to tribal sovereignty."[10]

Ultimately, land privatization is an ill-fit for the Navajo Nation.[11] First, while land privatization can take many forms and need not recreate the off-reservation land market, it nonetheless would be a dramatic break from the ways that Diné traditionally and culturally think of land rights. Second, land privatization would threaten the tribe's continued vitality and the basic survival of very low income Diné families. Families that for generations have scraped out a livelihood based on subsistence farming and animal husbandry might find it difficult to resist selling their land to access much-needed cash income. It also might be difficult for such families to pay any privatization-associated land taxes, which could jeopardize ongoing ownership even if they did not sell their land. Of course, if the price is right and the family is able to transition to the wage economy or start a new business, things could work out – yet a substantial risk remains that privatization writ large would make many families who sold (or were pushed off) their land even more vulnerable.

The idea that reservations should be broken up and parceled out in fee simple chunks is not new; the federal government imposed a version of privatization during the allotment era, with disastrous consequences for tribes subjected to the policy.[12] By allowing non-Indians to purchase land from Indian allottees and by opening up "surplus" land to non-Indian settlement, allotment significantly reduced tribal land holdings and fundamentally reshaped reservation life.[13] For some tribes, whole areas became predominantly non-Indian, while other tribes were left with checkerboard areas with land held in a wide variety of forms.[14] The Navajo Nation was largely spared allotment's devastating effects because non-Indians were less covetous of Diné land at the time, and there was recognition that the tribal land base was inadequate given the size of the tribe and the nature of the land.[15]

At first blush, the creation of limited land markets through the selective privatization of land might appear to be a middle ground between the untenable status quo and the risks of full-bore privatization. But details matter. People concerned about possible loss of the tribal land base are likely to agree that any sales take place only between Navajo Nation citizens. This intra-tribal limitation sounds simple, but given the Navajo Nation's requirement of one-quarter blood quantum for citizenship, it quickly can become complex and require line drawing that either challenges the intra-tribal limitation or challenges rights held through descent.[16] Consider a child raised on the reservation whose biological parents are a non-Indian and a Navajo Nation citizen with one-quarter blood quantum. Even if the tribal member "owned" the family land under the partial privatization scheme in some sort of "tribal fee" arrangement, should the child be allowed to come into ownership of the land when his or her parents die?

The complexity only increases when details of a partial land privatization structure are considered. Depending on how the partial alienation right is defined, the amount of land families hold rights to, and the proximity of parcels to more developed areas, some families would experience a windfall from privatization not available to other families. A family with extensive grazing or customary use lands allowed to convert their holdings into tribal fee land could benefit disproportionately. Families holding land within easy commuting distance of border towns or reservation population centers stand to gain the most financially from privatization. Remote agricultural land, even land that has not been destroyed by overgrazing, is likely to be worth only a fraction of the value of land close to formal sector jobs. On the other hand, if privatization is accomplished by a central tribal authority simply "taking" land and then offering it for sale, the costs of privatization are likely to fall disproportionately on families that control larger amounts of land.

Divergence in the benefits and costs across Diné families creates harm that must be taken into account, whatever the theoretical advantages of land privatization. Inattention to the winners and losers of partial privatization not only would reshape the tribe and community in ways that are not "fair" (to use an English word) and not keeping with "k'e" or "hozho" (to use Navajo concepts of kinship and balance) but would also increase the political difficulty of land reform.[17] As Robert Miller explained in a recent article, land privatization "is not guaranteed to be a better solution than traditional Indian institutions, or even the best solution to economic development issues in Indian country. Moreover, the argument ignores historical and cultural principles."[18] For the Navajo Nation, land privatization writ large would undermine the central government, lead to tribal land loss through direct sales to outsiders or through tax foreclosures, and increase inequality within Diné society. There likely will always be non-Indians, and some Diné as well, who believe that land privatization is the solution to Indian poverty. Seeing the development found off-reservation compared to the lack of development on trust land, these "friends of the Indian" will conclude that tribes should pursue land privatization. But such a path is the wrong one for the Navajo Nation and for Diné. Just because it can be challenging to chart a course that both preserves the tribal land base and allows for greater economic development does not mean that the Navajo Nation should reach for trite, ahistorical solutions.

8.2 THE GOOD PATH: RECLAIMING LOCAL AUTHORITY

Rather than abandoning the reservation as a concept and practice, as full-scale land privatization would, Diné are experimenting with structural reform as a way to make progress on their governance challenges. The self-determination era is nearing the mid-century mark, but red tape in Washington and in Window Rock continues to frustrate economic growth. Tribal members' ability to change Washington's oversight role may be limited, but they can push for structural reform within the Navajo Nation. Dissatisfaction with the central government has led to various efforts to reassert and strengthen the role of local institutions, creating space for economic development and responding to community needs.[19] These efforts are ongoing and iterative, with occasional stalls or roadblocks. It is too early to know how successful Diné will be in reforming the Navajo Nation government. In part, efforts to strengthen local authority over economic development and land use reflect the mismatch between the Navajo Nation's current central government and the tribe's tradition of hyper-local decision-making. These efforts reflect Diné awareness that their current form of government is not working and a willingness to experiment until they see better results on the ground.

This section focuses on two mechanisms – the Local Governance Act (LGA) and municipal home rule – which localities have used to expand their role in shaping their communities. After the Navajo Nation passed the LGA in 1998, chapters responded by seeking the additional powers that come from LGA certification. Similarly, in Kayenta, a group of civic-minded professionals, frustrated by the central government's bureaucracy, pushed for separate township status as a way to gain greater independence and to pursue a more pro-development approach. Both LGA certification and the Kayenta Township model are efforts to check Window Rock's heavy control over local governance and land use decisions, but they are not complete breaks from the central government. Although LGA-certification and recognition as a township afford local communities greater freedom to operate independently and set their own development agenda, Window Rock retains important oversight functions.

8.2.1 *The Local Governance Act (LGA)*

The brainchild of Albert Hale, first introduced during his 1994 campaign for Navajo Nation President, the LGA initially seemed like the biggest change in how Diné govern themselves since the formation of the Navajo Business Council in the 1920s. When it was enacted in 1998, the LGA established a mechanism for chapters to become certified to manage their own affairs. LGA-certified chapters were promised the ability to do everything from levy taxes and issue bonds to exercise the power of eminent domain to acquire land and enact zoning regulations.[20] Significantly, certified chapters are empowered to "[i]ssue home and business site leases or permits," a critical power that addresses an ongoing source of frustration on the reservation.[21] Devolution of governance authority to the chapters, it was thought, would empower local communities, strengthen democratic participation, and cut through Window Rock's red tape.[22] Once certified, chapters can "reshape their governing infrastructure," which includes moving away from existing quorum requirements and resolution processes that often bog down chapters and make meetings frustrating.[23] But, so far, the LGA has not lived up to such expectations. The certification process proved both expensive and time-consuming, which prevented many chapters from taking advantage of the expanded authority provided for under the Act. Chapters that managed to get certified have found that they still need Window Rock, which retains an oversight role even over certified chapters, to sign-off on many of their activities.[24] Two decades after it was enacted, power still radiates from the central tribal government rather than being significantly devolved to local communities. But it is too early to know whether these challenges make LGA akin to a dead-end street or are mere hiccups on the path toward tribal governance reform.[25] Slowly, additional chapters continue to get certified and their experience operating as LGA-certified chapters continues to mature. Though the LGA did not set in motion an immediate, radical change to how the tribe governs itself, it did provide a structured way for local communities to reclaim some of their sovereignty from Window Rock.

Chapters that want to assume greater authority through LGA certification have to first jump through a number of hurdles. They have to demonstrate to the satisfaction of the Navajo Auditor General that they have sufficient internal controls in place to handle the additional responsibilities that come with certification. Under the rubric of a "Five Step Management System," chapters have to show the adequacy of their policies and practices related to accounting, personnel management, records management, procurement, and property control.[26] Chapters also have to file comprehensive land use plans as part of the certification process.[27] The LGA therefore demands much from chapters and chapter officials. And the ability of chapters to rise to meet the LGA requirements differs across the reservation. For chapters located in rural parts of the reservation, human capital constraints limit the ability of the chapter to get certified. Even chapters located near one of the Navajo Nation's urban centers still struggle to find people active in local governance who have the right combination of skills and commitment.[28] Outside consultants can fill in gaps, whether those gaps relate to familiarity with accounting processes or preparing a land use plan, but consultants are expensive. The Navajo Nation provided limited start-up funding for the chapters so they could work towards certification; not surprisingly, much of that money flowed to off-reservation firms. Bolstering its support, in 2015, the tribe also hired more than a dozen planners to work with chapter officials.[29] Though the LGA was meant to allow chapters to escape Window Rock's red tape, certification ironically involved imposing *greater* bureaucratic requirements and oversight pressures on chapters.

To be clear, there is nothing wrong with the idea that chapters must first demonstrate their competence before they get the benefit of LGA-based powers. Just as corruption is a problem in Window Rock, the possibility of nepotism, unjustified preferences, and corruption is at least as high at the local level, where family ties can play an even bigger role and corrective forces may not exist. As Michelle Hale notes, "The mishandling of chapter funds has been an unremitting issue."[30] The powers that come from certification, including the power to tax and to establish land use districts within the chapter, almost invite favoritism and corruption. Therefore, it makes sense to require a demonstration that chapters have systems in place to keep track of money and property purchased by the local officials on behalf of the chapter. Even the requirement that chapters submit land use plans as part of the certification process can be justified. A well-thought-out land use plan signals that chapter officials have engaged the public to some extent, have an awareness of the needs of their community, and have ideas about how they hope to use their LGA powers after certification. The problem is not with any of the requirements individually. The problem is that, at the time the LGA was enacted, few chapters were in a position to comply with the requirements. The certification process involved too much paperwork, too much money, and too much time.

Of the Navajo Nation's 110 chapters, only forty-four were certified as of December 2019, more than twenty years after the LGA was enacted.[31] Though the first chapter, Shonto, received certification quickly (1999), a decade later, only ten chapters were certified.[32] Since January 2010, however, thirty-four additional chapters have been certified. Delays at the chapter level and long queues for audits (and follow-on audits) by the Navajo Office of the Auditor General partly explain why sixty-six chapters remain uncertified. Satellite offices of the Navajo Nation Division of Community Development provide local chapter officials with guidance related to general chapter governance as well as LGA certification.[33] In order to incentivize chapters to pursue certification, the Navajo Nation provides a one-time payment of $160,000 to chapters when they receive certification.[34] Even with such technical assistance and the incentive payment, for a variety of reasons – including lack of capacity, lack of interest, and other priorities – not all chapters have chosen to pursue certification.

Although certification delays are important, the most significant reason the LGA has not yet transformed Diné politics and development is perhaps the fact that certified chapters have been slow to take full advantage of LGA-recognized powers. At least on its face, the LGA envisions chapters playing a large role in setting the agenda for their community, determining how land should be used, and jump-starting development within their territory. Yet, LGA certification has not unleashed a flurry of experimentation, entrepreneurship, or governance reforms. One contributing factor is that even after certification, Window Rock retains its oversight authority.[35] Certified chapters remain sub-units of the Navajo Nation government apparatus headquartered in Window Rock rather than truly independent actors.[36] Chapters may not have to wait for a quorum to conduct business, but Window Rock still has to sign off on major decisions.[37] But considering the challenges faced by tribal members across the reservation, the trepidation of certified chapters to assert their LGA-sanctioned authority is surprising. It may be that certified chapters are just moving deliberately; slowly working up to when they flex their muscles. Just as tribal governments ramped up the number of programs they took over from the BIA during the self-determination period, so too chapters may need time to gain momentum. A more pessimistic perspective is that governance reform can only do so much. Unless there are economic forces that can provide a tailwind to chapters, LGA powers alone will not be enough for local officials to bring development and opportunity to their chapters.

The LGA is both a new direction in tribal governance and a return to a more traditional governance model. Formally, chapter houses are no more "traditional" than the central Navajo Nation government structure. There were no chapter houses before Diné were imprisoned in Bosque Redondo: chapters were instead created in 1927 by John G. Hunter, the Superintendent of the Leupp Agency, as a way to more effectively manage rural parts of the reservation.[38] Chapters are, therefore, foreign impositions much as was the creation of the Navajo Business Council.[39] Informally though, chapters are a better cultural match with traditional Diné governance norms, which were based on small community groups and dispute resolution through mediation and consensus.[40] Though much has been made of the infrequent larger gatherings of Diné leaders, called the *Náádchid*, hyper-local, largely independent governance by small community groups was the principle characteristic of Diné governance prior to conquest.[41] Indeed, it arguably was not until livestock reduction of the 1930s that the central tribal government superseded informal local governance as the most important site of political control and authority for most tribal members. If the baseline is the modern Navajo Nation government, with its centralization of control and administrative bureaucracy in Window Rock, then devolution to chapters through the LGA appears to be a new, potentially destabilizing, direction in Diné politics. But perhaps the LGA is simply correcting an imbalance between centralization and local authority, an imbalance that has existed since the imposition of the Navajo Business Council in the 1920s. Seen in this light, LGA devolution offers a way for local communities across the reservation to return to a more traditional relationship with their government.[42]

8.2.2 *The Township Model*

Kayenta Township provides another model for how to shift authority from Window Rock to local communities. One of the larger cities on the reservation, Kayenta is located a half hour drive from both Monument Valley and from the coalmine entrance on Black Mesa. Today, Kayenta has both BIA and public schools, a new Indian Health Service hospital, three hotels, a shopping center with a grocery store, gas stations, a laundromat, a post office, numerous restaurants, and a small airport. Black Mesa Twin Cinema, located in the same shopping center as the Bashas' grocery, is one of only three operating movie theaters on the reservation.[43] In addition to Whoppers, Kayenta's Burger King features a great collection of World War II artifacts connected to the Navajo Code Talkers. Compared to many other reservation communities, Kayenta is thriving. Tourism, education, health services, and, until recently, mining support a solid middle class that resides in distinct housing compounds that stand somewhat apart from the normal mix of hogans and double-wides that dot the rest of the town. That said, it is still a small town by off-reservation standards; the 2010 census recorded a total population of just over five thousand people.

Through a series of legislative actions by the Navajo Nation Council, beginning in 1985, Kayenta Township was granted unique home rule municipal authority with particular confirmed powers.[44] To establish the town, Kayenta was authorized to withdraw 3,606.43 acres of Navajo trust land. In 1996, the council signed off on a Kayenta-specific sales tax and a 1999 memorandum by the Navajo Nation Attorney General concluded that Kayenta had been delegated the power to issue leases within

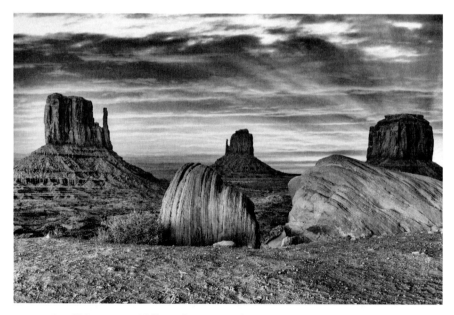

FIGURE 8.2 "Monument Valley after sunset, long exposure of West and East Mitten Buttes." (Photo by: Gagliardi Giovanni /REDA&CO/Universal Images Group via Getty Images)

the township boundaries.[45] (Kayenta Township did not replace chapter governance, it just formed a unique institution within Kayenta Chapter.) Although one opinion letter by the Attorney General in 2006 muddied the waters, questioning the township's ability to issue business site leases, that authority was confirmed by Economic Development Committee action later in 2006 and by a subsequent 2010 Attorney General memorandum. Though Kayenta initially received home rule authority on a provisional basis, collectively, these actions confirm the Navajo Nation's commitment to Kayenta Township's relative independence.

The problem with thinking of the township model as a path toward greater local autonomy for Diné communities across the reservation is that Kayenta is just one town. No other community has followed Kayenta's lead. A partial explanation for Kayenta's status as the sole township perhaps can be found in Kayenta's unique advantages in terms of economic drivers and location.[46] Kayenta is far enough away from border towns that it can support some local services that would be less viable in communities located closer to off-reservation shopping options. It is a long way from Kayenta to Cortez, Durango, Farmington, or Flagstaff; according to the Wetherills, "[t]heir desert post office, they boasted, was farthest distant from a railroad of any in the United States" at the time they established their trading post in Kayenta in 1910.[47] But Chinle is also quite remote. And while Kayenta is close to Monument Valley, which is a bigger tourist draw than Canyon de Chelly, Chinle's local attraction, Chinle can count on some tourist dollars. Tuba City and Shiprock likewise could benefit from home rule authority and would seem to have the human capital necessary to assume such municipal powers. Yet, Kayenta remains a one-off experiment.

Dedicated administrators and community buy-in are both needed for Kayenta Township to work. Over the years, as the *Navajo Times* reports, "There have been multiple moves to revoke the township status, mostly by local businesses tired of paying taxes no one else on the Nation has to pay."[48] Like the reservation as a whole, Kayenta continues to have significant challenges, especially when it comes to unemployment and poverty, and those problems should not be glossed over. The public high school has to offer a day care center to cope with student pregnancies and, more generally, the schools in Kayenta struggle to attract and retain quality teachers. According to the American Community Survey, Kayenta Township's median household income for the period from 2012 to 2016 was $32,000, a $12,000 decline from what it had been in 1990.[49] This household income decline can be traced largely to mining-related employment shocks. With a 41 percent poverty rate, Kayenta is an area of "concentrated poverty," a classification researchers use to describe extreme-poverty areas where more than 40 percent of the population falls below the poverty line.[50] But these structural problems do not diminish what Kayenta Township has managed to accomplish as a governing body. From big things, like facilitating upscale housing and creating a town dump,[51] to small things, like street lights and township events, Kayenta Township has been active in improving life in the town and creating the conditions necessary for greater economic development.

8.3 RECLAIMING AUTHORITY

The pressure to reform the Navajo Nation's system of governance is building. Though a centralized government serves non-Indian interests in having a single entity to negotiate with, Window Rock struggles to respond to the needs of local communities across the reservation. For decades, the central government could use extractive industry royalties to purchase the buy-in of tribal members. Even though power was traditionally diffuse in Diné society, appreciation for the services and employment provided by the central government helped build support for the Navajo Nation political institutions that emerged out of the tumultuous, formative livestock reduction period of the 1920s and 1930s. The Navajo Nation evolved over time, becoming increasingly independent from the federal government. Especially under the charismatic leadership of Peter MacDonald, buoyed by a wave of Navajo nationalism, the central government came to have ever greater importance in the lives of ordinary Diné. But fissures between centralization and local authority have existed ever since the Treaty of Bosque Redondo was signed. The LGA and Kayenta's assumption of home rule authority did not come out of nowhere; they reflect an awareness that the central government was not meeting the needs of local communities. Something had to change and, to its credit, the Navajo Nation created space for greater local autonomy. Fissures between the central and local authority are likely to become even more pronounced in the next decade, as the Navajo Nation passes through a contraction period occasioned by the shuttering of a number of coal mines and coal-fired power plants. The central government likely will have to lay off staff, cut services, and reduce grants to chapters, actions that will come as a shock to the Navajo economy and intensify the political environment. Such economic hardship will likely force tribal members to confront more directly the cultural mismatch between concentration of authority in a central government and Diné traditional governance structures.

For Diné activists frustrated by the corruption, inefficiency, and politics of Window Rock, the question about local empowerment is not about whether to pursue it, but how to go about it. In 2015, the Navajo Nation established the "Title 26 Task Force" and charged it with considering reforms to the LGA. The task force floated regionalization – multiple chapters working collectively – as one way of addressing some of the human capital limits plaguing the existing LGA certification and governance processes. The task force's regionalization proposal dovetails well with the 2010 reduction in the size of the Navajo Nation Council and offers greater economies of scale while still devolving some authority from Window Rock. It also addressed the fact that chapter boundaries can be somewhat arbitrary; as a practical matter, many projects already require the cooperation of neighboring chapters. But in hindsight, regionalism seems like an idea that was dead-on-arrival. As a Diné Policy Institute report noted:

> Regionalization will result in the loss of local democracy. In the elimination of chapter officials for one at-large representative, community members will lose the chapter meeting as a forum to discuss and decide on local affairs. Although imperfect, chapter house meetings are a cultural staple of the Navajo political process and one that cannot be replaced in technocratic governance represented in the regional centers.[52]

Whatever the problems with implementation of the LGA, chapters are not going anywhere for the time being. The authors of the report, Andrew Curley and Michael Parrish, tellingly concluded that the best way for the tribe to promote local empowerment is not through streamlining the LGA but through "expansion of the Kayenta Township model as an immediate policy solution for larger Navajo communities."[53]

But local empowerment need not be set up as a binary choice between the LGA and municipal home rule. What works in one community might not work in another, which means local success arguably will depend more on an openness to experimentation than on finding the perfect governance structure. All across the reservation, some Diné local leaders and grassroots activists – either separately or in coordination with their chapter government – have bypassed government reform in favor of nonprofit institutions (NGOs) as a third way of addressing local challenges.[54] Though they fall outside the tribal governance structure, the ease of establishing NGOs and their flexibility allows them to contribute to local empowerment. Sometimes these NGOs operate completely independent of the Navajo Nation government and of chapter officials, sometimes they take on roles that ordinarily might be considered part of the function of government. Just as the Red Cross comes in to aid communities following a natural disaster and does so in coordination with government partners, so too one of the roles NGOs on the reservation can play is to fill in service gaps. Where the tribal government is failing or unable to meet particular community needs, Diné-focused NGOs can and do step in. But civic society organizations can also take on different roles, not coordinating with government but pressuring the Navajo Nation to do better for its people. Grassroots activists, often united under the banner of cause-specific NGOs, have pushed back when they felt elected leaders were going down a bad path. Activists and cause-related NGOs have been particularly vocal when it comes to tribal economic development, natural resource extraction, water rights, and the environment.

NGOs are by definition *nongovernmental organizations*, which arguably makes them an awkward fit with the possibilities offered by LGA certification and the township model. But civic organizational work can also support local empowerment. Structurally, there are significant advantages to channeling local initiatives and local concerns through NGOs. While there are filing requirements to form a charitable organization, 501(c)(3) or otherwise, and the accounting and personnel management issues can be difficult, those requirements are minimal compared to LGA certification or township formation. NGOs typically file paperwork with the state, not the tribe, and are subject to state and federal oversight. Fortunately, it is relatively easy to form a corporation, including a nonprofit corporation, so would-be social entrepreneurs can get started quickly. NGOs also have the advantage of being nimble in ways few government bodies can be. Under the right leadership and with a good grant writer, local NGOs can marshal as much financial support for community objectives as can the local chapter government. NGOs are not a panacea: many problems require the coordination and financial wherewithal of government. Even with the best of intentions and a committed staff, NGOs can only do so much. What is clear is that local, civic society NGOs, along with the LGA and municipal home rule, emphasize the rising importance of local institutions in building a better future for Diné communities.

There is no turning back the clock. Diné were forced into recognizing the authority of headmen to speak on behalf of the entire tribe as part of the treaty process after their defeat by the US army. The US government imposed a central tribal authority on the Diné in the 1920s in response to extractive industry demands. Though the tribe has pushed through numerous reforms to their government, and the current Navajo Nation government is quite different than the Navajo Business Council, external forces continue to favor centralization of Diné tribal authority. As a matter of convenience, efficiency, and consistency, the Navajo Nation's relationships with external sovereigns are likely to remain almost exclusively within the purview of Window Rock. The tribe cannot return to being a loose constellation of locally governed bodies, united by culture and language but not subject to a shared coercive government.[55] Those days are gone. But the balance, pushed by external demands arguably, swung too far toward centralization and is in need of correction.[56] Just as the United States struggles with the conflicting demands of federalism, continually rebalancing national and state authority, so too the Navajo Nation – unlike smaller tribes – must manage tribal federalism. Rather than being the final word, the LGA and Kayenta Township are merely the tribe's first steps along a path of empowering localities to reclaim their authority.[57]

9

Reclaiming the Land

The Navajo Nation controls over seventeen million acres of land but has a relatively small population.[1] In some parts of the reservation you can drive for miles without seeing a house. Even in the middle of the bigger metropolitan areas, those few cities with more than three thousand people, it is common to see large plots of unused land and the occasional wild mustang or goat. Put differently, there is no shortage of reservation land. And yet, it is often difficult for tribal members to find land on which to build a house or start a business. The Navajo Nation's inability to effectively control reservation land management frustrates tribal economic growth and hurts tribal members. Ironies abound. Traditionally, Diné land rights were based on, and dependent on, actual use. Today, such customary use and grazing rights block development. Families with past use rights to tribal trust land freeze out newcomers, even if they are not making present use of the land. Meanwhile, those working in the wage economy are, in practice, denied land access even though they have the resources and desire to invest in the land. Fortunately, poor land use management is a barrier that the Navajo Nation, acting within its own authority, can fix. But land reform will require attention and should be a top priority of the tribe.

This chapter focuses on what the Navajo Nation can do to reclaim authority over the land and create space for development.[2] Experts and tribal officials routinely blame the United States for the land use problems that plague the Navajo reservation. Such attacks are warranted. In its role as co-trustee of reservation trust land, the United States has failed to establish conditions for broad-based growth. Military and bureaucratic attacks on Indian nations have given way to inattention and indifference to reservation poverty. Excessive red tape and the chronic understaffing of Indian-focused positions makes it hard for tribal members to gain formal rights to use land and reflect the federal government's general disregard of Indian issues. But the Navajo Nation is not off the hook; there is plenty of fault to go around. Though tribal members and the Navajo Nation government have long recognized the need for land use reform, little has changed, despite the tribe's ability to exercise its authority over the land.

Ultimately, the Navajo Nation is going to have to reclaim its authority over the land, for the good of the people as a whole. Currently, a small minority of tribal members with customary use and grazing rights hold veto powers over tribal development.[3] These veto powers have been around for so long that they appear natural, but such power exists only because the Navajo Nation has chosen to acquiesce in these assertions. The prioritization of these vested, but often dormant, claims is not supported by tribal traditions regarding land rights nor by Diné cultural norms involving societal change. Governance reform (discussed in Chapter 8) will only do so much. Devolution alone will not necessarily solve the problem of reservation land paralysis, though local empowerment could be part of a larger strategy to promote development. Tribal leaders in both Window Rock and local chapter governments tend to defer to the land use status quo and are reluctant to push for change that might disrupt local communities. To overcome this, the costs imposed by the current system must be fully understood and leaders must be willing to courageously experiment with alternatives.

Reforming land management is politically dangerous, which is likely why the tribe has made so little progress addressing land issues. Land reform threatens to upset the expectations of tribal members who may have few resources to call their own aside from their customary use or grazing land claims. The stakes are high and tribal members are likely to push back on proposals that undermine their land claims, regardless of whether such rights are formally permitted by the tribe or only informally recognized by the local community. Politicians understand the costs of upsetting settled land rights expectations and have been reluctant to step in. But the costs associated with doing nothing likely exceed any adjustment costs associated with meaningful reform. Creating space for local experimentation and inter-local competition could break the political logjam that currently blocks efforts at comprehensive solutions. Reclaiming the land and making it available for tribal members and for economic development will take courage and a sense of collective responsibility on the part of both elected leaders and community organizers. The easy path is to do nothing: for politicians to continue to neglect land issues and for activists to block any proposal that falls short of perfection. But the easy path will only perpetuate the problems of brain drain, commercial underdevelopment, and poverty.

Localism offers a path forward; local experimentation promises to create space for development, provided that local communities have an incentive to invest in transforming the way they manage their land. By allowing local communities to capture a portion of the gains possible from land reform, the Navajo Nation can foster local governance innovation. If communities begin to see the advantages of reform, some of them will likely compete to free up land for housing and for commercial enterprise. Fostering such locally driven experimentation will require that the Navajo Nation turn over some authority to local chapters and towns. This is not a small ask. But the alternative way forward – Window Rock coming up with a grand land reform bargain that addresses the concerns of both grazing permittees and formal sector employees – seems unlikely. This chapter looks first at the Navajo Nation's recent effort to reform the homesite lease process. It then turns to the perennial problem of overgrazing and discusses the hold that grazing permittees have over reservation land. It ends by highlighting the stakes of land reform and by offering local experimentalism as a way for tribal leaders to address the challenges of land reform.

Whether Diné are able to transition to a more flexible structure of property rights in land depends on the vision that leaders offer and the degree to which there is collective buy-in for transformation. The politics of change, including the question of how to respond to those tribal members who suffer real or perceived losses as a result of change, is fraught and has largely stalled meaningful reform since the 1950s. But continuing to put such a heavy thumb on the scale in favor of grazing and customary use rights breaks from the traditional Diné emphasis on *use* as the basis for, and limitation upon, property rights. By returning to traditional understandings of land rights, Diné can reassert their rights over the public domain, freeing up space for economic growth and improving the lives of tribal members who want to make the reservation home.

9.1 HOME

Traditionally, Diné land rights were tied to clustered familial groups and grounded in use. Extended family units herded and farmed together, and land rights were allocated among families according to their use of land. Land was not held separately from use; land that was not being used was available to others. As a study of Navajo land use observed, "Navajo individual tenure differed from the American capitalist form of private ownership in two ways, both holdovers from communal tenure. Anyone could take land from someone who claimed it but did not use it, and land in general could never be bought or sold."[4] A recent comprehensive report on Navajo land reform by the Diné Policy Institute, a research entity located within Diné College, highlighted the traditional importance of use, noting, "There was rarely a permanence to any one family's control of land. If a family moved on, another family could move in and occupy the land."[5] Similarly, the Navajo Supreme Court emphasized that an "aspect of traditional Navajo land tenure is the principle that one must use it or lose it."[6]

Since the end of World War II, control over small-scale development – farming, grazing, and homesites – largely has been in the hands of the tribal government. During this period, relatively little attention has been paid to routine land governance challenges. When outside interests sought access to the rich coal of Black Mesa and made plans to build and operate power plants just off the reservation, the US government and the Navajo Nation came together to make it happen. Meanwhile, "smaller" issues – like lengthy title searches, overlapping grazing and customary rights, and minimal land availability for local development – festered.

Land holdings and grazing rights previously were the primary source of Diné wealth and inequality. But just as merchant-capitalism undermined feudalism and the security of the landed elite in Europe, so too the wage economy disrupted the connection between land and inequality in Diné society. Today, formal sector employment, not control over land, is the primary driver of income and wealth among reservation residents. Grazing permits and herd size still matter, but a job with a mining company or with the Navajo Nation government pays significantly more than a family can make selling their sheep or wool. Diné urbanization mirrored that of the rest of the United States over the last one hundred years, but for Diné that move often meant leaving their extended families' traditional lands and moving to the towns – Chinle, Kayenta, Shiprock, Tuba City, and Window Rock – that are the reservation equivalent of cities. Financial wealth is concentrated in these towns, especially in Window Rock, but many members of this new Diné elite are land poor; having left their ancestral lands, they have a hard time gaining access to even small lots. In contrast, those Diné who still live in remote parts of the reservation often control vast amounts of land but live well below the poverty line. In many cases, these individuals are the parents and grandparents of those who moved to a reservation town or to a border town for career purposes. This inverse relationship between land and inequality suggests there is an opportunity for land reform and that at least a subset of tribal members would support such an effort.

The home is the center of family life on and off the reservation, so it is not surprising that the Navajo Nation's most significant effort in recent years to push land reform came in the form of an effort to modernize and internalize tribal homesite leasing. On October 4, 2016, the Navajo Nation Council approved "Homesite Lease Regulations 2016" (HLR 2016) which were prepared by the Division of Natural Resources Navajo Land Department. The previous regulations dated from 1993 and an update was sorely needed. According to the findings of the Council resolution approving the changes, the amendments "will benefit qualified applicants who are seeking housing assistance and/or utility infrastructure assistance."[7] In part, HLR 2016 simply memorialized and formalized the sovereign authority under "the Navajo Nation General Leasing Regulations of 2013, which authorizes the Navajo Nation to issue leases, except [M]ineral Leases and Rights-of-way, without the approval of the Secretary [of the Interior]."[8] The ability of the Navajo Nation to "unilaterally issue [l]eases," was confirmed by the Secretary of the Interior under the Navajo Nation Trust Land Leasing Act of 2000, 25 U.S.C. §415 (e).[9] For decades, tribes rightly complained that Bureau of Indian Affairs (BIA) red tape, in particular title search delays, hampered development. Bypassing the BIA is a central feature of HLR 2016 and reflects the extent to which, after more than a century of the federal government exercising a heavy hand, the Navajo Nation now sits in the driver's seat when it comes to land use regulation.

FIGURE 9.1 "Pictorial Rug, Reservation Scene" (Bequest of William R. Wright, 1995. Image © President and Fellows of Harvard College, Peabody Museum of Archaeology and Ethnology, 995–29-10/73825)

At first glance, HLR 2016 demands little from tribal members seeking a homesite lease. Though the regulations provide for a homesite *lease* rather than outright ownership, the monthly rental rate is only $1.00 for a renewable seventy-five-year lease term.[10] HLR 2016 did not include a provision for incremental increases in the rental rate, which presumably would be a good idea when contemplating a seventy-five-year lease agreement between the tribe and tribal members, but it nevertheless cracks open an important door for the tribal government. Ever since the formation of the Navajo Business Council, the bulk of funding for the Navajo Nation government came from royalties from gas, oil, uranium, and coal leases. But the shuttering of the coal-fired power plants on and near the reservation has led to a gradual withdrawal of extractive industry companies from the Navajo Nation. Some mines and power plants are still limping along, but the writing is on the wall.[11] For its own survival, the Navajo Nation needs to find alternative ways of generating revenue. Though $1.00 a month will not do all that much, homesite lease rental payments in the future might play a role similar to that of property taxes in the budgets of off-reservation local governments.

The problem with the homesite lease process envisioned by HLR 2016 is that it fails to recognize the significant limits on the ability of the tribe to implement its provisions – the process is cumbersome, the depth of reservation poverty makes it difficult to tax or collect fees from tribal members, and the process invites political pushback by placing the central government between Diné families and land they have long considered "theirs." In order to help tribal members understand what is required to get a homesite lease, the Land Department prepared a flowchart detailing the steps applicants have to follow.[12] After obtaining the application packet, applicants must:

(1) Contact their Grazing Official / Land Board Member in order to identify the coordinates of the homesite location with a handheld GPS unit and identify grazing permittees with rights over the area for consent of the homesite location.

(2) Submit the completed Homesite Lease (HSL) application with a $30 money order payable to the tribe.

(3) Submit a completed Homesite Biological Clearance Form (HSBCF) so that Navajo Fish and Wildlife can complete the Biological Resource Compliance Form.

(4) Hire a private archeologist to conduct a cultural investigation that is then sent to the Navajo Heritage & Historical Preservation Department so that a Cultural Resource Compliance Form can be completed.

(5) Hire a certified land surveyor to conduct a legal survey plat of the proposed homesite to be submitted to the Navajo Land Department.

(6) Collect all these forms and send them to the General Land Development Department for Environmental Review.

(7) Submit a completed packet to the Navajo Land Department for review by the department's director on behalf of the Navajo Nation; the packet must include (a) the Homesite Lease; (b) Certificate of Indian Blood (and Marriage License, if applicable); (c) Archaeological Inventory Report Compliance Form; (d) Biological Resource Compliance Form; (e) Cultural Resource Compliance Form; (f) Environmental Review Letter; (g) Certified Legal Survey Plat and TOPO Maps.

(8) If approved, pay $12.00 to the tribe to release the homesite lease to the applicant.

Every step in the process presented above can be justified – environmental reviews are important, archeological artifacts matter, surveys set the boundaries of the leased land – but the end result is a complex multistage process. For some tribal members, particularly those whose primary language is Navajo and who may not read or write in either English or Navajo, the layers of written submissions that must be given to different offices, sequentially, serve as a significant barrier. As one letter writer noted about HLR 2016, "[s]ubmitting at least 10 forms for clearances by everyone but your mother (oh, wait you need that, too), and waiting up to ten years is not acceptable."[13]

The process is also expensive. While the listed $42 in application and lease-release fees are modest, the fee schedule also includes a $350 resurvey fee and a $1,000 fee for a half-acre adjustment or a $2,000 fee for a full acre adjustment for tribal members who need adjustment to an existing homesite lease.[14] Additionally, applicants must hire a private archaeologist and a certified land surveyor. For tribal members living at or below the poverty line, such expenses virtually close the door to obtaining a formally recognized homesite lease.

These complexity and cost challenges of HLR 2016's homesite lease process are compounded by practical limits on the Navajo Nation's authority over tribal members. Though the Secretary of the Interior and the Navajo Nation Council agree that the tribe has the authority to unilaterally lease trust land, such authority means relatively little if tribal members do not feel bound by land use regulations promulgated by the central tribal government. As *The Navajo Times* reported, "When the five compliance officers for the new home site regulations are hired, they will face a daunting task – enforcing laws that nearly everyone on the Navajo Nation is violating."[15] Resistance to tribal authority need not be overt; a simple belief that the tribe is unlikely to enforce lease regulation against tribal members who are out of compliance is enough to undermine the tribe's ability to require that people follow the homesite lease process. HLR 2016 is not just about formalizing existing rights, it also imposes costly fines on tribal members for unauthorized improvements. Significantly, HLR 2016 provides for a $200 monthly fine for illegal parking of a trailer or mobile home, and the same hefty fine for storage sheds or corrals constructed without a permit.[16] These fees may make sense in urban areas or even in developing rural areas, but strike against long-standing norms on the reservation, where informal housing abounds (and is even traditional), permits are virtually unheard of, and animals often are kept close to the home. Beyond that, depending on their circumstances and connection to the land, some tribal members may think that having to apply for permission to live on land that has "belonged" to their family for generations is an unfair imposition by Window Rock.

Perhaps not surprisingly, there was grassroots resistance when HLR 2016 was rolled out. Western Navajo Agency Council pushed back with a resolution that argued that tribal members were neither adequately consulted nor given a meaningful chance to participate.[17] The strongly worded resolution accused the Resources and Development Committee of continuing "a regime of authoritarian paternalistic policies and laws originally initiated years ago by the federal government to control the Diné ... the central Navajo Nation government has copied and applied this attitude and behavior towards their own people." Western Navajo Agency Council also argued that the LGA requires chapter-level participation in homesite lease approval and the drafting of tribal land use regulations. "Everything here is going against k'e," complained Marvin Chee, an attendee at a homesite lease public hearing.[18] Part of the pushback the new homesite lease process encountered can be traced to the love/hate relationship Diné have with their central government.

A letter to the editor published by *The Navajo Times* linked HLR 2016 to these problems, asserting that "[t]he current home-site lease regulations are intended to harass and intimidate Diné to force them to pay fees to a greedy and corrupt Navajo Nation government."[19]

The Navajo Nation's effort to assert authority and impose order through the new homesite lease process was likely done for good reasons, even if today it is unclear whether the tribe will succeed in imposing a top-down structure. From a planning perspective, it is prohibitively expensive for the tribe to be constantly in a reactionary position. When tribal members drag a trailer to land they choose, place it where they want, and then complain because of poor road maintenance or lack of utilities such as water and electricity, the tribal government is placed in an untenable position. Similarly, in the absence of meaningful land use regulations, when one family builds a compound without permission on land claimed by another family, disputes arise that are needlessly complicated and difficult to resolve. Navajo Nation home-site leasing procedures not only further tribal sovereignty, but, by cutting out the federal government and related BIA red tape, should also speed up the lease approval process.

Off-reservation, land-use regulation and its attendant permits, fines, and fees are an ordinary part of local governance as it relates to homeownership, and they are arguably a necessary part of tribal governance as well. For its part, the Navajo Nation Land Department hopes to employ five compliance officers, a modest staff given the size of the reservation. Alone, homesite lease regulatory reform will do little to free up or reallocate unused land. Though, traditionally, land rights were tied to use, grazing rights today often exist more in theory, or on paper, than in practice. For a variety of reasons – everything from deterioration of the range and the expense of raising animals, to changing traditions and the loss of labor as younger family members opt for the wage economy – it is not uncommon that extensive claims to land are not supported by the behavior of the family or families asserting their grazing rights. This is not to suggest that the land has additional carrying capacity – much of the reservation is at risk of further deterioration and desertification – just that some assertions of grazing rights that block newcomers or development, including new homesites, may be based primarily on historical memory and not recent use.

More comprehensive land reform on the Navajo reservation will not be easy. As challenging as homesite lease reform has proven to be, homesite leases are low-hanging fruit compared to grazing and customary use rights. The 2017 comprehensive land reform report published by the Diné Policy Institute makes the connection between homesite leases and grazing rights clear:

> [W]e voice the collective complaint of everyday Navajo people and speak to our tribal government and elected officials, give us land reform. We need to break up the concentration of land from a few users and provide access to all Navajo people.

More importantly, we need to move away from the unsustainable permitting system we have inherited (or that was mandated) from the Bureau of Indian Affairs and reclaim sovereignty over our land ... We call for a new permitting system that focuses on the needs of livestock owners and frees up everything else for other forms of development. In the end, we argue for a renewal of Navajo community life through land policy.[20]

In this light, the Navajo Nation's attempt to bring the homesite lease process entirely within the tribe and to establish centrally-dictated approval requirements is a natural first move when it comes to land reform. But it cannot not be the last move.

9.2 GRAZING RIGHTS

As time passes, fewer and fewer Diné have direct memories of livestock reduction. But that does not mean that that era has been forgotten by Diné families. Reflecting the collective trauma of livestock reduction, many families continue to view grazing permits as their most important assets. When grazing permittees die without a clear line of succession, grazing right contests can lead to deep family resentments and the need for court involvement. Livestock, in particular sheep and goats, remain a fundamental part of the lifestyle and identity of many Diné. This makes it particularly difficult for tribal leaders to assert a right over land that is subject to grazing rights-based claims.

But if the Navajo Nation is going to create space for tribal members to build homes, start businesses, and remain on the reservation, it needs to more aggressively assert meaningful control over grazing and customary use rights. In some circumstances, the tribe will need to limit some of the rights held by tribal members. This is a contentious idea given the tribe's experience with livestock reduction in the 1930s. Though the federal government stepped away from active management of the Navajo range after World War II, the trauma of livestock reduction continues to paralyze land reform efforts. What began as a familiar story of external domination soon became a problem of tribal governance as well. This chapter connects the pain of livestock reduction, detailed in Chapter 3, with the myriad ways that grazing and customary use rights block economic development on the reservation.

Resolution of the conflict between grazing rights and development ultimately belongs to the Navajo Nation. The most likely path for reform is through local governance experiments at the chapter level, but the central government also could accomplish it if land reform becomes a priority for the Navajo Nation and for tribal members. There are costs and benefits associated with either of these options, but what is most important is that Diné find a way to break the impasse that exists. Livestock reduction was a cruel policy that would never have been imposed on white ranchers, but the memory of that period should not continue to cripple land reform efforts. It is an almost impossible task to locate precisely the moment when, for most practical purposes, the Navajo Nation gained effective control over the use of tribal land. Was it when the federal government backed away from livestock reduction, when President Nixon officially launched the self-determination era in a Special Message to Congress,[21] or much more recently with the passage of the Hearth Act of 2012?[22] Reasonable minds can differ. For the Navajo Nation, the relative authority of the federal government and the tribe arguably switched during the Peter MacDonald era.[23] But what is clear is that today the tribe cannot deflect blame onto the federal government for ongoing regulatory failures or mismanagement.

Land management problems "belong" to the tribe and it is the tribe that has the authority to implement a better approach. One possible solution is to reaffirm the tribe's traditional understanding that "use" is the proper basis for individual property rights in land. Reclaiming "use" would allow the tribe to right-size land holdings where customary use and grazing claims not supported by actual use of the land are harming Diné interests.[24]

Livestock feature prominently both in Diné identity and in the history of the Navajo Nation. Extended family dynamics and gatherings often revolve around livestock in some way. Horses, goats, and sheep occupy a central place culturally, as can be observed in everything from the reservation rodeo circuit to the beautiful handmade woolen rugs that many Diné produce. On the reservation, drivers know to look out for sheep moving under the watchful eyes of shepherds and sheep dogs. For many Diné families, a grazing permit is their most prized, most defining, and most contentious possession. Livestock reduction was the major crisis faced by the nascent Navajo Council and left an indelible mark on Diné.[25] The Navajo Nation has struggled with grazing rights ever since because of the long shadow cast by that trauma.[26] Partly as a result, since World War II, there has not been a serious effort to deal with the continued destruction of the Navajo range.[27] The wage economy replaced grazing in terms of economic importance for most Navajo families. The inability of the Navajo range to provide a suitable livelihood for the entire tribe was an additional contributing factor.[28] These push-and-pull factors, combined with Window Rock's almost singular focus on using extractive industry development to maximize tribal revenue over the past six-plus decades, left matters of grazing regulation and enforcement neglected.[29]

The neglect has taken a number of forms. First, because the permit system was allowed to become ossified, the importance of inherited rights has correspondingly increased.[30] Second, tribal politicians balk at pursuing land reform because of the high political cost of proposing changes to the existing system.[31] Though the federal government backed off after World War II, creating space for much-needed tribally led reform, memories of the stock reduction program paralyzed efforts by the tribal government to address the problems of overgrazing.[32] Tribal members resist efforts, by the central tribal government and by their chapter, to rein in herd size or deal with the wild mustang problem.[33] Council delegates assume that grazing and customary use rights reform is untouchable and thus avoid real engagement with

FIGURE 9.2 Young sheep in Pauline J. Garnenez's corral, at Red Lake, just north of Navajo, New Mexico. Photo by Elvia Castro, Copyright 2008.

the issue; indeed, tribal agency work rarely advances beyond the planning stage.[34] Meanwhile, not only does deterioration of the range and desertification of the reservation continue, but nonagricultural development also remains bottled up, trapped by the hold that the existing system has on unused land.[35]

The Navajo Nation requires that tribal members have a grazing permit in order to graze their animals on the Navajo range.[36] Measurements in the system are based on sheep units, with one horse, mule, or burro equal to five sheep; one cow equal to four sheep; and one goat counted as one sheep unit.[37] Grazing permits are limited geographically, and in theory permittees cannot have more than ten horses or more than 350 total sheep units.[38] However, when the tribe conducted a livestock inventory of select grazing districts in 2001, there were 403,138 sheep units found even though the number of permitted sheep units in those districts was only 285,346.[39] Because these figures did not include feral or penned animals, even these elevated figures do not reflect the actual number of sheep units in these districts.[40] Grazing regulation and enforcement generally falls upon district grazing committees.[41] Their authority extends to the question of whether tribal members can fence portions of the range.[42] The Navajo Nation Code directly incorporates language from the 1957 Navajo Reservation Grazing Handbook,[43] which lists as one of the purposes of the grazing regulation "[t]he adjustment of livestock numbers to the carrying capacity of the range in such a manner that the livestock economy of the Navajo Nation will be preserved."[44] The regulations allow for the issuance of new permits to tribal members over age eighteen whenever the district's carrying capacity has not been exceeded.[45] Finally, though there are grazing fees associated with the use of non-trust land owned by the Navajo Nation, tribal members are not charged grazing fees for permitted use of trust land.[46]

The cultural significance of grazing, coupled with limits on the issuance of new permits, makes grazing permits a highly valued possession on the reservation.[47] Conflicts involving grazing permits, between both neighbors and family members, are frequent and often heated. The Navajo Supreme Court, in *Begay v. Keedah*, established five factors for determining who should be awarded a contested grazing permit: first, animal units in grazing permits must be sufficiently large to be economically viable; second, land must be put to its most beneficial use; third, the most logical heir should receive land use rights; fourth, use rights must not be fragmented; and fifth, only those who are personally involved in the beneficial use of land may inherit it.[48] Navajo law thus emphasizes economic viability, beneficial use, and concern with the risks that come from overly fragmented rights. The fifth *Begay* factor demonstrates a departure from off-reservation understandings of property because, for Diné, ownership interests in grazing permits are dependent upon personal use.[49] Factor five's use requirement does not square easily with non-Indian property rights, which largely accept the severability of use and ownership.[50] But by including use as a prerequisite for being awarded a contested grazing permit, the Navajo Supreme Court affirmed traditional Diné practices, which emphasize use as the basis of property rights.[51] As the Court noted in *Begay*, "[a]nother aspect of traditional Navajo land tenure is the principle that one must use it or lose it."[52]

When the inheritance of grazing rights came before the Navajo Supreme Court again in 2007, the Court reaffirmed traditional Diné understandings of property, even where they break from non-Indian notions of equality.[53] In 2002, the Navajo Nation Council passed *Diné Bi Beenahaz'áanii*, or, in English, The Foundation of the Diné, Diné Law, and Diné Government, discussed previously in Chapter 6.[54] Though Navajo Fundamental Law, as it is also called, does not include provisions that expressly address how courts should resolve conflicts involving land rights, it emphasizes tradition and kinship (*k'é*).[55] Applying the *Begay* factors in a subsequent case, the Navajo Supreme Court added a preference for women when it comes to grazing permits.[56] The Navajo Supreme Court ruled that the *Begay* factors had to be interpreted in light of Navajo Fundamental Law, which recognizes that "Navajos maintain and carry on the custom that the maternal clan maintains traditional grazing and farming areas."[57] To outsiders, such overt sexism might seem jarring, but matrilineal control over the homestead and overgrazing is very much a part of Navajo culture.[58] The gender-modified *Begay* factors remain the law today. These cases highlight both the challenge of determining what to do with grazing rights following the death of the previous permittee and the importance of grazing rights in defining land rights more generally on the reservation.

Grazing rights permit the holder to graze their animals on tribal trust land; they do not grant formal ownership rights. However, permittees typically understand their grazing rights as providing them an ownership interest in the underlying land.[59]

"[Grazing] permittees view themselves as the de facto owners of the land and therefore believe they have the right to decide how the land is to be used. The permittees pass their rights from generation to generation, and they are often conservative."[60] Though at times the tribe has tried to impose limits on the power of permittees to determine how "their" land is used, the tribe has largely gone along – except when such claims conflict with the interests of extractive industry – with permittees' expansive understanding of the nature of grazing rights. What this means in practice is that development proposals which threaten, or seem to threaten, the rights of permittees often die on the drawing board. Even though a particular project, say a new school or store, might use only a small amount of land relative to the reservation's seemingly endless supply, grazing permittees often thwart such projects.[61] Opposition by a single permittee can derail a project irrespective of the extent to which the project responds to recognized community needs. Multiple legal and political factors empower grazing permittees to block development in this way.

Grazing permittees currently can exploit the "raw"[62] status of most reservation land to block development. Because most reservation land has not been zoned, it remains "raw" land, meaning that any proposed change invites a fight with those who prefer the status quo. If each locality used zoning to set aside some areas for residential or business development, grazing permittees would have less ground to contest development proposals. They could, of course, contest the initial zoning decision and the appropriateness of development generally, but zoning would front-load such debates, making planning permission less contentious for individual entrepreneurs or tribal members seeking permission for their particular proposals. Zoning also would help depoliticize the process of approving development proposals. In many rural chapters, families with the longest, deepest connection to the area have the most political power. Rivalry at the family or clan level can lead chapters, using grazing rights as cover, to reject development proposals – regardless of the merits of the proposal – if they come from the "wrong" family or clan. Zoning could provide a check on the power grazing permittees have over all forms of development.

In some respects, the secondary interest in land tied to grazing provides permit holders *greater* ability to maintain the range undisturbed than if they owned the land outright. Land ownership typically comes with rigid boundary lines that serve to define the space over which owners enjoy presumptive control.[63] Off-reservation landowners enjoy broad exclusionary and development rights within the four corners of their individual plot, but they have much more limited authority when it comes to what happens beyond their property. Grazing rights are different. The territory over which a grazing right attaches is often defined loosely, based on informal understandings of family claims to the range rather than formal boundaries.[64] Most significantly, it is common for land to be subject to multiple grazing and customary use claims, with different families claiming an interest in the same area of land. Grazing rights are also amorphous enough to support even long dormant claims. Even though it might have been years since sheep grazed over a particular part of the range because grazing permittees had been keeping their sheep closer to their homesite, they could plausibly move their animals to that part of the range in the future. Any land that is withdrawn for development is a loss not only to the family or families with grazing rights over that part of the range, but to all families who use the land and rightly fear that territory within their grazing district might have to be adjusted as a result.[65] There is a certain logic to resisting development. As Michelle Hale notes, "For some Indigenous people, the best 'use' of land is non-use, to effectively keep exploitation and extraction at bay."[66] But for tribal members seeking development permission, layers of potential claimants means they may face objections not just from those with secondary land rights directly at stake, but also from grazing permittees whose rights are not directly implicated.[67] Consequently, the secondary nature of grazing rights enables permittees to control a larger area than they would if the rights were explicitly tied to land instead of grazing.

Commentators agree that, as a practical matter, grazing permittees enjoy broad veto power over reservation development.[68] Permittee approval is required in order for projects to go forward.[69] How tribal members experience permittee power can be seen in Louise Litzen's struggle to open a laundromat near Diné College in Tsaile, Arizona:

> For eleven years, she has navigated in good faith through a maze of processes to obtain a business site lease. Some of her neighbors own grazing permits on land surrounding Diné College, much of which has not been used for grazing for generations. The refusal of any of these individuals to waive their grazing rights can single-handedly prevent Louise from opening her business.[70]

Litzen's story is not unique. To get a business site or home site lease requires first getting approval from grazing or chapter officials. Those officials, fearful of trampling on the rights of permittees, typically require all permittees in the area (including those with nearby rights whose land is not directly impacted) to sign off on any development proposal. This arrangement results in pervasive hold-out problems. Rights holders with petty disagreements or grievances can block even the most community-centered forms of development, locking up land with marginal grazing utility.

Though the grazing permit system initially was federally imposed and the federal government retains an active role, today Diné have authority over the general direction of reservation development at the community level. This authority is exercised though hyper-local decision-making institutions and structures. Local chapter officials, grazing committees, and democratic processes in each chapter are involved in even relatively small changes that might affect the range. Proposals to move from elected grazing officials towards enforcement of grazing regulations by paid professional staff have been floated by the central government, but, so far, such

a transition has not happened. Partly as a consequence, permittees hold disproportionate political power. Grazing rights holders are actively engaged in chapter
politics. They attend meetings, serve on committees, and vote to protect their
interests. They are often older and more tied to the existing power dynamics in the
community than younger Diné who may live and work off-reservation. They also
tend to be relatively conservative, protective of their grazing rights, and reluctant to
see their community change. Such a state of affairs means that even fairly routine
proposals – for example, to create a formalized car repair business or small restaurant – involve the whole community. Entrepreneurs cannot rely upon background
rules or zoning regulations to provide them with a presumptive right to develop
a parcel of land; instead grazing permittees typically exercise their power such that
the default is to block development. In rural chapters, the status quo of strong
grazing rights reigns supreme, choking off other forms of development.

9.3 REASSERTING USE AS THE BASIS OF DINÉ PROPERTY RIGHTS

What should be done to check the extent to which grazing rights permittees can
block other forms of land use? This chapter does not give a full answer to that
question. As discussed in Chapter 8, one of the biggest sticking points in Diné
politics today is whether local decision-making should drive policy or whether the
central government in Window Rock should be in charge. Traditionally, the different levels of government have had different spheres of primary responsibility. For
example, extractive industry fell under the purview of Window Rock while local
institutions handled grazing. But tribal members often discover that the lines
between local and national authority can blur, and spheres often overlap in frustrating ways. When tribal members seek permission to use land for a business venture or
even when they try to secure a homesite lease, for example,[71] it is all but inevitable
that they will confront multiple hurdles. Chapter politics and the Window Rock
bureaucracy can hamper even determined efforts by individuals to obtain formal
land rights. Part of freeing up portions of the range for development is resolving the
conflict between the decentralization and centralization impulses that complicate
Navajo Nation governance.

This chapter avoids giving an answer to whether land use should be governed
primarily by chapters or primarily by the central government. As discussed in
Chapter 8, good arguments can be made on both sides of the Navajo-federalism
debate. Chapters that are closer to the people in theory provide a more meaningful
form of direct democracy and can offer a land use approach better tailored to the
needs of their particular community. On the other hand, decentralization efforts in
the past, especially the LGA,[72] did not live up to their promise,[73] in part because
rural chapters often have a thin talent pool from which to take on complex land
management issues. Outside consultants can fill some of the planning and accounting gaps but are a prohibitively expensive option for long-term governance.

Economies of scale – how many local land departments can the Navajo Nation realistically support – also favor centralization. But governance reform is perhaps a precondition for grazing and land use reform. At some point, Diné will decide that the costs of the current bifurcated approach – in which tribal members seeking to use land encounter high barriers at both the chapter level and in Window Rock – are too great and something must change.[74] But, mindful that "a smothering kind of paternalism" by friends of the tribe can harm Diné as much as direct attacks on tribal sovereignty,[75] this chapter is deliberately agnostic as to whether decentralization or centralization forces should prevail.

Where this chapter does stake a claim is on the principles that should guide land reform. By returning to the traditional Diné *use* requirement as central to the recognition and protection of land rights, the Navajo Nation (whether at the chapter level or in Window Rock) can right-size grazing rights.[76] The grazing permit system, though initially imposed on top of existing land holdings, transformed Diné understandings of property rights in land. While use continues to be the basis for assertions of a right over land, the inverse – that land rights can be lost through disuse – has been lost. Families continue to base their interest in land on past (customary) use, but the traditional understanding that land rights depend on use – that rights can be lost through nonuse after initial acquisition – is under pressure. Families whose right is based on having used the land in the past often assert an interest in land that they have not used in years. Complicating matters further, the same area can quickly become subject to the claims of neighboring families who start using the land for grazing or other purposes after observing that the prior family appeared, through nonuse, to have abandoned their interest. The grazing permit system introduced into even the most remote parts of Diné society a more fixed understanding of property rights in land, rights that depended primarily on formal recognition in the form of a permit and only secondarily upon use. Lessening the hold grazing permittees have over land, including the problems of overlapping claims and of general resistance to nonagricultural development, will not be easy. Returning to the traditional understandings – that use is not only a precondition for acquiring land rights but also for maintaining an interest in the land itself – would help open land for development.

As a descriptive matter, the authority of grazing permittees is typically wielded by an older generation that seeks to maintain the vast majority of tribal land as grazing land, even land in prime locations. Such protection of the status quo harms would-be entrepreneurs, typically younger members of the tribe, as well as Diné who move to a different part of the reservation and seek land for a home site. Ironically, strong assertions of the need to protect grazing rights and the traditional sheep-centric way of life reflect more the Anglo-American emphasis on ownership than the traditional Diné use-dependent approach to property rights.

Anglo-American law is certainly concerned with use, but the focus is the exclusionary rights of owners and not the possibility that there could be a dynamic relationship between use and rights.[77] Put differently, the grazing permit system pushed reservation land use governance towards non-Indian notions of relatively fixed ownership interests.[78] Anglo-American property law is not indifferent to non-use, but it is fair to say that property doctrine struggles with nonuse and abandonment, erring on the side of strong ownership interests.[79] The common law goes so far as to prohibit the abandonment of real property.[80] Of course, there are exceptions – such as ways in which rights are undermined through nonuse – but the exceptions found in Anglo-American property law provide imperfect solutions for the challenges presented by Navajo grazing rights.

The most direct way in which Anglo-American property law deals with nonuse is through the doctrine of adverse possession. Adverse possession works to transfer title from an owner who has slept on his or her rights, through nonuse and failure to guard against intruders, to an adverse possessor who has earned a right to the property by possessing the property continuously for a statutory period.[81] The doctrine thus prioritizes use over nonuse and, through the statutory period, establishes when nonuse (coupled with nonenforcement of the owner's right to exclude) can result in loss of property. But many people, including judges, dislike the idea that title should be given to an adverse possessor. The whole thing feels too much like theft, especially when the adverse possessor knew from the start that the land was not his or her property.[82] Courts, consequently, are reticent to follow the doctrine; rather than sign off on adverse possession-based transfers, they often find excuses to protect the original property owner.[83]

Adverse possession arguably has limited import on the Navajo reservation because the doctrine is about more than just nonuse. It also requires entry and use by an adverse possessor. In the Navajo context, the adverse possession doctrine could facilitate productive transfers of land between people with grazing rights, from an inactive to an active user of the range, for example. But the majority of Diné cases are marked by only one side (nonuse) of the two-sided adverse possession relationship (nonuse by the original rights holder coupled with use by an intruder). In short, there are no bona fide "intruders" on much of the range. Consequently, the traditional adverse possession doctrine does little to clear the Navajo range of underlying grazing rights claims. A modified version of adverse possession that required only nonuse might work; the Navajo Nation could justify such a modification by the fact that the tribe holds ultimate title (in trust with the federal government) to the land. One could argue, for example, that land not withdrawn from the range "belongs" in some way to all tribal members. There is a collective interest in freeing up rangeland for development, or at least in checking the veto power enjoyed by grazing rights holders, and a modified version of adverse possession might serve this interest. On the other hand, part of the beauty of the adverse possession doctrine is that it places the burden of proof on the adverse possessor. If the doctrine changed so that nonuse alone was enough, then the tribe itself would bear the burden to establish that the grazing permittee had failed to use his or her portion of the range for the statutory period. Such a modification would change adverse possession from an Anglo-American doctrine that forces transfers between private parties into a tool of the Navajo Nation to strip tribal members with grazing rights of those very rights.

If the goal is to claw back dated, unused grazing rights, Anglo-American law offers a more direct mechanism – tax liens – that could theoretically accomplish much the same. Off-reservation, when a property owner fails in his or her obligations (the main one being the payment of property taxes) to the state, the solution is not some version of adverse possession by the state, but instead a lien on the property.[84] Property taxes encourage – and, in practical terms, may require – productive use of property. Enforcement through a tax lien allows the state to reclaim property when owners fail to pay their property taxes.[85] Another way to think about this is as a collective claim connected to nonuse that disciplines owners and, like adverse possession, punishes those who do not live up to the basic requirements of ownership. Superficially, with the exception of isolated fee simple properties located within the larger reservation, tax liens would seem to have little relevance in the Navajo Nation. After all, the Navajo Nation and the US government hold most of the reservation land in joint trust. Tribal members typically have only use rights to the land. But the Navajo Nation can certainly impose a system of user fees that make grazing rights conditional on payment. In the event of nonpayment, the tribe could reclaim rangeland, checking the power permittees have to block other forms of use.

In theory, fees enforced through tax liens offer the Navajo Nation an effective way to free up the range, but the politics of imposing fees would likely derail any proposal as it advanced beyond the planning stage. Given the poverty of the reservation, fees would have to be set at amounts that are low relative to off-reservation standards. But even a relatively low fee could convince tribal members to disclaim those portions of their customary use areas that they do not actually use. After all, few people will want to pay for something if they see no benefit in the payment, no matter how small the per acre fee. Of course, if the tribe were more aggressive, if it set user fees closer to the costs of herding, including environmental damage and governance costs, then more land would be freed from grazing rights claims. However, and this is the challenge, the imposition of *any fee* is likely to be politically dead on arrival if raised in the Navajo Nation Council. The weight of memory from livestock reduction is just too great. Even if they were set artificially low, user fees would be an extra burden on those Diné families already living close to subsistence levels. Just as the seemingly neutral culling requirements of the New Deal disproportionately harmed the most vulnerable, so too would Diné families experience user fees differently depending on their relative wealth. Families with outside income tied to formal sector employment would be less impacted than families more dependent on grazing. Taking a broader view, tax liens were one of the mechanisms through which Indians were dispossessed of their land following allotment. Unlike tax liens imposed by non-Indian governments, grazing fees would ensure that the land remains within the tribe; nevertheless, the history of Indian land loss limits the ability of the Navajo Nation to institute a meaningful grazing fee system.

Fortunately, Diné need not adopt an approach based on Anglo-American law; instead, they can revitalize their traditional practice of treating land rights as use-dependent. For while modified versions of adverse possession and tax foreclosure could help the Navajo Nation diminish the power that grazing permittees currently enjoy, the Diné tradition of insisting on use provides a better solution in terms of political feasibility and cultural match. Reservation land, though largely free from off-reservation fee simple ownership claims, is subject to strong claims tied to past use. In *Dreaming of Sheep in Navajo Country*, a comprehensive and beautifully written exploration of Navajo grazing practices and history, Marsha Weisiger notes:

> Matrilocal residence meant that most pastures and springs became associated with particular matrilineages. Certainly Diné did not conceive of land – unlike stock – as something people "owned"; it was communally held, and unused land was available to whoever preempted it. But practically speaking, families tended to graze their livestock in the same general areas year after year, so that over time, they acquired generally recognized, though often overlapping, use-rights to particular areas.[86]

The challenge is squaring the sense of ownership – which enjoys community support – with the idea that "unused land" is generally available to others who can use it. What should have to give when generally recognized rights to particular areas conflict with Diné traditional land use practices? Traditionally, as the Diné Policy Institute's 2017 report, *Land Reform in the Navajo Nation*, highlights, "[t]here was rarely a permanence to any one family's control of land. If a family moved on, another family could move in and occupy the land."[87] There is no simple answer to this conflict between tradition and generally recognized use-rights. Land rights have ossified, and there is little incentive for Diné families to make land concessions from their customary use and traditional grazing area for the greater good of the tribe. At some point, a choice has to be made. Though the tribe could improve how the range is governed and how development proposals are dealt with through selective incorporation of aspects of Anglo-American property law, ultimately, a better option would be to revitalize the traditional Diné emphasis on use.

Making land rights use-dependent once more will not be easy. Some tribal members will experience a loss if told that land they considered "theirs" is no longer theirs to control because the land has been unused for a long time.[88] To revitalize the traditional use-dependent understanding of rights over land, the tribe might need to make compensating payments or provide allowances to tribal members who suffer a loss when the range is freed from dated grazing permit-based claims. But as tempting as it is to focus only on the loss that grazing permittees may experience, it is worth keeping in mind the hidden losses the current system is imposing on the tribe as a whole.

Given the trauma of livestock reduction, it is no wonder that both the Navajo Nation and the federal government are reticent about trying to tackle, once again, the problem of overgrazing. The original problem that motivated the livestock reduction program during the New Deal has not gone away – creeping desertification continues to be a problem – but revisiting grazing (or even making headway on related issues, such as the need to cull the wild horses that roam across the reservation and destroy vegetation) has been a political nonstarter.[89] There are significant costs associated with the ongoing neglect of land reform as it relates to the Navajo range.[90] The current system is not working. Not only does overgrazing continue, but grazing enforcement problems abound, nonagricultural development opportunities are being lost because of grazing permittees' veto power, and very little land is available without a fight.[91]

9.4 THE FUTURE OF LAND REFORM

It is up to Diné to decide for themselves the right balance between local control and centralized land management and how they might incentivize change. What should be uncontroversial is that reform is needed. It may be that meaningful reform must begin at the chapter level and work its way to Window Rock. Or, it may be that until tribal members are presented with a comprehensive land reform package, they will reject piecemeal efforts. But what is certain is that there are significant costs associated with letting the status quo remain unchallenged.

If the Navajo Nation finds a way to right-size existing grazing and customary use claims, it will free up land for residential and small-scale commercial development. There is enough land that the tribe need not infringe on the use rights of those Diné families who are actually using their land. Simply returning to the idea that land not being used can be claimed by others in the community will go a long way. A heavy-handed way to do this would be to impose a sufficiently high per-acre tax on rangeland, such that tribal members might be conservative when asserting land claims. Such an approach would be controversial and invite a backlash. It may be that that is a price that has to be paid, but such a top-down approach may not be required.

Ultimately, Diné will decide what Navajo land governance looks like.[92] That the Navajo Nation now has the power to set the agenda is itself a significant victory considering the history of heavy-handed federal involvement in even relatively local land use decisions. Bringing back the tribe's traditional use-dependent understanding of the land rights tribal members enjoy would help the Navajo Nation regain control over the range and would create space for Diné to take more advantage of growth opportunities that respond to the needs of all tribal members.

One of the most remarkable things about the Navajo Nation today is the continued vitality of what Charles Wilkinson called "measured separatism," or what might colloquially be labeled tribal identity.[93] The Navajo Nation remains overwhelmingly Diné and "Diné identity remains strong" in ways that are both readily apparent and more subtle.[94] Even though the Navajo Nation Council and the Navajo Nation Supreme Court have battled in recent years over the place of Navajo fundamental law in the courts,[95] reservation life in many ways continues to reflect the importance of connections and mutual interdependence. Hopefully, if those Diné harmed by the high degree of deference given to grazing and customary use rights raise their voices, showing how they are being locked out of homesites and the reservation itself, then collectively Diné will prioritize rather than resist land reform.

10

Creating Space for Experimentation

One way to think about the past two decades of Navajo land use reform efforts is as a series of policies that aim to free up land for development. Of course, when the stakes are high enough, as in the case of large-scale extractive industry and power generation, grazing and customary use rights claims give way.[1] But it is often difficult for tribal members who want to engage in smaller-scale (including individual) residential and commercial development to find available land.[2] The LGA was supposed to allow chapters to address such challenges, but it has not yet accomplished all that much from a land reform perspective. One way of creating space for development is by incentivizing local experimentation and ensuring that local reservation communities capture some of the benefits of development, as opposed to those benefits accruing centrally to the tribe as a whole. This chapter examines the benefits of local experimentation in two contexts: public housing and business site leasing.

10.1 PUBLIC HOUSING

Simply driving into Chinle, Shiprock, Tuba City, or Kayenta can be an emotionally draining experience. Dilapidated housing is everywhere. In 2017, the Urban Institute published the most comprehensive study of Indian housing to date. The study, commissioned by HUD, noted that 6 percent of American Indian and Alaska Native (AIAN) households in tribal areas have plumbing deficiencies compared to 1 percent nationwide; 12 percent have heating deficiencies compared to two percent for the United States as a whole; and 16 percent suffer from overcrowding compared to 2 percent for the country as a whole.[3] The report concluded that altogether "34 percent of AIAN households had one or more physical problems compared with only 7 percent for US households," meaning that AIAN households are almost five times as likely to live with such problems.[4] But these dire national statistics about Indians and Alaska Native households paint too rosy a picture compared with the situation on the Navajo Nation. As David Listokin notes, Navajo housing problems effectively drag down the statistics for tribes as a whole: "in the absence of the Navajo data, the share of Native American households in Indian country confronting housing space and quality problems would drop substantially."[5] The most recent in-depth survey of Diné housing conditions was completed in 2011. The study found that most homes, fully 89 percent, still rely on wood or pellet stoves for heat.[6] Additionally, "[h]alf of all individuals living on Navajo tribal lands have incomplete bathroom facilities and more than half have incomplete kitchen facilities."[7] Thirty-nine percent of households deal with overcrowding.[8] Perhaps most troubling, "5% of all children on the reservation live in housing classified as 'available shelter,' which is defined as non-typical and non-standard housing of the lowest quality. This housing is lower quality than tents or shacks and may be interpreted to indicate a possibly desperate housing situation."[9] The study authors concluded, "More than half of individuals living on the Navajo Nation live in structures that are either dilapidated or require serious repairs."[10]

But what do such poor housing conditions mean to families living with them? A brief personal aside: my mother's house when I was in seventh grade and living on the reservation just outside St. Michaels, a suburb of Window Rock, did not have running water, proper insulation, or proper electricity. The outhouse was roughly 100 feet from the house, near the edge of the property line. What did all of this mean to me, a seventh grader, and my brother, a sixth grader? It meant we bathed infrequently because we had to haul in all the water and do sponge baths in a small bucket. It meant we tried our best not to have to go to the bathroom in the middle of the night and we were careful around the length of orange extension cord that provided electricity to the house. There is a danger that raw housing quality statistics for the Navajo Nation will overstate the hardships of the conditions. But no matter how it may be expressed, poor housing quality certainly makes life more difficult. For the approximately 40 percent of households on the Navajo reservation that lack running water,[11] water is a much bigger issue than it is for the typical American household. Though the average American uses 100 gallons of water a day, some Diné families, reliant on trucked in water, make due with 400 gallons a month.[12] Other families haul their own water, driving an average of twenty-eight miles roundtrip (but with some driving as many as eighty miles roundtrip) to fill their water jugs and portable water tanks.[13] Lack of running water not only costs more – up to "twenty times more than water for non-water haulers in neighboring communities"[14] (including gas and car usage) – but it also makes everyday life more difficult. Bathing, washing dishes, cleaning, and even having a drink of water become decisions made in the shadow of water scarcity and with full recognition of the difficulty involved in getting water. Contrast that experience with the assumptions made by most Americans that water will be readily available, relatively cheap, and largely unlimited for most household uses. The 400 gallons per month per household that some Diné families have to work with makes California's water rationing amount of 50 gallons per person per day starting in 2030 seem luxurious.[15]

What is true of water is also true for other amenities taken for granted off-reservation, from heat and electricity to telephone service and internet access.[16]

The government entity tasked with addressing the tremendous need for decent housing on the Navajo reservation is the Navajo Housing Authority (NHA). In 1996, Congress recognized the importance of tribal sovereignty and local decision-making when it passed the Native American Housing Assistance and Self-Determination Act (NAHASDA). NAHASDA brought principles of self-determination to the Indian housing realm.[17] It permitted tribes to either run their own housing authority or assign their rights and responsibilities to a tribally designated housing entity (TDHE). NAHASDA enjoyed bipartisan support in Congress when it passed. A damning 1996 Urban Institute study on the housing needs of Indians and Alaska Natives, like the later 2016 Urban Institute study, highlighted the critical housing needs in tribal areas.[18] But perhaps the biggest push for change came from the work of reporters at the *Seattle Times* who put together a Pulitzer-prize winning series, *Tribal Housing: From Deregulation to Disgrace*, on the problems that plagued Washington's pre-NAHASDA approach to Indian housing.[19]

Since its passage, NAHASDA has been considered "a moderate-to-strong success by many in Indian Country."[20] According to the National Congress of American Indians, "NAHASDA has resulted in tens of thousands more housing units being constructed as well as increased tribal capacity to address related infrastructure and economic development challenges."[21] NAHASDA primarily operates through a block grant program, though it also provides for a loan guarantee program to support private housing finance on trust land as well as funding for training and technical assistance.[22] HUD distributes block grant funding to tribes according to a formula meant to take into account each tribe's number of pre-existing public housing units (in order to cover maintenance and renovation costs) and the tribe's need for new units.[23] In practical terms, this formula advantaged the Navajo Nation, which had a large number of units built prior to NAHASDA as well as a significant need for more housing.[24] The original formula, as well as subsequent revisions to the program, were the result of a process of negotiated rulemaking involving both the federal and tribal officials. The program is heralded as a success for a number of reasons: First, under NAHASDA, tribes have done at least as well as the federal government did in delivering new units.[25] Second, the program also is quite flexible; NAHASDA funds can, of course, be used for housing construction and maintenance, but there is allowance for other uses as well. Tribes can use their block grants to build senior centers, fund crime prevention efforts, and provide housing counseling, reallocating funds as needed.[26] Tribes do not have an entirely free hand, since HUD supervises tribal housing programs through its Office of Native American Programs (ONAP). On the front end, ONAP works with tribes to put together their funding applications, reviews those applications, and sets grant amounts. On the back end, ONAP monitors and audits TDHEs to ensure they spend funds appropriately and that their housing projects are successful. And third, even though HUD continues to play a role, NAHASDA put tribes in the driver's seat when it came to setting priorities and deciding how public housing programs should address the challenges of reservation housing. Taking a broad view, the Urban Institute's 2017 comprehensive study notably concluded, "the housing assistance system established under NAHASDA appears to be functioning reasonably well and doing what it was intended to do. It represents a marked improvement over the previous approach."[27]

Unfortunately, NAHASDA's structural reliance on block grants allows the federal government to back away from its responsibilities when it comes to Indian housing. By virtue of both specific treaty promises and the general trust relationship between tribes and the federal government, the United States is under a legal obligation to provide housing to Indians.[28] HUD has, for example, described the NAHASDA block grant as "the principal means by which the United States fulfills its trust obligations to low-income American Indian and Alaska Natives to provide safe, decent, and sanitary housing."[29] Even if such a strong claim is not accepted, the federal government should not use programs designed to further tribal self-determination as an excuse for stripping those same programs of financial support. Yet that is exactly what is happening. By fixing the nominal amount provided to tribes at the amount provided when NAHASDA was created, the federal government has effectively made significant cuts in the real amount of money dedicated for tribal housing.

> Since 1998, the first year that [the NAHASDA block grant] became operational, Congress has provided a consistent level of funding annually in nominal terms – an average of about $667 million per year from 1998 through 2014. During 17 years, however, inflation has seriously eroded that level. The 2014 amount ($637 million in nominal dollars) represented only $440 million in 1998 purchasing power.[30]

The reduction in real funding cut the average amount available for tribal housing development nearly in half for the period of 2011 to 2014 when compared to the average between 1998 and 2006.[31] As the US Commission on Civil Rights observed, "The flat-funding of the Block Grant program – combined with inflation in construction costs over time – has resulted in a sharp decrease in the number of affordable housing units developed in Indian Country in recent years."[32] The 2018 federal budget increased NAHASDA funding by $100 million – not enough to get NAHASDA back to where it was when the program was created, but a step in the right direction.[33] Inadequate, indeed declining, funding means that even though NAHASDA serves Indian country better than pre-NAHASDA federal housing programs, HUD reports that between 2003 and 2015, "the number of overcrowded households, or households without adequate kitchens or plumbing, grew by 21 percent."[34]

Inflation has taken a significant bite out of the federal commitment to tribal housing programs, but it would be a mistake to treat this as inadvertent change or a case of neglect. It is instead a design feature and part of the attraction of these sorts of block grants, affecting all tribal programs. Taking a broad view, the US Commission on Civil Rights in 2018 concluded, "Native American program budgets generally remain a barely perceptible and decreasing percentage of agency budgets. Since 2003, funding for Native American programs has mostly remained flat, and in the few cases where there have been increases, they have barely kept up with inflation or have actually resulted in decreased spending power."[35] Federal support for tribal housing is but a particular example of this larger phenomenon.[36] Just as welfare reform was sold as a way of devolving authority to states with the federal government capping the amount paid to states to run their now state-specific welfare programs,[37] so too the federal government sold NAHASDA. Under the guise of returning control to native communities via block grants, the federal government successfully reduced its spending on Indian housing.

Devolution to tribes provides the federal government with a convenient excuse when tribal projects falter or needs go unaddressed: converting the government's trust responsibility into a block grant payment makes it possible for federal officials to claim that such problems are beyond the scope of their authority and that any blame should fall on tribal governments. Not surprisingly, lack of administrative capacity on the tribal side is routinely highlighted as one of the factors limiting housing development in Indian country.[38] And it's true: administrative capacity is a significant problem for most TDHEs, as tribes of all sizes struggle with a lack of human capital. But it is important not to mischaracterize human resource problems as problems with tribal self-determination. It cannot be forgotten that the federal government struggled at least as much as the tribes do in terms of building and managing Indian housing. Lack of capacity on the tribal side arose as a structural feature of relying on tribal management of federal block grant funds. None of this suggests that tribal administration of federal programs is bad; indeed, such arrangements may be invaluable in terms of both supporting self-determination and improving the lives of tribal members who rely on these services. But it is important to keep in mind that these problems are the predictable result of the way NAHASDA was designed. Attention here now shifts to leadership problems at NHA and ways the tribe might do a better job of facilitating the construction of new public housing units.

In 2009, Chester Carl was the face of Navajo housing, and arguably the face of Indian housing nationwide when he was indicted for accepting bribes and fell from grace. According to the indictment, a contractor, William Aubrey (whose company, Lodgebuilder, received $38 million in NAHASDA funds to build housing on the reservation) illegally gave Carl $194,950 in casino chips over a four-year period.[39] Lodgebuilder also did unpaid work on Carl's house.[40] Carl was CEO of NHA for nine years, until October 2007, when he resigned after admitting taking gifts from Aubrey.[41] Notably, Carl had also served two terms as Chairman of the National American Indian Housing Council (NAIHC), the umbrella organization that provides training and technical assistance to TDHEs.[42] But beyond formal titles, Carl was involved in all the important conversations, was a featured speaker at NAIHC's annual conferences, and was one the foremost experts on both NAHASDA and Indian housing. A jury ultimately gave a split verdict, convicting Aubrey of embezzlement and conversion of funds but acquitting Aubrey and Carl of the bribery charges.[43] Despite Carl's acquittal, real damage was done to NHA, including the disruptions that followed Carl's leadership, the development projects that were delayed, the projects that failed entirely, and HUD's subsequent "intense scrutiny" that NHA had to deal with.[44] Carl made an effort to reclaim his position atop NHA but was rebuffed, though he went on to serve as Executive Director of the Hopi Tribal Housing Authority for a number of years. Sadly, years after Carl's departure and subsequent indictment, NHA as an entity is still struggling.

In 2016, the Arizona Republic published a series of lengthy articles attacking the Navajo Housing Authority (NHA). As the paper noted, between 1988 and 2016, the Navajo Nation received $1.66 billion in public housing funds through NAHASDA.[45] During that same period, housing projects stalled and hundreds of millions of dollars were left unspent by NHA. The series highlighted a number of particularly troubled projects:

- In Aneth, Utah, NHA tore down an old HUD development, promising the displaced residents that they would get new units. But eight years later, when the units were finally completed, residents found that the project was rife with construction defects.
- In Kayenta, Arizona, NHA built a women's shelter that remained shuttered for eighteen years after it was completed because the tribe could not find a nonprofit with the resources necessary to run the shelter (partly because of disputes between NHA and the nonprofit that was supposed to operate the shelter).
- In Tolani Lake, Arizona, NHA built approximately three dozen units using a clustered dome design, for teacher housing. But when the school closed, the units were left vacant and vandalized. Even after NHA spent another $2.5 million to refurbish them, they remained vacant eyesores.[46]
- In Shiprock, New Mexico, of ninety-one units of new low-income housing built by Lodgebuilder, only one was opened for occupation. The others were left abandoned until NHA eventually tore them down.[47]

Citing these failed projects, construction problems, and an inability to get new housing built, reporters Craig Harris and Dennis Wagner concluded that NHA "has failed in ways almost too numerous to count."[48] To the credit of this investigative series, the newspaper published a description of the challenges of building on the reservation and a defense of NHA offered by then-NHA CEO, Aneva Yazzie.[49] But, as the series explained, "Staff turnover is chronic. New employees often lack expertise. Lack of decent housing and jobs creates a brain drain, siphoning away the tribe's most educated and employable members."[50] NHA's track record largely speaks for itself. The Arizona Republic detailed the cost overruns, poor planning, and shoddy construction that led to four failed projects,[51] but the most damning indictment came in the form of an earlier GAO report that found that as of July 2013, NHA had a backlog of half a billion dollars in unexpended, previously awarded funds.[52] Though NHA made progress in dealing with that backlog after the GAO report – in part because the tribe faced the very real danger that the federal government would recapture all those funds – in the end, NHA was made to return $26 million to the federal NAHASDA pool.[53] Notably, no other TDHE had "ever faced an enforcement action for failing to comply with its IHP," which shows both how reluctant HUD is to sanction its grantees and the depth of NHA's failings.[54] NHA's inability, even with significant sums of money available, to effectively build and manage housing is a tragic governance failure.

NHA's difficulties continue into the present. After publication of the Arizona Republic series, NHA reconstituted its board and Aneva Yazzie resigned, replaced by Roberta Roberts, NHA's Director of Government and Public Affairs, who became an interim CEO.[55] Roberts's permanent replacement, Craig Dougall, took over in July 2018. Soon after, Dougall fired Roberts, along with two other whistleblowers, after they complained to NHA's board about pornographic material Roberts discovered on an NHA phone used by Dougall.[56] Roberts is now suing NHA for wrongful termination, while Dougall was eventually fired, though he received a $176,000 payout as part of a separation agreement.[57] As of August 2019, NHA has a new interim CEO, which means there has been considerable leadership turnover in the organization. Compounding matters, five new members of the NHA board decided to pay themselves a total of $114,000 over two months, a figure well above the maximum amount that the Navajo Nation permits tribal board members to be paid annually ($2,500).[58] This is not the first time the NHA board has found itself in hot water: the late-Senator John McCain issued a report in 2017 critiquing NHA for, among other things, excessive travel – to Hawaii and Las Vegas – by the NHA board, which "created at least an appearance of impropriety."[59] Following the media attention to the excessive stipends, Sean McCabe, the Secretary/Treasurer of the board resigned and returned some of the money, but the other members kept the money.[60] A second year law student at Arizona State University, the chairman of the board in 2019, and the other members of the board have resisted calls for their resignation brought by the Navajo Nation government.[61]

Navajo Nation efforts to check NHA and attempts by tribal members to make NHA pay for its mistakes have not been particularly successful. The Navajo Nation has considered stripping NHA of its authority.[62] NHA is the Navajo Nation's TDHE and is therefore subordinate to the Navajo Nation government, which could remove NHA's TDHE designation, making NHA ineligible for NAHASDA funding. In both 2012 and 2013, members of the Council attempted to do just that, but they did not have enough votes.[63] Sovereign immunity generally protects NHA from having to pay monetary damages should residents of NHA units sue the housing authority.[64]

What this means in practice is that there is little recourse when NHA neglects Diné families living in units that are poorly constructed or in need of repair.[65] Sovereign immunity effectively blocks housing law as a practice area for DNA-Peoples' Legal Services, reducing the degree to which residents can hold NHA accountable for problems in the units it manages.

Despite all of NHA's recent personnel issues, there are significant innate barriers that make it difficult to build public housing on the reservation. The land's trust status, the environmental reviews required for construction, the reservation's remoteness, the small number of qualified construction companies, the reporting requirements HUD imposes, and the inevitable local siting disputes combine to blunt or even thwart many NHA projects. But the fact that construction is inherently difficult on the reservation to begin with just makes NHA's self-inflicted wounds all the more painful. Enough has been said in this book about tribal corruption already, but even as this chapter transitions from NHA to commercial development, it is worth emphasizing that even the best laid plans will fail if the right people are not in place to implement them.

10.2 BUSINESS DEVELOPMENT

Diné spend most of their money off-reservation. According to the Navajo Nation's 2018 Comprehensive Economic Strategy report, for every dollar earned on the reservation, $0.53 "leaks" off-reservation.[66] Such spending supports both off-reservation businesses and local and state governments, through sales tax collection.[67] Once income taxes are taken into account, Diné spend less than $0.35 of every dollar on the reservation.[68] But why? For many Diné families, it can take hours to drive to the nearest border town, yet weekend drives to Gallup, Farmington, and Flagstaff have become a routine part of life on the reservation, even part of Diné culture. Part of the explanation can be found in the same report, in a chart that describes the status of the Navajo Nation's undeveloped commercial tracts. The smallest local unit of the Navajo Nation is the chapter, but the tribe is also divided into six agencies, each encompassing multiple chapters. The Western Agency consists of 18 chapters and has a total of 2,359,122 acres, or roughly 3,686 square miles,[69] and includes within its boundaries two of the larger reservation cities, Kayenta and Tuba City. Yet, across the agency, project after project either "needs funding for infrastructure" or "needs [to either submit or finalize various] plans."[70] The chart is remarkable in several respects. It highlights how the combination of inadequate infrastructure and tribal red tape can harm economic growth. Even more remarkable is that the Navajo Nation's central government directly handles every proposed development project. True, the township model allows Kayenta a partial exit from Window Rock's control, but all commercial and light industrial development proposals for the rest of the reservation must pass through the Window Rock bureaucracy.

Window Rock serves as both the regulator and landlord for most of the reservation's industrial parks and commercial real estate developments. The Navajo Nation

Division of Economic Development manages the tribe's 11 industrial parks, which range in size from 20 acres to 320 acres, and provides a listing of the units available for incoming tenants.[71] Navajo Nation Shopping Centers, Inc. (NNSC) owns and operates ten grocery-anchored outdoor shopping centers (akin to strip malls, with small shops such as "Pizza Edge" and "Sonic," as well as laundromats and cell phone stores, aligned next to a large grocery store) across the reservation.[72] Along with the local school, these shopping centers are often the center of community life in their town. Though some trading posts are still operational, these shopping centers have largely taken their place.[73] NNSC separated from direct tribal control and now operates as an independent tribal enterprise, which means that while it still works for the benefit of the tribe, it is protected from political interference by virtue of its designation.[74]

The shopping centers that dot the Navajo Nation today grew out of a highly successful partnership between the tribe and a relatively small grocery store chain, Bashas'.[75] "By 1976," according to Professor Susan Carder's excellent history, "a system of trade that had been in place for more than one hundred years was now in ruin. Fewer than fifty posts remained offering some basic goods. For the most part, the Navajo people were left with limited options: a convenience store or a trip off the reservation to Fed Mart or later, Wal-Mart."[76] In 1979, a Navajo Nation delegation met with the management of three larger grocery chains, including Safeway, but failed to secure an anchor grocery store for a shopping center the tribe hoped to build in Chinle, a city particularly removed from off-reservation towns.[77] The delegation then met with "Edward (Eddie) Basha, Jr. owner of the unknown Bashas' Markets," and, according to one of the Navajo negotiators, when the Navajo delegation started setting up their presentation, Basha, Jr. "told us to put that (expletive) away. He said he had been waiting for us, and was ready to build a grocery store for the Navajo people."[78] The Tséyi Shopping Center is not managed by NNSC, which the Navajo Nation did not create until 1983,[79] but instead by Dineh Cooperatives, Inc. (DCI), a nonprofit formed in 1971 as a co-op that morphed into a community development corporation (CDC) in order to secure federal grant money. A $2 million grant from the Community Services Administration and an additional $1 million from HUD provided the initial funding for Tséyi Shopping Center.[80] Without a grocery store agreeing to operate out of the shopping center, Tséyi Shopping Center would not be able to deliver the services to the community that it was designed for, nor would it have ever gotten off the ground.[81]

Today, Bashas' is part of reservation life because the chain has been deliberate about weaving itself into the community. The initial lease provided that the tribe had a right to 25 percent of the store's profits and that 95 percent – with a goal of 100 percent within five years – of employees would be Diné.[82] Bashas' did not simply transplant a store from Phoenix and plop it down on the reservation; instead, the stores are tailored to meet Diné-specific needs. Parking spaces are extra-wide because many shoppers drive pickup trucks, the stores "stock more mutton than beef," and, as the Chinle store director asked, "Where else would you find fifty-pound sacks of Bluebird flour?"[83] In 2015, when Professor Carder published her research, only five of the 355 full-time-equivalent employees were non-Navajo, and all the store directors were Diné women.[84] According to Johnny Basha, when he was named director of real estate for the chain, Eddie Basha, Jr. told him "to always conduct myself as a guest on the Navajo Nation and realize that it is a privilege for us to serve the Navajo people. Second, if I perceive a cultural barrier in my work on the Navajo [reservation], I must always remember the cultural barrier is mine to overcome, not the Navajo's."[85] There is something incredibly beautiful about the self-awareness and humility of such advice, especially coming from the then-CEO of the reservation's most successful retail enterprise.

For non-Indians unfamiliar with the reservation, it can be hard to appreciate the importance of a grocery store. Bashas' significance reflects, in part, the extent to which commercial development is truncated on the reservation. A glaring example of the failure of non-Indians to understand what life is like on the reservation came in 2001, when the US Supreme Court held that the Navajo Nation could not impose a hotel occupancy tax on Cameron Trading Post, a combined trading post/hotel located in Cameron, Arizona.[86] The hotel sits on an island of fee land within the reservation at the intersection of one road that leads to the south rim of the Grand Canyon and another that connects Flagstaff, Arizona with Lake Powell, Monument Valley, and other sites to the northeast. Chief Justice Rehnquist, writing for the unanimous Court, held that the tribe's hotel occupancy tax did not fit into either of the *Montana* exceptions and, therefore, the tribe could not impose the tax on the hotel. The first *Montana* exception provides that a "tribe may regulate, through taxation, licensing, or other means, the activities of nonmembers who enter consensual relationships with the tribe or its members, through commercial dealings, contracts, leases, or other arrangements."[87] The second *Montana* exception provides that a "tribe may ... exercise civil authority over the conduct of non-Indians on fee lands within its reservation when that conduct threatens or has some direct effect on the political integrity, the economic security, or the health or welfare of the tribe."[88] The Court held that the Navajo Nation "failed to establish that the hotel occupancy tax is commensurately related to any consensual relationship with petitioner or is necessary to vindicate the Navajo Nation's political integrity."[89]

From an outsider's perspective, this holding makes sense: this is a case about just a single hotel in an area the size of West Virginia. Yes, part of the attraction of staying at Cameron is the "overwhelming Indian character" of the hotel and the area,[90] but the main attraction for more tourists staying at the hotel is likely the Grand Canyon. No wonder not a single justice rose to the defense of the tax. But what all nine justices failed to appreciate is the relationships involved in operating a business of this sort on the reservation and the importance of such a business to the tribe. The hotel not only had a large Diné workforce but also relied on Navajo Nation government services. Even though the hotel is located on fee land, for most visitors to the area, it is part of the Navajo Nation, an impression the hotel/trading post promoted through its product choices and overall design. Moreover, the hotel does have a direct effect on the tribe. When a restaurant or hotel goes through a remodel or closes in an off-reservation city, local residents may not even notice. There are plenty of alternatives and no area is defined by a single retail business, much less by a modest hotel and trading post. But for remote parts of the Navajo Nation, that just is not true. For Diné living in the area, the hotel/trading post is the center of life in that part of the reservation. Though *Atkinson* has been relegated to a minor status in Indian law textbooks, the case highlights the Justices' profound ignorance of what life is like on the Navajo Nation. Just as Bashas' doubles as a grocery store and an integral part of Diné life, so, too, Cameron Trading Post is much more than it appears in the pages of the Court's opinion.

But why are there so few retail businesses on the reservation? Part of the explanation comes, of course, from the overall weakness of the reservation economy. The significant percentage of the population that is either unemployed or living below the poverty line (or both) limits the number and type of businesses that can operate successfully on the reservation. But that is only a partial explanation for the dearth of formal businesses and storefronts. Though the reservation may not be a good location to open a Tiffany's, even the poorest communities have needs *and* resources. Across America, entrepreneurs have shown that money can be made providing goods and services in poor areas that had previously been neglected. Wal-Mart remade the country through a vast network of stores catering to the bottom and middle of the market, flooding communities with relatively inexpensive goods.[91] In 2018, the chain had more than 500 billion dollars in revenue, an amount just above the total GDP of Belgium.[92] More than ninety percent of all Americans live within fifteen miles of a Wal-Mart, and Wal-Mart's website even offers a decal with the Navajo Nation seal for $4.99.[93] Yet, there is not a single Wal-Mart on the Navajo Nation. This is not to say that Navajos do not shop at Wal-Mart, only that their considerable collective spending flows to off-reservation locations. Gavin Clarkson, a former professor turned politician, noted, "[t]he largest Wal-Mart on the planet, in terms of dollar sales per square foot is in Gallup, New Mexico, on the edge of the Navajo Nation."[94] There have been efforts to bring Wal-Mart to the reservation, but according to then-Navajo Nation Vice President Ben Shelly, "lack of electrical infrastructure to sustain a Wal-Mart warehouse" forced the tribe to abandon a store planned for Chinle.[95] Wal-Mart is as controversial on the reservation as it is off the reservation. In a somewhat unusual move, the Diné Policy Institute published two position papers, one supportive of locating a store on the reservation and one opposed,[96] though ironically the author of the pro-Wal-Mart brief has since recanted.[97] The absence of Wal-Mart and other retail options means that families across the reservation have to travel for several hours to reach the nearest border town whenever they want something unavailable in the local community. A consumer preference survey conducted in 2011–12 found that over 80 percent of Navajos purchased their groceries off-reservation, with Wal-Mart the top choice for such consumers, and that 75 percent of those consumers drove at least 50 miles to do such shopping.[98]

Lack of capital, of course, plays a role. Opening a large store requires capital that off-reservation banks are often reluctant to advance for development opportunities on trust land. Inability to access credit is often given as *the* reason reservation development is stalled. Reservation land is held in joint trust by the Navajo Nation and the United States. Though the land's status protects it from alienation out of the tribe, it also means that entrepreneurs cannot put up the land as collateral, which harms their access to capital. The solutions, discussed in Chapter 7, that have been offered in the past – including alternative guarantees provided for by either the US government or the Navajo Nation – help, but they also add additional hoops for any would-be entrepreneur, as well as for their prospective off-reservation finance partners. Academics and quasi-academics have turned the reservation-access-to-capital conundrum into a cottage industry, decrying it at every turn as the cause of tribal poverty and underdevelopment. That debate is not worth revisiting here, but finding the capital to start a new business is a significant hurdle for new business ventures on the reservation.

The Navajo Nation's business site lease process can also make it challenging to start a formal business on the reservation. Just as was the case with the homesite lease process, to get a business site lease, an applicant must obtain a long series of permissions and file a seemingly endless number of forms. Below is an overview of the business site lease process created by Catapult Design,[99] a Navajo nonprofit, with help from the Navajo Nation's Western Regional Business Development Office (RBDO):

Step 1: Interview with local Regional Business Development Offices
- Review and screen your business plan with your local RBDO. The plan must show feasibility of potential success of proposed business.

Step 2: Obtain Land Withdrawal
- Consult with your local RBDO on the steps to obtaining a land withdrawal from the Navajo Land Department.

Step 3: Obtain Land Consent
- 3.1 Check with RBDO on Land Status
   - Hopi consent is also required for lands associated with the 1934 Statutory Freeze Area ("Bennett Freeze").
- 3.2 Secure customary land user's consent
   - Request a consent form from your local RBDO and then consult the Grazing Permit Representative at your Chapter. This process often varies from RBDO to RBDO.
- 3.3 Pass Chapter Resolution
   - (1) Work with your RBDO to draft a Chapter resolution. You may also need to provide proof of land consent and approval for right of way. Your RBDO can help you with both;

    (2) During a scheduled Chapter meeting, you will put forward a resolution and request clearance from the Grazing Committee to start your business;

    (3) A hearing will be scheduled to present your resolution, during which the Chapter will vote to either approve or deny your proposed resolution.

  3.4 Fill out Business Site Lease Application
- If you[r] resolution passes, you have six months to complete and file a final business site lease application, including all clearances. If you wait more than six months, you will have to start over.

Step 4: Securing Site Clearance

  4.1 Environmental Assessment
- Your RBDO conducts the environmental assessment and submits it to the Division of Economic Development (DED) for their review.

  4.2 Appraisal Report
- This step only applies to businesses with a certain revenue and is carried out by the DED Real Estate Department . . .

  4.5 Land Survey
- A Navajo Land Department conducts a land survey to identify the legal boundaries of the business. As the business owner, you can also hire a private surveyor.

  4.6 Procurement Clearance
- Navajo Credit Services conducts a credit check.

  4.7 Certificate of Good Standing
- This step is required for Corporations or LLC/L3C businesses. Domestic businesses may request a Certificate of Good Standing from the Navajo Business Regulatory Department. Foreign businesses may request one from the Secretary of State in US state business is registered.

Step 5: Negotiating Lease Terms
- Work with your RBDO to negotiate the terms and conditions of the lease

Step 6: Final Lease Approvals
- On your behalf, your RBDO will submit Form 164 (Previously Signature Approval Sheet) to receive final lease approvals from Navajo agencies and the Office of the President.
- The chain of approval includes: 1. DED, 2. Office of the Controller, 3. Department of Justice, 4. Business Site Lease – approving committee in the DED, 5. DED Real Estate Department, 6. Office of the President.

Step 7: Ongoing Responsibilities
- After the approval of the business site lease, the following must be submitted annually to stay compliant: 1) Rent, as stated in the lease; 2) Financial statement of gross receipts; 3) Form 200 – Declaration of Interest in Lease, submitted on the 15th of May to the Navajo Tax Commission.

Though the process is divided into seven steps, the number is misleading, considering the significant subparts and roadblocks along the way. Indeed, an alternative characterization of the same process, the Navajo Nation's "Business Site Lease Application Requirement and Procedures Check List" has 56 different line items.[100] Two "steps" in the "simplified version" above are particularly fraught for would-be entrepreneurs: Step 3: Obtain Land Consent and Step 6: Final Lease Approvals. Obtaining land consent requires local chapter officials and Diné with existing land use rights to agree that a business can operate on land that most likely was previously subject to a customary use or grazing rights claim. The permission game moves from the local to the nation at step six, with final lease approvals required from seemingly every conceivable office responsible for economic development, including the Office of the President!

At each of the steps that requires permission, the prospective entrepreneur faces the possibility that their business site lease application will be denied outright, even arbitrarily, or sit in limbo for months. Direct and indirect application fees, including the cost of environmental and archeological site work, are the major barrier to the successful implementation of the Navajo Nation's Homesite Lease Regulations of 2016. Application fees should be less important, at least in theory, in the business lease context because adequately capitalized businesses should be able to cover such fees. However, delays and uncertainty weigh heavily upon would-be entrepreneurs hoping to start a business; delays can kill off even the best ideas. As a recent report from the Diné Policy Institute noted, "Business site leases are obtained through the central government, which goes through several offices, where the process for approval often stalls for months. This extremely slow application process affects financing and development, keeping many business from developing."[101] Red tape is so pervasive and all-consuming that part of a 2009 Navajo Nation Council resolution approving the business site management plan goes so far as to specify the sequence "in a two-divider folder" that lease files are to be maintained, complete with visual aid setting forth the correct order and placement for twenty-two different documents.[102]

Entrepreneurship on reservation is not monolithic even though the business site leasing process largely assumes it is. Tribal members hoping to obtain a location to operate a business must all pass through the same business site leasing process despite the tremendous range in Diné business types and sizes. It does not matter whether someone wants to open a Chic-Fil-A franchise location in Tuba City or open a small frybread stand, both ventures, at least as a formal matter, require a business site lease. Of course, things are different in practice: small businesses operate informally, without a business site lease, while larger businesses, especially those that require outside capital, go through the process. Though small businesses are not brought into the formal economy, and might, technically, be using the land in violation of Navajo law, they operate with the tacit blessing of the Navajo Nation. The tribe typically does not enforce prohibitions on operating a business out of one's home or on customary use land. Indeed, by having separate categories for homesite leases and business site leases, the tribe discourages some tribal members from pursuing a business site lease. According to the tribe's land use regulations, if the business that is operating on an approved business lease site fails, the land reverts to the Navajo Nation. Consequently, a family running a business operating out of their home that obtains permission to operate a business on their land faces the possibility of losing that land precisely because they sought a business site lease. Paradoxically, their de facto land rights are more secure by *not* seeking a business site lease. Moreover, the tribe's regulations do not envision mixed use development, which means that obtaining a business lease requires tribal member entrepreneurs live elsewhere. Diné entrepreneurs therefore face a choice between a homesite and a business lease.

Imagine an auto mechanic, Darren Yazzie, who has built a good reputation repairing cars directly in front of his hogan. In time, Yazzie may want to expand his business, predicting that he can make more money if he replaces the hole dug into the ground with a proper car lift under a protective roof. Yazzie realizes that to cover the costs of such improvements he will need to relocate the business from its current location at the end of a dirt road to a spot along the paved road near the local trading post. Besides, he does not want to risk his home. The community would also benefit: Yazzie could service more vehicles and take on some of the work that people currently take to off-reservation shops. But precisely because Yazzie wants to build his new shop on land that has not traditionally been his, the application will predictably generate more community debate and resistance from neighbors who feel such business development comes at the expense of their traditional rights over the plot of land along the paved road. Yazzie is caught in a catch-22. Formalizing his business at its original location is likely to be less controversial at the chapter level, but Window Rock would force him to give up some of his land rights at his homestead should the business lease application be approved. If Yazzie is particularly ambitious and has the capital necessary to wait out the business site lease process, he might eventually be able to build at a new location, but not until after the wait and uncertainty have exacted a financial and emotional toll.

Perhaps the difficulties in obtaining a business site lease are simply a natural consequence of the trust status of the land. Superficial comparisons of border town development versus the absence of retail businesses on reservation seem to provide empirical support for this view. Trust status complications provide the Navajo Nation with convenient excuses for underdevelopment and an ability to deflect blame toward the US government. As an explanation, however, such a view fails to recognize both the power the tribe has to set the terms for use of reservation land and the potential that regulatory reform in the land use context has to create economic opportunity within the Navajo Nation. This is not to deny that trust status complicates and suppresses development, it only serves to highlight that there is space for a more assertive and proactive land policy on the part of the Navajo Nation. As the self-determination era matured, the federal government, through legislation as well as agency practice, progressively removed itself from day-to-day supervision of the reservation. Regulation has been devolved, or returned, to the Navajo Nation. So far, the tribe has been reluctant to embrace its full authority, preferring instead various half measures that attempt to bring the informal market in from the cold without radically altering the relationship between tribal members and the tribal government.

Examples of these half measures abound. In Window Rock, for example, the tribe built small permanent structures designed so that vendors can have a permanent base from which to sell food. For Diné families who previously sold their frybread or burritos from the back of a truck or perhaps a small trailer, these structures offered limited recognition by the tribe of their rights to the space that they had previously just occupied. But there was no displacement involved. By the time that the Navajo Nation decided to beautify and formalize this area, the vendors and their use of space already enjoyed the support and acceptance of the capital region's office workers and community members. A similar story, albeit one still in progress, can be told of the Navajo Nation's relationship with the flea markets that dot the reservation. Part of Diné life for decades, flea markets provide supplemental income to vendors and offer consumers a place to buy food, traditional medicine, clothing, jewelry, and other goods.[103] Through a combination of carrots (infrastructure upgrades such as electrical connections and signage) and sticks (enforcement against vendors who operate elsewhere) the Navajo Nation and individual chapters have sought to channel existing informal markets into regulated flea markets. Vendors, who may not be able to afford a permanent business location or the expense of the business site lease process, can operate at a flea market for a relatively low fee.[104] Taking a more proactive role when it comes to industrial development, the Navajo Nation manages eight industrial sites, areas where permissions and utilities are already in place.[105] The sites – located in or near Chinle, Fort Defiance, Leupp, Church Rock, Gallup, Shiprock, Farmington, and Navajo, NM – are a mix of legacy sites, places with a history of industrial development and undeveloped land.[106] The process to obtain a lease in one of these industrial parks is relatively easy compared to the homesite lease and business site lease processes.[107] Prospective lessees do not need to go through the land withdrawal process, which means they do not need permission from the local chapter nor from many of the administrative offices in Window Rock, though sign-off by the BIA area director is required.[108] Yet, even with this simplified process, most of the tribe's industrial acreage in these parks remains vacant, unable to attract tenants. At various points, the Navajo Nation has experimented with industrial subsidies as a way of enticing particular companies to locate on the reservation. Even as the tribe molded itself to wave after wave of extractive industry (most recently coal mining), small- to medium-scale industries such as light manufacturing largely bypassed the Navajo Nation.

What fixed food stands, designated areas for flea markets, industrial parks, and reservation shopping centers have in common is that they are products of the central government. Window Rock acts as promoter, owner, landlord, and regulator, all in one. One could look at these sites and conclude that the Navajo Nation is doing all that it can, that would-be entrepreneurs have all the space they need. Not only can commercial enterprises operate on the tribe's industrial parks – the Shiprock Business/Commercial Park includes an office building, a structural steel company, a hardware store, and a Subway restaurant[109] – but each region's business development office maintains a list of available business sites.[110] These are sites, like those in the industrial parks, which have already gone through the land withdrawal process, meaning these sites are not subject to conflicting grazing or customary use claims. Driving past these sites, one might not recognize them as business sites, for many appear to be little more than dirt, sand, and weeds. Nevertheless, the tribe is seeking applicants to fill these sites. If there were pent up demand for business sites, one might expect these sites to be snatched up across the reservation. It is noteworthy, however, that the Fort Defiance regional office, which includes the greater Window Rock area (perhaps the most desirable area) does not have available sites.[111] Nevertheless, an argument can be made that the Navajo Nation is doing all that it can to make land available to would-be entrepreneurs. The problem with this perspective is that it mistakenly assumes that the availability of land controlled by Window Rock is the same as land use regulation that creates an environment conducive to business development. Starting a new venture is inherently risky. For Diné entrepreneurs and families interested in forming their own business, such risk is often personal because outside capital is hard to come by. There are no easy answers, but moving from a permission-based system to a rights-based system of business development could help.

10.3 FORWARD THROUGH LOCAL EXPERIMENTATION

The biggest barrier to effective use of NAHASDA funds and to business development is not the land's trust status but the inaccessibility of that land. Part of the LGA-certification process, discussed in the previous chapter, is the creation of a community land use plan (CLUP). Certified chapters can using zoning and eminent domain authority to create areas set aside for NHA use and other areas where Diné would have a presumptive right to open new businesses. That zoning is not the norm and that grazing rights holders continue to enjoy a de facto veto right over proposed developments at the chapter level is more a function of politics than of legal authority. Lack of political will, not lack of power, is why the Navajo Nation does not have zoning.[112] The lone exception, Kayenta Township, demonstrates that zoning on the reservation is possible and that zoning can help growth. Zoning differs from a list of available business sites or spaces in an industrial park because it establishes presumptive rights thereby reducing the uncertainty that currently undermines development proposals.[113]

There are downsides to zoning. Certainty about what is permitted typically comes at the expense of equal certainty regarding what has been prohibited, which can be experienced as a loss by land rights holders facing new limitations on what they are allowed to do with their land. And zoning creates mismatches between rights holders of particular parcels and the ideal users of that same land. Some zones are likely going to be more valuable. For example, two Diné families with adjoining rights to land based on grazing, the Begays and Chees, might find themselves in different financial situations if one area is zoned for business and the other for continued grazing. If zoning results in the Begay family, but not the Chee family, having a right to use their land for business purposes, the Begays might experience a windfall, especially if the regulations permit the transfer of land rights among tribal members. Indeed, without a right to transfer land between tribal members, zoning regimes may fall apart or be of limited utility. Zoning and transferability, however, need not take the form they do off-reservation. The tribe could decide to spread the gains and losses associated with zoning across the population rather than concentrating them upon families based on their traditional use areas. Off-reservation, rezonings typically benefit particular landowners, even though the value created by such rezoning is largely a function of government action. The Navajo Nation need not have the same approach: a local chapter could, for example, use its eminent domain authority to create business zones, compensating displaced land rights holders for their loss of grazing land.

The idea here is not that there is a single right way that chapters and the Navajo Nation should assert their eminent domain and zoning powers to create opportunity for economic development, only that they should be more assertive and proactive with these powers. Given the extent to which land dispossession and changes in land rights, especially during the livestock reduction period, are part of the history of oppression of Diné by the United States government, it is not surprising that the Navajo Nation has been reticent about upsetting the expectations tribal members have regarding their land. But reticence has become neglect. Overprotection of the interests of customary use and grazing rights holders harms other members of the tribe. Reluctance by chapter officials and by the Navajo Nation central government to challenge the status quo ultimately serves neither the families with existing rights nor the tribe as a whole. Righting the ship cannot be done overnight, nor perhaps can it be done by the central government. Federal recognition of the tribe's powers of self-determination, coupled with devolution of significant land use authority from

Window Rock to LGA-certified chapters, means that today's Navajo Nation is well-positioned to see what can be achieved through local experimentation and competition across chapters.

Not all chapters will agree that they need to free up land to site new public housing or businesses, nor will all chapters succeed in challenging the political dominance of grazing interests. But some chapters, likely through the dedication and political charisma of select politicians and advocates, likely can break through the logjams. Chapters where things work – where business site leases can get past the chapter approval stage and where the chapter can come together to find land upon which to locate other community projects – should get rewarded when Window Rock considers alternative development proposals. There is need for public housing and business development across the whole reservation; the Navajo Nation is not yet in a position to have areas where development should be constrained. It would, of course, be problematic if local experimentation and competition ended up favoring the greater Window Rock area, which enjoys a comparative advantage in terms of human capital, to the exclusion of the rest of the reservation. Kayenta Township's independence as well as Shonto's place as the first chapter to achieve LGA certification, however, provide reasons to believe that the rewards will not be fully captured by the area surrounding Window Rock.

To put things in concrete terms, local experimentation could provide a solution for one of the largest barriers facing NHA: approval for local land withdrawal necessary to site new public housing developments. Currently, NHA takes the lead regarding siting decisions, which means that it bears the risk and added costs associated with construction delays tied to missing approvals or inadequate infrastructure. Indeed, poor coordination between NHA and public utility providers (transportation, water, and electric) routinely leaves NHA in the awkward position of not being able to move residents into newly completed units because the units lack basic utilities. Putting chapters in the driver's seat could lower delays, and associated delay costs, on both the front and back end. Instead of having NHA select sites, or pay expensive consultants to pick sites and put together ideal development proposals that may or may not go anywhere,[114] chapters could compete with each other for NHA projects. Chapters that bring "shovel-ready" projects forward, with permissions finalized and a demonstrated community commitment to the project, would beat out proposals subject to greater uncertainty. Fairness concerns might require NHA to deviate from an approach that is truly location-neutral across the reservation. But even unequal distribution of need or utilities could be built into the completion across chapters. NHA could give chapters with greater need for new housing extra credit in their application. In order to account for utility gaps, the tribe could prioritize spending on utility improvements in currently underserved chapters or otherwise equaling out whatever competition process NHA implements. The details of the competition are less important than the move from Window Rock control to local empowerment and experimentation. Window Rock's inability to spend down hundreds of millions of dollars in federal housing assistance highlights the need for the tribe to try a new approach, especially when it comes to housing.

Compared to housing, chapter-level experimentation with regard to business development is easier politically but more challenging economically. Problems delivering Navajo housing can be partly, though not fully, smoothed out by the annual NAHASDA grant. The tribe does not have access to a dedicated funding stream for business development and, even more significant, the rural character of much of the Navajo Nation puts a natural cap on market development for many chapters. But retooling housing development so that it incorporates inter-chapter completion requires cooperation between chapter houses and NHA, as well as multiple other agencies in Window Rock. On the other hand, chapter governments can do a lot on their own to improve the business environment within the chapter without needing Window Rock's buy-in. A community that worked together to create a business district through voluntary concessions of land for the collective good or through compensating payments might be able to create the conditions for a new auto repair shop or a new restaurant. The current business site lease process requires that proposals, following local approval, obtain permission from multiple offices in Window Rock, meaning that a chapter is not able to act unilaterally. But chapters that succeed in speeding up their local process will have a competitive advantage over chapters where politics and uncertainty dominate. Chapters interested in flexing their muscles might go even further. Chapters, for example, could approve zoning rules that permit tribal members to combine homesite and business site leases, so that Diné could operate formal ventures out of or next to their homes without risking dispossession should the business fail. A chapter-initiated mixed use zoning of this sort would invite a confrontation with the land management offices in Window Rock, but openness to experimentation would likely pay dividends at both the local and national level.

Revisiting the tribe's standard operating assumption that profits and taxes from businesses flow to the national government similarly might encourage business development. It is one thing, arguably, to assert that the Navajo Nation's mineral wealth belongs to the whole tribe, and quite another for Window Rock to capture the tax value generated by a local store. The size and strength of the Navajo Nation's central government can be traced in part to the decision in the 1920s and continuing to the present to funnel extractive industry royalties and taxes to Window Rock according to the basic bargain that the tribe would provide jobs and services in return.[115] But the decline of coal is already having ripple effects on the tribe's general operating budget. The Diné should consider whether it is time for a new bargain on taxes in recognition of the role local development can play in taking up some of the slack as both extractive industry and the central government shrink. Recalibrating the distribution of benefits from development so chapters see greater benefit from zoning and from business site approvals could provide the political push needed to create an environment conducive to small-scale entrepreneurship.

Chapter-level experimentation may not work; it may be that human capital constraints and a century of channeling Diné decision-making through a centralized tribal government ultimately will doom chapter-based development solutions. If chapters do not embrace their land use powers, the same entrenched groups and interests that have historically thwarted development on the reservation as a whole will block change at the chapter level. What local experimentation offers, when coupled with a willingness by some chapters to push the boundaries of their authority, is a way out of the circle of blame and recrimination used to avoid accountability for the Navajo Nation's poverty and underdevelopment. Chapters blame Window Rock and Washington for their problems, Window Rock blames Washington and chapters, and Washington blames the Navajo Nation and sometimes the Navajo people. Though this chapter has offered a few suggestions about what could be done, what matters most is adoption of an orientation that permits and encourages local experimentation when it comes to land reform and governance. None of this is a panacea. Fixing NHA's dysfunction, clearing land for development, providing entrepreneurs with greater certainty regarding their business proposals, and adopting chapter-level zoning will not necessarily result in rapid growth. Some features of the Navajo economy are structural and highly resistant to change. Much of the reservation is rural, lacks infrastructure, and is far removed from off-reservation population centers. No matter how well organized or creative some chapters are, they likely will struggle to attract commercial and industrial development. Even "soft" cultural institutions, such as the weekend trips to off-reservation border towns, will limit the impact of local experimentation. But that does not mean local experimentation should not be tried. LGA-certification offers chapters the ability to exercise broad powers over their land. It is worth seeing what local communities can accomplish if given the right incentives and encouragement.

11

Sovereign Assertions

The Navajo Nation's interests do not end at the reservation border. As a matter of both economic development and cultural survival, the Navajo Nation must concern itself with off-reservation threats, including the competing interests and values of non-Indians. As discussed in Chapters 6–10, the Navajo Nation should improve tribal governance, reduce corruption, deal with development red tape, and support local experimentation. But internal reforms do not take place in a vacuum; the economic and cultural vitality of the tribe also depends on its ability to assert its interests beyond the reservation boundary. This chapter explores three ways that the Navajo Nation must push the physical and legal boundaries of sovereignty.

First, the Navajo Nation must protect its interest in water; without doing so, even the best internal land use policies will inevitably fail. Though securing and safe-guarding the tribe's water rights largely benefits on-reservation users of water, a full assertion of the water rights theoretically held by the Navajo Nation would have a tremendous external impact, particularly on development in Arizona, California, and New Mexico. For the Navajo Nation, water truly is life. As Professor Robert Anderson, the foremost scholar on Indian water law, notes, "In the arid West, the right to use land without a right to use water is nearly valueless."[1] Non-Indian use (and overuse) threatens to undermine Diné rights to water, both as a legal and practical matter.

Second, the Navajo Nation must continue to protect its citizens from industrial and commercial harms originating in adjacent or nearby lands not controlled by the tribe. Uranium mining, fracking, and industrial pollution have significant effects on the Navajo Nation even when companies operate on off-reservation land not subject to tribal regulation. The tribe is not powerless, however, and in some circumstances can assert its authority to counter adverse off-reservation land use proposals. Indeed, Diné have used soft power to oppose the amorphous – compared to quantifiable environmental degradation – harm of border town racial and economic discrimination.

Third, the Navajo Nation and nongovernmental Diné organizations must continue to push back against non-Indian land uses or policies off-reservation that
threaten areas of particular cultural importance. Though the Diné succeeded in
securing a right to return to their homeland within the four sacred mountains
through the 1868 Treaty of Bosque Redondo, the current reservation does not
include all the land and territory that the Diné hold sacred.[2] Over the last decade,
in addition to standing with other tribes in protesting the Dakota Access Pipeline,
Diné fought against the desecration of one of their sacred mountains, the San
Francisco Peaks. Diné urged the federal government to protect the sacred land in
southern Utah from development, which was designated by President Obama as
Bears Ears National Monument in 2016. Often acting alongside other tribes, the
Navajo Nation's effort to protect sacred sites is something that non-Indians and non-
Indian courts have trouble fully understanding, yet the outcome of these efforts is
critical to Diné cultural survival.

Diné water rights, conflicting neighboring land uses, and sacred sites could each
fill entire chapters or even books, but are discussed here together because collectively they show how the Navajo Nation is reaching beyond its borders to protect
Diné interests. Not all these efforts have been successful. The inability of tribal
members to access reliable water should be a national embarrassment for the United
States. Companies continue to exploit the fee status of land next to the reservation to
move forward with environmentally harmful projects. And the staunch protection of
non-Indian religious traditions, in contrast with indifference to Indian sacred sites,
can only be explained by ethnocentricity and religious intolerance. Regardless, the
interests of the Navajo Nation and of Diné advocates, who at times support and at
times oppose actions by the Navajo Nation government, extend well beyond the
reservation and have significant impacts on the often conflicting land use plans of
non-Indian communities. Reflecting both ambition and the interconnectedness of
non-Indian and Indian claims, Diné are expanding de facto sovereignty by demanding that non-Indians recognize rights that extend well beyond the reservation line.

11.1 WATER RIGHTS

On July 5, 2012, following months of intense pressure from Diné activists opposed to
the deal, the Navajo Nation Council rejected the Navajo-Hopi Little Colorado
River Settlement (NHLCRS).[3] Senator Jon Kyl characterized the proposed settlement as a "birthday gift" to Arizona when he introduced the NHLCRS legislation on
the 100th anniversary of Arizona's statehood.[4] For a while, it looked like NHLCRS
would get finalized. Senator Kyl and the late Senator John McCain traveled to Tuba
City in April 2012 to rally support for the settlement.[5] Navajo Nation President Ben
Shelly and Stanley Pollack, the lawyer responsible for negotiating on behalf of the
tribe, argued that NHLCRS was a good deal for the Diné and for the Navajo
Nation.[6] Yet, as the *Arizona Republic* noted in May 2012, within months of its

introduction, opposition "swelled."[7] Diné activists, rallying around the slogan that "water is life," argued that NHLCRS was "a geopolitical giveaway to Arizona and the city of Phoenix."[8] Joining ordinary tribal members were former tribal leaders. Peter MacDonald, who still enjoyed considerable political power following his release from prison, "used an analogy of a thief stealing sheep and then trying to sell them back to you for a profit."[9] In this instance, with its "No" vote, the Council listened to the voices of protesters who "intuitively knew that the Navajo Nation was getting a bad deal."[10] As Professor Andrew Curley explains, "Through mobilization around a collective right to water and a sense of impending injustice, the Diné people defeated the proposed settlement agreement."[11]

But what exactly was defeated? One answer is the NHLCRS, which followed the standard pattern of tribal water settlements: Indians are given money to build water infrastructure and non-Indians receive disclaimers from tribes of a portion of their otherwise unquantified water rights.[12] According to the Senate legislation that would have implemented the NHLCRS, the agreement

> settles the water rights claims of the Navajo Nation, allotees of the Navajo Nation, the Hopi Tribe, and allotees of the Hopi Tribe by providing drinking water infrastructure to the Navajo Nation and the Hopi Tribe in exchange for limiting the legal exposure and litigation expenses of the United States, the States of Arizona and Nevada, and agricultural, municipal, and industrial water users in the States of Arizona, Nevada, and California.[13]

Both sides of this deal had reasons to support it. The Navajo Nation and the Hopi Tribe have a desperate need for water infrastructure and non-Indians face tremendous uncertainty connected with possible Indian water rights claims. NHLCRS, therefore, represented an accommodation by both sides, an awareness that Indians and non-Indians alike have something to gain through negotiated settlement of these claims.[14]

In theory, the Navajo Nation has a right to a tremendous amount of the water flowing through the Colorado River and its tributaries. In 1908, the US Supreme Court handed down its decision in *Winters v. United States*, coming down strongly in support of Indian water rights.[15] The dispute in *Winters* was whether an upstream user of water from the Milk River in Montana had superior rights to Indians living on the downstream Fort Belknap Reservation.[16] Like most western states, Montana bases water rights recognition on prior appropriation. While water rights in eastern states are tied to riparian rights, meaning rights associated with having land next to a river or waterway, in the arid west, a different system developed. Prior appropriation means that whoever first puts water to productive use gets rights to that water.[17] So if one person starts diverting water from a river for irrigation in 1902 and another person (upstream or downstream) diverts water from the same waterway in 1903, in years without enough water for both users, the person who first diverted the water gets priority. Under prior appropriation, timing of use determines who gets water in a drought and who is left high and dry. The United States, acting in its trust capacity, sued Henry Winter (whose name was misspelled Winters) on behalf of the Gros Ventres and Assiniboines living on the Fort Belknap Reservation, arguing that Winter's upstream use of water was thwarting the very purpose for which the reservation was established in 1888. The Court agreed, after first observing, "It was the policy of the government, it was the desire of the Indians, to change those habits and to become a pastoral and civilized people. If they should become such, the original tract was too extensive; but a smaller tract would be inadequate without a change of conditions. The lands were arid, and, without irrigation, were practically valueless."[18] Though the 1888 Treaty did not mention water rights, the Court reasoned that the Indians did not give up the one thing, water, which would make their smaller reservation habitable.[19] According to the holding in *Winters*, the 1888 treaty amounted to a reservation of adequate water to support the purposes of the reservation, effective as of the date of the treaty. The Court added that according to the canons of construction applied to Indian treaties, any "ambiguities occurring will be resolved from the standpoint of the Indians" and rejected the argument that Montana statehood took away these water rights.[20] *Winters* was a huge victory for tribes and continues to be the basis for tribes' ability to assert *Winters* rights or Indian "reserved" water rights.

It would be more than half a century after *Winters* before the US Supreme Court would once again wade into the complications of Indian water rights. In 1963, the US Supreme Court issued its holding *Arizona* v. *California*,[21] a landmark case "dealing primarily with the division of the water in the Colorado River among the affected upper and lower basin states."[22] But the Special Master (an outside expert selected to advise courts on complicated topics) tasked with sorting out the competing state claims to the river did not ignore Indian water rights. As the Supreme Court explained in *Arizona*, "[the Special Master] found that the water was intended to satisfy the future as well as the present needs of the Indian Reservations and ruled that enough water was reserved to irrigate all the practically irrigable acreage on the reservations."[23] The Court agreed, and with that, "practically irrigable acreage" (PIA), the amount of water needed to irrigate the land that could practically be farmed on each reservation, became the default standard for determining Indian water rights.[24] Or it did so at least in theory. Under *Winters* and *Arizona*, Indian reserved water rights "had priority over the rights of most white settlers in the American West," yet, in practice, "Indians found it hard to actually obtain the water to which they had legal claim."[25]

For more than a century, Western states and the US Bureau of Reclamation have largely ignored Indian water rights, preferring to facilitate non-Indian development. Western cities, supplied by massive energy and water projects drawing upon Indian resources, grew exponentially. Politicians at the federal and state level plowed money into projects along the Colorado River, designed to ensure that cities such as Phoenix, Las Vegas, and Los Angeles had reliable supplies of cheap water.

FIGURE 11.1 "Glen Canyon Dam," by Norman Rockwell. Oil on Canvas. Glen Canyon Dam, Colorado River Storage Project, northern Arizona. 1969. Used with permission of the Bureau of Reclamation.

Though plans to build dams on both ends of the Grand Canyon were eventually scrapped,[26] Glen Canyon Dam, Hoover Dam (discussed previously in Chapter 3), and Parker Dam harness the Colorado, providing dependable power and water to non-Indians.

Fearing that water scarcity would cut off southern Arizona's growth, Arizona politicians pushed through the Central Arizona Project (CAP), a series of aqueducts and pumps that push 1.5 million acre feet of water uphill from the Colorado River, along the Arizona-California border, to south central Arizona, home of Phoenix, Tucson, and more than eighty percent of the state's population.[27] This "engineering marvel" took 20 years to build, cost more than $4 billion, and uses up to 2.8 million megawatt hours per year of energy to power its massive pumps, roughly the same amount of energy as is used by a quarter of a million homes per year.[28] As discussed in Chapter 4, CAP is closely linked with Navajo Generating Station (NGS), a coal-fired power plant located near Page and Glen Canyon Dam that provided CAP with the power it needed and that was constructed largely to provide this dedicated power. Though NGS was decommissioned at the end of 2019, the CAP pumps continue their endless operation thanks to power from other diverse sources. The impressive scale and expense of CAP, and the related growth of Tucson and Phoenix, shows what can be done to support the economic development of favored non-Indian communities. It also reflects a larger truth acknowledged by the National Water Commission in 1973:

> During most of [the period since *Winters* (1908)], the United States was pursuing a policy of encouraging the settlement of the West ... In retrospect, it can be seen that this policy was pursued with little or no regard for Indian water rights and the *Winters* doctrine. With the encouragement, or at least the cooperation, of the Secretary of the Interior – the very office entrusted with the protection of all Indian rights – many large irrigation projects were constructed on streams that flowed through or bordered Indian Reservations ... With few exceptions the projects were planned and built by the Federal Government without any attempt to define, let alone protect, prior rights that Indian tribes might have had in the waters used for the projects.[29]

Considering the inadequate amount of water that Indian nations receive, as well as the poor state of the water infrastructure on many reservations, the investments and diversion of water to benefit off-reservation development is particularly troubling.[30] This is not a case of neglect but of indifference and theft.[31]

The Navajo Nation and the Diné know they have water rights that the tribe does not currently enjoy. In an article about the NHLCRS, Professor Melanie Yazzie argues that the Navajo Nation should *"enforce* rights such as those outlined in the *Winters* Doctrine – rather than meekly pay[ing] lip service to them in political rhetoric."[32] At one point, Navajo Nation attorney Stanley Pollack estimated that the tribe had a right to more than five million acre feet of water per year from the Colorado River, more than either Arizona or California's entitlement.[33] Tellingly, "almost all of Arizona's lands within the Upper Basin [of the Colorado River] are within the boundaries of the Navajo Reservation."[34] In 2008, taking an even more aggressive stance, one based on all the land within the four sacred mountains, not just within the reservation, Peter MacDonald told a reporter, "Navajo has claim to every drop of the water that's presently being used by New Mexico, Arizona, California, Nevada, Utah, Colorado and Wyoming."[35] Even if MacDonald's claim is a bit excessive, so too is the position of non-Indians across the western United States.[36] It would be tremendously disruptive to non-Indian communities if Indian nations succeeded in converting their "paper" *Winters* Doctrine water into "wet" or actual water on their reservations. A 1978 GAO report noted that "the normal flow of most western streams has been fully appropriated," and that "[a]ssertion of the reserved rights could pose a threat to investments and economies which are dependent on the water sources in which the Federal Government and Indians have undetermined but potentially extensive rights."[37] And that was written forty years ago, when the population of the Phoenix metropolitan region was approximately a third of what it is now.[38] As Dean April Summitt warned in her history of the Colorado River, *Contested*

Waters, "Already over-allocated, future quantifications of Indian shares guarantee that someone will experience a shortage."[39]

Getting from *Winters'* imprecisely defined water rights to particularized rights to water that trump existing non-Indian uses of water is challenging. The US Supreme Court has done very little to protect those rights it recognized in *Winters*, taking on very few cases that deal with Indian water rights and saying "precious little directly on the merits" of Indian water rights' claims.[40] Instead, the Court has used an expansive reading of the McCarran Amendment, 43 U.S.C. § 666, legislation which waived the United States' immunity in order to allow state adjudication of federal water rights, as an excuse to permit state court jurisdiction over Indian water rights claims.[41] Moving Indian water rights claims from the federal court system to the state courts undermined the ability of tribes to secure water through litigation. As Professor Robert Anderson noted in a 2018 article, "While the forum should not – at least in theory – make a difference to the outcome, state courts have traditionally been hostile forums for Indian rights litigation, and that has held true for the modern water cases."[42] Tribes in Arizona, for example, know in advance that however unlikely it is that a federal court will cut off a portion of Phoenix's water, it is almost unimaginable that a state court would close the valves. The effect of recognizing state court jurisdiction is to push Indian nations to settle their water rights claims rather than risk litigation, leaving litigation as a second-rate fallback option.[43] Again, Professor Anderson explains: "Tribal rights to water are firmly established, although for any tribe, claiming such rights is [an] arduous, lengthy, and expensive process. Still, the model – one that has resulted in 32 settlements approved by Congress – has a large role for the tribes and others who rely on a common water resource."[44] Non-Indians, whose "rights are far from secure," also have reasons to prefer negotiated settlements to the uncertainty of litigation.[45] Though it is hard to imagine the Navajo Nation, for example, getting rights to all the water in the Colorado River, even a substantially lower amount could threaten the continued vitality of western cities. These dynamics are replicated across the West, leading to settlements through which Indians "trade some water for infrastructure."[46]

The proposed NHLCRS fit the standard settlement pattern. Under it, the Navajo Nation and Hopi Tribe gave up some of their water rights claims and in return were promised a relatively small amount of money to cover infrastructure costs.[47] Also built into the deal was a controversial provision that would recognize the tribe's rights to 6,411 acre feet per year of water from the San Juan River *if* the lease between the tribe and Navajo Generating Station was renewed through 2044.[48] Proponents of the deal argued that "it would guarantee water rights for the Diné people, rights that were in jeopardy of being lost if not quantified."[49] If water is thought of as a fixed, or even diminishing resource, then the more time that passes without water quantification, the more likely that Diné water rights will be reduced. Non-Indian cities continue to grow and, from a realist's perspective, it seems unlikely that courts will recognize Indian water rights that threaten non-Indian expectations. The US

Supreme Court, in a 2005 decision, *City of Sherrill* v. *Oneida Indian Nation of New York*, for example, held that Indian land rights had to give way to non-Indian expectations because too much time had passed.[50] The Court explained, "This long lapse of time, during which the Oneidas did not seek to revive their sovereign control through equitable relief in court, and the attendant dramatic changes in the character of the properties, preclude [Oneida Indian Nation] from gaining the disruptive remedy it now seeks."[51] Navajo water rights are similar. It is one thing for the Navajo Nation to claim a specific amount of water from the Colorado River and its tributaries when there is enough water to go around, it is quite another thing for the Navajo Nation to insist on its right to water that previously flowed to non-Indian cities such as Phoenix, Las Vegas, and Los Angeles. The investment in the infrastructure supporting these cities and the resulting growth in the non-Indian population means that "water rights decisions have already been made simply through the process of water development."[52] According to this view, the Navajo Nation should get what it can now, while there is still water to be had.

One way to view the defeat of NHLCRS is as a rejection, not of a single water settlement, but of the entire logic of the Winters' settlement framework. Despite the promise of infrastructure funding and "wet" water, Diné activists rallied against any surrender of the tribe's water rights. The work of three Diné scholars show the depths of opposition to water settlements generally. Andrew Curley explains, "Diné opponents of the settlement did not misunderstand western water law; they challenge[d] its legitimacy."[53] Melanie Yazzie concluded that NHLCRS "is yet another attempt by complicit parties to surrender the tribe's sovereignty to the economic interests of both outsiders and insiders who have clear contempt for a tribal legal standing that stands between them and the fulfillment of an insatiable desire for unfettered growth and territorial acquisition."[54] The defeat of NHLCRS, Yazzie argues, reflects a larger Diné frustration with powerful insiders and outsiders:

> The passionate opposition expressed by these citizens at town hall meetings, at protests that continued from the spring into the summer, and in countless posts, photographs, and links that erupted on the Internet, is the latest instance of Navajos' long-held dissatisfaction with the tribal government's history of collusion with non-Indian interests, and especially in areas related to economic development.[55]

And Benjamin Bahe Jones, in his dissertation, emphasized that understanding and negotiating water rights involve a discourse of power that prioritizes prior appropriation, a principal that clashes with the idea of "water as a public resource."[56] Jones explains:

> In essence, the Navajos are forced to appropriate discourses that enable their exclusion and de-legitimatize their cultural identities that inform the designs of their political organization as they struggle to articulate their own differences with the dominant political discourse. It is not so much that the Navajos have an unfathomable water claim in terms of their paper water rights. The challenge is

about becoming fully knowledgeable about converting their "paper water" to "wet water" and developing their expertise in the water discourse. The dominant discourses and practices continue to re-inscribe themselves thus limiting the Navajo self-determined possibilities that may incorporate their culture.[57]

The prior appropriation standard, even with *Winters* layered awkwardly on top of it,[58] forces Diné to think of water in a limited way that is based primarily on scarcity, not cooperation. The imagined Indian in *Winters* narrows Indian water rights to that necessary for irrigation and only grudgingly admits other water uses, such as maintenance of instream flows and sales of water to off-reservation buyers. The law of prior appropriation and *Winters* also inserts a degree of discursive expertise and scientific knowledge that makes water negotiations the realm of experts rather than of the Diné communities who will be directly impacted by any finalized settlement.[59]

Although the discourse of water settlements can be dry, the effect of the discourse is anything but for Indigenous communities whose water is at stake. Curley provocatively writes, "Water settlements between states and tribes are a final realization of enclosures that began at the advent of colonialization."[60] Just as Dina Gilio-Whitaker, in her book, *As Long as Grass Grows*, situates environmental degradation of Indian country as part of the larger story of colonialism, so too Curley connects water settlements to other forms of subjugation. "Although language and demeanor of water settlement discourse is different from the violence of bullets and bayonets," Curley continues, "the effects are the same – to enclose upon Indigenous lands and resources for the benefit of settler communities."[61] Holding nothing back, Curley describes *Winters* – a case ordinarily held up as a tremendous victory for tribes – as "colonial law."[62] After questioning whether water settlements actually benefit Indigenous communities, Curley calls them "part of one of the last great enclosures on the continent, the enclosure of Indigenous water resources."[63] Descriptively, Curley is right.[64] By converting unquantified Indian water rights into quantified water rights, settlements not only drastically reduce the amount of water tribes can claim but also provide non-Indian water users with certainty they would not otherwise have. In theory, the *Winters* Doctrine put Indian water rights ahead of non-Indians. Even though most of the water in the Colorado River basin has been used for the benefit of non-Indians, "the assertion of *Winters* rights by Indian tribes can act as a cloud over economic development in the West."[65] Settlement quantification solves that for non-Indians, providing them with security that Indians will not be able to convert all their paper water rights into wet water. Just as most Indian treaties read as if the US government was creating a reservation when in fact the opposite was true, Indians were giving land to the federal government in return for recognition of the limited amount of land they retained, the same is true of Indian water rights settlements. Water settlements often come with infrastructure dollars and a right to a subset of the tribe's theoretical rights under *Winters*, but non-Indians are the primary beneficiaries of these agreements. Because federal funding underpins these agreements, states and their non-Indian residents often receive the benefits of the agreements without even having to pay the infrastructure costs. In other words, the settlements are unearned windfalls to non-Indian communities, allowing people in Phoenix, Las Vegas, and Los Angeles the peace of mind that comes from not recognizing that their water rights exist, in part, because of the ongoing colonial relationship between non-Indians and the area's first inhabitants.[66]

The critiques Diné scholars have leveled at water settlements are damning and accurate, but to what purpose? What alternative is there for the Diné and for the Navajo Nation than to engage in settlement negotiations; negotiations where a positive result would still likely take the form of water quantification, infrastructure projects, and disclaimer of any additional water? As the Diné protests against NHLCRS show, "colonialism is not complete and indigenous peoples resist enclosure,"[67] but that does not necessarily mean that the Navajo Nation government is wrong to pursue negotiated settlements. The theoretical possibility that a court would award a tribe their full *Winters'* based PIA amount of water is a powerful tool to improve the negotiating position of tribes, but the US Supreme Court's disinclination to assume a lead role in such litigation and deference to state courts has weakened the bargaining strength of Indian nations. One radical alternative would be for the Navajo Nation, or Diné activists, to exercise their upstream position to divert water so it does not reach the CAP aqueduct. If done to irrigate trust land, the Navajo Nation could claim it was simply exercising its rights to water. The prior appropriation regime should accommodate this since Diné rights should have a priority date of time immemorial. Even if Diné water rights are understood solely in terms of the *Winters* Doctrine, the tribe's water rights priority date would still be 1868, well before the exponential growth of non-Indian population centers in the West over the last century.[68] The problem with this diversion strategy, as well perhaps as with Curley's critique that settlements are a form of colonial enclosure, is that Diné water rights do not exist in a vacuum.

Non-Indian government bodies, including courts, are unlikely to tolerate actions that could leave major off-reservation cities without the water they have come to rely upon. It might be great for the Navajo Nation if the existing prior appropriation/ *Winters* paradigm was replaced with a cooperative approach to water management that placed equal importance on tribal members and off-reservation businesses.[69] It would also be both a boon to life on the reservation and a reflection of the country's moral obligation to its fellow (Indigenous) citizens if the federal government unilaterally sponsored a massive water hookup and infrastructure program similar to what was done for poor whites in Appalachia during the New Deal under the banner of the Tennessee Valley Authority. But there is little reason to think non-Indian governments will embrace a cooperative and morality-informed relationship with the Navajo Nation.[70] Instead, politicians are likely to continue prioritizing the interests of their non-Indian constituents and, at best, paying only lip service to the rights of their Diné constituents living on the reservation.[71] Put differently, even though Diné scholars and tribal members are right to be critical of water settlements, trading away the tribe's "paper" rights for "wet" water might be the only realistic option available to tribal leaders. Insistence on justice – in this case, full and meaningful recognition of the Navajo Nation's water rights – risks the tribe being forever cut off from the water of the Colorado River basin.[72] The academic insight that water settlements are a form of enclosure is correct, but that does not mean that tribal leaders should avoid any quantification-based deal with non-Indian parties. For Indian nations in the southwestern United States and elsewhere, "climate change implicates an increasingly competitive, water-scarce environment in which it is urgent to secure tribal groundwater rights and protect groundwater sources serving tribes."[73] Securing those rights – moving beyond theoretical rights – likely will require that the Navajo Nation accept the need to compromise in ways not acceptable to all tribal members.

11.2 NEIGHBORING FEE LAND

Like other governments, the Navajo Nation recognizes the negative impact that development beyond its borders can have on tribal members and on its territory. When a company or locality seeks to engage in harmful activities near the reservation, the Navajo Nation sometimes asserts its interests even though the location is not technically under the tribe's regulatory jurisdiction. The same is true after the fact: when the Navajo Nation becomes aware of harms to tribal members or other interests of the tribe from existing off-reservation activities, the Navajo Nation occasionally takes it upon itself to extend its influence beyond the reservation border. Federal Indian law and environmental law recognizes that Indian nations should be able to regulate some activities occurring on neighboring fee land. In *Brendale v. Confederated Tribes and Bands of the Yakima Indian Nation*, a divided US Supreme Court affirmed the power of tribes to regulate activities on fee land located within the reservation, provided that the part of the reservation being regulated was still primarily Indian.[74] Going a step further, the US Environmental Protection Agency (EPA), as part of an agency commitment to working with tribes on a government-to-government basis, permits Indian nations to carry out federal environmental programs, treating tribes as states for the purposes of setting environmental policy.[75] Treatment as a state famously allowed a small tribe to impose its water quality standards on the city of Albuquerque.[76] Never mind the trust or fee status of the land, under ordinary principles of trespass and nuisance, landowners typically have the right to prevent neighbors using land in a way that harms them. Accordingly, the Navajo Nation, as a co-trustee of reservation land, has a property right to block harmful forms of development that have spillover effects on neighboring reservation land. But even though there is some legal support that the Navajo Nation can draw upon when it takes a stand against an off-reservation activity, its authority is much weaker than if the proposed activity were to take place on the reservation. This section looks at three examples – uranium mining, water pollution from a gold mine, and border town discrimination – where the Navajo Nation has sought to protect itself and tribal members from dangers originating just beyond the edges of the reservation.

11.2.1 *Uranium Mining*

Not all of the tribe's efforts have been successful. The market for uranium cooled in the 1980s, and by 1986, companies left the Navajo reservation. In 2005, the Navajo Nation banned uranium mining on tribal land and "on any sites within the Navajo Indian Country" as defined by both Navajo law and federal law.[77] The tribe was reacting to renewed federal and industrial interest in nuclear energy and took this stance despite possessing "25% of the recoverable uranium in the country."[78] In this century, uranium is recovering from the price slump associated with relative over-supply during the Cold War. The value of uranium reflects a number of competing factors: global awareness that carbon-based energy production contributes to climate change; attention to the risk that natural disasters (such as the Fukushima, Japan tsunami) pose to nuclear power plants; and the relative cost of solar and wind energy. When the price of yellowcake rises, mining companies become increasingly interested in exploiting the large supply of uranium on or near the Navajo Nation, ban or no ban.

Through a series of cases, Hydro Resources, Inc. (HRI), a subsidiary of Uranium Resources, Inc. (which changed its name to WestWater Resources, Inc. in 2017), won the right to mine uranium on land in the eastern checkerboard of the Navajo Nation.[79] HRI's position was that the Navajo uranium ban applied only to reservation land. HRI owns 183,000 acres of land in northwestern New Mexico, including one particularly important site in the Church Rock Chapter of the Navajo Nation, which "holds more uranium than any other site" owned by HRI.[80] In fact, the two HRI parcels in the Church Rock checkerboard area – areas with a mix of tribal and nontribal land – are estimated to contain 7.8 tons of uranium.[81] Though the Navajo Nation continues to suffer from health and environmental problems associated with past uranium mining on the reservation, HRI argued that it can mine uranium in the checkerboard area so long as the company had an ownership interest in the land it wanted to mine. And in 2010, the Tenth Circuit Court of Appeals agreed, ruling that the Navajo Nation did not have the authority to regulate checkerboard land owned by HRI.[82] The holding, as well as a related decision upholding HRI's source materials license,[83] cleared the way for HRI's proposed in situ leaching operation. In situ leaching involves injecting a chemical into the underground water aquifer to free up uranium, which is then pumped to the surface.[84] While in situ leaching is the standard way of mining uranium today, restoring groundwater resources after mining operations cease takes decades (if such restoration is attempted at all).

In a bid to block the mine, the Navajo Nation and the EPA argued that the mine, though located on fee land owned by HRI, sat in a "dependent Indian community" and therefore was subject to the laws of the Navajo Nation. "Indian country" includes:

(a) all land within the limits of any Indian reservation under the jurisdiction of the United States government, notwithstanding the issuance of any patent, and, including rights-of-way running through the reservation, (b) all dependent Indian communities within the borders of the United States whether within the original or subsequently acquired territory thereof, and whether within or without the limits of a state and (c) all Indian allotments, the Indian titles to which have not been extinguished, including rights-of-way running through the same.[85]

The Navajo Nation, together with the EPA, argued that though the land was not tribal trust land and therefore did not fit into part (a), it was a dependent Indian community under part (b). Indeed, the Navajo Nation's definition of Navajo Indian Country, which includes land in satellite Navajo communities, arguably reaches even further, or is at least more specific, than the federal definition of Indian country.[86] The Church Rock population is almost entirely Navajo and outsiders would probably assume that the area was located on the reservation. Indeed, "eighty-eight percent of the land surrounding HRI's parcel is owned by the Tribe, tribal members or held in trust for the Tribe."[87] Additionally, the Church Rock population is 97 percent Navajo.[88] From the tribe's perspective, HRI was simply engaged in an end-run around the Navajo ban and Diné would still suffer the associated environmental and health harms. Tribal members, predictably, would be the ones who would extract the uranium and suffer the consequences of such proximity.[89] The Navajo Nation had enough experience to doubt that uranium mining would create lasting economic opportunities and knew that the proposed operation would once again scar the land around Church Rock, which already has "some of the largest piles of radioactive tailings in the world."[90] The 10th Circuit's holdings, by focusing only on the nature of the land title held by non-Indians, eviscerated the dependent Indian community subcategory in the definition of Indian country.[91] The federal circuit court gave HRI the green light.

Not all Diné agree with the Navajo Nation's anti-uranium mining position. In 2013, the Church Rock Chapter passed a resolution in support of HRI, citing the company's commitment to hiring 70 percent of the mine's workforce from the local community and the company's projection that $35 million would flow into the local area.[92] The Navajo Nation ban, in place since 2005, turns away companies interested in establishing mines on the reservation, even when they promise jobs and lucrative royalty payments. But the tribe's authority to reject these extractive industries located in checkerboard areas is limited. WestWater, Inc., has not yet begun extracting uranium from its Church Rock sites, but the pieces are in place. The mine is on hold for the moment as the company "await[s] a sustained improvement in the uranium price."[93] Unfortunately, as the HRI litigation highlights, the Navajo Nation often cannot fully protect itself from the harms of mining even when it takes a strong stance.

11.2.2 *Gold King Mine Spill*

A major pollution incident at the Gold King Mine in 2015 provided the Navajo Nation with another reminder that the Navajo Nation is vulnerable to mining harms even when the mine is located off-reservation. First staked out by Olaf Arvid Nelson in 1887, the Gold King Mine around the turn of the century employed hundreds of people and extracted millions of dollars in minerals from the side of a mountain near Silverton, Colorado.[94] But by August 5, 2015, the date of the mine spill, the mine had long since stopped operating. A company doing contract work for the EPA, and under the direction of EPA officials, accidentally removed a "plug" at a mine entrance and "inadvertently triggered a release of 3 million gallons of acidic, mine-influenced waters."[95] As the *Denver Post* reported, the leak "sent a yellow-orange plume of pollution" down Cement Creek and into the Animas River and the San Juan River.[96] It took weeks for the Animas River, which became an alarming yellow-orange color, to regain its natural color.[97] Communities downstream from the mine, including parts of the Navajo Nation near Farmington, saw rising levels of "arsenic, copper, manganese, cadmium and zinc" in the water, spiking to dangerous levels near Durango, Colorado.[98] To dilute the pollutants, extra water was released from Navajo Dam, upstream from where the Animas River joins the San Juan River, so that measurements in Shiprock, New Mexico showed no increase in acidity on August 10.[99] Though contested by a subsequent report issued by the EPA's Inspector General, a Department of Interior report on the mine blowout found that the EPA-directed contractors should have followed different procedures that would have prevented this large release of pollutants.[100] Part of the problem was that the EPA's on-site coordinator was on vacation the day of the spill and the interim coordinator authorized work to proceed without all the necessary equipment.[101]

The Navajo Nation reacted to the spill just like other downstream governments and private landowners did, by decrying the pollution and suing those responsible. Following the spill, "New Mexico, Utah, the [Navajo Nation] and about 300 individuals filed lawsuits seeking more than \$2 billion in damages" from the EPA.[102] The EPA contractor as well as the corporate owner of the mine were also sued.[103] One of the primary challenges the Navajo Nation faces is establishing a harm because water quality tests afterward suggest that the spill did not "result in the ecological calamity that many observers feared" initially when the water turned yellow-orange.[104] Yet, while it is tempting to see the Gold King Mine spill as a single event, more accurately it is just a dramatic moment in a stream of pollution emanating from the mine. The EPA Inspector General's report noted that prior to the August 5, 2015 mine blowout, "the Gold King already was leaking 200 gallons per minute of acid metals-laced discharge – equal to the disaster every 10 days."[105] And following the disaster, after a March 2019 major snowfall knocked out power to the plant treating mine wastewater, mine wastewater bypassed the treatment facility "at a rate of 250 to 300 gallons per minute," leading downstream users of the Animas and San Juan rivers to once again be warned to protect themselves from the pollution by limiting their water use.[106] Looking beyond this one mine highlights the scale of the problem of environmental harm associated with old mines and with any new mining operations.[107] As Professor Clifford Villa notes, thirty-three mines, including the Gold King Mine, discharge 5.4 million gallons of polluted mine water into the Animas River watershed every day.[108] In the wake of a spill event, suits might be the only option available to the Navajo Nation. But in advance of a crisis, treatment as a state might allow the tribe to better protect itself from off reservation harms; "TAS status for water quality can help tribes by facilitating both off-reservation and on-reservation enforcement."[109] Returning to the Albuquerque example mentioned previously, in that case, even though it impacted off-reservation users, the Pueblo of Isleta was allowed to set a standard for arsenic that was "1,000 times more stringent than the State of New Mexico standards."[110] Pushing tribal standards upstream, as TAS allows, can be "an extra-territorial strategy" to protect tribal interests in land and water that can be impaired by off-reservation pollution.[111]

11.2.3 *Border Town Discrimination*

The Navajo Nation's efforts to influence land use off-reservation include responding to the discrimination and abusive business practices that Diné experience in border towns. Such efforts rest on less solid legal ground than either water rights or nuisance type harms, both of which are backed by clear legal principles that support the Navajo Nation's interests. When it comes to border town discrimination and harmful practices, the tribe has little actual authority to draw upon. Just as there is relatively little that California can do to prevent Nevada from allowing businesses, even businesses situated close to the border between the two states, to sell fireworks that are not allowed to be sold in California, so too the Navajo Nation's regulatory reach is generally restricted to within the reservation. But that does not mean that the Navajo Nation does not have an interest in protecting its citizens beyond the reservation boundary. Given the lack of commercial development on the Navajo reservation and the cultural connection many Diné have with border towns, it is no wonder that the Navajo Nation has attempted to use soft power to fight back against the discrimination tribal members often encounter in Farmington, Gallup, and Flagstaff. Through investigations, lobbying, and relationship building, the Navajo Nation has pushed back on some of the abuses Diné face in border towns.

The Navajo Nation Human Rights Commission (NNHRC) in particular has attempted to use soft power to check border town mistreatment. After nearly a year of public hearings, from December 2008 to September 2009, the Commission released

Assessing Race Relations between Navajos and Non-Navajos: A Review of Border Town Race Relations.[112] The report highlighted discriminatory criminal sentences, predatory business practices, public accommodation violations, and failure to investigate suspicious deaths, among other issues.[113] The Commission recommended that the Navajo Nation "engage in serious dialogue with border town officials to ensure Navajo citizens are not discriminated against but given the same opportunities, benefits and services as non-Indians."[114] It is worth quoting at length the report's conclusion:

> We must stand firm, together and united as bila'ashdla'ii, the five fingered people and demand our existence and inherent rights be permanent, respected and equal to all other peoples of this world. This is the beginning to the end to an oppressive and subservient relationship that existed and exists between the Navajo and its non-indigenous neighbor. The human rights of the Navajo People will no longer be an impediment to change, but the impetus for change around us.[115]

This powerful conclusion gets at the heart of much of the discrimination Diné faced and still face: the idea that Diné interests must always give way to non-Indian interests. Though focused on border towns, the Commission took a broad view of both its mandate and authority. As professors Kristen Carpenter and Angela Riley observe, "The NNHRC's initial project, involving the investigation of hate crimes against Navajo people occurring in border towns, integrated tribal, domestic, and international norms."[116]

The first report on border town discrimination was published in 1975, following the murder of three Diné men in Farmington by three white male high school students engaged in "Indian rolling – the practice of abusing Navajo street inebriates."[117] Authored by the New Mexico Advisory Committee to the United States Commission on Civil Rights, the 1975 report noted that the Diné bodies had been "severely beaten, tortured, and burned."[118] After discussing the violence, the attitudes of non-Indians in Farmington, and alcohol-related problems impacting Diné and border towns, the 1975 report argued, "The reciprocity which binds Navajos to Anglos in Farmington and establishes the parameters for relationships between these two groups is oppressively unequal."[119] The Committee found "that many elected public officials in Farmington – as well as civic, business and professional leaders – have generally failed to assume a sense of active responsibility for promoting positive and productive relationships among the diverse segments of the population which they serve."[120] The report also recommended that the EEOC investigate whether private employers in Farmington and city and county governments were discriminating against Diné in hiring.[121] Thirty years later, the Committee found that relations had improved significantly on many fronts. Nevertheless, it reported that the Committee received detailed evidence "concerning predatory lending practices, payday loans, usurious interest rates, deceptive sales practices, misrepresentation, and other egregious financial arrangements."[122] The NNHRC report highlighted many of the same border town issues. The Commission, currently led by Professor Jennifer Nez Denetdale, has kept up the pressure on these border town business practices. Through hearings and distribution of know your rights documents and pamphlets, the NNHRC has worked to bring attention to ongoing challenges, such as predatory car sales practices and vehicle repossessions, the rights of inebriates, loan sharks, and violence against Native women.[123]

These are not easy issues and the Navajo Nation's ability to address them is limited because of limits on the tribe's regulatory authority. Alcohol stores catering to Diné shoppers coming from the reservation, where alcohol is prohibited, are a ubiquitous sight as one enters any of the towns bordering the Navajo Nation. Dealing with these and other harmful businesses will require cooperation with the non-Indian governments tasked with regulating them. But there is reason for hope. Cooperative agreements have been shown to work in addressing some issues, especially policing.[124] Further, non-Indian governmental interest in safety and security off-reservation at times aligns with the interest Indian nations have in protecting their citizens. In 2017, four stores in Whiteclay, Nebraska, which sits across the state line from South Dakota's Pine Ridge Reservation, were forced to stop selling alcohol when the Nebraska Supreme Court upheld the decision of the state's Liquor Control Commission not to renew the stores' liquor licenses.[125] Neither Arizona nor New Mexico has followed Nebraska's example,[126] but that does not mean that only the Navajo Nation cares how border town businesses impact tribal members visiting or living in reservation border towns. Though the Navajo Nation has little power to mandate what types of businesses off-reservation towns permit, using its soft power to call attention to abuses and discrimination can improve Diné experiences in border towns.

Even though it can sometimes feel as if the Navajo Nation is far removed from the rest of the United States, the tribe is continually forced to interact with and occasionally defend itself from its off-reservation neighbors. In some respects, tribal actions such as seeking to block locally undesirable land uses (in the case of uranium mining), suing for compensation for pollution of the tribe's resources (in the case of the Gold King Mine), or protesting discriminatory treatment of its citizens are not different in type from the actions non-Indian governments routinely engage in. But the Navajo Nation's status as a domestic dependent nation, politically both an independent sovereign and part of the larger political fabric of the United States, complicates matters. Nowhere is the tribe's complicated status as a nested sovereign put into as much relief as it is in Navajo Nation's efforts to protect Diné sacred sites, covered in the next subsection.

11.3 SACRED SITES

The Navajo Nation's interest in off-reservation development and land use extends beyond protecting the tribe from economic or environmental harms to protecting Diné cultural and spiritual resources. Indeed, sacred site protection is perhaps the most important and far-reaching type of extraterritorial claim made by the Navajo Nation. The reservation lies within the four sacred mountains but includes far less land than the Diné used and valued prior to conquest. No wonder then that the tribe has a strong interest, tied to cultural and religious survival, in protecting Diné sacred sites, even when those sites exist outside the reservation boundaries. Because non-Indians place religious significance on buildings – churches, mosques, synagogues – as opposed to nature, it is often difficult for non-Indians to appreciate the signifi-cance that a mountain or rock outcropping can have in the Diné spiritual worldview. Sacred sites vary from "discrete geological formations" to "entire landscapes," but whatever the form, "[s]acred sites are integral to the *practice* of native people's land-based religions."[127] This dissonance frequently leads to conflicts between the non-Indian inclination towards development and the Indian interest in protecting sacred sites against exploitation. All across the world, governments must navigate these competing interests. Sometimes Indigenous peoples win, as when the Australian government decided to ban climbing on Uluru or Akers Rock, in recognition of its sacred status among Aboriginal groups.[128] But as shown by the construction of the Dakota Access pipeline, despite sizeable and sustained protests by Native Americans from across the country, non-Indian development interests often triumph over the interests that Indigenous peoples have in protecting resources and sites that they consider sacred.[129]

FIGURE 11.2 "Moonrise over San Francisco Peaks" (Photo by: Christopher Reed / FOAP via Getty Images)

For the last decade, the Navajo Nation has invested considerable time and energy trying to protect off-reservation sacred sites, but with limited success. This section starts by telling the story of the tribe's unsuccessful effort to prevent the further desecration of the San Francisco Peaks, one of the four sacred mountains. It then explores the ongoing political and legal contest over Bears Ears National Monument. Sacred site claims are challenging in part because they blur the line between the Navajo Nation as a sovereign nation and Diné cultural and religious rights. If Mexico asserted, on behalf of its citizens, a right to block development on the US side of the Rio Grande, the United States and most American citizens would probably just ignore such a claim. Similarly, when the Taliban destroyed a 1,700 year old statue of Buddha in 2001, United Nations Secretary General Kofi Annan pleaded with the Taliban's foreign minister, but there was little else that could be done.[130] Diné enjoy slightly more say in what happens off-reservation because courts will at least consider their religious and cultural claims. But courts are reluctant to stray from the idea that land owners, including the federal government in the case of government land, may do what they want with their land, even if tribes object. This reluctance stems partly from the inability of non-Indians to understand the place-based spiritual beliefs of many Native peoples and partly from a fear that tribal sacred site claims could be limitless.[131] Personally, I admit, I get nervous any time a religious or ideological group wants to impose its views on others. What is sacred to you may not be sacred to me, and there must be checks on the extent to which one group's notion of the sacred can trump how another group uses their land. But, at least in the case of the Navajo Nation's efforts to protect sacred sites, the greater danger is that Diné sites will not be protected even though there would be little question about protecting similar non-Indian sites.[132] Stated differently, continued colonialism, not excessive religious protectionism, is the best way to understand the many threats facing Indigenous sacred sites that sit beyond current reservation boundaries. Accordingly, when the Navajo Nation asserts its interest in protecting those sites and natural areas that are central to Diné belief systems, it is acting to protect both the interests of tribal members and its own legitimacy as a government.

The tension between Indian interest in sacred site protection and non-Indian interest in exploiting natural resources played out dramatically in the courts in a case involving the San Francisco Peaks, one of the traditional four sacred mountains of the Diné.[133] The Peaks have spiritual significance for many tribes, not just the Diné. As Professor Justin Richland explains, "If it were possible to compare the signifi-cance of different sites in the sacred Hopi landscape (though I am quite sure one cannot, at least from a Hopi perspective), few would be more significant than *Nuvatukya'ovi*, the mountains known in English as the San Francisco Peaks."[134] But, unfortunately for the tribes who view Arizona's highest peak as sacred, the mountains, called *Dook'o'oosłííd* in Navajo, are now part of the federal government's Coconino National Forest.[135] In 2002, Snowbowl Ski Resort, which has a special use permit to use *Dook'o'oosłííd*, sought permission to expand the resort and to spray the ski areas with artificial snow.[136] Rather than use fresh water, which is in limited supply in the high desert surrounding the peaks, Snowbowl wanted to spray up to 1.5 million gallons of recycled sewage water onto the mountain as artificial snow.[137] After the Forest Service approved Snowbowl's permit, the Navajo Nation, and other tribes for whom the Peaks are sacred, sued, claiming that such use of wastewater would violate their religious rights.[138] For the tribes, this would be desecration, quite literally the spraying of feces and dead bodies unto the sacred Peaks and preventing them from accessing soils and herbs used in healing ceremonies.[139] Feces because of the use of toilet waste water and dead bodies because of run-off from funeral parlors.[140] Such treatment of a place of religious significance is, according to the plaintiffs, a substantial burden on the free exercise of religion and a violation of the Religious Freedom and Restoration Act of 1993 (RFRA).[141]

When a three-judge panel of the Ninth Circuit initially ruled in their favor in 2007, tribal advocates breathed a sigh of relief.[142] But, "[a]las, the victory was short-lived," reversed after the full Ninth Circuit panel of judges held that the harm did not meet the "special burden" on religion required by the RFFA.[143] The Ninth Circuit decision highlighted the lower court's findings that "highly variable snow-fall" had resulted in operating losses for the owners of the ski resort and that artificial snow was "needed to maintain the viability of the Snowbowl."[144] The Ninth Circuit characterized the tribal claim as being based upon "diminishment of spiritual fulfillment," which it held did not amount to RFRA's "substantial burden."[145] The court focused on the relatively small amount of land impacted – 1 percent of the Peaks – by the ski area and applied a restrictive reading of RFRA's requirements.[146] Additionally, the court found comfort in Arizona's classification of the treated sewage water that would be used as being of an A+ grade, the highest mark possible under state law, which signaled that it is suitable for irrigation of school grounds and crops.[147]

In his dissent, Judge William Fletcher noted that the Forest Service's environmental impact assessment failed to "discuss the health risks resulting from ingestion of the treated sewage effluent or the likelihood that humans – either adults or children – will in fact ingest the artificial snow."[148] Moreover, as Fletcher highlighted, the current owner of the ski resort purchased it in 1992, "with full knowledge of weather conditions in northern Arizona."[149] After an extended critique of the majority's treatment of the RFRA, Judge Fletcher concluded by highlighting the irony of the court protecting everyone's recreational interest in "public park land" to justify "spraying sewage effluent over holiest of the Indians' holy mountains," which was originally taken by force from Indians.[150] Despite the strength of the dissent[151] and the importance of the case to the tribes involved, the Supreme Court decided *against* hearing arguments on the matter.[152] Sewage effluent was not endangering the National Cathedral or a Judeo-Christian sacred site.[153] Snowbowl began making snow out of recycled waste water on December 24, 2012, Christmas Eve, but when it did so, "the snow that blasted onto the mountain was yellow."[154] The ski resort has since had to deal with the "yuck factor" of using wastewater to create snow.[155] Nevertheless, its snow guns continue to operate, alongside signs warning skiers not to eat the snow.[156] Indians have not simply resigned themselves to the desecration of San Francisco Peaks: they continue to fight against further expansion of the ski resort. The Navajo Nation, with the assistance of the University of Arizona's Indigenous Peoples Law and Policy Program, citing the "irreparable harm" the artificial snow would have on the tribe's "religious and cultural rights," brought the matter to the Inter-American Commission on Human Rights.[157] But in terms of protection of Indigenous sacred sites, when it comes to the San Francisco Peaks, the last ten years have not been good ones.

A much more promising development in terms of non-Indian appreciation of the importance of Indigenous sacred sites occurred when President Obama established the Bears Ears National Monument on December 28, 2016, in the twilight of his presidency. The Presidential Proclamation establishing the monument begins on an almost poetic note:

> Rising from the center of the southeastern Utah landscape and visible from every direction are twin buttes so distinctive that in each of the native languages of the region their name is the same: Hoon'Naqvut, Shash Jáa, Kwiyagatu Nukavachi, Ansh An Lashokdiwe, or "Bears Ears." For hundreds of generations, native peoples lived in the surrounding deep sandstone canyons, desert mesas, and meadow mountaintops, which constitute one of the densest and most significant cultural landscapes in the United States. Abundant rock art, ancient cliff dwellings, cere-monial sites, and countless other artifacts provide an extraordinary archaeological and cultural record that is important to us all, but most notably the land is profoundly sacred to many Native American tribes, including the Ute Mountain Ute Tribe, Navajo Nation, Ute Indian Tribe of the Uintah Ouray, Hopi Nation, and Zuni Tribe.[158]

The proclamation was historic not only because it protected an enormous area, 1.35 million acres or an area approximately the size of Delaware,[159] but also because the proclamation seemed to recognize the importance of sacred sites. As Professor Charles Wilkinson explains, "the tone and tenor of the Proclamation is central to its meaning. The writing is powerful and often lyrical … [It] glows with respect for tribal culture, tribal experience, tribal expertise, and tribal knowledge without ever being romantic."[160]

The Bears Ears designation did not just happen, instead it was the result of a concerted effort by tribal advocates and Indian nations. Responding to an invita-tion by Utah Senator Robert Bennett to participate in an effort by the Public Lands Initiative (PLI) to resolve disputes over use of public land in the state, Diné from Utah formed a Navajo nonprofit, Utah Diné Bikéyah (UDB), to gather information about the area.[161] As Professor Sarah Krakoff's excellent history of Bears Ears highlights, even though conservation groups supported UDB's proposal to protect

1.9 million acres of land around Bears Ears, the proposal was unlikely to advance under the PLI process because it conflicted with San Juan County's preferred use of the land: mining development.[162] The best path forward appeared to be through the White House, and "[i]n order to get this proposal off on the right track, Indian people and UDB leaders agreed that the tribes should spearhead the effort."[163] Accordingly, the Inter-Tribal Coalition (ITC) was formed in 2015, taking the reins from UDB.[164] The final ITC proposal, submitted to President Obama on October 15, 2015, noted the efforts of tribal advocates leading up to the proposal but explained, "[t]he need for protecting the Bears Ears landscape has been broad and heartfelt for well over a century."[165] Collaborative management of the protected land, with a built-in role for officers of the ITC tribes, was a central feature of proposal.[166] The Bears Ears Proclamation did not accept the proposal wholesale. It reduced the land protected from the 1.9 million acres envisioned by ITC to a final 1.35 million acres, and it modified the role of the Bears Ears Commission.[167] But it did embrace "tribal ecological knowledge in various places" and created a structure that draws upon that knowledge through the requirement that the federal government engage with the Commission.[168]

A little less than a year after President Obama's historical proclamation, President Trump released his own "Presidential Proclamation Modifying the Bears Ears National Monument."[169] Arguing that the Antiquities Act, the legal basis for presidential declarations of new national monuments, "requires that any reservation of land as part of a monument be confined to the smallest area compatible with the proper care and management of the objects of historic or scientific interest to be protected," Trump radically reduced the amount of land protected by 1.15 million acres.[170] Rather than an area the size of Delaware, the Trump administration protected an area the size of Dallas, opening much of the rest for development.[171] Even within the reduced area, the Trump administration pushed for more intensive development in terms of roads and utilities than was originally envisioned.[172] This battle between President Trump and President Obama, between development and protection, is not over yet. Immediately after President Trump's proclamation, tribes, environmental groups and others sued; those lawsuits, now combined into a single challenge, continue to advance through the courts.[173] And there is room for optimism: President Trump arguably lacked the authority to do what he did. "There is no law directly on point simply because no previous President has attempted to tear apart the national monument system, a foundation stone of American conservation law and policy."[174] Even if President Trump arguably succeeded in reducing the monument to a hollowed out version of the Bears Ears National Monument created by President Obama, much less the larger area included in the initial ITC proposal, the effort to get non-Indians to recognize the value of Indigenous sacred sites and environmental resources "has enduring lessons for how to heal human and environmental wounds, and how to conceive of those as interconnected."[175]

For Diné, protecting the sacred requires continual vigilance. And not only against non-Indian interests. Navajo Nation President Ben Shelly, for example, supported the construction of an aerial tramway that would bring tourists from cliffs on the eastern edge of the Grand Canyon down to the water's edge at the confluence of the Colorado and Little Colorado Rivers.[176] The centerpiece of the Grand Canyon Escalade project was to be the 1.6 mile long gondola ride, but the development would have also included retail space, a hotel, and an RV park.[177] Among the principals of Confluence Partners, the developer that pushed the project, was former Navajo Nation President Albert Hale.[178] Hale argued that the project would gener-ate between $50 and $90 million for the tribe annually.[179] Under the banner "Save the Confluence," Diné who would be directly affected came together to protest the project. They were joined by environmental groups from across the country who saw the project as threatening the sanctity of the Grand Canyon. "The Confluence Project would free ride on the Grand Canyon's visual and raw beauty," Professor Lynda Butler argues, "drawing many visitors to a secluded and unique natural wonder that would be forever changed."[180] Fortunately for those horrified by the proposal,[181] the Navajo Nation Council rejected the proposal by a vote of 16–2 on October 31, 2017.[182] Given that the development offered jobs and revenues, the Navajo Nation Council's decision ultimately showed the tribe's interest in protect-ing sacred sites even when there are economic costs in doing so. The extremes that the Navajo Nation will go to protect its interests in sacred sites can be seen in the tribe's 2017 purchase of the Wolf Springs Ranch and Boyer Ranch in Westcliffe, Colorado. Though Westcliffe is a six hour drive from the nearest reservation city, Shiprock, NM, the ranches sit just to the east of Blanca Peak, the Diné sacred mountain of the east, known to Diné as Tsisnaasjini' or Dawn or White Shell Mountain. In total, the tribe became the owner of nearly 29,000 acres.[183] There are little direct benefits to the tribe in owning such land so far removed from the rest of the reservation. Leases and revenue from permits issued cover the costs of maintaining the properties, but today the land serves no pecuniary purpose.[184] Such revenues do not allow the tribe to recoup the $23 million spent to purchase the properties.[185] But profit is not the point.

11.4 NATION AND PEOPLE

This chapter looked at ways the Navajo Nation pushes the physical and legal boundaries of tribal sovereignty. When the tribe asserts its right to water currently dedicated to off-reservation uses, protests uses of neighboring fee land that have spillover effects on the reservation, or pushes the federal government to protect sacred sites located beyond the reservation border, the Navajo Nation challenges the notion that Diné should only concern themselves with what happens within the reservation. Even though not all of these efforts have been successful, they do show the ways the Navajo Nation is reaching beyond its borders in order to protect Diné interests, including interests that non-Indians have a hard time fully understanding. It is tempting to push back against the tribe's off-reservation assertions. Perhaps the tribe ought to maintain a rigid line between areas where it should have authority and areas that are under the control of other governments. After all, the Navajo Nation is quick to protest whenever state or local governments claim to have a right to regulate or police activity on the reservation. Indeed, one of the principal complaints Diné have is against the constant intrusion of non-Indian interests. It might seem almost hypocritical, then, for the Navajo Nation to make demands on neighboring non-Indian governments. But why should the Navajo Nation be any different from other nations? The United States looks to protect its interests across the globe, regardless of political boundaries. The same is true of states and counties. Lines on a map can make it harder for a government to successfully promote the interests of its citizens, but they rarely stop governments from attempting to do so. Especially where there is strong legal support, as is the case of the Navajo Nation's claims to water in the Colorado River basin, governments at times need to be aggressive in asserting their interests. Conquest and the other forms of subjugation have made it hard for Diné to make demands on neighboring non-Indians. It is a testament to the tribe's strength and perseverance that today it is in a position to reach out well beyond the reservation in order to protect Diné interests. The Navajo Nation is a government, but it also is the institutional voice of a people who have survived and whose interests are necessarily and quite appropriately felt by non-Indians throughout the Southwest.

12

Conclusion

The Navajo Nation faces serious challenges. Much of the reservation cannot support agriculture and is straining under excess grazing demands. Though it took environmentalists and scientists decades to accomplish, western states are shifting away from their dependence on Navajo coal. In the short term, the tribal government is likely to be faced with severe budget shortfalls as mining revenue dries up. Governance disputes between the different branches in Window Rock and between the central government and local chapters remain ever-present and could become more pronounced as the tribe enters an age of austerity. And on a more fundamental level, with each passing generation, Diné must continually reimagine and redefine their identity within the four sacred mountains.

Fortunately, as the chapters in this book show, Diné have a long history of overcoming challenges. Tribal leaders met the existential threat of capture and removal to Fort Sumner by negotiating a treaty that allowed the Diné to return to their homeland. Tribal members then created the conditions for the expansion of the reservation by increasing the size of their herds, spreading outward into areas beyond the original reservation boundary. The federal government's livestock reduction policy imposed severe hardship on Diné families but also served as a crucible in the formation of the Navajo Nation government and the transition of Diné from a loosely organized sovereign constellation to a nation with a strong central government. Non-Indian demand for Diné resources led first to the creation of the Navajo Tribal Council and later to the emergence of Diné leaders who fought back against inequitable leases and other unfair limitations on Diné sovereign authority. Today, the Navajo Nation faces other challenges, principal among them matters related to poverty and economic development. Land governance reform is needed to create the conditions that will enable economic growth and that will provide greater opportunities for Diné families that choose to make the reservation home. But just as Diné overcame past difficulties, there is reason for some optimism that the tribe will continue to survive and, at times, thrive, even in the face of tremendous external, and internal, pressure.[1]

Like peoples across the globe, the year 2020 was a difficult one for Diné. The coronavirus (COVID19) hit the reservation hard. By mid-May 2020, the Navajo

Nation had a higher per capita infection rate than anywhere else in the United States, beating out areas like New York City that saw earlier case spikes.[2] The Navajo Nation responded to COVID19 in part by implementing weekend curfews as a way to enforce social distancing, enforced through traffic patrols and checkpoints.[3] The University of California San Francisco sent multiple waves of doctors and nurses to assist in the response to the crisis.[4] *The Navajo Times* published public safety advertisements from Indian Health Service urging tribal members to keep a "two sheep" distance apart from other people.[5] The fact that the Navajo Nation is particularly vulnerable to the virus is not necessarily surprising for those familiar with the reservation.[6] "Decades of negligence and billions of dollars in unmet need from the federal government have left tribal nations without basic infrastructure like running water and sewage systems, along with sparse internet access and an under-funded Indian Health Service," *High Country News* noted, which "compounds the life-threatening danger the virus poses to the elderly and immunocompromised."[7] Even as health experts advised Americans about the importance of frequent hand-washing and of sanitizing surfaces, approximately 40 percent of Diné families do not have running water.[8] Lack of infrastructure coupled with a population facing a long list of health disparities, including obesity and diabetes, predictably turned the reservation into "one of the worst-of-the-worst American hot spots" when it comes to COVID19.[9]

Government response to the coronavirus, at least initially, was delayed. Not only was the US President, Donald Trump, deliberately downplaying the pandemic,[10] but also tribes experienced significant delays getting access to the $8 billion in funds that were earmarked for them under the Coronavirus Aid, Relief, and Economic Security (CARES) Act.[11] After the Navajo Nation was given just over $600 million, an amount that later increased to $714 million, as its share of CARES Act funding, the fault for delays shifted from the federal government to the tribal government.[12] Disagreement between the Navajo Nation President's Office and the Navajo Nation Council about how to spend the pot of money left Diné "wondering why our leaders in Window Rock are not moving more quickly."[13] It was not until August 2020, well into the pandemic, that the bulk of the CARES Act funding was allocated, which included: $130 million for water projects, $76 million for the Navajo Department of Health, $60 million for the Navajo Nation Division of Economic Development, $44 million for powerline projects, $53 million for broadband and telecommunica-tion projects, $35 million for residential solar, $24.6 million for Navajo Gaming Enterprise, and a fund to pay individual Navajo families $1,000 in hardship assistance.[14]

Fortunately, when COVID19 struck the Navajo Nation, a new generation of Diné leaders stepped up, operating outside of the government early on to bring supplies and hope to even the most remote parts of the reservation. Ethel Branch, a Harvard-trained lawyer who served as Navajo Nation Attorney General under the previous administration, organized a GoFundMe campaign that had raised more than

$3.6 million by mid-May 2020.[15] Donations poured in, including a large number of gifts from Irish donors as a way of repaying Native Americans for financial assistance that the Choctaws gave Ireland 173 years ago in response to the potato famine.[16] Celebrities, including Jason Momoa (Aquaman) and Mark Ruffalo (The Hulk), joined in efforts to provide relief to the reservation.[17] Branch decided to act in part because she "felt like the government wouldn't be able to respond quickly, and definitely not at the individual family level."[18] Branch's group, Navajo & Hopi Families COVID-19 Relief Fund, mobilized an army of volunteers who bought supplies, sewed masks, bundled foodstuffs and cleaning materials, and delivered relief supplies throughout the reservation.[19] As several news organizations noted, it was Diné women who took the lead.[20]

The pandemic highlighted many of the governance weaknesses that tribal members knew about pre-COVID. Not only did the Navajo Nation government dither, but also aid groups fought, struggling to coordinate with each other and with Navajo Nation officials.[21] More importantly, many of the stressors that made the Navajo Nation especially vulnerable to the pandemic – lack of utility connections and pre-existing health disparities – will require far more time and resources than just the CARES Act funding and the work of relief groups. And yet, the fight was waged and progress was made. Tellingly, during a September 21, 2020 town hall organized by Navajo Nation President Jonathan Nez, Dr. Anthony Fauci praised the Navajo Nation's response to the virus: "You have been very successful. You rose to the occasion, despite the difficulties you were having, to bring down the level of new cases to a very low number."[22] Ultimately, the verdict on the Diné response to the COVID19 pandemic was not written by the time this book had to be sent to press, but given the work of grassroots organizations and eventually of the Navajo Nation government, there is room for optimism about both how the tribe responds to serious crisis and how it can handle future challenges.

A similar story can be told about previous crisis moments the tribe faced. Though Chapter 6 focused on corruption scandals and focused on Diné leaders who abused their offices, seen from a different angle, those same scandals reflect the tribe's resiliency. After the 1989 Senate hearings aired all of Peter MacDonald's (and, in some respects, the tribe's) dirty laundry, the Tribal Council voted to place MacDonald on involuntary administrative leave, a move that was subsequently upheld by the Navajo Nation Supreme Court.[23] Though turmoil followed the Council's decision,[24] when the dust settled, the Council amended Title 2 of the Navajo Tribal Code in order to split legislative and executive functions, significantly reducing the power of the office which MacDonald had abused.[25] When faced with executive misconduct, the Navajo Nation's legislative and judicial branches, in other words, accomplished what the United States has been unable to do in reaction to the continued violations of the Constitution and abuses of power by President Trump. Such a statement might seem overly provocative, but abuse of office is common to all governments and the Navajo Nation's response to incidents of corruption is relatively robust compared to non-Indian responses to high level corruption by elected officials at the federal level. The same holds for true for the discretionary fund crisis. After *The Navajo Times* coverage revealed the extent to which Council members were abusing the Council's discretionary fund, the tribe named an independent prosecutor to uncover the facts and to hold Council members accountable. Even though Chapter 6 emphasized the degree to which voters in the subsequent election seemed to pardon Council delegate abuse of power, not only did the public learn of the abuses, but also the Navajo Nation Supreme Court and the Navajo Nation President acted to check the Council's power.[26] Again, such responsiveness to corruption and abuses of authority is not a given when it comes to any government, including the non-Indian governments that surround the Navajo Nation.

Taking a broader view of the political fights involved in any crisis, it is important to keep in mind that there is no single "authentic" or shared Diné perspective. The tribe is not a monolith and there is no one Diné answer to how land should be used or the appropriate development path for the Navajo Nation. On nearly every issue explored in this book, there are different perspectives and competing voices within the tribe. Just as civic society organizations such as Doodá Desert Rock and Diné CARE help elevate the voices of those opposed to environmentally destructive projects, unions lead rallies of Diné mine and power plant workers who hope to save the coal-based economy.[27] The passion that some Diné families have when it comes to protecting their traditional grazing lands does not diminish the frustration felt by other Diné families unable to find decent housing because land is unavailable for development. Just as no one political party or social group in the United States defines what it means to be American, so too the disagreements among Diné can be strongly felt and result in ugly political battles without those disagreements resulting in a splintering of the tribe's structure. Put differently, there is space within the Navajo Nation for a multitude of perspectives among tribal members.

The fact that Diné have a diversity of perspectives on land use and development does not lessen their sense of identity. Story-telling, religious and cultural teachings, string and shoe games, multigenerational clustered living, values transmitted through the Diné language, and, even, cooking and eating practices combine to inculcate the Diné identity in each new generation. Significant past traumatic experiences, including conquest and livestock reduction, as well as past triumphs, such as the return to Dinétah and expansion of the reservation following that return, contribute to that collective identity. Although it can be more attenuated for those living off the reservation, shared lifeways, language exposure, and community ties help create a distinctly Diné culture and way of interacting with the world. Again, this does not mean that Diné have homogeneous views, but diversity of perspectives does not erase the tribe's collective sense.

Going forward, the Navajo Nation is going to have to create a political environment that builds on tribal members' collective identity to resolve the significant challenges that it faces. It is worth pausing to appreciate the seriousness of these challenges. Part of why there is such diversity within the tribe on how to manage reservation land is that the nature of the land itself, on much of the reservation, is inherently difficult. Though there are parts of the Navajo Nation, particularly in the Chuska mountains, with lush vegetation and sufficient water resources, much of the reservation is arid and in a process of desertification. Top soil is limited and of poor quality. Rain is infrequent. Without significant investments and extensive irrigation, intensive agriculture is not feasible. Even herding, a typical use of land that does not get enough water to support agriculture, is a marginal activity on much of the reservation. Even families who rely on sheep for subsistence often find that, with the amount they have to pay to provide supplemental hay to keep their animals alive, their herds often end up being a resource drain. An ongoing drought and overgrazing (attributable to sheep herds as well as, in part, to feral horses) together make much of the reservation unable to support even small-scale for-profit family grazing operations. Any government, Native or non-Native, would struggle with these physical challenges, with these features of the land itself.

But even as these physical challenges are acknowledged, it is important not to think of these challenges as destiny. The current condition of the land and the lack of development on the reservation instead reflect an ongoing choice to prioritize non-Indian spaces. If anything, Phoenix and Tuscon, lying as they do in a hotter, dryer part of Arizona than the high desert of the reservation's section of northern Arizona, have even more difficult realities when it comes to the nature of their land. Yet they, like Las Vegas, Nevada to the West, are thriving despite these challenges. The biggest explanation for the contrast between the Navajo Nation and these neighboring communities is that for a century resources were poured into non-Indian communities to move electricity and water from areas closer to the Navajo Nation to more remote places on the map. Phoenix, Las Vegas, Albuquerque, and even Los Angeles would not be what they are today if it were not for federal and state funding that facilitated their growth. That those same governments prioritized non-Indian development while choosing to not invest in Navajo development illustrates the second type of inherent challenge the Navajo Nation confronts: its position as a domestic dependent nation.

Arguably, US government policy is the most serious and consistent impediment to positive Diné land use and development. Ever since 1848, when Mexico relinquished much of the Southwest through the Treaty of Guadalupe Hidalgo, the United States government has undertaken actions that undermine tribal sovereignty and that make development more difficult. Kit Carson's scorched earth campaign that led to the tribe's internment at Bosque Redondo destroyed Diné orchards, fields, and water sources. Livestock reduction during the New Deal drastically reduced the average wealth of Diné families. The Secretary of the Interior worked behind the scenes to weaken the tribe's bargaining position with coal mining companies, effectively reducing the royalty rate those companies paid the Navajo Nation for

Navajo coal. More fundamentally, the US government continues to tolerate levels of poverty, unemployment, and other socioeconomic disparities – including bad housing conditions, lack of running water and electricity, and poor health outcomes – that would raise national alarms and a sense of urgency if they occurred off-reservation. As Diné know too well, settler colonialism is alive and well. Though one can point to positive things the US government has done, navigating the relationship with the United States remains the biggest challenge the Navajo Nation faces in terms of managing its land and supporting economic development.

Acknowledging these structural challenges, both physical and political, is crucial to correct for the harsh judgment outsiders can pass on the Navajo Nation for its many land use and economic development struggles. Though those struggles are detailed in this book, non-Indians need to be careful not to assume that non-Indian leadership or methods of decision-making would have led to better outcomes for the tribe. This is true whether the non-Indian viewing the Navajo situation is a policy-maker or an academic; regardless of their role, humility is a critical trait when Bilagáanas opine on Diné issues and on reservation life. This book tackles controversial matters of Diné governance. It does so because to shy away from such controversies – whether they involve the choice to pursue environmentally destructive forms of development or the recurrent problem of corruption by elected officials – is to give an incomplete and misleading account of Navajo land use and economic development. But it is worth emphasizing that any suggestions, whether implicit or explicit, made in previous chapters are merely that: suggestions. Ultimately, Diné will solve Diné problems. The most that non-Indians can or should do is offer suggestions. And sometimes even offering suggestions is an overreach. Personally, not only am I a Bilagáana, but my connection to reservation life diminishes with every year I live on the east coast. This book reflects both the love I have for the Navajo Nation and the hopes I carry that life on the reservation can become easier for those Diné currently struggling. Where I let my frustration show too much and failed to demonstrate the humility appropriate for a non-Indian offering suggestions, I apologize.

If non-Indian humility regarding the best path forward for Diné is one side of the coin, the other side is appreciation of the power, arguably unique among Indian nations in the United States, of the Navajo Nation to set its own course. Although more than four decades have passed since the self-determination era began, tribes are still treated interchangeably by the federal government even though no single land use or economic development model will work for every tribe. It is time for institutional and situational differences between tribes to be taken seriously.[28] As much as federal Indian law is built around the idea that all tribes are the same, they are not.[29] The Navajo Nation – because of its size, the extent to which it remains separate from neighboring non-Indian communities, and its natural resource wealth – arguably is *uniquely* well-positioned to take on full nationhood, to assume full control over reservation land and development.

An oft-repeated slogan of the self-determination era is that tribes enjoy a nation-to-nation relationship with the United States, but this claim is undermined by the degree of paternalistic control over Indian reservations still exercised by US government entities such as the Bureau of Indian Affairs and the Environmental Protection Agency. Ever since President Nixon's 1970 Special Message to Congress,[30] tribes have incrementally expanded their range of authority. The form such expansion takes varies, from tribal takeover of programs formerly administered by the federal government to creation of novel, tribally determined initiatives. Diné still receive some services from the federal government – the most high profile being the Bureau of Indian Education schools and Indian Health Service healthcare facilities – but the face of "government" for Diné living on the reservation is the Navajo Nation government. As much as tribal leaders critique Washington red tape or federal rules, the Diné experience of local government – their interactions with police, with permitting processes, and with politics – is an experience rooted primarily in the Navajo Nation experience.

Unfortunately, neighboring non-Indian governments, at the state and federal level, have not caught up with this reality. This is where tribal difference comes in. It may be bad policy to completely unshackle all tribes from federal oversight, but the Navajo Nation is different. The size of the Navajo Nation bureaucracy already allows the tribe to take on more matters of a modern administrative state than can be handled by smaller tribes. Not only does the Navajo Nation have an ever-expanding array of departments, but, crucially, most of the positions, from entry-level staffers to department leadership roles, are held by tribal members, not by outsiders brought in because there is not enough local expertise. No wonder that some Navajo leaders have suggested that the Navajo Nation should consider pursuing statehood: the tribe already operates much like a state. For now, statehood is little more than a brainstormed idea. But the larger point, that the Navajo Nation is capable of a greater degree of independence, remains true even if the tribe's sovereignty continues to fall within the "domestic dependent nation" paradigm rather than being structured as a state of the United States.

What does greater independence for the Navajo Nation look like? My answer is that independence and sovereignty are only meaningful if the Navajo Nation is allowed to fail; if it can make decisions and has to suffer the consequences of those decisions.[31] For all the governance progress that has been made by the Navajo Nation over the last fifty years, the United States remains the big brother in the relationship. When things go wrong, tribal leaders tend to blame Washington. And it is often fair to blame Washington. The Navajo Nation continues to operate as a constrained sovereign. Partly, this is structural and will be hard to break from: the Navajo Nation depends on federal funds to run many of the programs it took over from the federal government. Precedent from the US Supreme Court limits the tribe's governance authority, especially when it comes to regulating and policing non-Indians.[32] But not everything can be attributed to hard law limits on tribal sovereignty. Even without direct federal oversight of particular programs, the memory of past federal attacks on the tribe – everything from military conquest to livestock reduction – arguably works to dampen the willingness of the tribe to push the boundaries of its sovereignty. And the federal government has done very little to distance itself from past wrongs committed against the tribe,[33] which helps explain and justify Diné fears about what could happen if the federal government disapproves of something the tribe does.[34]

Nevertheless, my view – expressed most forcefully in the latter half of this book – is that the Navajo Nation should be more assertive in claiming and exercising its authority over the reservation. It should experiment, push, and demand as a matter of right its ability to determine how land is used and the nature of economic development on the reservation. Sometimes the Navajo Nation will stumble and such missteps, unfortunately, likely will harm tribal members. There has to be a floor, forms of federal protection that are permanent and protect tribal members against major governance failures that harm Diné families. But that floor need not be a federal Indian law floor, it could instead be a floor provided by federal welfare programs that Diné have access to as US citizens. Paternalism towards tribes is often justified under the theory that tribal members need US protection, but such paternalism already finds expression through the welfare state.[35] When it comes to a nation as large and as sophisticated as the Navajo Nation, such paternalism should have no place. Presumably, Diné leaders know better than DC bureaucrats what works and what does not work on the reservation and what risks are worth pursuing and what risks are too great. Even if they do not, even if the federal government's preferred policy is best in an objective sense, the Navajo Nation should be able to make mistakes.

For those who live on the reservation, the point being made here could cause confusion; after all, the tribe already makes lots of mistakes. True. But meaningful independence involves the ability to do big things, to set national priorities, even if those priorities conflict with the interests of neighboring non-Indian governments. For the past hundred years, the tribe in some respects has done the bidding of off-reservation interests. Especially with regard to energy development, the Navajo Nation was open for business even when the terms of exchange were unfair to the tribe. There are notable exceptions, moments when the tribe resisted non-Indian expectations. In the energy space, Chairman Peter MacDonald's formation of the Council of Energy Resource Tribes and President Joe Shirley's uranium ban, stand out. But overall the Navajo Nation remains, in my view, overly cautious about setting its own course. Bureaucrats and elected officials in Washington or in the neighboring states do not know more about the reservation than do Diné. Further decoupling funding from paternalism will be hard, but the biggest lesson from the self-determination era is that tribes do better when they are in control and when they assert their power.[36]

If there is one message I would like Diné readers to get from this book, it is the idea that there is space for the Navajo Nation to more aggressively assert its sovereignty over the land. For Bilagáana readers, the main message I hope was conveyed in this book is that the non-Indians should respect Diné and the Navajo Nation enough to respect their right to set their own course.[37] Yes, as with any change or assertion of authority, mistakes will be made, some entrenched interests will suffer losses, and there will be political battles. The best way to regain control over the land might not always be through the central government, and on some matters Window Rock should further empower local initiatives and local experimentation. But in the long run, I think that the tribe will be better off if the tribe reclaims its authority over the land. More Diné families will find ways to stay on the reservation and find ways to live fuller, less impoverished lives. That is the dream of good government and I believe that Diné and the Navajo Nation are up to the challenge.

Notes

PREFACE

1. *See* Maureen Trudelle Schwarz, *Navajo Lifeways: Contemporary Issues, Ancient Knowledge* (Norman, Oklahoma: University of Oklahoma Press, 2001), 5 ("Neutral or pure history does not exist. As with all things cultural, histories are partial and biased, constructed by positioned subjects to know certain things and not others.").
2. Vine Deloria, Jr., *Custer Died for Your Sins: An Indian Manifesto* (New York: Macmillan, 1988), 78.
3. *Id.* at 79–81.
4. *Id.* at 93.
5. *Id.* at 94.
6. *Id.* at 100 (emphasis changed on the word "pure," which is all capitalized in the original).
7. As one author noted, "Many Indians would be satisfied if only Indians wrote about Indians." Devon A. Mihesuah, "Introduction," in *Natives and Academics: Researching and Writing about American Indians*, ed. Devon A. Mihesuah (Lincoln: University of Nebraska Press, 1998), 1–22, at 14.

1 INTRODUCTION

1. Rogue Madrid, "The Journal," in *The Navajos in 1705: Roque Madrid's Campaign Journal*, eds. Rick Hendricks and John P. Wilson (Albuquerque: University of New Mexico Press, 1996), 13–38, at 13.
2. Navajos fought colonists almost from the moment of encounter: "In 1580, Spanish explorers reached the Diné near Mount Taylor. The Diné asked that some of their people, stolen by the Hopi and in turn by the Spanish, be returned. The Spanish refused. A battle ensued." David Treuer, *The Heartbeat of Wounded Knee: Native America from 1890 to the Present* (New York: Riverhead Books, 2019), 57. But Navajos lived on the effective edge of the Spanish holdings in the new world and it took at least another century for Spain to engage in a more sustained effort at conquest of Navajo land. *See* Rick Hendricks and John P. Wilson, "Conclusion," in *The Navajos in 1705: Roque Madrid's Campaign Journal*, eds. Rick Hendricks & John P. Wilson (Albuquerque: University of New Mexico Press, 1996), 89–100, at 100 ("Beginning with Rogue Madrid's 1705 campaign and for more than a decade thereafter, full-scale Spanish military expeditions were carried out against the Navajos almost without

surcease."). *See also* Michael Lerma, *Guided by the Mountains: Navajo Political Philosophy and Governance* (New York: Oxford University Press, 2017), 64 (noting that the first contact between Navajos and the Spanish likely occurred in 1583 and that by the 1620s the Spanish were engaged in slave raids that targeted Navajos).

3. Traci Brynne Voyles, *Wastelanding: Legacies of Uranium Mining in Navajo Country* (Minneapolis: University of Minnesota Press, 2015), 34.

4. The conditions at Fort Sumner and the surrounding Bosque Redondo reservation are sometimes described as "a concentration camp." Lawrence David Weiss, *Development of Capitalism in the Navajo Nation: A Political-Economic History* (Minneapolis: MEP Publications, 1984), 37.

5. For a collection of documents related to the treaty as well as images of the treaty as originally signed, see Bernhard Michaelis, *The Navajo Treaty 1868: Treaty Between the United States of America and the Navajo Tribe of Indians* (Flagstaff, Arizona: Native Child Dinetah, 2014).

6. William Haas Moore, *Chiefs, Agents and Soldiers: Conflict on the Navajo Frontier, 1868–1882* (Albuquerque: University of New Mexico Press, 1994), 24 (quoting Barboncito's speech to Sherman on May 27, 1868).

7. *See* Jacqueline Phelan Hand, "Co-operating to Protect the Shining Big Sea Water and Its Siblings: Consultation with Native Peoples in Protecting the Great Lakes," in *Tribes, Land, and the Environment*, eds. Sarah Krakoff and Ezra Rosser (Burlington, Vermont: Ashgate, 2012), 151–170.

8. In July 2020, a district court ruled that the Dakota Access Pipeline, which had been operational at that point, had to be shut down pending an environmental review. *See* Jacey Fortin and Lisa Friedman, "Dakota Access Pipeline to Shut Down Pending Review, Federal Judge Rules," *New York Times*, July 6, 2020.

9. Mitch Smith, "Standing Rock Protest Camp, Once a Home to Thousands, Is Razed," *New York Times*, Feb. 23, 2016.

10. For more on the particular resonance of the Standing Rock protests, see Sarah Krakoff, "Standing with Tribes Beyond Standing Rock," *Harvard Civil Rights-Civil Liberties Law Review Amicus Blog*, Apr. 21, 2017, http://harvardcrcl.org/sarah-krakoff-standing-with-tribes-beyond-standing-rock/.

11. President Richard Nixon, Special Message on Indian Affairs to Congress (July 8, 1970).

12. Rennard Strickland, *Tonto's Revenge: Reflections on American Indian Culture and Policy* (Albuquerque: University of New Mexico Press, 1997), 14.

13. For the canonical work on Indian treaties, see Francis Paul Prucha, *American Indian Treaties: History of a Political Anomaly* (Berkeley: University of California Press, 1997).

14. This is particularly the case with the Navajo reservation. *See* Dana Powell, *Landscapes of Power: Politics of Energy in the Navajo Nation* (Durham, North Carolina: Duke University Press, 2018), 14 ("Colonial perceptions initially found Navajo landscapes marginal for settlement, but industrial capitalism later found them crucial for resource development.").

15. Shawn E. Reganf and Terry L. Anderson, "The Energy Wealth of Indian Nations," *Louisiana State University Journal of Energy Law and Resources* 3 (2014): 195–223, at 206.

16. Maura Grogan, *Native American Lands and Natural Resource Development* (New York: Revenue Watch Institute, 2011).

17. Valerie L. Kuletz, *The Tainted Desert: Environmental Ruin in the American West* (New York: Routledge, 1998), 13.

18. *See* Peter Meisen and Trevor Erberich, *Renewable Energy on Tribal Lands* (San Diego: Global Energy Network Institute, 2009), 3 (noting that "[t]ribal lands contain enormous

potential for renewable energy" and emphasizing in particular wind and solar); Thomas Elisha Jones and Len Edward Necefer, *Identifying Barriers and Pathways for Success for Renewable Energy Development on American Indian Lands*, SAND2016-311J (Albuquerque: Sandia National Laboratories, 2016), 3 (noting the richness and "great potential" of the renewable energy resources possessed by tribes).

19. *See Winters v. United States*, 207 U.S. 564 (1908).

20. "Water," in *Between Sacred Mountains: Navajo Stories and Lessons from the Land*, eds. Sam Bingham et al. (Tucson: University of Arizona Press, 1982), 236.

21. As Rennard Strickland noted, "The ideological heart of the current Indian issues is the startling, shocking realization that the Indian has neither faded nor died." Strickland, *Tonto's Revenge, supra* note 12, at 105. *See also* Donald L. Fixico, *Indian Resilience and Rebuilding: Indigenous Nations in the Modern American West* (Tucson: University of Arizona Press, 2013), 218 ("Certainly not over night, but within a century's stretch, the Native nations arose from the ashes of near ethnic cleansing and third-world neglect.").

22. A much longer list of abuses and assaults on Indian peoples is possible. *See* Larry W. Emerson, "Diné Sovereign Action: Rejecting Colonial Sovereignty and Invoking Diné Peacemaking," in *Navajo Sovereignty: Understandings and Visions of the Diné People*, ed. Lloyd L. Lee (Tucson: University of Arizona Press, 2017), 165 ("Even with outright genocide that annihilated many Tribes, disease blankets, our Trails of Tears, concentration camps, forced assimilation and the handouts, relocation, cultural genocide, federal government control of our lands, destructive exploitation of our lands/ resources with or without sham consultation, some of us are STILL here.").

23. *See, e.g.*, Jeffrey Ostler, *Surviving Genocide : Native Nations and the United States from the American Revolution to Bleeding Kansas* (New Haven, Connecticut: Yale University Press, 2019). For a critical look at use of the term genocide when discussing wrongs done to different tribes, see Alex Alvarez, *Native America and the Question of Genocide* (Lanham, Maryland: Rowman & Littlefield, 2014).

24. Sandra Day O'Connor, "Lessons from the Third Sovereign: Indian Tribal Courts," *Tulsa Law Journal* 33, no.1 (1997): 1–6, at 1.

25. As noted in a recent book about tribal economic development, "[e]ven today . . . many non-Indians continue to assume that American Indians live only in the past." Susan L. Smith and Brian Frehner, "Introduction," in *Indians & Energy: Exploitation and Opportunity in the American Southwest*, eds. Susan L. Smith and Brian Frehner (Santa Fe, New Mexico: School for Advanced Research Press, 2010), 3–19, at 5.

26. President Richard Nixon, Special Message on Indian Affairs to Congress (July 8, 1970).

27. *See* Nicholas Christos Zaferatos, *Planning the American Indian Reservation: From Theory to Empowerment* (Syracuse, New York: Syracuse University Press, 2015), 16 ("Indians continue to be the most impoverished and economically deprived segment of our population").

28. Bernadette D. Proctor et al., *Income and Poverty in the United States, 2015: Current Population Reports* (Washington, DC: United States Census Bureau, 2016).

29. *Id.*

30. *Id.*

31. Figures from December 2015. National Conference of State Legislatures, National Employment Monthly Update, http://www.ncsl.org/research/labor-and-employment /national-employment-monthly-update.aspx.

32. For the Navajo figures: My Tribal Area website, https://www.census.gov/tribal/. For the national figure on income: Proctor et al., *Income and Poverty in the United States, supra* note 28.

33. Nancy Pindus et al., *Housing Needs of American Indians and Alaska Natives in Tribal Areas: A Report From the Assessment of American Indian, Alaska Native, and Native Hawaiian Housing Needs* (Washington, DC: US Department of Housing and Urban Development Office of Policy Development and Research, 2017), xviii.

34. Indian Health Service, *Indian Health Disparities* (Washington, DC: Indian Health Service, 2019).

35. *Id.*

36. Barack Obama, "On My Upcoming Trip to Indian Country," *Indian Country Today*, June 5, 2014.

37. Burke A. Hendrix, *Ownership, Authority, and Self-Determination* (University Park: Pennsylvania State University Press, 2008), 174 ("the great variety among indigenous groups makes any general statements likely to be mistaken in multiple ways, with potentially limiting consequences for any groups that do not comfortably fit the template.").

38. *See, e.g.,* Philip P. Frickey, "Transcending Transcendental Nonsense: Toward a New Realism in Federal Indian Law," *Connecticut Law Review* 38 (2006): 649–666, at 650–661 (arguing that Indian law legal scholars should focus on how law works, taking a ground up approach, and not on how it is described in doctrinal theory).

39. *See* "Introduction," in *Between Sacred Mountains: Navajo Stories and Lessons from the Land*, eds. Sam Bingham et al. (Tucson: University of Arizona Press, 1982), xi. ("In Navajo Country one sees many miles of land that looks quite empty, but someone who has learned enough to recognize even one plant will see life right to the horizon.").

40. Andrew Needham, *Powerlines: Phoenix and the Making of the Modern Southwest* (Princeton, New Jersey: Princeton University Press, 2016), 29.

41. Note: this is the translation that was given to me by my stepmother, Zelma King, who taught college level Navajo for years. Definitions from other sources tend to be more neutral, referring just to "whites." *See* Robert W. Young and William Morgan, Sr., *The Navajo Language: A Grammar and Colloquial Dictionary* (Albuquerque: University of New Mexico Press, rev. ed. 1987) ("Bilagáana, white man").

42. For an excellent history of Columbus, see Laurence Bergreen, *Columbus: The Four Voyages* (New York: Viking Penguin, 2011).

43. *See generally* Paul G. Zolbrod, *Diné Bahane': The Navajo Creation Story* (Albuquerque: University of New Mexico Press, 1984). For short summaries of the Navajo creation story, *see* Donald L. Fixico, "Understanding the Earth and the Demands on Energy Tribes," in *Indians and Energy: Exploitation and Opportunity in the American Southwest*, eds. Susan L. Smith and Brian Frehner (Santa Fe, New Mexico: School for Advanced Research Press, 2010), 21–34, at 25–26; Lloyd L. Lee, *Diné Identity in a Twenty-First-Century World* (Tucson: University of Arizona Press, 2020), 19–24.

44. Robert S. McPherson, *Sacred Land Sacred View: Navajo Perceptions of the Four Corners Region* (Salt Lake City, Utah: Brigham Young University Press, 1992), 15.

45. *Id.*

46. United States Commission on Civil Rights, *The Navajo Nation: An American Colony* 20 (Washington, DC: Commission on Civil Rights, 1975), 20 (report written by Carol J. McCabe and Hester Lewis).

47. *See* Frank Pommersheim, "The Reservation as Place: A South Dakota Essay," *South Dakota Law Review* 34 (1989): 246–270, at 351 ("This notion of homeland [tied to the austere beauty of the prairie and the land] is not, of course, unique to Indians alone, and despite the obvious irony, it is valued by many non-Indians, including non-Indian residents of the reservation.").

48. *See, e.g.,* Lee, *Diné Identity in a Twenty-First-Century World, supra* note 43, at 72 (quoting teacher and tribal member John Morgan, who relates that his mother told him that even if he went away to university, "your umbilical cord is still buried here in the sheep coral, so you're from here no matter what").

49. *See* McPherson, *Sacred Land Sacred View, supra* note 44, at 73. For more on the Hero Twins, see Jim Kristofic, *The Hero Twins: A Navajo-English Story of the Monster Slayers* (Albuquerque: University of New Mexico Press, 2015).

50. New Mexico Advisory Committee to the United States Commission on Civil Rights, *The Farmington Report: A Conflict of Cultures* (Washington, DC: US Commission on Civil Rights, 1975), 14.

51. *See* Lee, *Diné Identity in a Twenty-First-Century World, supra* note 43, at 77 ("The land is part of the core of what it means to be human and Diné. The land's energy and power are reflected in the origin narratives and Diné philosophy.").

52. Pommersheim, "The Reservation as Place," *supra* note 47, at 362.

53. Though this is subject to debate, as Kevin Noble Maillard writes, "Marriage, affinity or even lifelong residency may change the white man, but he will always be a foreigner in Indian Country." Kevin Noble Maillard, "What's So Hard About Casting Indian Actors in Indian Roles," *New York Times*, Aug. 1, 2017.

54. *See Johnson v. M'Intosh,* 21 U.S. (8 Wheat.) 543 (1823). *See also* Lindsay G. Robertson, *Conquest by Law: How the Discovery of America Dispossessed Indigenous Peoples of Their Lands* (Oxford, England: Oxford University Press, 2005) (discussing the Johnson case and the Doctrine of Discovery in detail); Blake A. Watson, *Buying America from the Indians: Johnson v. McIntosh and the History of Native Land Rights* (Norman, Oklahoma: University of Oklahoma Press, 2012) (same); Robert A. Williams, Jr., *The American Indian in Western Legal Thought: The Discourses of Conquest* (Oxford, England: Oxford University Press, 1990) (describing the history of European thought that led to the Johnson decision).

55. *Cherokee Nation v. Georgia,* 30 U.S. 1, 13 (1831).

56. Two Supreme Court cases in particular that illustrate this preference for development and callous treatment of Indian land rights are *Tee-Hit-Ton Indians v. United States,* 348 U.S. 272 (1955) (taking land from Alaska Natives for timber harvesting without compensation), and *City of Sherrill, New York v. Oneida Indian Nation of New York,* 544 U.S. 197 (2005) (denying the Oneida Indian Nation the right to unite fee and aboriginal title in part because of the extent of non-Indian development in the area).

57. Legal scholars also largely ignore tribes despite their being the third type of sovereign within the United States. For articles critiquing this erasure, see Elizabeth Reese, "The Other American Law," *Stanford Law Review* 73 (2021); Maggie Blackhawk, "Federal Indian Law as Paradigm Within Public Law," *Harvard Law Review* 132, no. 7 (2019): 1787–1877.

58. Felix S. Cohen, *Handbook of Federal Indian Law* (Washington, DC: United States Government Printing Office, 1941), 123.

59. An expanding literature explores the challenges of such deviation from off-reservation norms. Recent notable articles include Angela R. Riley, "(Tribal) Sovereignty and Illiberalism," *California Law Review* 95, no.3 (2007): 799–848; Bethany Berger, "Reconciling Equal Protection and Federal Indian Law," *California Law Review* 98 (2010): 1165–1197; and Sarah Krakoff, "They Were Here First: American Indians, Race, and the Constitutional Minimum," *Stanford Law Review* 69 (2017): 491–548.

60. *See* Matthew L. M. Fletcher, *American Indian Tribal Law* (New York: Aspen Publishers, 2011).

61. Tina Norris, Paula L. Vines and Elizabeth M. Hoeffel, *The American Indian and Alaska Native Population: 2010, 2010 Census Briefs* (Washington, DC: US Census Bureau, 2012), 14.
62. *Id.* at 14 Table 6.
63. *Id.*
64. *Id.*
65. Rebecca Fairfax Clay, "Tribe at a Crossroads: The Navajo Nation Purchases a Coal Mine," *Environmental Health Perspectives* 122, no.4 (2014): A104–A107, at A105.
66. *See, e.g.*, Robert S. McPherson, *Dinéjí Na 'Nitin: Navajo Traditional Teachings and History* (Boulder: University Press of Colorado, 2012); Lawrence D. Sundberg, *Dinétah: An Early History of the Navajo People* (Santa Fe, New Mexico: Sunstone Press, 1995); John R. Farella, *The Main Stalk: A Synthesis of Navajo Philosophy* (Tucson: University of Arizona Press, 1990); Zolbrod, *Diné Bahane', supra* note 43.
67. See Steve Pavlik, *The Navajo and the Animal People: Native American Traditional Ecological Knowledge and Ethnozoology* (Golden, Colorado: Fulcrum Publishing, 2014).
68. *Cherokee Nation v. Georgia*, 30 U.S. 1, 20 (1831) ("The court has bestowed its best attention on this question, and, after mature deliberation, the majority is of the opinion that an Indian tribe or nation within the United States is not a foreign state in the sense of the constitution, and cannot maintain an action in the courts of the United States.").
69. Raymond I. Orr, *Reservation Politics: Historical Trauma, Economic Development, and Intratribal Conflict* (Norman, Oklahoma: University of Oklahoma Press, 2017), 40. Despite the considerable attention given to Supreme Court decisions, especially decisions that undermine tribal sovereignty, "tribal Indians remain in the most desperate human need. And the kind of help they need doesn't always come from just the courthouse or the casebook." Strickland, *Tonto's Revenge, supra* note 12, at 56.
70. Orr, *Reservation Politics, supra* note 69, at 40 ("Scholarship that reveals intratribal politics leaves a scholar vulnerable to anti-Indian criticisms that portray American Indian reservations as dysfunctional political units.").
71. *Id.*
72. Similarly, Philip Frickey, before his untimely death, argued that Indian law scholarship should turn its gaze from endless theorizing about Supreme Court jurisprudence to empirical, grounded work on reservation life – what he called "realism." Frickey also wrote, "I hope I have made the case that more grounded work would be very helpful to federal Indian law. To be sure, the results of such work must be objective; the scholar needs to take the subject and inquiry where it goes. Not all such work will document facts and reach conclusions that tribes will like, and this kind of work will be intrusive into tribal matters in a way that at least some tribes will find troubling." Philip P. Frickey, "Tribal Law, Tribal Context, and the Federal Courts," *Kansas Journal of Law and Public Policy* 18 (2008): 24–33, at 32.
73. As Elizabeth W. Forster, a Bilagáana, living on the reservation wrote in 1931, "Throughout the desert landscape, between the mountains and the highway thirty miles to the east, there is, to the casual eye, no sign of human dwelling until one notices here and there a small structure resembling in shape an Esquimo igloo. It is built of logs covered with desert soil, which makes it practically invisible from a distance. This is a Navaho house – or Hogan it is called." Letter from Elizabeth W. Forster to Emily, Oct. 10, 1931, in *Denizens of the Desert: A Tale in Word and Picture of Life Among the Navaho Indians, The Letters of Elizabeth W. Forster / Photographs of Laura Gilpin*, ed. Martha Sandweiss (Albuquerque: University of New Mexico Press, 1988), 39–43, at 41.

74. As a particularly troubling use of this notion, consider the US Supreme Court's claim that "[t]o leave [Indians] in possession of their country was to leave the country a wilderness," which it used to deny a tribe sovereign rights over land within its reservation boundary. *City of Sherrill v. Oneida Indian Nation of New York*, 544 U.S. 197, 215 (2005).

75. I have explored these examples in previous works. *See* Ezra Rosser, "Ahistorical Indians and Reservation Resources," *Environmental Law* 40 (2010): 437–545; Ezra Rosser, "The Trade-off Between Self-Determination and the Trust Doctrine: Tribal Government and the Possibility of Failure," *Arkansas Law Review* 58 (2005): 291–352.

76. Robert J. Miller, *Reservation "Capitalism": Economic Development in Indian Country* (Denver, Colorado: Praeger, 2012), 10.

77. *Id.*

78. Jessica A. Shoemaker, "No Sticks in My Bundle: Rethinking the Indian Land Tenure Problem," *Kansas Law Review* 63 (2014): 383–450, at 400.

79. Miller, *Reservation "Capitalism," supra* note 76, at 15–16.

80. *See* Fixico, *Indian Resilience and Rebuilding, supra* note 21, at 171 ("Prior to modernity, Native nations practiced what might be called moral economy. In such an economy, communities functioned to take care of their members with food supplies and whatever was needed that could be acquired through trade … The moral economies of tribes centered on sharing wealth and distributing goods to make sure everyone had enough to eat, were comfortable, and were secure.").

81. Rebecca Tsosie, "Cultural Sovereignty and Tribal Energy Development: Creating a Land Ethic for the Twenty-first Century," in *Indians and Energy: Exploitation and Opportunity in the American Southwest*, eds. Susan L. Smith and Brian Frehner (Santa Fe, New Mexico: School for Advanced Research Press, 2010), 262–279, at 263.

82. *See* Hope Babcock, "A Possible Solution to the Problem of Diminishing Tribal Sovereignty," *North Dakota Law Review* 90 (2014): 13–86, at 19 ("Adding insult to injury, at various points, perhaps out of a sense of collective guilt, we have romanticized Indians beyond all recognition."); Frederick E. Hoxie, *This Indian Country: American Indian Activists and the Place They Made* (New York: Penguin Press, 2012), 3 ("why is it that American so easily accept the romantic stereotype of Indians as heroic warriors and princesses? Why don't we demand a richer, three-dimensional story?").

83. Reservation basketball, or rezball, has gotten considerable attention in the last few years, with both a Netflix documentary series and a book by a *New York Times* journalist covering the topic. *See Basketball or Nothing* (Netflix, 2019); Michael Powell, *Canyon Dreams: A Basketball Season on the Navajo Nation* (New York: Blue Rider Press, 2019). *See also* Lee, *Diné Identity in a Twenty-First-Century World, supra* note 43, at 82–83 (highlighting the significance of Spanish and Mexican "introduction of livestock").

84. *See* Lee, *Diné Identity in a Twenty-First-Century World, supra* note 43, at 95 ("Diné people have always adapted to their environment. This adaptation does not make Diné identity and way of live unoriginal but rather shows a vibrant group.").

85. *See* Aubrey W. Williams, Jr., *Navajo Political Process* (Washington, D.C.: Smithsonian Institution Press, 1970), 2 ("The cultural history of the Navajo is replete with references concerning the various cultural items and techniques borrowed and incorporated from other people. Yet, each of the historical and cultural accounts … mentions the distinctive character of Navajo culture through time, in spite of the influx of ideas from different cultures.").

86. As Diné professor Lloyd Lee notes, one of the more significant adaptations made by many members of the tribe is the incorporation of external religious beliefs, especially those of

Christianity and of the Native American Church. Lee, *Diné Identity in a Twenty-First-Century World, supra* note 43, at 14–15.

87. *See* Williams, Jr., *Navajo Political Process, supra* note 85, at 59 ("the most outstanding feature of the integrative process undergone by the Navajo has been a major trend toward structural incorporation of Anglo-American principles of political organization without a corresponding strong tendency to integrate the cultural content of these principles.").

88. Haas Moore, *Chiefs, Agents and Soldiers, supra* note 6, at xxii.

89. Madrid, "The Journal," *supra* note 1, at 20.

90. *Id.* at 27.

91. Rick Hendricks and John P. Wilson, "The Route," in *The Navajos in 1705: Roque Madrid's Campaign Journal*, eds. Rick Hendricks and John P. Wilson (Albuquerque: University of New Mexico Press, 1996), 63–87, at 63.

92. Naomi Schaefer Riley, *The New Trail of Tears: How Washington Is Destroying American Indians* (New York: Encounter Books, 2016), 66.

93. Williams, Jr., *Navajo Political Process, supra* note 85, at 5.

94. *See* Haas Moore, *Chiefs, Agents and Soldiers, supra* note 6, at xiii. ("If the vanishing Indian myth was true, the Navajos should have suffered extinction or assimilated into the greater North American population. The fact is that they survived as Navajos.").

95. *See* Jennifer Nez Denetdale, "Foreword," *in Navajo Sovereignty: Understandings and Visions of the Diné People*, ed. Lloyd L. Lee (Tucson: University of Arizona Press, 2017), viii ("The Navajo Nation, its leaders and citizens, might be constrained by the "domestic dependent" relationship with the United States, but it has not stopped Diné from being what it means to be Diné, and to reach into the past to the teachings of our ancestors who used their knowledge and experiences to survive the American war waged on them, and to perpetuate the teachings that have kept our people vibrant and alive.").

2 THE NAVAJO NATION

1. *See* David Treuer, *The Heartbeat of Wounded Knee: Native America from 1890 to the Present* (New York: Riverhead Books, 2019), 61 ("Attempts to negotiate with the Diné were also complicated by the lack (or at least the apparent lack) of a centralized government. Different clans and bands of Diné took their own counsel, and there was no single government, much less a spokesperson, for the thousands of Diné living within the borders of their four sacred mountains.").

2. For more about the Pueblo Revolt, see David Cutter and Iris Engstrand, *Quest for Empire: Spanish Settlement in the Southwest* (Golden, Colorado: Fulcrum Publishing, 1996), 91–118.

3. *See* Klara B. Kelley and Peter M. Whiteley, *Navajoland: Family Settlement and Land Use* (Tsaile, Arizona: Navajo Community College Press, 1989), 16 ("Whoever 'the Navajos' were before the revolt and reconquest, afterward they comprised a fusion of Navajo Apaches and Pueblo refugees.").

4. Peter Iverson, *Diné: A History of the Navajos* (Albuquerque: University of New Mexico Press, 2002), 12.

5. As Farina King notes, "[a]lthough American authorities forced Navajos to relocate to Hwééldi, their removal from their homeland ironically strengthened their sense of home and identity as a people." Farina King, *The Earth Memory Compass: Diné Landscapes and Education in the Twentieth Century* (Lawrence: University Press of Kansas, 2018), 57.

6. Jennifer Nez Denetdale, "Chairmen, Presidents, and Princesses: The Navajo Nation, Gender, and the Politics of Tradition," *Wicazo Sa Review* 21, no.1 (2006): 9–28, at 11.

7. *Id.* Some historians have questioned whether naachid gatherings actually took place or were merely invented parts of Navajo history. *See* Andrew Curley, "The Origin of Legibility: Rethinking Colonialism and Resistance among the Navajo People, 1868–1937," in *Diné Perspectives: Revitalizing and Reclaiming Navajo Thought*, ed. Lloyd L. Lee (Tucson: University of Arizona Press, 2014), 129–150, at 138 ("However, anthropologists Kluckhohn and Leighton arrived at the opposite conclusion when writing about this same thing fifty years earlier. Finding it difficult to document the naachid, they reasoned in the mind-1940s that this ceremony was an act of 'retrospective falsification' rather than an actual even that had ever taken place.").

8. Aubrey W. Williams, Jr., *Navajo Political Process* (Washington, DC: Smithsonian Institution Press, 1970), 6.

9. Iverson, *Diné, supra* note 4, at 16.

10. *See* Marren Sanders, "Genetic Research in Indian Country," *Oklahoma City University Law Review* 39 (2014): 1–43; Kim TallBear, *Native American DNA: Tribal Belonging and the False Promise of Genetic Science* (Minneapolis: University of Minnesota Press, 2013).

11. For an example of just how much is *not* known, consider the uncertainty regarding when such a crossing might have taken place: "Archaeologists generally agree that proto-Asiatic people first migrated into the Western Hemisphere across the Bering Strait from Siberia to Alaska sometime between 50,000 and 20,000 B.C." Cutter and Engstrand, *Quest for Empire, supra* note 2, at 8.

12. *Id.* at 11.

13. *See* Jared Diamond, *Collapse: How Societies Choose to Fail or Succeed* (New York: Penguin Group, 2005), 137–156; George Johnson, "Vanished: A Pueblo Mystery," *New York Times*, Apr. 8, 2008.

14. Iverson, *Diné, supra* note 4, at 20.

15. *Id.* at 21–22.

16. Williams, Jr., *Navajo Political Process, supra* note 8, at 6.

17. For an overview of the treaties signed between Navajos and the Spanish, and later the Mexican governments, see David M. Brugge and J. Lee Correll, *The Story of the Navajo Treaties* (Window Rock, Arizona: Navajo Parks and Recreation, 1971), 1–14.

18. Williams, Jr., *Navajo Political Process, supra* note 8, at 4.

19. *See* Richard C. Hopkins, "Kit Carson and the Navajo Expedition," *Montana: The Magazine of Western History* 18, no.2 (1968): 52–61, at 54 (noting that "reciprocal raid and reprisal became the norm" in the relationship between Navajos and New Mexicans and Pueblans).

20. Kelley and Whiteley, *Navajoland, supra* note 3, at 22.

21. *Id.* at 38.

22. Traci Brynne Voyles, *Wastelanding: Legacies of Uranium Mining in Navajo Country* (Minneapolis: University of Minnesota Press, 2015), 200.

23. *Id.* Some sources have 1852 as the year Fort Defiance was established. Mary Stephenson, *Navajo Ways in Government: A Political Process* (Menasha, Wisconsin: American Anthropological Association, 1963), 10.

24. *See* Voyles, *Wastelanding, supra* note 22, at viii. *See also* Klara Kelley and Harris Francis, *A Diné History of Navajoland* (Tucson: University of Arizona Press, 2019), 137 ("Forts Wingate and Defiance were military posts meant to control the Diné.").

25. Voyles, *Wastelanding, supra* note 22, at 200.

26. Kelley and Whiteley, *Navajoland, supra* note 3, at 40–41. *See also* William Haas Moore, *Chiefs, Agents and Soldiers: Conflict on the Navajo Frontier, 1868–1882* (Albuquerque: University of New Mexico Press, 1994), 26 ("By 1862 the estimated number of Navajo captives held by New Mexicans ranged between fifteen hundred and three thousand."). *See also* Frank McNitt, *Navajo Wars: Military Campaigns, Slave Raids, and Reprisals* (Albuquerque: University of New Mexico Press, 1972, 1990), 12 ("Traffic in Indian slaves not only was enjoyed by the upper levels of secular authority but also extended at this time or soon after into every home of moderate means – even, if in a lesser degree, to the Franciscan clergy. By no means did all of the clergy become involved, but enough of them were dependent upon Indian labor that the line between benevolent Christian effort and outright exploitation often was scarcely discernible."). For a July 1865 list of Indian captives in Conejos County, Colorado Territory, and Costilla County, Colorado Territory, see *id.* at 442–446 Appendix D. Most captives listed were children or young adults and most were female. *Id. See also* Marie Mitchell, *The Navajo Peace Treaty 1868* (New York: Mason & Lipscomb Publishers, 1973), 15 ("Women and children from ages six to 16 were bringing $200 each on the slave market, which encouraged more and more raiders to invade Navajo country.").
27. Williams, Jr., *Navajo Political Process, supra* note 8, at 6.
28. Stephen J. Rockwell, *Indian Affairs and the Administrative State in the Nineteenth Century* (New York: Cambridge University Press, 2010), 225.
29. Stephenson, *Navajo Ways in Government, supra* note 23, at 11 ("Even though perhaps as many as 3,000 Navajos were able to hide out in remote canyons and thus elude the captors (a famous example is Hoskinini of Monument Valley), Kit Carson effected the conquest of the tribe. Once and for all, Navajo traditional war patterns were destroyed, and the ultimate authority of the United States Government was imposed upon the people.").
30. Hopkins, "Kit Carson and the Navajo Expedition," *supra* note 19, at 57.
31. McNitt, *Navajo Wars, supra* note 26, at xi ("So unquestionably certain were the Americans of their right to seize land or anything else owned by Indians that, by 1861, the matter had been so resolved that Navajos were allowed but one option: they could choose between unconditional surrender and extermination. It is necessary to emphasize that the literal meanings of the words actually were intended.").
32. Moore, *Chiefs, Agents and Soldiers, supra* note 26, at 2.
33. *Id.* at 2.
34. *See* Kelley and Whiteley, *Navajoland, supra* note 3, at 43 ("Kit Carson's defeat of the Navajos ended their political and economic autonomy forever. All at once they were forced to depend on the developing capitalist economy and federal government bureaucracy of the United States.").
35. Hopkins, "Kit Carson and the Navajo Expedition," *supra* note 19, at 61.
36. Voyles, *Wastelanding, supra* note 22, at viii.
37. *Id.*
38. Lynn R. Bailey, *The Long Walk: A History of the Navajo Wars, 1846–68* (Tucson, Arizona: Westernlore Press, 1988), 170. *See also* Howard W. Gorman, "Howard G. Gorman," in *Navajo Stories of the Long Walk Period*, eds. Broderick H. Johnson & Ruth Roessel (Tsaile, Navajo Nation, Arizona: Diné College Bookstore/Press, 1973), 23–42, at 30. Note: Gorman was member of the Tribal Council and served as Vice Chairman from 1938–1942. ("It was inhuman because the Navajos, if they got tired and couldn't continue to walk farther, were just shot down . . . They had to keep walking all the time, day after day.").

39. *See* Lloyd L. Lee, *Diné Identity in a Twenty-First-Century World* (Tucson: University of Arizona Press, 2020), 84 (providing the translation for Hwéeldi). *See also* Treuer, *The Heartbeat of Wounded Knee, supra* note 1, at 62 (describing Bosque Redondo as, "in short, a hell").

40. Moore, *Chiefs, Agents and Soldiers, supra* note 26, at 3 (writing of Bosque Redondo, "The Navajos would have to abandon their pastoral ways and become sedentary. They would learn Euro-American farming and methods and congregate in settled communities. Their children were to attend schools run by Catholic priests. In such a manner, they would become independent yeomen and eventually take their place among the American citizenry.").

41. Mitchell, *The Navajo Peace Treaty 1868, supra* note 26, at 57.

42. Moore, *Chiefs, Agents and Soldiers, supra* note 26, at 3.

43. *Id.* at xii.

44. United States Commission on Civil Rights, *The Navajo Nation: An American Colony* 20 (Washington, DC: Commission on Civil Rights, 1975), 15 (report written by Carol J. McCabe and Hester Lewis).

45. Bailey, *The Long Walk, supra* note 38, at 226. *See also* Peter Nabokov, *Where the Lightning Strikes: The Lives of American Indian Sacred Places* (New York: Viking Press, 2006), 95 (describing Fort Sumner as "a concentration camp").

46. Kelley and Francis, *A Diné History of Navajoland, supra* note 24, at 16.

47. *See* Voyles, *Wastelanding, supra* note 22, at 35 ("Diné leaders had tirelessly negotiated with their captors to protest their incarceration, and local authorities were under pressure from their constituents because of the cost of keeping the camp open.").

48. *Report of the Commissioner of Indian Affairs,* Nov. 23, 1868, at 4, http://images .library.wisc.edu/History/EFacs/CommRep/AnnRep68/reference/history .annrep68.i0003.pdf.

49. *See* Norman J. Bender, *"New Hope for the Indians": The Grant Peace Policy and the Navajos in the 1870s* (Albuquerque: University of New Mexico Press, 1927), 13 ("Crop failures caused by droughts and insects had dealt crippling blows to the plans for agricultural self-sufficiency.").

50. *See* Williams, Jr., *Navajo Political Process, supra* note 8, at 7 ("The Government had spent about two million dollars on the Fort Sumner experiment.").

51. Rockwell, *Indian Affairs and the Administrative State in the Nineteenth Century, supra* note 28, at 226. Navajo-related expenses were but part of a larger government effort and expense: "The *New York Times* report in 1882 that 80 percent of the War Department's budget and 73 percent of its personnel were being used to pacify Indians in the West." *Id.*

52. *Report to the President by the Indian Peace Commission,* Jan. 7, 1968, *in Annual Report of the Commissioner of Indian Affairs for the Year 1868* (Washington: Government Printing Office, 1868), Appendix p44.

53. Moore, *Chiefs, Agents and Soldiers, supra* note 26, at 22 (quoting a letter from Sherman to Grant).

54. *Id.* at 22.

55. *Id.* at 21.

56. Brugge and Correll, *The Story of the Navajo Treaties, supra* note 17, at 19.

57. Robert S. McPherson, *Sacred Land Sacred View: Navajo Perceptions of the Four Corners Region* (Salt Lake City, Utah: Brigham Young University, 1992), 1–2.

58. Curley, "The Origin of Legibility," *supra* note 7, at 133.

59. Klara B. Kelley, *Navajo Land Use: An Ethnoarchaeological Study* (New York: Academic Press, Inc., 1986), 23.

60. Williams, Jr., *Navajo Political Process, supra* note 8, at 18.
61. *See* Moore, *Chiefs, Agents and Soldiers, supra* note 26, at 27 ("The reservation, once surveyed, was approximately half of what the general indicated [verbally on May 30, 1868 in the negotiations].").
62. Voyles, *Wastelanding, supra* note 22, at 36 ("The land that was excluded from the reservation to make way for the railroad stretched from Tsoodzil, the sacred mountain of the south, to present-day Gallup, New Mexico, and was 'the best of the Navajos' traditional winter range.'").
63. Brugge and Correll, *The Story of the Navajo Treaties, supra* note 17, at 30.
64. *Id.*
65. *See* Voyles, *Wastelanding, supra* note 22, at 36; Moore, *Chiefs, Agents and Soldiers, supra* note 26, at 28.
66. *See* Curley, "The Origin of Legibility," *supra* note 7, at 133 ("It was the Navajo people themselves who voiced opposition to these plans and pleaded with US authorities to let them go back to their homeland on the Colorado plateau. The US government eventually relented and decided to allow the Navajo people to return to their homes. This was the biggest accomplishment for those headmen who were negotiating on behalf of the Navajos, perhaps the most significant diplomatic event in Navajo history.").
67. " Reservation: The Old Paper," in *Between Sacred Mountains: Navajo Stories and Lessons from the Land*, eds. Sam Bingham et al. (Tucson: University of Arizona Press, 1982), 144.
68. Curley, "The Origin of Legibility," *supra* note 7, at 131.
69. *Id.* at 130 ("My argument is twofold. First, the US government created the Navajo tribe and the Navajo tribal government in order to make the Navajo people into what James C. Scott (1998) has described as a 'legible' population subject to the simplification and manipulation of 'the state,' or powerful interests within the US federal government. Second, the Navajo people resisted these efforts in both overt and subtle ways because they interfered with their own senses of personal autonomy, livelihood, and collective independence."). *See also* Michael Lerma, *Guided by the Mountains: Navajo Political Philosophy and Governance* (New York: Oxford University Press, 2017), 172 ("Contemporary Diné governance did not arrive by accident. Many would argue that it is the legacy of centuries of US federal Indian policy.").
70. As former Navajo Nation Supreme Court Justice Raymond Austin notes, "The Diné language does not have a single word that translates to sovereignty, but that does not mean our ancestral traditional Diné did not exercise sovereignty." Justice Raymond D. Austin, "Diné Sovereignty, a Legal and Traditional Analysis," in *Navajo Sovereignty: Understandings and Visions of the Diné People*, ed. Lloyd L. Lee (Tucson: University of Arizona Press, 2017), 32. *See also* Manley A. Begay Jr., "The Path of Navajo Sovereignty in Traditional Education: Harmony, Disruption, Distress, and Restoration of Harmony," in *Navajo Sovereignty: Understandings and Visions of the Diné People*, ed. Lloyd L. Lee (Tucson: University of Arizona Press, 2017), 59 ("Sovereignty has been too often portrayed strictly in the European political and legal sense, which consequently severely diminishes and dismisses traditional Navajo (and other Indigenous) cultural views and conceptions of it.").
71. *See* Lee, *Diné Identity in a Twenty-First-Century World, supra* note 39, at 85 ("The impact of Hwéeldi was traumatic and life altering. The people began to see themselves as one nation.").
72. It is important not to paint too rosy a picture of the treaty relationship. As Larry Emerson explains, "While a treaty between two countries signifies mutual sovereignty, the 1868 treaty was also a colonizing document." Larry W. Emerson, "Diné Culture, Decolonization, and the Politics of Hózhó," in *Diné Perspectives: Revitalizing and*

Reclaiming Navajo Thought, ed. Lloyd L. Lee (Tucson: University of Arizona Press, 2014), 49–67, at 54.

73. *See* Curley, "The Origin of Legibility," *supra* note 7, 129–150, at 134 ("The basic point is that the Treaty of Bosque Redondo created the Navajo Tribe of Indians.").

74. Robert W. Young and William Morgan, Sr., *The Navajo Language: A Grammar and Colloquial Dictionary* (Albuquerque: University of New Mexico Press, rev. ed. 1987) ("Navajo Country, Navajoland").

75. Moore, *Chiefs, Agents and Soldiers, supra* note 26, at 33.

76. *Id.* at 40.

77. *See id.* ("One writer has concluded that they number who never surrendered was between fifteen hundred and two thousand."); Marsha Weisiger, *Dreaming of Sheep in Navajo Country* (Seattle: University of Washington Press, 2009), 90 ("When the Diné finally returned home, some found that those family members who escaped imprisonment had relocated to more secluded western locales, and others discovered strangers in their favorite places.").

78. Moore, *Chiefs, Agents and Soldiers, supra* note 26, at 284.

79. Voyles, *Wastelanding, supra* note 22, at viii.

80. Moore, *Chiefs, Agents and Soldiers, supra* note 26, at 56.

81. Kelley, *Navajo Land Use, supra* note 59, at 23.

82. Moore, *Chiefs, Agents and Soldiers, supra* note 26, at 36.

83. Caleb Michael Bush, "Land, Conflict and the 'Net of Incorporation': Capitalism's Uneven Expansion into the Navajo Indian Reservation, 1860–2000" (PhD diss., Binghamton University, State University of New York, 2005), 5.

84. Voyles, *Wastelanding, supra* note 22, at 37 ("Estimates of Navajo livestock between 1868 and 1890 show a remarkable increase in herd sizes."); Denetdale, "Chairmen, Presidents, and Princesses," *supra* note 6, at 13 ("With their return to Dinetah, Navajos rebuilt their herds to pre-Bosque Redondo levels and struggled to restore a measure of self-sufficiency to their lives, although they remained wards of the US government.").

85. *See* Andrew Needham, *Powerlines: Phoenix and the Making of the Modern Southwest* (Princeton, New Jersey: Princeton University Press, 2016), 43 ("As was the case with horses for plains tribes, sheep converted energy stored in grass into a new, mobile form that could supply Navajos with sustenance in the form of milk and meat as well as wool for clothing and blankets.").

86. Kelley, *Navajo Land Use, supra* note 59, at 24.

87. *Id.* at 26.

88. Willow Roberts Powers, "Trading Posts of the Four Corners," in Edward Grazda, *A Last Glance: Trading Posts of the Four Corners* (Brooklyn, New York: Powerhouse Books, 2015), 111–115, at 111.

89. To see reproductions of trading post script or tokens, see Bill P. Acrey, *Navajo History: The Land and the People* (Shiprock, New Mexico: Department of Curriculum Materials Development Central Consolidated School District No. 22, 1978), 140. *See also* Frank McNitt, *The Indian Traders* (Norman: University of Oklahoma Press, 1962), 86 ("Whether intended or not, the widespread use of tokens often had the effect of encouraging Indians – if not compelling them – to continue going back to the same trader. In some instances this placed the Indians at a disadvantage, particularly when a trader who enjoyed such a monopoly may have been dishonest, charged too much, or carried a poor line of trade goods.").

90. *See* Edward Grazda, *A Last Glance: Trading Posts of the Four Corners* (Brooklyn, New York: Powerhouse Books, 2015), 13 ("Starting around the 1870s, in an area that

would come to be known as the Four Corners, there were places where Native Americans interacted with the Anglo world, their commodities and culture. They were called trading posts.").

91. Kelley, *Navajo Land Use, supra* note 59, at 19.

92. Moore, *Chiefs, Agents and Soldiers, supra* note 26, at 237.

93. "Peace and Livestock," in *Between Sacred Mountains: Navajo Stories and Lessons from the Land*, eds. Sam Bingham et al. (Tucson: University of Arizona Press, 1982), 155.

94. Voyles, *Wastelanding, supra* note 22, at xii.

95. Garrick Bailey, "Foreword," in *Washington Matthews: Studies of Navajo Culture, 1880–1894*, eds. Katherine Spencer Halpern and Susan Brown McGreevy (Albuquerque: University of New Mexico Press, 1997), ix–xi, at x.

96. Moore, *Chiefs, Agents and Soldiers, supra* note 26, at 145.

97. Kelley, *Navajo Land Use, supra* note 59, at 19 ("The growing herds of *ricos* like Narbona perhaps forced not only *pobres*, but also the ambitious children of *ricos*, to colonize new land, most of which was to the west.").

98. *See* Curley, "The Origin of Legibility," *supra* note 7, at 140 ("Simply put, Navajos ignored many of the carefully established provisions found in the Treaty of Bosque Redondo. They refused these new modes of order and regimentation. Between 1868 and 1937 there were scattered reports of Navajos not holding themselves to the terms of this treaty. They did this by living beyond reservation lines, openly defying tribal and federal authority, and using ceremonial knowledge, or what some have dubbed 'witchcraft,' against government officials.").

99. Moore, *Chiefs, Agents and Soldiers, supra* note 26, at 253.

100. Elmer R. Rusco, *A Fateful Time: The Background and Legislative History of the Indian Reorganization Act* (Reno: University of Nevada Press, 2000), 51.

101. *See* Donald L. Fixico, *Indian Resilience and Rebuilding: Indigenous Nations in the Modern American West* (Tucson: University of Arizona Press, 2013), 5 ("the so-called Indian Problem arose as good-hearted reformers – Friends of the Indian – wanted the government to alleviate the impoverished living conditions on reservations.").

102. Rockwell, *Indian Affairs and the Administrative State in the Nineteenth Century, supra* note 28, at 246.

103. *See* Lewis Meriam et al., *The Problem of Indian Administration* (Baltimore: Johns Hopkins Press, 1928), 7 ("When the government adopted the policy of individual ownership of the land on the reservations, the expectation was that the Indians would become farmers. Part of the plan was to instruct and aid them in agriculture, but this vital part was not pressed with vigor and intelligence. It almost seems as if the government assumed that some magic in individual ownership of property would in itself prove an educational civilizing factor, but unfortunately this policy has for the most part operated in the opposite direction."). *See also* Ezra Rosser, "Anticipating de Soto: Allotment of Indian Reservations and the Dangers of Land-Titling," in *Hernando de Soto and Property in a Market Economy*, ed. D. Benjamin Barros (New York: Ashgate, 2010), 61–75 (critiquing the argument that private property will solve poverty and using allotment as the historical example).

104. Jessica A. Shoemaker, "No Sticks in My Bundle: Rethinking the Indian Land Tenure Problem," *Kansas Law Review* 63 (2014): 383–450, at 403–404.

105. Judith Royster, "The Legacy of Allotment," *Arizona State Law Journal* 27 (1995): 1–78, at 12; Leonard A. Carlson, "Federal Policy and Indian Land: Economic Interests and the Sale of Indian Allotments, 1900–1934," *Agricultural History* 57, no. 1 (Jan. 1983): 33–45, at 33–34.

106. Shoemaker, "No Sticks in My Bundle: Rethinking the Indian Land Tenure Problem," *supra* note 104, at 440 ("For example, the tribes of the arid southwest largely escaped allotment because, in that climate and landscape, federal officials acknowledged that 'tribes such as the Navajo had to live communally to survive,' and '[t]hese nomadic herdsmen who followed the grass and rain could not exist on 80 or even 320 acres.' Therefore, the Navajo today still operate with some of their own indigenous property systems and tenure rules on remaining reservation lands."); Rusco, *A Fateful Time, supra* note 100, at 54 ("In dry areas of the West (which included the very large Navajo Reservation) 160-acre parcels would have been useless to individuals for farming purposes."). Though "the vast majority of its land was not allotted to individuals," the Navajo Nation was not entirely spared; as David Listokin reports, "about 5 percent of the land base of the Navajo Nation (more than 700,000 acres) is individually allotted." David Listokin et al., *Housing and Economic Development in Indian Country: Challenge and Opportunity* (New Brunswick, New Jersey: Center for Urban Policy Research Press, 2006), 345, 334.

107. For more on the history and impact of this change, see George William Rice, "Indian Rights: 25 U.S.C. § 71: The End of IndianSovereignty or a Self-Limitation of Contractual Ability," *American Indian Law Review* 5, no. 1 (1977): 239–53.

108. Moore, *Chiefs, Agents and Soldiers, supra* note 26, at 203.

109. *Id.* at 203–204.

110. Lloyd L. Lee, "The Navajo Nation and the Declaration on the Rights of Indigenous Peoples," in *Diné Perspectives: Revitalizing and Reclaiming Navajo Thought,* ed. Lloyd L. Lee (Tucson, Arizona: University of Arizona Press, 2014), 170–186, at 178–179.

111. *Id.* at 178–179 (listing the years as 1880, 1884, 1886, 1900, 1901, 1905, 1907, 1913, 1930, and 1934).

112. *See* Peter Iverson, "Land," in *"For Our Navajo People": Diné Letters, Speeches and Petitions 1900-1960,* ed. Peter Iverson, photo ed. Monty Roessel (Albuquerque: University of New Mexico Press, 2002), 3 ("The treaty provided an initial land base. This acreage would be more than quadrupled over the next seventy years. At a time when many Indian nations in the West lost much of their land, the Navajos increased their base.").

113. Voyles, *Wastelanding, supra* note 22, at 37.

114. *See* "Winning the Peace," in *Between Sacred Mountains: Navajo Stories and Lessons from the Land,* eds. Sam Bingham et al. (Tucson: University of Arizona Press, 1982), 146 ("How did the Navajo win back in peacetime land that they lost in war? The won it with livestock. Sheep and cattle held land that guns and arrows could not.").

115. *See* Bush, "Land, Conflict and the 'Net of Incorporation,'" *supra* note 83, at 6 ("Ultimately, the barren quality was the reason why so much land was given over to the Navajos; such land was not much good for anything, it seemed, so why not give it to the Indians clamoring for more land?").

116. Curley, "The Origin of Legibility," *supra* note 7, at 146.

117. Kelley and Whiteley, *Navajoland, supra* note 3, at 68.

118. Williams, Jr., *Navajo Political Process, supra* note 8, at 27. For good maps showing the expansion of the Navajo Nation, see *Id.* at 13; "Winning the Peace," *supra* note 114, at 147.

3 A NEW AND OLD DEAL FOR NAVAJOS

1. Klara B. Kelley and Peter M. Whiteley, *Navajoland: Family Settlement and Land Use* (Tsaile, Arizona: Navajo Community College Press, 1989), 71 ("In 1921 several oil

companies asked the Commissioner of Indian Affairs if they could meet with the 'Navajo Council' to negotiate oil leases. Unfortunately, there was no Navajo Council.").

2. Aubrey W. Williams, Jr., *Navajo Political Process* (Washington, DC: Smithsonian Institution Press, 1970), 21–23.

3. Andrew Needham, *Powerlines: Phoenix and the Making of the Modern Southwest* (Princeton, New Jersey: Princeton University Press, 2016), 44. For more on Chee Dodge's life, *see* Klara Kelley and Harris Francis, *A Diné History of Navajoland* (Tucson: University of Arizona Press, 2019), 183–184.

4. Williams, Jr., *Navajo Political Process, supra* note 2, at 22.

5. As Dana Powell explains: "The pressure to develop the vast reserves of oil discovered beneath Diné land is what fueled the construction of 'the Navajo Nation' as a newly formed, centralized, all-male Navajo Business Council/Tribal Council to represent all of the reservation, especially in regard to negotiating access to oil." Dana Powell, *Landscapes of Power: Politics of Energy in the Navajo Nation* (Durham, North Carolina: Duke University Press, 2018), 39.

6. Larry W. Emerson, "Diné Culture, Decolonization, and the Politics of Hózhó," in *Diné Perspectives: Revitalizing and Reclaiming Navajo Thought,* ed. Lloyd L. Lee (Tucson: University of Arizona Press, 2014), 49–67, at 54 ("The real purpose of this new council was to sign oil and gas leases."); Michael Lerma, *Guided by the Mountains: Navajo Political Philosophy and Governance* (New York: Oxford University Press, 2017), 118 (arguing that "the Business Council of 1922 was a rubber-stamp mechanism meant to ensure the vitality of parties interested in royalties related to oil on the Navajo reservation").

7. *See* Andrew Curley, "The Origin of Legibility: Rethinking Colonialism and Resistance among the Navajo People, 1868-1937," in *Diné Perspectives: Revitalizing and Reclaiming Navajo Thought,* ed. Lloyd L. Lee (Tucson: University of Arizona Press, 2014), 129–150, at 135 (noting in connection with the early Council, "This was a formula that British colonial officials in Africa called indirect rule – an arrangement in which a seemingly legitimate authority figure among a colonized people enacted colonial policies on behalf of the colonists in order to imbue these policies with an air of local acceptance and legitimacy.").

8. "Jacob C. Morgan, Mar. 7, 1939, Radio Broadcast KTGM," in *"For Our Navajo People":* *Diné Letters, Speeches and Petitions 1900–1960,* ed. Peter Iverson, photo ed. Monty Roessel (Albuquerque: University of New Mexico Press, 2002), 181–184, at 182–183.

9. Williams, Jr., *Navajo Political Process, supra* note 2, at 60.

10. *See* Elmer R. Rusco, *A Fateful Time: The Background and Legislative History of the Indian Reorganization Act* (Reno: University of Nevada Press, 2000), 28 ("The Navajo Tribal Council organized by Hagerman lasted and gained the support of the Navajos, no doubt in part because at the time of its formation there was no other governing structure at the level of the nation.").

11. Writing about Indian tribes in general, Nicholas Zaferatos explains, "Resource development of Indian lands served as the primary mechanism for transforming tribal communities from captive nations into internal colonies." Nicholas Christos Zaferatos, *Planning the American Indian Reservation: From Theory to Empowerment* (Syracuse, New York: Syracuse University Press, 2015), 113.

12. *See* Kelley and Francis, *A Diné History of Navajoland, supra* note 3, at 10 (highlighting the difficulty non-Indians had in recognizing traditional forms of Diné governance: "[l]ocal groups chose their leaders by consensus, notwithstanding the colonizer stereotype of Diné having no central leadership").

13. *See* Elizabeth Reese, "The Other American Law," *Stanford Law Review* 73 (2021), 32 (pagination from draft of manuscript available at https://papers.ssrn.com/sol3/papers.cfm

?abstract_id=3660166) ("Although the Navajo (or Diné, as they call themselves) people, culture, and elements of their political identity and laws are very old, the Navajo Nation is relatively new, existing as a unified state for only the last century.").

14. Jennifer Nez Denetdale, "Chairmen, Presidents, and Princesses: The Navajo Nation, Gender, and the Politics of Tradition," *Wicazo Sa Review* 21, no. 1 (2006): 9–28.

15. *See* Kathleen P. Chamberlain, *Under Sacred Ground: A History of Navajo Oil 1922–1982* (Albuquerque: University of New Mexico Press, 2000), at 84 ("Navajos relegated royalties to the tribe, not individuals – a far-sighted choice").

16. *See* Andrew Curley, "Constitutionalism," *in Navajo Nation Constitutional Feasibility and Government Reform Project* (Tsaile, Arizona: Diné Policy Institute, 2008), 19 (the Navajo Nation's "entire tribal government has been largely created by and for extractive industries"); Lerma, *Guided by the Mountains*, supra note 6, at 12 ("Navajo Nation was put under tremendous pressure to create governments with a singular purpose of signing land leases."); Klara B. Kelley, *Navajo Land Use: An Ethnoarchaeological Study* (New York: Academic Press, Inc., 1986), 9 ("In the Navajo country, industrial capital made its emerging dominance felt first through the creation, in 1922, of the Navajo Tribal Council, a representative body of Navajos that was to sign leases arranged between the Bureau of Indian Affairs (BIA) and private oil companies.").

17. Chamberlain, *Under Sacred Ground*, *supra* note 15, at 29–30.

18. *Id.* at 65 (the resolution failed to have effect because the council's ability to cancel such leases depended on the companies being in breach of contract).

19. *Id.* at 30.

20. *Id.* at 113 ("from 1923 forward, the Interior Department repeatedly failed to maximize revenues").

21. Russel Lawrence Barsh, "Indian Resources and the National Economy: Business Cycles and Policy Cycles," in *Native Americans and Public Policy*, eds. Fremont J. Lyden and Lyman H. Legters (Pittsburgh, Pennsylvania: University of Pittsburgh Press, 1992), 193–221, at 211.

22. Michael Joseph Francisconi, *Kinship, Capitalism, Change: The Informal Economy of the Navajo, 1968–1995* (Shrewsbury, Massachusetts: Garland Publishing, Inc., 1998), 70.

23. *Id.* at 69.

24. Philip Reno, *Mother Earth, Father Sky, and Economic Development: Navajo Resources and Their Use* (Albuquerque: University of New Mexico Press, 1981), 124.

25. Brian Jackson Morton, "Coal Leasing in the Fourth World: Hopi and Navajo Coal Leasing, 1954-1977" (PhD diss., University of California, Berkeley, 1985), 272.

26. Chamberlain, *Under Sacred Ground*, *supra* note 15, at 111.

27. Philip Reno, *Mother Earth, Father Sky, and Economic Development*, *supra* note 24, at 126 (quoting from Tom Barry, "Aneth People Tired of Exploitation: Oil Wealth Has Not Brought Them Better Life," *Navajo Times*, Apr. 13, 1978).

28. Chamberlain, *Under Sacred Ground*, *supra* note 15, at 111–112.

29. Jackson Morton, "Coal Leasing in the Fourth World: Hopi and Navajo Coal Leasing, 1954-1977," *supra* note 25, at 272.

30. *See* Williams, Jr., *Navajo Political Process*, *supra* note 2, at 19 ("Yet it was not until oil was discovered, on land originally set aside by the Treaty of 1868, that the need was sufficiently compelling to overcome the inertia that had previously prevented the establishment of a representative tribal government.").

31. *See, e.g.*, Kelley and Whiteley, *Navajoland*, *supra* note 1, at 139 ("Because these industries [referring to oil, gas, and coal extraction] are capital intensive, they furnish relatively few jobs. But lease monies, royalties, and bonuses, comprise most tribal government

revenues – seventy percent in 1975 – which support the core of tribal bureaucracy administering infrastructure development, social services, and some tribal enterprises.").

32. *See also* Lawrence C. Kelly, *The Navajo Indians and Federal Indian Policy: 1900–1935* (Tucson: University of Arizona Press, 1968), 139 ("This Meriam report, so named from the director of the project, Lewis M. Meriam, has become a classic in the field of Indian administration. Thoughtful and sober, it was the product of specialists in the fields of education, health, administration, law, and Indian history. In general the report was highly critical of the Bureau but, unlike many of the Bureau's critics, it found the roots of the Bureau's troubles not in the personalities of its leaders but in tradition."); David Treuer, *The Heartbeat of Wounded Knee: Native America from 1890 to the Present* (New York: Riverhead Books, 2019), 201–202 ("When they were done they had managed to create a comprehensive, detailed, and impartial document that offered a damning assessment of how Indians had fared over the forty years the assimilation machine had been gobbling them up and churning out Americans.").

33. Lewis Meriam et al., *The Problem of Indian Administration* (Baltimore: Johns Hopkins Press, 1928), 3.

34. *Id.* at 100 ("The evidence warrants the conclusion, however, that in the past fee patents have been issued too freely, that they have been given before the Indian has given sufficient demonstration of his capacity to make his own way. Too much reliance has been placed on the theory that the way to teach a boy to swim is to throw him overboard and let him swim or drown. The Indian faces too swift and treacherous a current for such an experiment at this period of his development.").

35. *Id.* at 7.

36. *See Id.* at 352.

37. *Id.* at 547.

38. *Id.* at 563.

39. *Id.* at 6.

40. *Id.* at 14.

41. *Id.* at 504.

42. *Id.* at 431.

43. *United States* v. *Kagama*, 118 U.S. 375, 384 (1886). For a critique of this view today, see Matthew L. M. Fletcher, "Retiring the 'Deadliest Enemies' Model of Tribal-State Relations," *Tulsa Law Review* 43 (2007): 73–87.

44. For more on John Collier's background, see Treuer, *The Heartbeat of Wounded Knee*, *supra* note 32, at 204–205.

45. *See* Traci Brynne Voyles, *Wastelanding: Legacies of Uranium Mining in Navajo Country* (Minneapolis: University of Minnesota Press, 2015) 51 ("Collier himself, an avowed liberal, felt he stood in opposition to prior federal Indian policies of forced assimilation into white language and culture, but the policies during his tenure merely translated into new forms of the old assimilationist ideology.").

46. Donald L. Fixico, *Indian Resilience and Rebuilding: Indigenous Nations in the Modern American West* (Tucson: University of Arizona Press, 2013), 88.

47. Needham, *Powerlines*, *supra* note 3, at 49.

48. *Id.*

49. There are conflicting vote tallies in the literature. *See* Fixico, *Indian Resilience and Rebuilding*, *supra* note 46, at 87 ("Of 15,600 votes cast, the margin of defeat was only 134 votes."); Williams, Jr., *Navajo Political Process*, *supra* note 2, at 23 ("The Navajos voted by a slim margin of 7,992 to 7,608 to reject the Indian Reorganization Act.").

50. Williams, Jr., *Navajo Political Process*, *supra* note 2, at 23.

51. For more on Diné Fundamental Law, see Kenneth Bobroff, "Diné Bi Beenahaz'áanii: Codifying Indigenous Consuetudinary Law in the 21st Century," *Tribal Law Journal* 5, no.4 (2004–2005). *See also* Ezra Rosser, "Displacing the Judiciary: Customary Law and the Threat of a Defensive Tribal Council," *American Indian Law Review* 34, no.2 (2011): 379–401 (highlighting an unsuccessful effort by the Council to undermine Fundamental Law).

52. *See* Kelley and Whiteley, *Navajoland, supra* note 1, at 75 ("Chapters did not become widespread until around 1930 when the Tribal Council began to allocate money for chapter house construction and other local projects.").

53. Williams, Jr., *Navajo Political Process, supra* note 2, at 37 ("The chapters were integrated into preexisting, local sociopolitical structures which had at their core the extended family structure that functioned as the basic unit of social control among the Navajo people.").

54. *See* Chamberlain, *Under Sacred Ground, supra* note 15, at 75–76 ("While the council addressed matters raised by the dominant society – like oil royalties – chapters dealt with internal or local issues.").

55. The livestock reduction section of this chapter draws heavily upon Ezra Rosser, "Reclaiming the Navajo Range: Resolving the Conflict Between Grazing Rights and Development," *Connecticut Law Review*, Vol. 51 (2019): 953–981.

56. *See* Robert S. McPherson, *Sacred Land Sacred View* (Salt Lake City, Utah: Brigham Young University, 1992), 61 ("Interestingly, perhaps the most influential animal to affect the life of the Diné was not native to the American Southwest but was introduced by the Spanish. Soon after their arrival, sheep became a major economic, social, and religious consideration in traditional Navajo life. People measured their status in society, the welfare of their family, and the blessings from the holy beings by taking stock of their herds.").

57. Kevin Tehan, "Of Indians, Land, and the Federal Government: The Navajo-Hopi Land Dispute," *Arizona State Law Journal* 1976 (1976): 173–212, at 177 ("Animal husbandry has been part of the Navajo social structure since its earliest days; sheep serve as a measure of wealth and a means of exchange. The relationship between the Navajo and their sheep transcends a simple owner-object owned situation, for the Navajo is 'linked to his herds' by ties 'in which he and his family's continuity and well being, as well as his own self-image are symbolized by his herds.'").

58. Melanie K. Yazzie, "Decolonizing Development in Diné Bikeyah: Resource Extraction, Anti-Capitalism, and Relational Futures," *Environment and Society* 9, no.1 (2018): 25–39, at 32.

59. Kelley, *Navajo Land Use, supra* note 16, at 9 ("The industrial growth of southern California required that Navajos reduce their livestock to stem overgrazing and the resulting soil erosion, which threatened to silt up Boulder Dam, the source of electricity that was to power California's growth.").

60. Needham, *Powerlines, supra* note 3, at 47.

61. *See, e.g.,* J. W. Hoover, "Navajo Land Problems," *Economic Geography* 13, no.3 (1937): 281–300, at 286–289 (explaining the problem of erosion due to overgrazing and providing photos of arroyo development).

62. *See* Voyles, *Wastelanding, supra* note 45, at 28 ("The notion that indigenous relationships to the land had driven it to ruin, in short, promoted colonial agendas of control, coercion, and assimilation. In the context of livestock reduction on Navajo land in the 1930s, this colonial declensionist narrative was compounded by the culture of conservationism in federal resource management, an efficiency-oriented approach to resources that was

starkly juxtaposed against what was seen as an irrational Navajo land use that produced a landscape desperately in need of salvation."); Marsha Weisiger, "Gendered Injustice: Navajo Livestock Reduction in the New Deal Era," *Western Historical Quarterly* 38, no.4 (2007): 437–455, at 440 ("Collier believed that if the range continued to deteriorate, sheep and goats would starve, and ultimately, so would Navajos.").

63. For a skeptical take on Navajo overgrazing, see Kelley and Francis, A *Diné History of Navajoland*, *supra* note 3, at 250–255.

64. See "Tom Dodge, Oct. 30, 1933, Speech," in *"For Our Navajo People": Diné Letters, Speeches and Petitions 1900–1960*, ed. Peter Iverson, photo ed. Monty Roessel (Albuquerque: University of New Mexico Press, 2002), 166–169, at 168. ("I know from my own observations that the reservation as a whole is very much over-grazed. We Navajos should organize in some way or other to at least stop the process of erosion. We ourselves should take the lead in dealing with this question of erosion. We should not be driven to it by outside people. We ourselves should take the initiative. We should not hold back hoping that the conditions will be better themselves without our help. Certainly the conditions will not be improved if we graze our sheep as we have been doing in the past. One way of dealing with the question is range control. And certainly there is a great need of range management or control. Those who own sheep and goats should organize or agree among themselves to establish some form of range control. Thos[e] who own livestock should take the lead. This should not be forced upon them from Washington.").

65. Kelley, *Navajo Land Use*, *supra* note 16, at 98.

66. See Williams, Jr., *Navajo Political Process*, *supra* note 2, at 28 ("The Navajo Tribal Council, in a meeting at Tuba City in November 1933, passed a resolution sanctioning a voluntary stock reduction program with the stipulation that the Government attempt to secure additional grazing lands outside of the reservation."). *See also* Kelley and Francis, *supra* note 12, at 20 (arguing that the Council's "consent to the stock reduction program" destroyed Diné respect for the Council).

67. Voyles, *Wastelanding*, *supra* note 45, at 47 ("During the stock reduction period, a veritable flood of federal experts, ranging from ecologists, conservationists, agronomists, and cartographers, to social workers, anthropologists, and economists, descended on the reservation.").

68. O. N. Hicks, "The First American and His Range Resource," *Journal of Range Management* 23, no.6 (1970): 391–396, at 393.

69. See Kelley, *Navajo Land Use*, *supra* note 16, at 100; Williams, Jr., *Navajo Political Process*, *supra* note 2, at 39. *See also* Lawrence David Weiss, *Development of Capitalism in the Navajo Nation: A Political-Economic History* (Minneapolis, Minnesota: MEP Publications, 1984), 99 (noting that "[m]uch of the reduction was effected by the government offering prices substantially above market value for Navajo stock" and explaining the market prices were relatively low because of the Great Depression).

70. Kelley, *Navajo Land Use*, *supra* note 16, at 100.

71. Williams, Jr., *Navajo Political Process*, *supra* note 2, at 39.

72. *Id.*

73. *Id.*

74. The favored definition of the US government was based on residence, but such a standard worked to incentivize the breaking up of large family units. *See* "Interview with E. R. Fryer and Tribal Council Members (May 15, 1939)," in *"For Our Navajo People": Diné Letters, Speeches and Petitions 1900–1960*, ed. Peter Iverson, photo ed. Monty Roessel (Albuquerque: University of New Mexico Press, 2002), 20. Fryer explained

how the Indian Service defines family for the purpose of stock reduction: "Usually we name the head of the family. If they live together and share things and operate as a family it is considered a family. They may have a son-in-law who does not own any sheep but has two or three horses. He is part of that family group if he lives with his father-in-law and shares income." *Id.*

75. See Weiss, *Development of Capitalism in the Navajo Nation, supra* note 69, at 101 ("The effect of these inequities against smaller herders were such that, in the aggregate, smaller herders were reduced by 23.1 percent while larger herders were reduced by only 5.4 percent of their prereduction size.").

76. *See* Chamberlain, *Under Sacred Ground, supra* note 15, at 73 (discussing the goat reductions of 1934); Kelley and Whiteley, *Navajoland, supra* note 1, at 103 ("Thirty-five hundred goats from Navajo Mountain area 'were shot and left in heaps to rot' near Inscription House because the cost of driving them to the railroad was prohibitive."); *see also* Needham, *Powerlines, supra* note 3, at 48 ("Furthermore, some BIA officials carried out reduction with marked cruelty. On occasion, agents shot animals and burned their carcasses in front of astonished families that had formed lifelong relationships with those animals.").

77. Kelly, *The Navajo Indians and Federal Indian Policy: 1900-1935, supra* note 32, at 162.

78. *See* Kelley, *Navajo Land Use, supra* note 16, at 101 ("Between 1939 and 1943, the Indian Service secured court judgments against several Navajos accused of violating the grazing regulations, and those judgments broke the Navajo resistance.").

79. "Letter from Tom Dodge to John Collier (May 7, 1936)," in *"For Our Navajo People": Diné Letters, Speeches and Petitions 1900-1960,* ed. Peter Iverson, photo ed. Monty Roessel (Albuquerque: University of New Mexico Press, 2002), 176.

80. Williams, Jr., *Navajo Political Process, supra* note 2, at 29.

81. Meriam et al., *The Problem of Indian Administration, supra* note 33, at 504.

82. "Letter from Scott Preston, Julius Begay, Frank Goldtooth, and Judge Many Children to Rep. John R. Murdock (Feb. 14, 1940)," in *"For Our Navajo People": Diné Letters, Speeches and Petitions 1900-1960,* ed. Peter Iverson, photo ed. Monty Roessel (Albuquerque: University of New Mexico Press, 2002), 23–24.

83. "Speech by Manuel Denetso at the Navajo Council (July 5, 1940)," in *"For Our Navajo People": Diné Letters, Speeches and Petitions 1900-1960,* ed. Peter Iverson, photo ed. Monty Roessel (Albuquerque: University of New Mexico Press, 2002), 27.

84. Voyles, *Wastelanding, supra* note 45, at 39, 52.

85. Kelley, *Navajo Land Use, supra* note 16, at 99.

86. Needham, *Powerlines, supra* note 3, at 48.

87. "Peace and Livestock," in *Between Sacred Mountains: Navajo Stories and Lessons from the Land,* eds. Sam Bingham et al. (Tucson: University of Arizona Press, 1982), 55 ("The cutting down of livestock is known as *Stock Reduction,* and people remember it with sadness the way they remember Fort Sumner."). *See also* Chamberlain, *Under Sacred Ground, supra* note 15, at 83 (explaining that "stock reduction rivaled the Long Walk in its devastating consequences"); Powell, *Landscapes of Power, supra* note 5, at 49 ("The livestock reduction of the 1930s is remembered almost as bitterly as the displacement during the Long Walk of the 1860s."); Mary Stephenson, *Navajo Ways in Government: A Political Process* (Menasha, Wisconsin: American Anthropological Association, 1963), 115 ("for the Navajos the 'Indian New Deal' was the period of greatest coercion since Bosque Redondo.").

88. *See* "Letter from Chee Dodge to James Stewart, Land Dep't, Indian Office, Dep't of Indian Affairs (Apr. 20, 1936)," in *"For Our Navajo People": Diné Letters, Speeches and Petitions 1900-1960,* ed. Peter Iverson, photo ed. Monty Roessel (Albuquerque: University

of New Mexico Press, 2002), 173 ("The Indians have all been excited for the last two or three years anyway, because they didn't know whether they were going to lose their stock, whether they were going broke or would have anything to eat.").

89. Richard Wright, *The Roots of Dependency: Subsistence, Environment, and Social Change among the Choctaws, Pawnees, and Navajos* (Lincoln: University of Nebraska Press, 1983), 313 ("Coming to the Navajos with a program promising economic rehabilitation, Collier had crippled their way of life and accelerated the onset of dependency.").

90. Chamberlain, *Under Sacred Ground, supra* note 15, at 73. *See also* Franconi, *Kinship, Capitalism, Change, supra* note 22, at 58 ("Stock reduction of the 1930's reduced by fifty percent the total number of sheep on the reservation and dramatically changed the economic livelihood and social status of many families. Before the livestock cuts, Diné were self-sufficient, but following them, supplemental income from wage labor and/or welfare became sufficient.").

91. "Letter from Deshna Clah Cheschillige to Senator Dennis Chavez (Dec. 8, 1940)," in *"For Our Navajo People": Diné Letters, Speeches and Petitions 1900-1960*, ed. Peter Iverson, photo ed. Monty Roessel (Albuquerque: University of New Mexico Press, 2002), 143.

92. *See* Fixico, *Indian Resilience and Rebuilding, supra* note 46, at 85, 87.

93. In his account of livestock reduction, former Navajo Nation Council member Henry Zah noted, "the government took away much of our stock when it increased too much, after the government had warned the Diné about the conditions of the land. This had been warned when the sheep were given. The Diné had increased their livestock, and it was thought of as if the sheep still belonged to Wááshindoon." Henry Zah, "Henry Zah," in *Navajo Stories of the Long Walk Period*, ed. Broderick H. Johnson (Tsaile, Navajo Nation, Arizona: Navajo Community College Press, 1973), 156–157, at 157 (Diné pronunciation of Washington in the original).

94. Marsha Weisiger, *Dreaming of Sheep in Navajo Country* (Seattle: University of Washington Press, 2009), 7 ("With missionary zeal, they imposed on the Navajos an experimental program based on the emerging sciences of ecology and soil conservation, while disparaging local knowledge and ignoring the importance of long-established cultural patterns.").

95. Reno, *Mother Earth, Father Sky, and Economic Development, supra* note 24, at 29.

96. *See* "Letter from Scott Preston, Julius Begay, Frank Goldtooth, and Judge Many Children to Rep. John R. Murdock (Feb. 14, 1940)," in *"For Our Navajo People": Diné Letters, Speeches and Petitions 1900-1960*, ed. Peter Iverson, photo ed. Monty Roessel (Albuquerque: University of New Mexico Press, 2002), 23 ("282 sheep units is not sufficient for even the bare existence of a moderate size Navajo family without additional income, and such a policy will mean the impoverishment of the entire Navajo Tribe.").

97. Kelley, *Navajo Land Use, supra* note 16, at 102.

98. *See* Franconi, *Kinship, Capitalism, Change, supra* note 22, at 50 ("Stock reduction was perhaps one of the most poorly managed programs of the New Deal era. To begin with, it was imposed upon the Diné from the outside, and, in spite of the proclaimed good intentions, clearly represented the colonial nature of reservations in the U.S.").

99. *See, e.g.*, Lynn Fuller, "Desertification on the Navajo Reservation: A Legal and Historical Analysis," *Stanford Environmental Law Journal* 8 (1989): 229–292, at 258 ("Navajo governmental authorities were politically unwilling or unable to enforce the grazing regulations . . .").

100. *See* Willow Roberts Powers, *Navajo Trading: The End of an Era* (Albuquerque: University of New Mexico Press, 2001), 127 (discussing the decline of sheep and rise of

wage labor in the 1960s and 1970s); Colleen O'Neill, *Working the Navajo Way: Labor and Culture in the Twentieth Century* (Lawrence: University Press of Kansas, 2005), 81–141 (describing the rise and form of Navajo wage labor).

101. *See, e.g.*, Fuller, *supra* note 99, at 231–232 (discussing the extreme desertification of Navajo lands due to overgrazing by livestock and the impacts on the Navajo people).

4 WAR PRODUCTION AND GROWING PAINS

1. *See, e.g.*, President George W. Bush, "Remarks by the President in a Ceremony Honoring the Navajo Code Talkers," *White House*, July 26, 2001, https://georgewbush-whitehouse.archives.gov/news/releases/2001/07/20010726-5.html.
2. Richard Ruelas, "Long Walk to Voting Rights for Navajos," *Arizona Republic*, Jan. 19, 2014. It is worth noting that Navajos, as well as members of other tribes, continue to face significant election-related barriers. *See generally* Jean Reith Schroedel, *Voting in Indian Country: The View from the Trenches* (Philadelphia: University of Pennsylvania Press, 2020); Patty Ferguson-Bohnee, "How the Native American Vote Continues to be Suppressed," ABA *Human Rights Magazine* 45, No. 1, Feb. 9, 2020, www.americanbar.org/groups/crsj/publications/human_rights_magazine_home/voting-rights/how-the-native-american-vote-continues-to-be-suppressed/. Physical address requirements and distance between polling stations serve to limit the Navajo vote. Native American Voting Rights Commission, Voting Barriers Encountered by Native Americans in Arizona, New Mexico, Nevada, and South Dakota (Jan. 2018), www.narf.org/wordpress/wp-content/uploads/2018/01/2017NAVRCsurvey-summary.pdf. In a particularly problematic example of non-Indian resistance to Navajo electoral might, after Navajos won two out of the three commission seats for San Juan County, Utah, those upset with the result began exploring ways of splitting the county in half and of changing the form of government. *See* Cindy Yurth, "Sea Change in the Desert," *Navajo Times*, Aug. 5, 2020.
3. David H. Getches et al., *Cases and Materials on Federal Indian Law*, 7th ed. (St. Paul, Minnesota: West Academic Publishing, 2017), 230.
4. Albert Einstein, Letter to President Roosevelt, Aug. 2, 1939, www.fdrlibrary.marist.edu/archives/pdfs/docsworldwar.pdf.
5. Barbara Rose Johnson, Susan Dawson and Gary Madsen, "Uranium Mining and Milling: Navajo Experiences in the American Southwest," in *Indians and Energy: Exploitation and Opportunity in the American Southwest*, eds. Susan L. Smith and Brian Frehner (Santa Fe, New Mexico: School for Advanced Research Press, 2010), 111–134, at 113 ("90 percent of the uranium eventually used in the Manhattan Project was imported from Canada and the Belgian Congo, with smaller amount obtained from mines in South Africa.").
6. Traci Brynne Voyles, *Wastelanding: Legacies of Uranium Mining in Navajo Country* (Minneapolis: University of Minnesota Press, 2015), 2.
7. *See id.*; Johnson, Dawson and Madsen, "Uranium Mining and Milling," *supra* note 5, at 113.
8. *See* Voyles, *Wastelanding*, *supra* note 6, at 85 ("By the mid-1950s, uranium exploration and leasing was well underway on Diné land.").
9. For more on the dangers posed by these tailing piles, see Bruce E. Johansen, *Resource Exploitation in Native North America: A Plague Upon the Peoples* (Denver, Colorado: Praeger, 2016), 3–5.

10. For a comprehensive history of uranium mining on the Navajo Nation, including photos of miners and mines, see Peter H. Eichstaedt, *If You Poison Us: Uranium and Native Americans* (Santa Fe, New Mexico: Red Crane Books, 1994).

11. *See id.* at 18 ("In Monument Valley, just outside of Kayenta, the valorization and degradation of the desert occurred simultaneously in the 1940s and 1950s; even as film crews shot the westerns that would underscore white Americans' collective 'imagined intimacy' with this part of Navajo country as the symbolic setting for their imagined community, uranium companies were busy blasting its famous red mesas into nonexistence for the uranium encased inside.").

12. Claire R. Newman, "Creating an Environmental No-Man's Land: The Tenth Circuit's Departure from Environmental and Indian Law Protecting a Tribal Community's Health and Environment," *Washington Journal of Environmental Law and Policy* 1, no.2 (2011): 352–411, at 378.

13. Keith Schneider, "A Valley of Death for Navajo Uranium Miners," *New York Times*, May 3, 1993.

14. *See* Voyles, *Wastelanding, supra* note 6, at 114 ("Likewise, in uranium mining, the bodily health of Native miners was exchanged for the national security needs of procuring uranium.").

15. Dana Powell, *Landscapes of Power: Politics of Energy in the Navajo Nation* (Durham, North Carolina: Duke University Press, 2018), 52 ("In the 1950s, before the uranium boom in the Southwest, cancer rates among Navajo people were so low that medical researchers published on a possible 'cancer immunity' in the Navajo population. By the 1980s however, cancer rates skyrocketed, especially among Navajo men who worked as miners and Navajo teenagers who had grown up living close to abandoned mines and other radioactive sites, historicizing the formerly assumed 'immunity.'").

16. Radiation Exposure Compensation Act, 42 U.S.C. § 2210 note (2012).

17. *See* Alice Segal, "Uranium Mining and the Navajo Nation—Legal Injustice," *Southern California Review of Law and Social Justice* 21 (2012): 355–397, at 385–386; Johansen, *Resource Exploitation in Native North America, supra* note 9, at 9–10.

18. William Jenney, "Having Your Yellowcake and Eating It Too: The Environmental and Health Impacts of Uranium Mining on the Colorado Plateau," *Arizona Journal of Environmental Law and Policy* 7 (2017): 27–55, at 52.

19. Klara B. Kelley, *Navajo Land Use: An Ethnoarchaeological Study* (New York: Academic Press, Inc., 1986), 152.

20. *Id.* at 152.

21. Andrew Needham, *Powerlines: Phoenix and the Making of the Modern Southwest* (Princeton, New Jersey: Princeton University Press, 2016), 146.

22. *See* Bethany R. Berger, "Paul and Lorena Williams: Sovereignty and Sheep on the Navajo Nation," in *"Our Cause Will Ultimately Triumph": Profiles in American Indian Sovereignty*, ed. Tim Alan Garrison (Durham, North Carolina: Carolina Academic Press, 2014), 51–64; Bethany R. Burger, "Williams v. Lee and the Debate Over Indian Equality," *Michigan Law Review* 109 (2011): 1463–1528.

23. Burger, "Williams v. Lee and the Debate Over Indian Equality," *supra* note 22, at 1501.

24. *Id.* at 1503.

25. 358 U.S. 217, 223 (1959).

26. Leah S. Glaser, "'An Absolute Paragon of Paradoxes': Native American Power and the Electrification of Arizona's Indian Reservations," in *Indians and Energy: Exploitation and Opportunity in the American Southwest*, eds. Susan L. Smith and Brian Frehner (Santa Fe, New Mexico: School for Advanced Research Press, 2010), 161–202, at 176.

27. *Id.*

28. Hal K. Rothman, "Pokey's Paradox: Tourism and Transformation on the Western Navajo Reservation," in *Reopening the American West,* ed. Hal K. Rothman (Tucson: University of Arizona Press, 1998), 90–121, at 106.

29. Kelley, *Navajo Land Use, supra* note 19, at 152.

30. Voyles, *Wastelanding, supra* note 6, at 104.

31. Arizona Department of Transportation Research Center, *Arizona Transportation History: Final Report 660* (Phoenix: Arizona Department of Transportation, Dec. 2011), 64, https://azdot.gov/docs/media/read-arizona%27s-transportation-history-in-its-entirety-.pdf?sfvrsn=0.

32. *See* Klara Kelley and Harris Francis, *A Diné History of Navajoland* (Tucson: University of Arizona Press, 2019), 22 ("Thus has Diné political sovereignty advanced, the price being dependence on resource extraction by and for outsiders.").

33. *See id.* at 25 ("Government agents and school people went into the countryside to round up children for the [BIA] schools, with or without their parents' consent."). For more on education systems imposed on Diné children during the twentieth century, see generally Farina King, *The Earth Memory Compass: Diné Landscapes and Education in the Twentieth Century* (Lawrence: University Press of Kansas, 2018).

34. For more on relocation, see Kasey Keeler, "Putting People Where They Belong: American Indian Housing Policy in the Mid-Twentieth Century," *Native American and Indigenous Studies* 3, no.2 (2016): 70–104.

35. Eric Shultz, "Report from Church Rock: A Uranium Legacy Update," *La Jicarita Magazine,* Sep. 10, 2012, https://lajicarita.wordpress.com/2012/09/10/report-from-church-rock-a-uranium-legacy-update/.

36. Rebecca Tsosie, "Indigenous Peoples and the Ethics of Remediation: Redressing the Legacy of Radioactive Contamination for Native Peoples and Native Lands," *Santa Clara Journal of International Law* 13, no.1 (2015): 203–272, at 216.

37. Marley Shebala, "Poison in the Earth: 1979 Church Rock Spill a Symbol for Uranium Dangers," *Navajo Times,* July 23, 2009.

38. United States Government Accountability Office, Uranium Contamination: Overall Scope, Time Frame, and Cost Information Is Needed for Contamination Cleanup on the Navajo Reservation (Washington, DC: United States Government Accountability Office, 2014), 10.

39. Laurie Wirt, *Radioactivity in the Environment—A Case Study of the Puerco and Little Colorado River Basins, Arizona and New Mexico* (Tucson: US Geological Survey Water-Resources Investigations Report 94-4192, 1994), 14.

40. Laurie Wirt, *Radioactivity in the Environment—A Case Study of the Puerco and Little Colorado River Basins, Arizona and New Mexico* (Tucson, Arizona: US Geological Survey Water-Resources Investigations Report 94-4192, 1994), 15.

41. Johansen, *Resource Exploitation in Native North America, supra* note 9, at 10–13.

42. Tsosie, "Indigenous Peoples and the Ethics of Remediation," *supra* note 36, at 214.

43. United States Government Accountability Office, *Uranium Contamination, supra* note 38, at 55.

44. Tsosie, "Indigenous Peoples and the Ethics of Remediation," *supra* note 36, at 207.

45. Philip Reno, *Mother Earth, Father Sky, and Economic Development: Navajo Resources and Their Use* (Albuquerque: University of New Mexico Press, 1981), 106.

46. Donald L. Baars, *Navajo Country: A Geology and Natural History of the Four Corners Region* (Albuquerque: University of New Mexico Press, 1995), 172.

47. M. R. Campbell and H. E. Gregory, "The Black Mesa Coal Field, Arizona," in *Contributions to Economic Geology (Short Papers and Preliminary Reports) 1909: Part*

II.—*Mineral Fuels,* Bulletin 431, Marius R. Campbell geologist in charge (Washington, DC: Government Printing Office, 1911), 229–238, at 229.

48. *Id.*

49. *Id.* at 236.

50. Mark Schoepfle et al., "Navajo Attitudes Toward Development and Change: A Unified Ethnographic and Survey Approach to an Understanding of Their Future," *American Anthropologist* 86 (1984): 885–904, at 885.

51. Brian Jackson Morton, "Coal Leasing in the Fourth World: Hopi and Navajo Coal Leasing, 1954–1977" (PhD diss., University of California, Berkeley, 1985), 1.

52. Kelley, *Navajo Land Use, supra* note 19, at 27.

53. Colleen O'Neill, *Working the Navajo Way: Labor and Culture in the Twentieth Century* (Lawrence: University Press of Kansas, 2005), 30–54 (describing the development and characteristics of truck mines of the 1930s).

54. Needham, *Powerlines, supra* note 21, at 45.

55. Morton, "Coal Leasing in the Fourth World," *supra* note 51, at 7.

56. *Id.* at 8.

57. *Id.* at 10. Peabody Coal Company operates mines across the United States, and in 1968 it was operating thirty-seven wholly owned mines in eight states in addition to its Arizona mining efforts. Peabody Coal Co., *Peabody Coal: The First One Hundred Years* (St. Louis, Missouri: Peabody Holding Company, Inc., 1983), 29 (on file with the Missouri History Museum Library). At the time, Peabody was responsible for "about 10 percent of the nation's total production of bituminous coal." *Id.*

58. Morton, "Coal Leasing in the Fourth World," *supra* note 51, at 56.

59. *See* Needham, *Powerlines, supra* note 21; Judith Nies, *Unreal City: Las Vegas, Black Mesa, and the Fate of the West* (New York: Nation Books, 2014).

60. Needham, *Powerlines, supra* note 21, at 1.

61. Bill Corcoran, "The Sierra Club's Shadowy History with the Navajo Generating Station," *Sierra Magazine,* Oct. 12, 2017, www.sierraclub.org/sierra/sierra-club-s-shadowy-history-navajo-generating-station.

62. *See* Powell, *Landscapes of Power, supra* note 15, at 10.

63. Martin Cruz Smith, *Nightwing* (New York: W. W. Norton & Company, 1977).

64. *See Lomayaktewa* v. *Hathaway,* 520 F.2d 1324, 1327 (9th Cir. 1975).

65. Charles F. Wilkinson, "Home Dance, the Hopi, and Black Mesa Coal: Conquest and Endurance in the American Southwest," *Brigham Young University Law Review* 1996 (1996): 449–482, at 459–467, 469–472.

66. Katosha Belvin Nakai, "When Kachinas and Coal Collide: Can Cultural Resources Law Rescue the Hopi at Black Mesa?," *Arizona State Law Journal* 35 (2003): 1283–1330, at 1290 (giving water usage amounts).

67. Johansen, *Resource Exploitation in Native North America, supra* note 9, at 179.

68. *See* John Dougherty, "A People Betrayed," *Phoenix New Times,* May 1, 1997; Evelyn Nieves, The Largest Coal-Fired Power Plant in the West Is Slated for Closure, *Sierra Magazine,* Oct. 12, 2017, www.sierraclub.org/sierra/2017-6-november-december/feature/largest-coal-fired-power-plant-west-slated-for-closure#;6.

69. Peter Nabokov, *Where the Lightning Strikes: The Lives of American Indian Sacred Places* (New York: Viking Press, 2006), 143.

70. United States Commission on Civil Rights, *The Navajo Nation: An American Colony* 20 (Washington, DC: Commission on Civil Rights, 1975), 17 (report written by Carol J. McCabe and Hester Lewis).

71. *Id.* at 30.

72. Eric Cheyfitz, "Theory and Practice: The Case of the Navajo-Hopi Land Dispute," *American University Journal of Gender, Social Policy and the Law* 10 (2002): 619–632, at 624.

73. *Id.*

74. *Healing* v. *Jones*, 210 F. Supp. 125, 134 (1962) (dividing the mineral rights to the contested portions of the 1882 Executive Order area equally between the Hopi and Navajo tribes). For more on the maneuverings of the Navajo and Hopi attorneys that led up to *Healing* v. *Jones*, see John Redhouse, *Geopolitics of the Navajo Hopi Land Dispute* (Flagstaff, Arizona: Indigenous Action Media, 1985), 9–12.

75. Cheyfitz, "Theory and Practice," *supra* note 70, at 627.

76. *See* Kate Linthicum, "Trying to Rebuild After 40 Frozen Years," *Los Angeles Times*, Nov. 5, 2009.

77. Reid Peyton Chambers, "Reflections on the Changes in Indian Law, Federal Indian Policies and Conditions on Indian Reservations since the Late 1960s," *Arizona State Law Journal* 46 (2015): 729–778, at 738 (following the Nixon speech, "promoting tribal self-determination has been the policy of every subsequent administration and bipartisan majorities in Congress.").

78. *See* Dana E. Powell and Dáilan J. Long, "Landscapes of Power: Renewable Energy Activism in Diné Bikéyah," in *Indians and Energy: Exploitation and Opportunity in the American Southwest*, eds. Susan L. Smith and Brian Frehner (Santa Fe, New Mexico: School for Advanced Research Press, 2010), 231–262, at 238 ("Since the industry's arrival in Navajo land in the early twentieth century, coal mining has become an integral part of Navajo livelihoods and cultural practices, perhaps because extractive industry is systematically embedded in the tribe's economic map as a result of the historical formation of the tribal government."). *See also* Rebecca Tsosie, "Indigenous Peoples and Epistemic Injustice: Science, Ethics, and Human Rights," *Washington Law Review* 87 (2012): 1133–1201, at 1171 (noting that coal, oil, and gas exploration "are often supported by tribal leaders as one of the sole mechanisms for tribal economic development").

79. *See* Melanie K. Yazzie, "Decolonizing Development in Diné Bikéyah: Resource Extraction, Anti-Capitalism, and Relational Futures," *Environment and Society* 9, no.1 (2018): 25–39, at 26.

80. For photos of the protest, see Bob Fitch Photography Archive, "New Mexico Navajo Protest, 1974," *Stanford Libraries*, https://exhibits.stanford.edu/fitch/browse/new-mexico-navajo-protest-1974.

81. United States Commission on Civil Rights, *The Navajo Nation*, *supra* note 70, at 23 (quoting Dr. Aberle).

82. Andrew Needham, "'A Piece of the Action': Navajo Nationalism, Energy Development, and Metropolitan Inequality," in *Indians and Energy: Exploitation and Opportunity in the American Southwest*, eds. Susan L. Smith and Brian Frehner (Santa Fe, New Mexico: School for Advanced Research Press, 2010), 203–230, at 211.

83. *Id.* at 211 (quoting from "They're Just Saying That," *Diné Baa-Hani*, Sept. 1970).

84. Morton, "Coal Leasing in the Fourth World," *supra* note 51, at 189 (quoting Peter MacDonald).

85. United States Commission on Civil Rights, *The Navajo Nation*, *supra* note 70, at 30 (quoting Peter MacDonald).

86. Needham, "A Piece of the Action," *supra* note 82, at 212–213.

87. *Id.* at 216 (quoting from "Indian Tribes Must Get Fair Return for Resources," *Navajo Times*, Apr. 22, 1976).

88. Donald L. Fixico, *Indian Resilience and Rebuilding: Indigenous Nations in the Modern American West* (Tucson: University of Arizona Press, 2013), 57.

89. For more on MacDonald's career, see Peter MacDonald, *The Last Warrior: Peter MacDonald and the Navajo Nation* (New York: Crown Publishers, 1993) (with Ted Schwarz).
90. Fixico, *Indian Resilience and Rebuilding, supra* note 88, at 156–157.
91. *See* Powell, *Landscapes of Power, supra* note 15, at 82 ("Despite CERT's many harsh critics, its significance as a model of anticolonial energy activism, modeled after global designs forged in Middle Eastern environmental governance, cannot be underestimated. Thirty-five years later, CERT continues to operate as a voice for mineral-rich native nations in addressing Congress and mobilizing individual native nations to control and protect their interests in energy development.").
92. Kent Demaret, "There's Fuel in Them Thar Hills, and Peter MacDonald's Indians May Now Get Theirs," *People Magazine*, Sept. 3, 1979.
93. Peter MacDonald, *The Last Warrior, supra* note 89, at 229.
94. *See United States v. Brown*, 763 F. Supp. 1518, 1520-24 (D.C. Az. 1991) (containing a brief overview of the nature of the bribery); *Navajo Nation v. MacDonald, Sr.*, No. A-CR-09-90 (Nav. Sup. Ct., Dec. 30, 1991) (upholding convictions on forty-one criminal counts). For Peter MacDonald's side of the story, see MacDonald, *The Last Warrior, supra* note 89, at 278–341.
95. Jerry Mander, *In the Absence of the Sacred: The Failure of Technology and the Survival of the Indian Nations* (San Francisco: Sierra Club Books, 1991), 279.
96. Much of the discussion of *Navajo Nation I and II* comes from Ezra Rosser, "The Trade-off Between Self-Determination and the Trust Doctrine: Tribal Government and the Possibility of Failure," *Arkansas Law Review* 58 (2005): 291–352.
97. Kathleen P. Chamberlain, *Under Sacred Ground: A History of Navajo Oil 1922–1982* (Tucson: University of New Mexico Press, 2000), 97.
98. *Seminole Nation v. United States*, 316 U.S. 286, 297 (1942).
99. 207 U.S. 564 (1908).
100. *See United States v. Navajo Nation*, 556 U.S. 287 (2009).
101. Much of the discussion of the proposed Desert Rock power plant comes from an earlier article: Ezra Rosser, "Ahistorical Indians and Reservation Resources," *Environmental Law* 40 (2010): 437–545.
102. Bureau of Indian Affairs, Desert Rock Energy Project Draft Environmental Impact Statement, DOI DES 07-23, May 2007 at § Appendix D, "Navajo Mine Extension Project: Background Information and Preliminary Mine Plans," p. D-1.
103. Powell, *Landscapes of Power, supra* note 15, at 127.
104. *See* Marley Shebala, "Desert Rock on the Rocks?," *Navajo Times*, May 1, 2009 (making the connection in the dates); Joe Shirley, Jr., "President's Statement on Sovereignty Day," *Navajo Nation Press Release*, Apr. 27, 2009.
105. Bureau of Indian Affairs, Desert Rock Energy Project Draft Environmental Impact Statement, *supra* note 102, at § 2.2.2.1.2, Ch. 2, p. 7–8. The DEIS also includes water use figures in acre-feet per year rather than gpm; 4950 af/yr is equivalent to the 3,070 gpm planned amount. This does not include the additional 600 af/yr "associated with the expansion of the surface mining operations at the Navajo Mine required to supply coal to the Desert Rock Energy Project." *Id.* at § 2.2.2.1.2, Ch. 2, p. 9.
106. *Id.* at 3-79 to 3-85.
107. Chuck Slothower, "Officials tout N.M.'s Desert Rock: Environmental Impact minimal from plant, they say," *Durango Herald*, Sep. 15, 2006. The Four Corners Air Quality Task Force felt that the statement "epitomizes our perception of the sensitivity of [USEPA] Region 9 personnel to the issues in the Four Corners Region." Four

Corners Air Quality Task Force, *Report of Mitigation Options* (Four Corners Air Quality Task Force, 2007), 228.

108. It is important to recognize that outside interests were on both sides of the debate about Desert Rock. *See* Powell, *Landscapes of Power, supra* note 15, at 164 ("While spokespeople for the DPA, along with former president Joe Shirley Jr., have been highly critical of tribal members who align with 'outside' environmental groups, activists criticize tribal leaders for failing to see their own peculiar 'outside' alignments with the developers and financiers who make the Desert Rock proposal possible.").

109. Dooda (No) Desert Rock Power Plant, *Petition* (June 2005) (on file with author) (signed by 1500 Four Corners residents).

110. San Juan Citizens Alliance, "Desert Rock Energy Project – Draft Environmental Impact Statement comment letter," Oct. 4, 2007, at 12 (sent to Harrilene Yazzie, NEPA Coordinator for BIA's Navajo Regional Office). *See also* Environmental Defense Fund, *Supplemental Comments on EPA's Proposed PSD Permit for the Desert Rock Energy Facility*, July 31, 2008 (sent to Joseph Lapka, Air Permitting Program USEPA Region 9) (on file with author) (arguing CO_2 is subject to EPA regulation when considering PSD permit applications). The figure which was given by the plant's developers was 10.9 million tons per year. To give some context to these amounts, consider that Yale University was responsible for more than 300,000 tons per year of CO_2 equivalent emissions from 2003 to 2008. Yale Office of Sustainability, *Yale University Greenhouse Gas Emissions Inventory Update 2003-2008* (New Haven, Connecticut: Yale University, 2009), 3.

   Note: the Environmental Defense Fund Supplemental Comments were contained in an online database, the Initial Prevention of Significant Deterioration Permit for the Desert Rock Energy Facility Docket Folder on regulations.gov, Docket ID: EPA-R09-OAR-2007-1110. But given the challenges of subsequent researchers finding particular letters from this database, citations are to copies of the letter on file with author.

111. Press Release, Bill Richardson, New Mexico Governor, Governor Richardson Issues Statement on Proposed Desert Rock Energy Facility (July 27, 2007), 1. Richardson's public statement preceded – arguably something it should not have – his formal request regarding Desert Rock for government-to-government consultation, a process the state and the tribe had previously agreed to in order to resolve disputes. Letter from Bill Richardson, New Mexico Governor, to Joe Shirley, Jr., Navajo Nation President (Aug. 20, 2007) (on file with author).

112. Press Release, Bill Richardson, *supra* note 111, at 2.

113. Letter from Bill Richardson, New Mexico Governor, and Gary K. King, New Mexico Attorney General, to Stephen L. Johnson, Administrator USEPA, and Wayne Nastri, Regional Administrator USEPA Region 9, June 19, 2008, 3 (on file with author).

114. *See e.g.* Letter from La Plata County [CO] Board of County Commissioners to Deborah Jordan, Air Division Director USEPA Region 9, July 16, 2008 (on file with author). Letter from Helen Kalin Klanderud, City of Aspen, CO, Mayor, to Robert Baker, USEPA Region 9, Mar. 20, 2007 (on file with author) (noting that the Aspen City Council was unanimously concerned with the effects of the Desert Rock on Aspen).

115. Letter from Dooda Desert Rock Power Plant Committee, signed by Lucy Willie et al., to Diné Power Authority and BHP Billiton, July 28, 2006 (on file with author). One member even signed the letter and a separate individualized response with a thumbprint. *Id.*; Letter from Louise Benally, Fruitland, N.M., resident, to Robert Baker, USEPA Region 9, Oct. 24, 2006.

116 *See* Shannon Shaw, "Documenting Desert Rock," *Santa Fe New Mexican*, July 19, 2006 (describing the origins of the photo exhibit).

117. Lisa Meerts, "Protestors Stop Work at Desert Rock," *Farmington Daily Times*, Dec. 13, 2006; Lisa Meerts, "Desert Rock Officials Get Court Order to Access Site," *Farmington Daily Times*, Dec. 21, 2006.

118. Lisa Meerts, "Desert Rock Protesters Reach Agreement," *Farmington Daily Times*, Jan. 3, 2007.

119. Moises Velasquez, "Before Regulation Hits, A Battle over How to Build New US Coal Plants," *Christian Science Monitor*, Feb. 22, 2007.

120. Leslie Linthicum, "A Question of Power: Coal-fired Plant on Navajo Land Called a Cleaner Energy Source, But Critics say Land, People Will Pay the Price," *Albuquerque Journal*, July 15, 2007.

121. *See* Cornelia de Bruin, "EPA Approves Desert Rock Permit," *Farmington Daily Times*, July 31, 2008 (quoting Dailan Long of Diné CARE as saying that "tribal elders are outraged," and including Elouise Brown of Dooda Desert Rock as among the outraged).

122. Elouise Brown, "Letter to the Editor: What's Next for Desert Rock?," *Farmington Daily Times*, Feb. 11, 2009.

123. Navajo Transitional Energy Company, "A Brief History" webpage, www.navajo-tec.com /history.html.

124. Press Release, "Navajo President Shelly States Support for NTEC Purchase of Mine," Navajo Nation Office of the President and the Vice President, Oct. 31, 2013, www.navajo -nsn.gov/News%20Releases/OPVP/2013/oct/103113%20PR%20Shelly%20NTEC% 20Navajo%20Mine%20Purchase.pdf.

125. Rebecca Fairfax Clay, "Tribe at a Crossroads: The Navajo Nation Purchases a Coal Mine," *Environmental Health Perspectives* 122, no.4 (2014): A104–A107, at A106, https:// ehp.niehs.nih.gov/doi/10.1289/ehp.122-A104.

126. *Id.*

127. Alastair Lee Bitsoi, "President Shelly Signs Energy Policy, $4.1 Million for NTEC to Acquire Navajo Mine into Law," *Navajo Times*, Oct. 24, 2013.

128. For a history of the mine, see United States Department of Interior Office of Surface Mining Reclamation and Enforcement, *Record of Decision: Four Corners Power Plant and Navajo Mine Energy Project* (Washington, DC: Department of the Interior, 2015), 2–10, www.wrcc.osmre.gov/initiatives/fourCorners/documents/ROD/RecordofDecisionFCPP .pdf.

129. Winona LaDuke, "Monster Slayers: Can the Navajo Nation Kick the Coal Habit?," *Indian Country Today*, July 31, 2013.

130. Clay, "Tribe at a Crossroads," *supra* note 125, at A106.

131. Alastair Lee Bitsoi, "Council Passes $4.1 Million to Acquire Navajo Mine," *Navajo Times*, Oct. 18, 2013.

132. Navajo Transitional Energy Company, "A Brief History" webpage, *supra* note 123.

133. United States Department of Interior Office of Surface Mining Reclamation and Enforcement, *Record of Decision*, *supra* note 128, at 13.

134. Jonathan Thompson, "What the Navajo Generating Station Will Leave Behind," *High Country News*, Mar. 20, 2017.

135. Peter Friederici, "Generating Controversy," *National Parks Conservation Association*, Spring 2015, www.npca.org/articles/941-generating-controversy.

136. Ian Frisch, "The End of Coal Will Haunt the Navajo," *Bloomburg News*, Oct. 13, 2017, www.bloomberg.com/news/features/2017-10-13/the-end-of-coal-will-haunt-the-navajo.

137. *See* Jonathan Thompson, "Why the Symbolism Behind Coal Is Still So Powerful," *Mother Jones*, Sep. 23, 2017; Andrew Curley, "T'áá hwó ají t'éego and the Moral Economy of Navajo Coal Workers," *Annals of the American Association of Geographers* 109, no.1 (2019): 71–86, at 72 ("Although environmental costs to the land and people are a factor, utility companies are divesting from coal because of its higher costs compared to natural gas.").

138. David Schlissel, *End of an Era: Navajo Generating Station Is No Longer Economic* (Cleveland: Institute for Energy Economics and Financial Analysis, 2017), 1, http://ieefa .org/wp-content/uploads/2017/05/End-of-an-Era_Navajo-Generating-Station_May-2017 .pdf.

139. Thompson, "What the Navajo Generating Station Will Leave Behind," *supra* note 134.

140. Johansen, *Resource Exploitation in Native North America*, *supra* note 9, at xi; Abrahm Lustgarten, "End of the Miracle Machines: Inside the Power Plant Fueling America's Drought," *ProPublica*, June 16, 2015, https://projects.propublica.org/killing-the-colorado /story/navajo-generating-station-colorado-river-drought.

141. Thompson, "What the Navajo Generating Station Will Leave Behind," *supra* note 134.

142. Lustgarten, "End of the Miracle Machines," *supra* note 140. For a map of the Central Arizona Project's connection to the power plant, see Roger Clark, "Navajo Generating Station's Next Chapter," *Grand Canyon Trust Advocate Magazine*, Spring/Summer 2017, www.grandcanyontrust.org/advocatemag/spring-summer-2017/navajo-generating-station.

143. Thompson, "What the Navajo Generating Station Will Leave Behind," *supra* note 134.

144. Frisch, "The End of Coal Will Haunt the Navajo," *supra* note 136.

145. *See* Powergrid International, "Navajo Generating Station Reaches Agreement to Keep Operating," *Powergrid.com*, Oct. 2, 2017, www.power-grid.com/2017/10/02/navajo-generating-station-reaches-agreement-to-keep-operating/.

146. Fixico, *Indian Resilience and Rebuilding*, *supra* note 88, at 158.

5 ALTERNATIVE ENVIRONMENTAL PATHS

1. Alexander Sammon, "A History of Native Americans Protesting the Dakota Access Pipeline," *Mother Jones*, Sep. 9, 2016.

2. Feliks Garcia, "Dakota Access Pipeline: Native American Protesters 'Attacked' with Pepper Spray and Guard Dogs," *The Independent* (UK), Sept. 4, 2016.

3. *See* Jack Healy, "Occupying the Prairie: Tensions Rise as Tribes Move to Block a Pipeline," *New York Times*, Aug. 23, 2016. For a well-written, longer telling of the Standing Rock protests, see Dina Gilio-Whitaker, *As Long as Grass Grows: The Indigenous Fight for Environmental Justice, from Colonization to Standing Rock* (Boston: Beacon Press, 2019), 1–12.

4. Gilio-Whitaker, *As Long as Grass Grows*, *supra* note 3, at 3.

5. *Id.* at 2; Lyndsey Gilpin, "These Maps Help Fill the Gaps on the Dakota Access Pipeline," *High Country News*, Nov. 5, 2016. According to the pipeline's developers, the pipeline moves an extra 100,000 barrels a day for a total of 570,000 barrels per day. Dakota Access Pipeline website, "Home," www.daplpipelinefacts.com/.

6. Paul VanDevelder, "Reckoning at Standing Rock," *High Country News*, Oct. 28, 2016.

7. For a powerful visualization of the original versus revised path of the pipeline, see Carl Sack, "A #NoDAPL Map," *Huffington Post*, Dec. 2, 2016, www.huffpost.com/entry/ a-nodapl-map_b_581a0623e4b014443087af35. *See also* Gregor Aisch and K. K. Rebecca

Lai, "The Conflicts Along 1,172 Miles of the Dakota Access Pipeline," *New York Times*, Mar. 20, 2017.

8. *See* Jeanette Wolfley, "Embracing Engagement: The Challenges and Opportunities for the Energy Industry and Tribal Nations on Projects Affecting Tribal Rights and Off-Reservation Lands," *Vermont Journal of Environmental Law* 19 (2018): 115–163, at 118 (discussing the relationship between the 1851 and 1868 treaties and subsequent treaties that split the Great Sioux Reservation into smaller reservations). *See also* Robert T. Anderson, "Indigenous Rights to Water and Environmental Protection," *Harvard Civil Rights-Civil Liberties Law Review* 53 (2018): 338–379, at 368–370 (describing the "duplicity" of the United States in its dealings with the Sioux following the treaty of 1868).

9. *See* David Archambault II, "Taking a Stand at Standing Rock," *New York Times*, Aug. 24, 2016.

10. *See* Troy A. Eid, "Beyond Dakota Access Pipeline: Energy Development and the Imperative for Meaningful Tribal Consultation," *Denver Law Review* 95, no.3 (2018): 593–607, at 594 (reporting that the numbers at the camps reached a peak of 10,000 people).

11. David Treuer, *The Heartbeat of Wounded Knee: Native America from 1890 to the Present* (New York: Riverhead Books, 2019), 435.

12. Rebecca Hersher, "Key Moments in the Dakota Access Pipeline Fight," *National Public Radio*, Feb. 22, 2017. *See also* Antonia Juhasz, "Paramilitary Security Tracked and Targeted DAPL Opponents as 'Jihadists,' Docs Show," *The Grist*, June 1, 2017, https://grist.org/justice/paramilitary-security-tracked-and-targeted-nodapl-activists-as-jihadists-docs-show/.

13. Jonah Engel Bromwich, "16 Arrested at North Dakota Pipeline Protest," *New York Times*, Nov. 21, 2016; Joshua Barajas, "Police Deploy Water Hoses, Tear Gas Against Standing Rock Protesters," *PBS News Hour*, Nov. 21, 2016; Sue Skalicky and Monica Davey, "Tension Between Police and Standing Rock Protesters Reaches Boiling Point," *New York Times*, Oct. 28, 2016. *See also* Press Release, "Native Americans Facing Excessive Force in North Dakota Pipeline Protests – UN Expert," *United Nations Human Rights Office of the High Commissioner*, Nov. 15, 2016.

14. Russell Begaye and Jonathan Nez, Letter to David Archambault II, Aug. 22, 2016 (on file with author). *See also* Ryan Heinsius, "Navajo Nation Among Dozens of Tribes to Oppose Dakota Access Completion," *KNAU Arizona Public Radio*, Feb. 28, 2017, www.knau.org/post/navajo-nation-among-dozens-tribes-oppose-dakota-access-completion.

15. *See* John H. Cushman, Jr., "Big Win for Dakota Pipeline Opponents, But Bigger Battle Looms," *Inside Climate News*, Dec. 5, 2016, https://insideclimatenews.org/news/05122016/dakota-access-pipeline-dapl-army-corps-standing-rock-sioux-reservation.

16. *See* Rozina Ali, "Will the Victory at Standing Rock Outlast Obama?," *The New Yorker*, Dec. 6, 2016.

17. Eid, "Beyond Dakota Access Pipeline," *supra* note 10, at 598.

18. *See* Andrew Restuccia and Josh Dawsey, "Trump Signs Executive Actions to Advance Keystone, Dakota Access Pipelines," *Politico.com*, Jan. 24, 2017; Rebecca Hersher, "Army Approves Dakota Access Pipeline Route, Paving Way For The Project's Completion," *National Public Radio*, Feb. 7, 2017.

19. Alan Taylor, "Dakota Access Pipeline Protesters Burn Their Camp Ahead of Evacuation," *The Atlantic*, Feb. 22, 2017.

20. Mitch Smith, "Standing Rock Protest Camp, Once Home to Thousands, Is Razed," *New York Times*, Feb. 23, 2017.

21. Julie Carrie Wong, "Police Remove Last Standing Rock Protesters in Military-Style Takeover," *The Guardian* (UK), Feb. 23, 2017.
22. Madison Park, "Oil Starts Gushing Through Controversial Dakota Access Pipeline," *CNN.com*, June 1, 2017.
23. Phil McKenna, "Standing Rock Asks Court to Shut Down Dakota Access Pipeline as Company Plans to Double Capacity," *Inside Climate News*, Aug. 20, 2019, https://insidecli matenews.org/news/20082019/standing-rock-dakota-access-pipeline-impact-assessment-court -double-capacity. *See also* The Takeaway, "Dakota Access Pipeline Leaks Start to Add Up," WNYC *Studios*, Jan. 11, 2018, www.wnycstudios.org/podcasts/takeaway/segments/across-country-smaller-pipeline-leaks-start-add.
24. For a Native perspective on the protests, see Kayla DeVault, "Four Ways to Look at Standing Rock: An Indigenous Perspective," *YES Magazine*, Nov. 22, 2016, www .yesmagazine.org/planet/four-ways-to-look-at-standing-rock-an-indigenous-perspective -20161122.
25. *See* Lauren P. Phillips, "Killing the Black Snake: The Dakota Access Pipeline's Fate Post-*Sierra Club v. FERC*," *Georgetown Environmental Law Review* 30 (2018): 731–747 (detailing the past litigation against DAPL and arguing in favor of the ongoing anti-DAPL litigation); Wolfley, "Embracing Engagement," *supra* note 8, at 121–125 (presenting the history of litigation against DAPL); Eid, "Beyond Dakota Access Pipeline," *supra* note 10, at 595–597 (same); Carla F. Fredericks, "Operationalizing Free, Prior, and Informed Consent," *Albany Law Review* 80, no.2 (2017): 429–482, at 474–476 (describing the litigation and connecting it to the internationally recognized right to free, prior, and informed consent).
26. For a list of those in prison as well as their prison sentences, see NoDAPLPoliticalPrisioners website, www.nodaplpoliticalprisoners.org/. *See also* Sam Levin and Julia Carrie Wong, "'Bogus charges': Standing Rock Activists Say They Face Campaign of Legal Bullying," *The Guardian* (UK), Nov. 30, 2016.
27. *See* Sam Levin, "'He's a Political Prisoner': Standing Rock Activists Face Years in Jail," *The Guardian* (UK), June 22, 2018.
28. Alix Bruce, "'Enough's Enough': Protest Law and the Tradition of Chilling Indigenous Free Speech," *American Indian Law Journal* 8, no.1 (2020): 53–126.
29. *See* Phil McKenna, "Standing Rock's Pipeline Fight Brought Hope, Then More Misery," *Huffington Post*, Apr. 5, 2017, www.huffpost.com/entry/standing-rock-pipeline-reservation_n_58e295dde4b03a26a364fb92.
30. According to a study of the economic effects of the protests, ETP's stock price underperformed during the protests, with social pressure contributing to these losses. Carla Fredericks et al., *Social Cost and Material Loss: The Dakota Access Pipeline* (Boulder: University of Colorado, First Peoples Worldwide, 2018), www.colorado.edu /program/fpw/sites/default/files/attached-files/social_cost_and_material_loss_0.pdf. *See also* Wolfley, "Embracing Engagement," *supra* note 8, at 131–134 (describing the costs to corporations of failing to meaningfully engage with affected Indigenous communities); Eid, "Beyond Dakota Access Pipeline," *supra* note 10, at 604–606 (arguing that energy companies are better off when they support tribal consultation).
31. *See* Tay Wiles, "What Standing Rock Meant to Those Who Took Part," *High Country News*, Jan. 23, 2017 ("Standing Rock, in other words, was more of a beginning than end. It was both a potent symbol for this American moment, and the start of something bigger. NoDAPL participants now hope the movement will raise the national consciousness on a broad array of Native American issues, from tribal sovereignty to environmental justice

to the local impacts of the extractive industry – issues often removed from public discourse and overlooked in history books.").

32. As Sam Deloria explains with his characteristic directness: "We must, of course, hold the government to standards of trusteeship and identify instances in which it shirks its responsibility. But if that analytical role slips into one of invariably passing all the blame to the federal government, the economic system, or the society at large, then Indian self-determination becomes a concept of power without responsibility." Philip S. Deloria, "The Era of Indian Self-Determination: An Overview," in *Indian Self-Rule: First-Hand Accounts of Indian-White Relations from Roosevelt to Reagan*, ed.Kenneth R. Philp (Salt Lake City: Howe Brothers, 1986), 191–207, at 195.

33. The affection progressives have for Indians is perhaps a continuation or the next generation's version of "the fascination of the hippie culture with the red man." Wilcomb E. Washburn, *Red Man's Land, White Man's Law*, 2nd ed. (Norman, Oklahoma: University of Oklahoma Press, 1995), 230. If tribes are successful in pushing their economic development priorities against non-Indian opposition, this may change. Lenora Ledwon argues that "[t]he increasing popularity of all things Indian is in inverse proportion to tribal autonomy." Lenora Ledwon, "Native American Life Stories and 'Authorship': Legal and Ethical Issues," *Saint Thomas Law Review* 9 (1996): 69–84, at 77. *See also* Stephen D. Osborne, "Protecting Tribal Stories: The Perils of Propertization," *American Indian Law Review* 28 (2003): 203–236, at 204–205 (noting that "Indians are hot" and that many Indians "view the continuing popularity of all things 'Indian' with more than a little skepticism").

34. James M. Grijalva, *Closing the Circle: Environmental Justice in Indian Country* (Durham, North Carolina: Carolina Academic Press, 2008), 19–20. The Keep America Beautiful and Ad Council advertisement won multiple awards and Iron Eyes Cody, the ad's actor, eventually was honored with a Hollywood walk of fame star. Advertising Educational Foundation's Social Responsibility, Ad Council Retrospective – Pollution Prevention webpage www.aef.com/exhibits/social_responsibility/ad_council/2278. The ad "appeared widely in print and on television" and was so successful because it "cleverly manipulated ideas deeply engrained in the national consciousness." Shepard Krech III, *The Ecological Indian: Myth and History* (New York: W. W. Norton & Company, Inc., 1999), 15. Robert Yazzie, former Chief Justice of the Navajo Nation, criticizes the ad as "totally false because it is based on the stereotyping of Indians as being 'stoic' and without emotions." Robert Yazzie, "Air, Light/Fire, Water and Earth/Pollen: Sacred Elements that Sustain Life," *Journal of Environmental Law and Litigation* 18 (2003): 191–207, at 191.

35. Robert H. Keller and Michael F. Turek note the dangers of the generalizing nature of stereotypes: "the 'Indian as Environmentalist' evokes powerful reactions. Like most stereotypes, its shard of truth can cause more harm than good. Indians who ride motorcycles instead of ponies, who fish with nylon gillnets instead of wooden weirs, who clear-cut tribal forests rather than seek visions . . . find that non-Indians, including environmentalists, can react with dismay, anger, and disbelief. The ecological mandate freezes Indians as an idea and artifact, a static and quaint people who have few economic needs." Robert H. Keller and Michael F. Turek, *American Indians and National Parks* (Tucson: University of Arizona Press, 1998), 178.

36. Frank Pommersheim, "The Reservation as Place: A South Dakota Essay," *South Dakota Law Review* 34 (1989): 246–270, at 246.

37. *Id.* at 350.

38. *Id.* at 368.

39. Armstrong Wiggins, "Indian Rights and the Environment," *Yale Journal of International Law* 18 (1993): 345–354, at 348.
40. Robert Laurence, "A Memorandum to the Class, in which the teacher is finally pinned down and forced to divulge his thoughts on what Indian law should be," *Arkansas Law Review* 46 (1993): 1–23, at 2.
41. Grijalva, *Closing the Circle*, *supra* note 34, at 19. *See also* Philip Reno, *Mother Earth, Father Sky, and Economic Development: Navajo Resources and Their Use* (Albuquerque: University of New Mexico Press, 1981), 3 (noting that Indians have "been called the first American ecologists"); Jace Weaver, "Introduction: Notes from a Miner's Canary," in *Defending Mother Earth: Native American Perspectives on Environmental Justice*, ed. Jace Weaver (Maryknoll, New York: Orbis Books, 1996), 1–28, at 4 (noting that "worshipful Whites" saw Indians as "the first environmentalists").
42. Mark David Spence, *Dispossessing the Wilderness: Indian Removal and the Making of the National Parks* (New York: Oxford University Press, 1999), 11–12.
43. Keller and Turek, *American Indians and National Parks*, *supra* note 35, at 177. They add that the thought behind such a stereotype is that "unless people heed the Indian, Western civilization may destroy the planet." *Id.* at 178.
44. *See, e.g.*, Carl H. Johnson, "Balancing Species Protection with Tribal Sovereignty: What Does the Tribal Rights-Endangered Species Order Accomplish?," *Minnesota Law Review* 83 (1998): 523–564, at 558 (arguing that because of their values, "tribes are more motivated to protect habitat" than non-Indians); Nancy B. Collins and Andrea Hall, "Nuclear Waste in Indian Country: A Paradoxical Trade," *Law and Inequality: A Journal of Theory and Practice* 12, no.2 (1994): 267–350, at 326 ("Many environmentalists homogenize and romanticize all Native Americans as environmentalists who desire to keep their land free of all economic development."); Wiggins, "Indian Rights and the Environment," *supra* note 39, at 354 ("Although Indian communities, like all others, have difficult decisions to make about their development, there is good reason to believe that if Indians are permitted to chart their own future they will continue to serve not only themselves, but also the global environment.").
45. Donald L. Fixico, *The Invasion of Indian Country in the Twentieth Century: American Capitalism and Tribal Natural Resources* (Boulder: University Press of Colorado, 1998), xvi. This holds true for traditional Navajos. Robert Begay, "Doo Dilzin Da: Abuse of the Natural World," *American Indian Quarterly* 25, no.1 (2001): 21–27, at 24.
46. Valerie L. Kuletz, *The Tainted Desert: Environmental Ruin in the American West* (New York: Routledge, 1998), 97 (discussing the US Nuclear Negotiator and US environmental policy).
47. Wolfley, "Embracing Engagement," *supra* note 8, at 130.
48. Rebecca Tsosie, "How the Land Was Taken: The Legacy of the Lewis and Clark Expedition for Native Nations," in *American Indian Nations: Yesterday, Today, and Tomorrow*, eds. George Horse Capture, Duane Champagne and Chandler C. Jackson (Lanham, Maryland: AltaMira Press, 2007), 240–279, at 246.
49. John P. LaVelle, "Rescuing Paha Sapa: Achieving Environmental Justice by Restoring the Great Grasslands and Returning the Sacred Black Hills to the Great Sioux Nation," *Great Plains Natural Resource Journal* 5 (2001): 40–101, at 96 ("Many commentators have noted the high solicitude for conventional values and ecological balance manifested in traditional American Indian tribal societies."). For more on traditional Indian environmental beliefs and relations with the land, see Rebecca Tsosie, "Tribal Environmental Policy in an Era of Self-Determination: The Role of Ethics, Economics, and Traditional Ecological Knowledge," *Vermont Law Review* 21 (1996): 225–334, at 272–287.

50. Keller and Turek, *American Indians and National Parks, supra* note 35, at 240. *See also* LaVelle, "Rescuing Paha Sapa," *supra* note 49, at 96–98 (arguing that "one should avoid endorsing conventional stereotypes about Indians and the environment" but also "recognize that environmental stewardship and reverence for nature are *central, pervasive,* and *normal* attributes of tribal societies").

51. Conceits that rely upon "ahistorical" ideas of Indians as people who live in an eden-esque state-of-nature are not limited to the area of Indians and the environment. *See* Kenneth H. Bobroff, "Retelling Allotment: Indian Property Rights and the Myth of Common Ownership," *Vanderbilt Law Review* 54 (2001): 1559–1623 (disproving the idea underlying allotment that Indian societies did not recognize property rights in individuals).

52. Weaver, "Introduction," *supra* note 41, at 7.

53. Terry L. Anderson, *Sovereign Nations or Reservations? An Economic History of American Indians* (San Francisco: Pacific Research Institute, 1995), xiv ("American Indian institutions were far from static but evolved in response to environmental and market conditions ... Indians readily adapted their institutions to meet changing economic and environmental conditions even before contact with Europeans.").

54. Krech III, *The Ecological Indian, supra* note 34, at 26–27.

55. Jana L. Walker et al., "A Closer Look at Environmental Injustice in Indian Country," *Seattle Journal of Social Justice* 1, no. 2 (2002): 379–401, at 379–380 (focusing on conceptions of environmentalists).

56. Robert D. Cooter and Wolfgang Fikentscher, "American Indian Law Codes: Pragmatic Law and Tribal Identity," *American Journal of Comparative Law* 56, no.1 (2008): 29–74, at 47.

57. For an extended discussion of Indians as environmentalists, see Fixico, *The Invasion of Indian Country in the Twentieth Century, supra* note 45, at 205–218.

58. Collins and Hall, "Nuclear Waste in Indian Country," *supra* note 44, at 325.

59. Dean Suagee, "Tribal People and Environmentalists: Friends of Foes?," *Great Plains Natural Resource Journal* 7, no. 1 (2002): 3–8, at 4 ("the easy case is dealing with environmental issues that arise outside of the reservation boundaries"). *See also* Grijalva, *Closing the Circle, supra* note 34, at 160 (noting that a proposal by non-Indian to build a landfill over a tribe's objections make environmental justice issues "more obvious" than when a tribe proposes a landfill).

60. A. Cassidy Sehgal, "Indian Tribal Sovereignty and Waste Disposal Regulation," *Fordham Environmental Law Journal* 5, no.2 (1994): 431–458, at 454. *See also* Rebecca Tsosie, "Indigenous Peoples and Epistemic Injustice: Science, Ethics, and Human Rights," *Washington Law Review* 87 (2012): 1133–1201, at 1151 ("It is not easy to reach a conclusion on the issue [of environmental justice] because tribal governments often depend upon the jobs and revenues that come to the reservation through mining operations.").

61. Deloria, "The Era of Indian Self-Determination," *supra* note 32, at 206. *See also* Keller and Turek, *American Indians and National Parks, supra* note 35, at 239–240 (arguing that it is "an unjust demand" that Indians not adapt to modern culture without risking the forfeiture of their rights).

62. For a brief history of the environmental justice movement, see Grijalva, *Closing the Circle, supra* note 34, at 4–8. Additionally, the EPA's environmental justice history webpage provides a brief, agency specific, history of the implementation of environmental justice efforts. US EPA Environmental Justice webpage, www.epa.gov/oecaerth/basics/ejbackground.html.

63. *See, e.g.,* US General Accounting Office, *Siting of Hazardous Waste Landfills and Their Correlation with Racial and Economic Status of Surrounding Communities* (Washington,

DC: US General Accounting Office, 1983); Commission for Racial Justice, United Church of Christ, *Toxic Wastes and Race in the United States* (New York: Commission for Racial Justice, United Church of Christ, 1987).

64. Jeffrey R. Cluett, "Two Sides of the Same Coin: Hazardous Waste Siting on Indian Reservations and In Minority Communities," *Hastings West-Northwest Journal of Environmental Law and Policy* 5, no.2 (1999): 191–206, at 192 (based on the Church of Christ study).

65. Grijalva, *Closing the Circle, supra* note 34, at 5.

66. *Id.*

67. Exec. Order No. 12898, *Federal Actions to Address Environmental Justice in Minority Populations and Low-Income Populations*, 59 Fed. Reg. 7629 (Feb. 11, 1994).

68. Rachel D. Godsil, "Remedying Environmental Racism," *Michigan Law Review* 90, no.2 (1991): 394–427, at 396. How much is being shouldered is contextual. A sewage treatment plant in a poor neighborhood that serves an entire city is a localized form of environmental injustice, a community bearing "the burden of an environmental problem that belongs to the entire nation" is a more national form. Collins and Hall, "Nuclear Waste in Indian Country," *supra* note 44, at 269 (discussing the storing of nuclear waste on Indian reservations).

69. After discussing the challenges of finding deliberate environmental racism, Rachel Godsil ends her section on the definition by simply concluding, "because hazardous waste sites must go *somewhere*, they are frequently placed in poor, minority communities." Godsil, "Remedying Environmental Racism," *supra* note 68, at 400 (italics in original).

70. *Id.* at 396.

71. Joshua Glasgow, "Not in Anybody's Backyard?: The Non-Distributive Problem with Environmental Justice," *Buffalo Environmental Law Journal* 13 (2005): 69–123, at 89–97 (arguing that political, educational, and informational limits among poor communities prevent them from imposing not-in-my-backyard type costs upon developers pursuing environmentally harmful activities, making such communities more attractive to those developers). Media indifference to environmental problems in minority communities is arguably another contributing factor. Cluett, "Two Sides of the Same Coin," *supra* note 64, at 196.

72. Collins and Hall, "Nuclear Waste in Indian Country," *supra* note 44, at 304.

73. Alice Kaswan, "Distributive Justice and the Environment," *North Carolina Law Review* 81, no.3 (2003): 1031–1148, at 1044 (describing the distributive environmental justice claim). Kaswan's thesis is that "distributional injustice is a matter of concern regardless of its cause." *Id.* at 1050.

74. Sarah Krakoff, "Standing With Tribes Beyond Standing Rock," *Harvard Civil Rights-Civil Liberties Law Review Amicus Blog*, Apr. 21, 2017, https://harvardcrcl.org/sarah-krakoff-standing-with-tribes-beyond-standing-rock/.

75. Fixico, *The Invasion of Indian Country in the Twentieth Century, supra* note 45, at xvi.

76. Most articles focus on environmental justice theory and not on providing examples – so they should not necessarily be faulted for not discussing Indian environmental justice issues – yet the absence of Indian examples is striking.

77. *See* Cluett, "Two Sides of the Same Coin," *supra* note 64, at 197 (noting that "American Indians are rarely treated as a separate group for the purposes of examining environmental racism.").

78. Wiggins, "Indian Rights and the Environment," *supra* note 39, at 349.

79. The notable counterexamples are James Grijalva's 2008 book, *Closing the Circle: Environmental Justice in Indian Country, supra* note 34, and Dina Gilio-Whitaker,

As Long as Grass Grows: The Indigenous Fight for Environmental Justice, from Colonization to Standing Rock, supra note 3.

80. Robert A. Williams, Jr., "Essays on Environmental Justice: Large Binocular Telescopes, Red Squirrel Pinatas, and Apache Sacred Mountains: Decolonizing Environmental Law in a Multicultural World," *West Virginia Law Review* 96, no.4 (1994): 1133–1164, at 1153.

81. Cluett, "Two Sides of the Same Coin," *supra* note 64, at 201 (describing the paternalistic position of Eleanor Metzger).

82. Members of Congress share the idea that industry might need to be controlled because of possibility "that tribal communities are being exploited by an unprincipled industry that takes advantage of poor communities." Jana L. Walker and Kevin Gover, "Commercial Solid and Hazardous Waste Disposal Projects on Indian Lands," *Yale Journal on Regulation* 10, no.1 (1993): 229–262, at 260. Tribes that decide to pursue harm-causing projects "face economic paternalism from those who believe ... that Tribes are simply incapable of making proper and intelligent decisions." Walker et al., "A Closer Look at Environmental Injustice in Indian Country," *supra* note 55, at 390.

83. Pommersheim, "The Reservation as Place," *supra* note 36, at 364.

84. Fixico, *The Invasion of Indian Country in the Twentieth Century, supra* note 45, at 190.

85. The paternalism of the original quote comes across when seen alongside the practice of tribes to "seek out" hazardous waste sites, even though such siting "generally seem[s] forced upon communities." Cluett, "Two Sides of the Same Coin," *supra* note 64, at 201.

86. "Indians" here refers to the collective rights of Indians as peoples, not Indians as individuals. The United States and other countries oppose the term "peoples" in relation to indigenous peoples and have sought to "delete the letter 's' from the term 'indigenous peoples.'" Dean B. Suagee, "Human Rights of Indigenous Peoples: Will the United States Rise to the Occasion?," *American Indian Law Review* 21, no.2 (1997): 365–390, at 376. Oren Lyons, a traditional chief of the Onondaga Nation, Iroquois Confederacy, explains, "[w]hen you say *peoples*, then we have to be recognized as separate nations and sovereigns. Consequently, the still refuse to add *s* to *people*." Oren Lyons, "Law, Principle, and Reality," *New York University Review of Law and Social Change* 20, no.2 (1993): 209–215, at 210. The issue took center stage at the 1993 U.N. World Conference on Human Rights and was dubbed "the battle of the 's'" by the Canadian press. Russel Lawrence Barsh, "Indigenous Peoples in the 1990s: From Object to Subject of International Law," *Harvard Human Rights Journal* 7 (1994): 33–86, at 51. For more on collective group rights of indigenous peoples and how these rights relate to US history and political structure, see Robert N. Clinton, "The Rights of Indigenous Peoples As Collective Group Rights," *Arizona Law Review* 32 (1990): 739–747.

87. Walker et al., "A Closer Look at Environmental Injustice in Indian Country," *supra* note 55, at 380.

88. Williams, Jr., "Essays on Environmental Justice," *supra* note 80, at 1154.

89. Grijalva, *Closing the Circle, supra* note 34, at 9 (describing the EPA position). *See also* Walker et al., "A Closer Look at Environmental Injustice in Indian Country," *supra* note 55, at 395 ("If Tribes are to achieve environmental justice within Indian country ... it is absolutely imperative that environmental justice issues affecting Tribes be viewed against the backdrop of tribal sovereignty"); Collins and Hall, "Nuclear Waste in Indian Country," *supra* note 44, at 313 (1994) ("In order to understand the position of Native Americans in environmental law, the twin issues of racism and sovereignty must be understood.").

90. Grijalva, *Closing the Circle, supra* note 34, at 4 (making this claim based on tribal sovereignty and the close connections of Indians with the natural environment);

Catherine A. O'Neill, "Environmental Justice in the Tribal Context: A Madness to EPA's Method," *Environmental Law* 38, no.2 (2008): 495–536, at 508 (arguing that Indians cannot be treated as any other "subpopulation" for environmental justice purposes because of tribal sovereignty and their government-to-government relationship with the United States).

91. *See e.g.* Oren Lyons, "Traditionalism and the Reassertion of Indianness," in *Indian Self-Rule: First-Hand Accounts of Indian-White Relations from Roosevelt to Reagan*, ed. Kenneth R. Philp (Salt Lake City, Utah: Howe Brothers, 1986), 243–250, at 244 ("We will determine what our culture is. It has been pointed out that culture constantly changes. It is not the same today as it was a hundred years ago. We are still a vital, active Indian society. We are not going to be put in a museum or accept your interpretations of our culture.").

92. For more on what environmental law stands to gain from Indian perspectives, see e.g. Grijalva, *Closing the Circle*, *supra* note 34, at preface x–preface xi (Tribes "bring a measure of human humility and respect for the natural world modern American environmental law seemingly lacks but, I think, desperately needs."); *Id.* at 11 (arguing that "western environmental law as implemented by federal and state agencies is generally unable to account for Indian visions of environmental justice that include the physical, social and spiritual relations affected by various land development uses.").

93. *Id.* at preface xi.

94. Gilio-Whitaker, *supra* note 3, at 138–140.

95. *Id.* at 91–108.

96. *Id.* at 69.

97. *Id.*

98. *Id.* at 71. *See also* Ezra Rosser, "Ahistorical Indians and Reservation Resources," *Environmental Law* 40 (2010): 437–545, at 521–544 (arguing that environmental groups should not channel their opposition to tribal government development policies through federal environmental review processes because doing so wrongly undermines tribal sovereignty).

99. Charles F. Wilkinson and John M. Volkman, "Judicial Review of Indian Treaty Abrogation: 'As Long as Water Flows, or Grass Grows Upon the Earth,' – How Long a Time is That?," *California Law Review* 63, no. 3 (1975): 601–661, at 617.

100. Philip P. Frickey, "Marshalling Past and Present: Colonialism, Constitutionalism, and Interpretation in Federal Indian Law," *Harvard Law Review* 107 (1993): 381–440, at 401. Frickey goes on to highlight the limitations of a contract of adhesion approach as compared to a sovereignty approach when interpreting Marshall's opinion in *Wooster*. *Id.* at 406–407 (focusing on timing of the *Wooster* decision, which pre-dates the development of the adhesion contract approach in contract law).

101. For more on the development of the Indian canons of construction, see Kristen Carpenter, "Interpretive Sovereignty: A Research Agenda," *American Indian Law Review* 33, no. 1 (2008): 111–152, at 117–120.

102. Congress in 1871 passed legislation providing that "hereafter no Indian nation or tribe within the territory of the United States shall be acknowledged or recognized as an independent nation, tribe, or power with whom the United States may contract by treaty" (providing further that the Act does not invalidate prior treaty obligations). Act of Mar. 3, 1871, ch. 120, 16 Stat. 544, 566. The Act reflected anger in the House of Representatives about not being involved in the treaty process; therefore, "abandonment of treatymaking was a matter of internal congressional politics." Philip P. Frickey, "(Native) American Exceptionalism in Federal Public Law," *Harvard Law Review* 119,

no.2 (2005): 431–489, at 441. Negotiated agreements, approved by Congress and signed by the President, replaced treaties. *Id.*

103. The photograph was taken by William Chaplis on May 20, 1948 and can be seen at www .newberry.org/lewisandclark/newnation/ranchers/flooding.asp.

104. Mandan Hidatsa Arikara (also known as the Three Affiliated Tribes) Nation website's history webpage, www.mhanation.com/main/history/history_garrison_dam.html.

105. Fixico, *The Invasion of Indian Country in the Twentieth Century, supra* note 45, at 191.

106. Collins and Hall, "Nuclear Waste in Indian Country," *supra* note 44, at 314 (emphasis added).

107. *Id.* at 320.

108. Robert D. Bullard et al., *Toxic Wastes and Race at Twenty: 1987–2007* (Cleveland: United Church of Christ, 2007), 155. A series of influential environmental justice articles by Vicki Been use the term "locally undesirable land uses" (LULUs for short) and much of the thinking about environmental justice is framed in terms of LULUs. *See e.g.* Vicki Been, "Locally Undesirable Land Uses in Minority Neighborhoods. Disparate Siting or Market Dynamics," *Yale Law Journal* 103 (1994): 1383–1422; Vicki Been, "What's Fairness Got to Do With It? Environmental Equity and the Siting of Locally Undesirable Land Uses," *Cornell Law Review* 78, no.6 (1993): 1001–1085. However, here the choice to describe this in terms of "undesirable characteristics" instead of LULUs is deliberate; some harmful activities may have little local effects, while still being of the sort that they are undesirable and will only be accepted with compensation.

109. Cluett, "Two Sides of the Same Coin," *supra* note 64, at 203 (arguing that "residents of minority and economically crippled communities, presented with promises of money and jobs, unwillingly receive hazardous waste facilities").

110. *See* Brian Jackson Morton, "*Coal Leasing in the Fourth World: Hopi and Navajo Coal Leasing, 1954–1977*" (PhD diss., University of California, Berkeley, 1985), 104 (citing Ruffing for the proposition that the Navajo Nation's dependence upon royalty payments is one reason for the "relatively low bargaining position" of the tribe); Russel Lawrence Barsh, "Indian Resources and the National Economy: Business Cycles and Policy Cycles," in *Native Americans and Public Policy*, eds. Fremont J. Lyden and Lyman H. Legters (Pittsburgh, Pennsylvania: University of Pittsburgh Press, 1992), 193–222, at 217 ("Even if Indian tribes were guaranteed absolute freedom of choice in land development, their dependence upon government aid and capital would continue to influence planning.").

It is beyond the scope of this chapter to define or defend an accounting of what counts as US government aid to tribes, for the purposes of this chapter it is enough to say that if the US ceased providing tribes funding government services would suffer markedly for many tribes. Some US government funding goes directly to tribal administrative agencies that have taken over work previously performed by the BIA (similar to federal block grants to states), some funding is used to meet obligations that the US agreed to through treaty, and some funding flows directly to individual tribal members as part of the government's welfare obligations to all citizens, regardless of Indian/non-Indian status. *See also* Deloria, "The Era of Indian Self-Determination," *supra* note 32, at 192 (discussing reservation welfare programs); Virginia Davis, "A Discovery of Sorts: Reexamining the Origins of the Federal Indian Housing Obligation," *Harvard Blackletter Law Journal* 18 (2002): 211–239 (arguing that there are treaty-based obligations that the US government provide reservation housing).

111. Jeff Radford, "Stripmining Arid Navajo Lands in the US: Threats to Health and Heritage," *Ambio* 11, no.1 (1982): 9–14, at 12 (parenthetical with dated per capita figures omitted).

112. Andrew Curley, "T'áá hwó ají t'éego and the Moral Economy of Navajo Coal Workers," *Annals of the American Association of Geographers* 109, no.1 (2019): 71–86, at 76.

113. *Id.* at 73, 78.

114. *See* Williams, Jr., "Essays on Environmental Justice," *supra* note 80, at 1153–1154 (arguing that given high unemployment rates Indians will consider siting a hazardous waste dump on an unused area but would not even think about such a dump if it were to be placed "where important spiritual, social, or physical values of the tribe are implicated").

115. Declaration of Joe Shirley, President of the Navajo Nation, Oct. 3, 2005, at p. 3, para. 11, for *Navajo Nation v. United States Forest Serv.*, 408 F. Supp. 2d 866 (D. Ariz. 2006).

116. Cluett, "Two Sides of the Same Coin," *supra* note 64, at 199–200.

117. Backcountry Against Dumps v. EPA, 100 F.3d 147 (D.C. Cir. 1996).

118. *Id.*

119. The article's "*" footnote acknowledges that the authors were the attorneys for the Campo Band. Walker and Gover, "Commercial Solid and Hazardous Waste Disposal Projects on Indian Lands," *supra* note 82, at 229.

120. *Id.* at 231.

121. This despite the fact that waste companies are attracted to Indian communities in part because of "the prospect of relaxed regulation in Indian Country." Mary Christina Wood, "Indian Land and the Promise of Native Sovereignty: The Trust Doctrine Revisited," *Utah Law Review* 1994 (1994): 1471–1569, at 1484. Walker and Gover's position rejecting a non-Indian role with regard to tribal environmental matters is shared by others. After identifying sources of law, including some available to non-Indians, Dean B. Saugee and John P. Lowndes' article on public participation in tribal environmental programs concludes by arguing that tribal courts and tribal officials bear the responsibility for establishing the right procedures and protections, thus implicitly favoring the resolution of all concerns through the tribal system. Dean B. Saugee and John P. Lowndes, "Due Process and Public Participation in Tribal Environmental Programs," *Tulane Environmental Law Journal* 13 (1999): 1–43, at 43.

122. Walker and Gover, "Commercial Solid and Hazardous Waste Disposal Projects on Indian Lands," *supra* note 82, at 231.

123. Cluett, "Two Sides of the Same Coin," *supra* note 64, at 200.

124. Walker and Gover, "Commercial Solid and Hazardous Waste Disposal Projects on Indian Lands," *supra* note 82, at 258.

125. Fortunately for the Campo Band, they were able to resolve disputes with the state of California in 1997 and the Golden Acorn Casino opened in 2001. Campo Kumeyaa Nation website's "History of the Modern Era" page, www.campo-nsn.gov/modernera .html.

126. For more on the controversy, see Dan McGovern, *The Campo Indian Landfill War: The Fight for Gold in California's Garbage* (Norman: University of Oklahoma Press, 1995).

127. Walker and Gover, "Commercial Solid and Hazardous Waste Disposal Projects on Indian Lands," *supra* note 82, at 262.

128. Collins and Hall, "Nuclear Waste in Indian Country," *supra* note 44 at 270 (focused on tribal–US relations and nuclear waste siting).

129. Anderson, *Sovereign Nations or Reservations?*, *supra* note 53, at 1. *See also* Walker et al., "A Closer Look at Environmental Injustice in Indian Country," *supra* note 55, at 384

("The economic condition and public health status of AI/ANs are among the lowest of any ethnic or minority group in the United States.").

130. Joseph P. Kalt and Stephen Cornell, "The Redefinition of Property Rights in American Indian Reservations: A Comparative Analysis of Native American Economic Development," in *American Indian Policy: Self-Governance and Economic Development*, eds. Lyman H. Legters and Fremont J. Lyden (Westport, Connecticut: Greenwood Press, 1994), 121, at 126. Backlash against gaming tribes impacts the cultural perception non-Indians have of Indian tribes seeking federal recognition. Renee Ann Cramer, "The Common Sense of Anti-Indian Racism: Reactions to Mashantucket Pequot Success in Gaming and Acknowledgment," *Law and Social Inquiry* 31 (2006), 313–341. Bethany Berger argues that protests arise when tribes violate the "racially fixed image" of Indians "as poor, traditional, and close to the earth." Bethany R. Berger, "Red: Racism and the American Indian," *UCLA Law Review* 56 (2009): 591–656, at 651. For a detailed account of the anti-Indian, anti-casino backlash focused on Connecticut, home of Foxwoods and the Mohegan Sun, see Jeffrey R. Dudas, *The Cultivation of Resentment: Treaty Rights and the New Right* (Stanford, California: Stanford University Press, 2008), 95–136.

131. David F. Aberle and Frank R. J. Flynn, "Education, Work, Gender, and Residence: Black Mesa Navajos in the 1960s," *Journal of Anthropological Research* 45, no. 4 (1989): 405–430, at 414.

132. For more on the causes of reservation poverty, see Walker et al., "A Closer Look at Environmental Injustice in Indian Country," *supra* note 55, at 287 ("These reasons include, but are not limited to, lack of money for new projects on Indian lands, as tribal and Indian trust land cannot generally be mortgaged or put up for collateral; the remoteness of most reservations which makes many projects not economically feasible; lack of infrastructure – electricity, communication systems, water, roads, and buildings – conducive to business; lack of skilled laborers and professionals; and the applicability of many federal, as well as tribal, laws to activities in Indian country that may make businesses reluctant to locate there."). Vine Deloria, Jr. writing about allotment, argued, "Indian poverty was deliberately planned and as predictable as the seasons." Vine Deloria, Jr., "Reserving for Themselves: Treaties and the Powers of Indian Tribes," *Arizona Law Review* 38 (1996): 963–980, at 978.

133. W. Roger Buffalohead, "Self-Rule in the Past and Future: An Overview," in *Indian Self-Rule: First-Hand Accounts of Indian-White Relations from Roosevelt to Reagan*, ed. Kenneth R. Philp (Salt Lake City, Utah: Howe Brothers, 1986), 265–277, at 273 (emphasis in original).

134. Philip S. Deloria, "What Indians Should Want: Advice to the President," in *Indian Self-Rule: First-Hand Accounts of Indian-White Relations from Roosevelt to Reagan*, ed. Kenneth R. Philp (Salt Lake City, Utah: Howe Brothers, 1986), 311–322, at 321.

135. *See* Cluett, "Two Sides of the Same Coin," *supra* note 64, at 201 ("As host to a uranium mine, Laguna Pueblo has become one of the best-educated tribes, having produced poets, doctors, writers, lawyers and academics.").

136. Hazel W. Hertzberg, "Federal Indian Policy Yesterday and Tomorrow," in *Indian Self-Rule: First-Hand Accounts of Indian-White Relations from Roosevelt to Reagan*, ed. Kenneth R. Philp (Salt Lake City, Utah: Howe Brothers, 1986), 278–288, at 283.

137. Collins and Hall, "Nuclear Waste in Indian Country," *supra* note 44, at 275.

138. Fixico, *The Invasion of Indian Country in the Twentieth Century*, *supra* note 45, at 189.

139. Fixico's treatment of this issue illustrates the difficulties of recognizing agency when tribes are also part of a larger system: "capitalist greed" is described as inconsistent with

Indian values regarding the environment at one point. *Id*. at 189. On the other hand, when describing Indian motivations in more detail, Fixico notes, "The Indians' reaction to the demand for their energy resources is twofold: reluctance to allow the mining operations to continue, on one hand, and a progressive attitude toward increased mining to help develop tribal programs on the other." *Id*. at 144.

140. Deloria, "The Era of Indian Self-Determination," *supra* note 32, at 200.

141. Hertzberg calls economics a "neglected subject," and notes, "We talk about Indian poverty, but there has not been enough analysis of the economic conditions on reservations." Hertzberg, "Federal Indian Policy Yesterday and Tomorrow," *supra* note 136, at 283.

142. Reno, *Mother Earth, Father Sky, and Economic Development*, *supra* note 41, at 2 (arguing that because of proximity, Indian tribes share the resource problems, though not the affluence). Though it sounds good to speak in terms of the "need to preserve our ecosystems from contamination so indigenous people can utilize those natural resources," the irony is that surrounding community contamination is what provides the market for on reservation waste siting. Russell Jim, "Federal Indian Policy Yesterday and Tomorrow," in *Indian Self-Rule: First-Hand Accounts of Indian-White Relations from Roosevelt to Reagan*, ed. Kenneth R. Philp (Salt Lake City, Utah: Howe Brothers, 1986), 278–288, at 281.

143. *See* Walker et al., "A Closer Look at Environmental Injustice in Indian Country," *supra* note 55, at 390 ("Tribes seeking to free themselves from federal dependence and poverty often must consider less desirable forms of economic development that may include potentially polluting industries and locally unwanted land uses ('LULUs').").

144. Joseph Kalt and Stephen Cornell of the Harvard Project on Indian Economic Development explain: "some American Indian tribes have enjoyed more extensive, complete, and secure property titles than private companies. That is, in a number of important respects, reservations are more 'deregulated' – at least with respect to non-tribal governments – than the vast bulk of the rest of the economy. This creates niches in the market that present American Indian tribes with classic opportunities for the exercise of comparative advantage. The question, of course, is how, and how well, tribes can respond to these opportunities." Kalt and Cornell, "The Redefinition of Property Rights in American Indian Reservations," *supra* note 130, at 126.

145. Kent Gilbreath, *Red Capitalism: An Analysis of the Navajo Economy* (Norman: University of Oklahoma Press, 1973), 55.

146. Al Henderson, "Introduction: What Economic Development Means to the Navajo," in Philip Reno, *Mother Earth, Father Sky, and Economic Development: Navajo Resources and Their Use* (Albuquerque: University of New Mexico Press, 1981), xii, xv.

147. *Id*. at xii.

148. *See* Karl Cates et al., *As Coal Economy Collapses, Imminent Public Budget Crisis Confronts Hopi-Navajo Tribes* (Lakewood, Ohio: Institute for Energy Economics and Financial Analysis, May 2019).

149. Ryan Randazzo and Noel Lyn Smith, "Navajo Nation Votes to End Efforts to Purchase Coal-Fired Power Plant, Sealing its Fate," *Arizona Republic*, Mar. 22, 2019.

150. *See* Joe Frazier, "NGS Begins Its Final Days," *Navajo Times*, Oct. 3, 2019; Krista Allen, "O'Halleran's Bill Plans for Future Without NGS," *Navajo Times*, Sep. 19, 2019.

151. Arlyssa Becenti, "NTEC's Coal Mine Purchase Draws Critics," *Navajo Times*, Aug. 29, 2019.

152. Karl Cates et al., *Proposed Navajo Acquisition of Bankrupt U.S. Coal Company Is an Ill-Timed Gamble* (Lakewood, Ohio: Institute for Energy Economics and Financial Analysis, Aug. 2019), 1.

153. Karl Cates, "Navajo Nation's Very Risky Bet on Coal," *The Hill*, Aug. 27, 2019.

154. Arlyssa Becenti, "A Deal 'That Cannot and Should Not Be Supported': Delegates, Nez Question NTEC Purchase of Coal Mines," *Navajo Times*, Sep. 27, 2019.

155. Press Release, "NTEC Expands its Conscientious Energy Development Efforts by Acquiring Three Coal Mines in the Powder River Basin," *Navajo Transitional Energy Company*, Aug. 19, 2019, https://cdn.website-editor.net/337bd928b7f54e51813e75f713453762/files/uploaded/Cloud%2520Peak%2520Purchase%2520PR.pdf.

156. Terry Bowman, "Tribal Utility Launches Renewable Energy Program," *Navajo Times*, Aug. 3, 2017.

157. Paul Ciampoli, "SRP, NTUA Officials Mark the Opening of New Solar Facility," *American Public Power Association*, Sep. 14, 2019, www.publicpower.org/periodical/article/srp-ntua-officials-mark-opening-new-solar-facility; Leslie Forero, "Navajo Tribal Utility Authority to Receive $94 Million Loan Supporting Renewable Energy," *Utah Public Radio*, June 6, 2019, www.upr.org/post/navajo-tribal-utility-authority-receive-94-million-loan-supporting-renewable-energy.

158. Ryan Heinsius, "Navajo Nation Opens Second Phase of Kayenta Solar Project," *KNAU Arizona Public Radio*, Sep. 27, 2019, www.knau.org/post/navajo-nation-opens-second-phase-kayenta-solar-project; Laurel Morales, "Navajo Receive Federal Loan to Complete Solar Farm," *KJZZ Fronteras Desk*, May 30, 2019, https://fronterasdesk.org/content/973856/navajo-receive-federal-loan-complete-solar-farm.

159. Adele Peters, "Solar is Starting to Replace the Largest Coal Plant in the Western U.S.," *Fast Company*, May 30, 2018, www.fastcompany.com/40577931/solar-is-starting-to-replace-the-largest-coal-plant-in-the-western-u-s; Sherralyn R. Sneezer, *An Assessment of the Potential for Utility-Scale Solar Energy Development on the Navajo Nation* (Albuquerque, New Mexico: Sandia National Laboratories Report SAND2020-1320, Jan. 2020), 9.

160. Sneezer, *supra* note 159, at 9.

161. Navajo-Hopi Observer, "Kayenta Solar Farm to Provide Power to More Homes on Nation," *Navajo-Hopi Observer*, Jan. 30, 2018, www.nhonews.com/news/2018/jan/30/kayenta-solar-farm-provide-power-more-homes-nation/.

162. Sneezer, *supra* note 159, at 14–15 ("the Navajo Nation has a significant solar resource compared to other regions outside of the Southwest that do not receive as much solar resources"); Garrit Voggesser, "The Evolution of Federal Energy Policy for Tribal Lands and the Renewable Energy Future," in *Indians & Energy: Exploitation and Opportunity in the American Southwest*, eds. Susan L. Smith and Brian Frehner (Santa Fe, New Mexico: School for Advanced Research Press, 2010), 55–88, at 74 ("Tribal lands contain many of the nation's renewable energy resources. Reservations in the West, particularly the Southwest, have the most direct solar radiation.").

163. Dana E. Powell and Dáilan J. Long, "Landscapes of Power: Renewable Energy Activism in Diné Bikéyah," in *Indians & Energy: Exploitation and Opportunity in the American Southwest*, eds. Susan L. Smith and Brian Frehner (Santa Fe, New Mexico: School for Advanced Research Press, 2010), 231–262, at 235.

164. Anelia Milbrandt, Donna Heimiller and Paul Schwabe, *TechnoEconomic Renewable Energy Potential on Tribal Lands* (Golden, CO: National Renewable Energy Laboratory. NREL/TP-6A20-70807, 2018), 15 Table 9. Installed capacity counts are necessarily estimates because not all solar systems on the reservations will be permitted nor in areas that are easily accessible even to tribal officials.

165. *Id.* at 7 Table 3.

166. Chris Deschene, "With the Navajo Generating Station Gone, We Need Help Luring Renewable Energy Investment to Our Land," *Arizona Republic*, May 23, 2020, www

.azcentral.com/story/opinion/op-ed/2020/05/23/we-can-replace-navajo-coal-plant-but-we-need-help/5225187002/.

167. Melanie Whyte, "As Coal Plant's Closure Looms, Navajo Nation Looks to the Future," *Arizona Highways,* Mar. 20, 2018, www.arizonahighways.com/blog/coal-plants-closure-looms-navajo-nation-looks-future.

168. Sneezer, *supra* note 159, at 11 (emphasis added). *See also* Benjamin Storrow, "Coal's Days in Navajo Country are Numbered," *E&E News,* Apr. 8, 2019, www.scientificamerican.com/article/coals-days-in-navajo-country-are-numbered/ (noting that when considering wind and solar facilities, "[f]inding suitable sites that do not conflict with grazing leases can be a challenge.").

169. Andrew Curley, "The Navajo Nation's Coal Economy Was Built to be Exploited," *High Country News,* June 28, 2017.

170. Tina Casey, "$3.6 Billion Energy Storage Project Rising From Ashes of Coal Power Plant," CleanTechnica.com, Jan. 22, 2020, https://cleantechnica.com/2020/01/22/3-6-billion-energy-storage-project-rising-from-ashes-of-coal-power-plant/.

171. Kavya Balaraman, "Proposed 2.2 GW Storage Project Plans to Use Navajo Coal Station Power-lines," *Utility Dive,* Jan. 21, 2020, www.utilitydive.com/news/2200-mw-storage-project-navajo-coal-facility-power-lines/570720/.

172. Daybreak Power, "Massive Battery Proposed Near Retired Navajo Coal Plant, Reports Daybreak Power," *Business Wire,* Jan. 17, 2020, www.businesswire.com/news/home/20200117005017/en/Massive-Battery-Proposed-Retired-Navajo-Coal-Plant.

173. *See* Krista Allen, "'We're Going to Fight': Another Developer, Another Project Near the Confluence," *Navajo Times,* Oct. 1, 2020 (discussing opposition to a pumped-water hydropower system being proposed for a tributary to the Little Colorado River above the Grand Canyon); Press Release, "Feds Urged to Deny Third Arizona Pumped-storage Project Threatening Humpback Chub, Little Colorado River," *Center for Biological Diversity,* July 30, 2020, https://biologicaldiversity.org/w/news/press-releases/feds-urged-deny-third-arizona-pumped-storage-project-threatening-humpback-chub-little-colorado-river-2020-07-30/email_view/ (critiquing a groundwater-based pumped storage proposal).

174. The Navajo Nation has to pay the US Bureau of Reclamation $1.9 million annually for use of the line. Alyssa Becenti, "Nation to Partner with SRP to Develop Solar Project," *Navajo Times,* Jan. 15, 2020.

175. Peters, *supra* note 159. As Uday Varadarajan, a principle at the Rocky Mountain Institute, noted, "An effort to develop solar at the site of the Navajo Generating Station would benefit from the significant existing transmission infrastructure at the site, and likely is only one of many such opportunities across the Navajo territory." Andrew Burger, "The Switch to Solar at Coal Power Plants and Mines is On," *Solar Magazine,* Apr. 25, 2019, https://solarmagazine.com/switch-to-solar-at-coal-power-plants-and-mines-is-on/. *But see* (noting that "[t]he Navajo's competitive advantage of using transmission lines paid for by the coal industry to connect clean energy generation on their land to the big cities might be fleeting.").

176. Grist Creative, "Building a Just and Renewable Future on the Navajo Nation," *Grist.com,* May 6, 2020, https://grist.org/sponsored/building-a-just-and-renewable-future-on-the-navajo-nation/.

177. Jeff Stanfield, "Navajo Nation Seeks Solar Deals with Coal Plant Owners," *S&P Global Market Intelligence,* Feb. 19, 2020, www.spglobal.com/marketintelligence/en/news-insights/latest-news-headlines/navajo-nation-seeks-solar-deals-with-coal-plant-owners-57162822.

178. Noel Lyn Smith, "Partnership Could Lead to Solar, Renewable Energy Projects on Navajo Nation," *Farmington Daily Times*, Feb. 20, 2020, www.daily-times.com/story/news/local/navajo-nation/2020/02/20/navajo-nation-los-angeles-examine-partnership-solar-energy/4812526002/. *See also* Sarah Donahue, "Clean Energy Produced on Navajo Land Could Help Power Los Angeles," *Salt Lake Tribune*, Mar. 5, 2020, www.sltrib.com/news/nation-world/2020/03/05/clean-energy-produced/.

179. Cindy Yurth, "NTEC Proposes Solar Array at Navajo Mine," *Navajo Times*, June 17, 2020.

180. *See* Duane "Chili" Yazzie, Op-ed, "Time to Face Realities, Take a Non-Western Tack," *Navajo Tmes*, Aug. 29, 2019.

181. For more on alternative energy development in Indian Country, *see e.g.* Bob Gough, "Revitalizing Economies, Preserving Cultures and Protecting the Environment: Striking the Balance in South Dakota and Indian Country," *Great Plains Natural Resource Journal* 7 (2002): 67–71; Patrick M. Garry et al., "Wind Energy in Indian Country: A Study of the Challenges and Opportunities Facing South Dakota Tribes," *South Dakota Law Review* 54 (2009): 448–459.

182. Jonathan M. Hanna, *Native Communities and Climate Change: Legal and Policy Approaches for Protecting Tribal Legal Rights* (Boulder: University of Colorado Law School Natural Res. Law Center, 2007), 1.

183. *Id.*

184. *Id.*

185. *Id.* at 32.

186. UN Permanent Forum on Indigenous Issues, Climate change and indigenous peoples webpage, www.un.org/esa/socdev/unpfii/en/climate_change.html.

187. International Work Group for Indigenous Affairs Conference on Indigenous Peoples and Climate Change Meeting Report, Copenhagen, Feb. 21–22, 2008, UN Doc. E/C.19/2008/CRP.3, at 3 (Mar. 10, 2008), *available at* www.un.org/esa/socdev/unpfii/documents/E_C_19_2008_CRP3_en.doc.

188. UN Permanent Forum on Indigenous Issues, Climate change and indigenous peoples webpage, *supra* note 186.

189. Hanna, *Native Communities and Climate Change*, *supra* note 182, at 23.

190. As Dean Speth writes, "If there is one country that bears most responsibility for the lack of progress on international environmental issues, it is the United States." James Gustave Speth, "International Environmental Law: Can It Deal with the Big Issues?," *Vermont Law Review* 28, no.3 (2004): 779–796, at 790.

191. Krech III, *The Ecological Indian, supra* note 34, at 216. *See also* Deloria, "The Era of Indian Self-Determination," *supra* note 32, at 205–206 ("But many scholars – who note the romantic view of Indians in earlier stages of Euro-American history – have themselves been blinded by the same romantic tradition today and deny us our political life and our humanity … We [Indians] have made mistakes, and you [Indian scholars] do us a disservice by almost uniformly shifting the blame elsewhere.").

192. *See* Hari M. Osofsky, "The Inuit Petition as a Bridge? Beyond Dialecticsof Climate Change and Indigenous Peoples' Rights," *American Indian Law Review* 31 (2006): 675–697 (discussing the significance of a climate change based Inuit petition to the Inter-American Commission on Human Rights); John H. Knox, "Climate Change and Human Rights Law," *Virginia Journal of International Law*, Vol. 50 (2009): 163–218, at 191–193 (summarizing the same petition); Rebecca Tsosie, "Indigenous People and Environmental Justice: The Impact of Climate Change," *Colorado Law Review* 78 (2007): 1625–1677, 1669–1674 (ditto).

193. Complaint, Native Village of Kivalina, Alaska v. ExxonMobil, et al., CV-08-1138, at p. 46, para. 188 (N.D. Cal. filed Feb. 26, 2008). For a brief summary of the case and motivation to sue, see Felicity Barringer, "Flooded Village Files Suit, Citing Corporate Link to Climate Change," *New York Times*, Feb. 27, 2008.

194. Public Hearing, Proposed Clean Air Act Permit for Prevention of Significant Deterioration of the Desert Rock Power Plant, Before the United States Environmental Protection Agency, Shiprock, N.M., Oct. 4, 2006 (Evening Session) (statement of Orion Yazzie, nineteen-year-old Navajo from Aztec, N.M.), at 57.

6 GOLF BALLS AND DISCRETIONARY FUNDS

1. For a recent effort to draw out traditional thinking about Diné governance, see Michael Lerma, *Guided by the Mountains: Navajo Political Philosophy and Governance* (New York: Oxford University Press, 2017).

2. For a historical example, see Ezra Rosser, "The Nature of Representation: The Cherokee Right to a Congressional Delegate," *Boston University Public Interest Law Journal* 15 (2005): 91–152.

3. Raymond I. Orr, *Reservation Politics: Historical Trauma, Economic Development, and Intratribal Conflict* (Norman: University of Oklahoma Press, 2017), 41.

4. David Wilkins, "Governance within the Navajo Nation: Have Democratic Traditions Taken Hold?," *Wicazo Sa Review* 17, no.1 (2002): 91–129, at 110.

5. Elizabeth Reese, "The Other American Law," *Stanford Law Review* 73 (2021), 37 (pagination from draft of manuscript available at https://papers.ssrn.com/sol3/papers.cfm?abstract_id=3660166).

6. Wilkins, "Governance within the Navajo Nation," *supra* note 4, at 110–111 ("By 1989 it was evident that while theoretically the Navajo Nation had a three-branch government, the actual state of affairs revealed that the [page break here] executive branch, under MacDonald, was vastly superior to the legislative branch and, in fact, dominated the law-making branch.").

7. Hearing before the Special Committee on Investigations of the Select Committee on Indian Affairs United States Senate, Feb. 2, 6, 7, 8, 9, 1989 Part 2: 12.

8. *Id*. at 12–13.

9. *Id*. at 14.

10. *Id*. at 15–16.

11. *Id*. at 16.

12. *Id*. at 17.

13. *Id*. at 18.

14. *Id*. at 19.

15. *Id*. at 22.

16. *Id*. at 26.

17. *Id*. at 30–31.

18. *Id*. at 44.

19. *Id*. at 48–49.

20. *Id*. at 49–50.

21. *Id*. at 50.

22. *Id*. at 51. Donaldson estimated that the improvements cost $60,000 in total. *Id*. at 69.

23. *Id*. at 52.

24. Robert Reinhold, "Charges of Corruption Divide Ancient Navajos," *New York Times*, Feb. 2, 1989.
25. Hearing before the Special Committee on Investigations of the Select Committee on Indian Affairs United States Senate, *supra* note 7, at 61.
26. *Id.* at 62.
27. *Id.* at 74.
28. *Id.*
29. *Id.* at 81.
30. *Id.*
31. *Id.* at 82.
32. *Id.*
33. *Id.* at 83.
34. *Id.*
35. *Id.* at 83–84.
36. *Id.* at 85.
37. *Id.* at 92–93 (testimony of Eugene (Pete) Twardowicz, Investigator, Special Committee on Investigations).
38. *Id.* at 80.
39. *Id.*
40. *Id.* at 94 (testimony of Eugene (Pete) Twardowicz, Investigator, Special Committee on Investigations).
41. *Id.*
42. *Id.* at 95 (testimony of Eugene (Pete) Twardowicz, Investigator, Special Committee on Investigations).
43. *Id.* at 96–97 (testimony of Eugene (Pete) Twardowicz, Investigator, Special Committee on Investigations).
44. *Id.* at 97 (testimony of Eugene (Pete) Twardowicz, Investigator, Special Committee on Investigations).
45. *Navajo Nation* v. *MacDonald*, 180 Ariz. 539, 542 (1994).
46. Hearing before the Special Committee on Investigations of the Select Committee on Indian Affairs United States Senate, *supra* note 7, at 99 (testimony of Eugene (Pete) Twardowicz, Investigator, Special Committee on Investigations).
47. *Id.*
48. *Id.*
49. *Id.* at 100 (testimony of Eugene (Pete) Twardowicz, Investigator, Special Committee on Investigations).
50. *Id.* at Appendix: 336.
51. *Id.* at 101 (testimony of Eugene (Pete) Twardowicz, Investigator, Special Committee on Investigations).
52. *Id.* In his testimony before the Select Committee, Brown reported a lower amount; that the profit to be shared with MacDonald after expenses and taxes was between $1.7 and $1.8 million. However, later the same day, Brown claimed his net profit on the $5 million gross profit was $3 million. *Id.* at 154, 166 (testimony of Byron T. ("Bud") Brown).
53. *Id.* at 102 (testimony of Eugene (Pete) Twardowicz, Investigator, Special Committee on Investigations).
54. *Id.* at 156 (testimony of Byron T. ("Bud") Brown).
55. *Id.* at 157 (testimony of Byron T. ("Bud") Brown).
56. *Id.* at 158 (testimony of Byron T. ("Bud") Brown).
57. *Id.* at 159 (testimony of Byron T. ("Bud") Brown).

58. *Id.* at 102 (testimony of Eugene (Pete) Twardowicz, Investigator, Special Committee on Investigations).
59. *Id.* at 143 (testimony of Byron T. ("Bud") Brown).
60. *Id.* at 103 (testimony of Eugene (Pete) Twardowicz, Investigator, Special Committee on Investigations).
61. *Id.* at 142–145 (testimony of Byron T. ("Bud") Brown).
62. *Id.* at 145 (testimony of Byron T. ("Bud") Brown).
63. *Id.* at 145 (testimony of Byron T. ("Bud") Brown).
64. *Navajo Nation* v. *MacDonald*, 180 Ariz. 539, 542 (1994).
65. Hearing before the Special Committee on Investigations of the Select Committee on Indian Affairs United States Senate, *supra* note 7, at 147 (testimony of Byron T. ("Bud") Brown).
66. *Id.* at 147 (testimony of Byron T. ("Bud") Brown).
67. *Id.* at 103 (testimony of Eugene (Pete) Twardowicz, Investigator, Special Committee on Investigations).
68. *Id.* at 104 (testimony of Eugene (Pete) Twardowicz, Investigator, Special Committee on Investigations).
69. *Id.* at 105 (testimony of Eugene (Pete) Twardowicz, Investigator, Special Committee on Investigations); *Id.* at 150 (testimony of Byron T. ("Bud") Brown).
70. *Id.* at 151 (testimony of Byron T. ("Bud") Brown).
71. *Id.* at 107 (testimony of Eugene (Pete) Twardowicz, Investigator, Special Committee on Investigations).
72. *Id.* at 107 (testimony of Eugene (Pete) Twardowicz, Investigator, Special Committee on Investigations).
73. *Id.* at 164 (testimony of Byron T. ("Bud") Brown).
74. *Id.* at 123–124 (testimony of Peter MacDonald, Jr.).
75. *Id.* at 124 (testimony of Peter MacDonald, Jr.).
76. *Id.*
77. *United States* v. *Brown*, 763 F. Supp. 1518, 1522 (1991).
78. Hearing before the Special Committee on Investigations of the Select Committee on Indian Affairs United States Senate, *supra* note 7, at 174 (testimony of Byron T. ("Bud") Brown, portion of a taped conversation from Nov. 22, 1988).
79. *Id.* at 176 (testimony of Byron T. ("Bud") Brown, portion of a taped conversation from Dec. 14, 1988).
80. *Id.* at 177 (testimony of Byron T. ("Bud") Brown, portion of a taped conversation from Dec. 14, 1988).
81. *Id.* at 179 (testimony of Byron T. ("Bud") Brown, portion of a taped conversation from Jan. 5, 1989).
82. *Id.* at 109 (testimony of Eugene (Pete) Twardowicz, Investigator, Special Committee on Investigations).
83. *Id.* at 153 (testimony of Byron T. ("Bud") Brown).
84. *Id.* at 154 (testimony of Byron T. ("Bud") Brown).
85. *Id.* at Appendix: 404 (Statement of Michael P. Upshaw, Feb. 7, 1989).
86. *Id.* at 113 (testimony of Eugene (Pete) Twardowicz, Investigator, Special Committee on Investigations).
87. *Id.* at 116 (testimony of Peter MacDonald, Jr.).
88. *Id.* at 118–119 (testimony of Peter MacDonald, Jr.).
89. *Id.* at 119 (testimony of Peter MacDonald, Jr.).
90. *Id.* at 120 (testimony of Peter MacDonald, Jr.).

91. *Id*. at 127 (testimony of Peter MacDonald, Jr.).

92. *Id*. at 125–126 (testimony of Peter MacDonald, Jr.).

93. *Id*. at 126 (testimony of Peter MacDonald, Jr.).

94. *Id*. at 183 (testimony of Byron T. ("Bud") Brown, portion of a taped conversation from Jan. 7, 1989).

95. Peter MacDonald, *The Last Warrior: Peter MacDonald and the Navajo Nation* (New York: Orion Books, 1993) (with Ted Schwarz), 301.

96. *Id*. at 302.

97. *Id*. at 294.

98. *Id*. at 303.

99. Raymond Darrel Austin, *Navajo Courts and Navajo Common Law: A Tradition of Tribal Self-Governance* (Minneapolis: University of Minnesota Press, 2009), 95. *See also* Eric Lemont, "Developing Effective Processes of American Indian Constitutional and Governmental Reform: Lessons from the Cherokee Nation of Oklahoma, Hualapai Nation, Navajo Nation,and Northern Cheyenne Tribe," *American Indian Law Review* 26, no.2 (2001/2002): 147–176, at 159 ("Council members split into two camps, those supporting and those opposing the Chairman. Consequently, day-to-day government operations became deadlocked.").

100. Sandy Tolan, "Showdown at Window Rock," *New York Times*, Nov. 26, 1989.

101. Peter Iverson, *Diné: A History of the Navajos* (Albuquerque: University of New Mexico Press, 2002), 294.

102. Lemont, "Developing Effective Processes of American Indian Constitutional and Governmental Reform," *supra* note 99, at 173 ("Many Navajos, for instance, credit their Supreme Court with helping to resolve the Nation's much-publicized government crisis in 1989. During the height of the controversy, political blocs loyal and opposed to the Council Chairman each claimed governing control over the Nation. Only when the Navajo Nation Supreme Court upheld the legality of the Council's removal of the Council Chairman from office did the turmoil begin to end and the opportunity presented itself for the Council to pass its Title 2 amendments. Although the turmoil peaked and ended a few months after the Court's ruling, many Navajo leaders credit the Court's respected stature and strong, independent decision making with preventing a protracted, violent stand-off between the two sides.").

103. Iverson, *Diné, supra* note 101, at 294.

104. *Id*.

105. Tolan, "Showdown at Window Rock," *supra* note 100.

106. *See* Bill Donovan, "The Riot of '89," *Navajo Times*, July 16, 2009 (showing MacDonald supporters advance on a tribal police officer).

107. Iverson, *Diné, supra* note 101, at 296. *See also* Wilkins, "Governance within the Navajo Nation," *supra* note 4, at 111 ("The conflict [between MacDonald and the Council] eventually escalated into a deadly confrontation that erupted in Window Rock on July 20, 1989, between MacDonald's supporters and the tribal council and the tribal police. Two Navajos died and ten others were injured.").

108. Iverson, *Diné, supra* note 101, at 296.

109. Donovan, "The Riot of '89," *supra* note 106. *See also* Albert W. Alschuler, "Bill Clinton's Parting Pardon Party," *Journal of Criminal Law and Criminology* 100, No. 3 (2010): 1131–1168, at 1148 fn. 121 (noting that "[f]ormer President Jimmy Carter and Representative Patrick Kennedy supported MacDonald's clemency application").

110. MacDonald, *The Last Warrior, supra* note 95, at 257.

111. *Id*., at 258.

112. *Id.* at 260.
113. Tolan, "Showdown at Window Rock," *supra* note 100.
114. MacDonald, *The Last Warrior, supra* note 95, at 265.
115. *Id.* at 278–279.
116. *See id.* at 286 ("The Big Boquillas land purchase was, to me, the most important decision I made at this time. The more than 700,000 acres would be the largest land acquisition the Navajo had made since 1934.").
117. *See id.* at 278–279 (arguing that only through such a mechanism could the tribe buy the land).
118. *Id.* at 291.
119. *Navajo Nation v. MacDonald*, 180 Ariz. 539, 544 (1994).
120. *Id.*
121. Iverson, *Diné, supra* note 101, at 297.
122. For an overview of the new structure of government put in place in 1989, *see* Charles Morris, "Navajo Nation Council Reforms," *American Indian Law Review* 16, no.2 (1991): 613–617; Lemont, "Developing Effective Processes of American Indian Constitutional and Governmental Reform," *supra* note 99, at 159–160.
123. Much of the discussion of the history of the reduction in the size of the Council is drawn from Ezra Rosser, "Displacing the Judiciary: Customary Law and the Threat of a Defensive Tribal Council," *American Indian Law Review* 34, no.2 (2011): 379–401.
124. Jason Begay, "Voters: 'Yes!': Majority of Diné Vote for 24-Member Council, Line-Item Veto for President," *Navajo Times*, Dec. 17, 2009.
125. The Council's suspension of President Shirley on a questionable corruption charge had been thrown out by a tribal district court the day before Navajos voted on the popular referendum to reduce the size of the Council.
126. Navajo Nation Tribal Council, *Amending Title 1 of the Navajo Nation Code to Recognize the Fundamental Laws of the Diné*, Resolution No. CN-69-02, at § 5 (A)–(B) (2002), www.navajocourts.org/Resolutions/CN-69-02Dine.pdf.
127. Navajo Nation Tribal Council, *Amending Title 1 of the Navajo Nation Code to Recognize the Fundamental Laws of the Diné*, Resolution No. CN-69-02 (2002), www.navajocourts.org/Resolutions/CN-69-02Dine.pdf. The resolution is now codified at Navajo Nation Code tit. 1, §§ 201–206 (2008). For more on the passage of the Fundamental Laws of the Diné, see Kenneth Bobroff, "Diné Bi Beenahaz'áanii: Codifying Indigenous Consuetudinary Law in the 21st Century," *Tribal Law Journal* 5, no.4 (2004–5).
128. *See* Ezra Rosser, "Customary Law: The Way Things Were, Codified," *Tribal Law Journal* 8 (2008): 18–33 (explaining why the Navajo courts prefer the term common law to customary law and the place of Navajo common law in relation to other sources of law).
129. Navajo Nation Tribal Council, Res. No. CN-69-02, at pmbl. ¶ 2 and tit. 1, § 2.
130. Navajo Nation Tribal Council, Res. No. CN-69-02, at §§ 2, 207(D).
131. *See Shirley v. Morgan*, No. SC-CV-02-10 (Nav. Sup. Ct., May 28, 2010): *Nelson v. Initiative Committee to Reduce Navajo Nation Council*, No. SC-CV-03-10 (Nav. Sup. Ct., May 28, 2010).
132. *Shirley v. Morgan*, No. SC-CV-02-10 (Nav. Sup. Ct., May 28, 2010), at 3.
133. *See* 5 U.S. 137 (1803).
134. *Shirley v. Morgan*, No. SC-CV-02-10 (Nav. Sup. Ct., May 28, 2010), at 12.
135. *Id.* at 15.

136. *Id.* at 17.
137. *Id.* at 18.
138. *Id.* at 19, 23.
139. *Id.* at 21–23.
140. *Nelson v. Initiative Comm. to Reduce Navajo Nation Council*, No. SC-CV-03-10, No. SC-CV-03-10, (Nav. Sup. Ct., Feb. 25, 2010) at 14–18.
141. *Id.*
142. *See, e.g.,* Bill Donovan, "Efforts Underway to Remove Herb Yazzie as Chief Justice," *Navajo Times*, Mar. 26, 2015.
143. *See* Levi Rickert, "Navajo Nation Supreme Court Chief Justice Herb Yazzie Announces His Retirement," *NativeNewsOnline.Net*, May 13, 2015, http://nativenewsonline.net/cur rents/navajo-nation-supreme-court-chief-justice-herb-yazzie-announces-his-retirement/.
144. *Id.*
145. *Id.*
146. Marley Shebala, "Discretionary Funds, First Lady's Office, to be Audited," *Navajo Times*, Dec. 3, 2009.
147. Marley Shebala, "Slush Funds Total Over $35 Million," *Navajo Times*, Nov. 12, 2009.
148. *Id.*
149. Bill Donovan, "New Special Prosecutor to Replace Balaran," *Navajo Times*, Sept. 26, 2011.
150. *See* Bill Donovan, "New Report Shows Bribery, Conspiracy, Abuse of Office in Slush Fund Case," *Navajo Times*, Sept. 12, 2013.
151. Alysa Landry, "Massive Navajo Corruption Case: Judge Sentences 11," *Indian Country Today*, Aug. 30, 2016.
152. *Evelyn Acothley, et al., v. Carol Perry*, No. SC-CV-08-11, (Nav. Sup. Ct., Feb. 25, 2011) at 3.
153. Marley Shebala, "Limit on Discretionary Aid to Individuals Shot Down by Delegates," *Navajo Times*, Sept. 24, 2009.
154. *See* Marley Shebala, "77 Delegates, VP Charged in Slush Fund Probe," *Navajo Times*, Oct. 28, 2010 (listing those charged and the amounts they stole).
155. *Id.*
156. *Id.*
157. Marley Shebala, "Call for Firm Action to Prevent Abuse Fades Away," *Navajo Times*, Sept. 10, 2009; Marley Shebala, "Limit on Discretionary Aid to Individuals Shot Down by Delegates," *Navajo Times*, Sept. 24, 2009.
158. Marley Shebala, "Legislative Relatives Received $100,000," *Navajo Times*, Oct. 8, 2009.
159. *Id.* For more details on money sent to these recipients, see Marley Shebala, "Trio Received Thousands in Council Aid," *Navajo Times*, Sept. 10, 2009.
160. Alysa Landry, "Massive Navajo Corruption Case," *supra* note 151.
161. Marley Shebala, "Limit on Discretionary Aid to Individuals Shot Down by Delegates," *supra* note 157.
162. David E. Wilkins, *The Navajo Political Experience*, 4th ed. (New York: Rowman and Littlefield, 2013), 38.
163. In 2016, Mel Begaye, who was still on the Council years later faced one of the rare criminal prosecutions stemming from having given $33,000 in discretionary funds to his own children, defended himself by arguing his actions were not criminal. Bill Donovan, "Delegate Claims Giving $33,000 to Children Was Not a Criminal Act," *Navajo Times*, Mar. 17, 2016. In 2017, a jury of six Navajos found Begaye guilty of 11 counts related to misuse of tribal funds and was sentenced to a three year prison sentence by the Window

Rock District Court judge, Carol Perry, who handled the discretionary fund cases. Bill Donovan, "Mel Begaye Out on $45,000 Bond," *Navajo Times*, Jan. 19, 2017.

164. Bill Donovan, "Another Slap on the Wrist?," *Navajo Times*, Nov. 11, 2010.

165. *Id.*

166. Marilyn Berlin Snell, "Navajo Monster Slayers: A Tribe Struggles to Fight Corruption," *High Country News*, Aug. 29, 2011, www.hcn.org/issues/43.14/navajo-monster-slayers-a-tribe-struggles-to-fight-corruption-while-keeping-its-traditions.

167. *Evelyn Acothley, et al., v. Carol Perry,* No. SC-CV-08-11, (Nav. Sup. Ct., May 4, 2011), at 3.

168. Cindy Yurth, "Central Voters Go With Native Son," *Navajo Times*, Nov. 3, 2010.

169. *See Navajo Nation v. Ben Shelly,* No. CP-CR-11-014/015/016, Order of Dismissal with Prejudice, Declaration of the Navajo Nation Prosecutor (Nav. Crownpoint Dist. Ct., Feb. 2, 2011).

170. Bill Donovan, "Ex-Speaker Pleads Guilty in Slush Fund Case," *Navajo Times*, Sept. 11, 2014.

171. Snell, "Navajo Monster Slayers," *supra* note 166.

172. *Id.*

173. *Id.*

174. *See* Bill Donovan, "Civil v. Criminal," *Navajo Times*, May 5, 2011.

175. *See* Reese, "The Other American Law," *supra* note 5, at 42 (noting that "many people continued to be enthralled with MacDonald long after his corruption seemed objectively indefensible").

7   IMPROVING TRIBAL GOVERNANCE

1. For more on protecting tribal businesses from government interference and setting up the relationship between tribal businesses and tribal governance, see Kenneth Grant and Jonathan Taylor, "Managing the Boundary between Business and Politics: Strategies for Improving the Chances for Success in Tribally Owned Enterprises," in *Rebuilding Native Nations: Strategies for Governance and Development,* ed. Miriam Jorgensen (Tucson: University of Arizona Press, 2007), 175–196.

2. This section draws heavily from an earlier article by the author that also includes supplemental citations. Ezra Rosser, "This Land is My Land, This Land is Your Land: Markets and Institutions for Economic Development on Native American Reservations," *Arizona Law Review* 47, no.2 (2005): 245–312.

3. Professor Lloyd Lee deserves particular credit for raising the profile of Diné Studies and providing space for Diné academic voices to find an outlet. *See, e.g.,* Lloyd Lee, *Diné Identity in a 21st-Century World* (Tucson: University of Arizona Press, 2020); *Diné Perspectives: Revitalizing and Reclaiming Navajo Thought,* Lloyd Lee ed. (Tucson: University of Arizona Press, 2014); *Navajo Sovereignty: Understandings and Visions of the Diné People,* Lloyd Lee ed. (Tucson: University of Arizona Press, 3rd ed., 2014).

4. *See* Michael Lerma, *Guided by the Mountains: Navajo Political Philosophy and Governance* (New York: Oxford University Press, 2017), 27 ("There is no unified single body of Diné philosophy of governance."). *See also id.* at 130 ("The research about Navajo Nation governance can be comprehensively dealth with briefly because not much exists.").

5. The organizers of the annual Diné Studies Conference, https://dinestudies.org/, play a significant role supporting and guiding the Diné Studies scholarly project.

6. For discussion of this assertion and presenting critical scholarly responses, see Ezra Rosser, "Destabilizing Property," *Connecticut Law Review* 48, No. 2 (2015): 397–472, at 432–434.
7. Harold Demsetz, "Toward a Theory of Property Rights," *American Economic Review* 62 (1967): 347–359.
8. Michael Joseph Francisconi, *Kinship, Capitalism, Change: The Informal Economy of the Navajo, 1868–1995* (New York: Garland Publishing, Inc., 1998), 92 (basing this conclusion on the description of this as an impediment to Navajo business growth in Daniel C. Shaffer, *Navajo Business Incubator Feasibility Study: Final Report* (1993)).
9. *See* Lorraine Turner Ruffing, "Navajo Economic Development: A Dual Perspective," in *American Indian Economic Development,* ed. Sam Stanley (Chicago: Mouton Publishers, 1978), 15–86, at 16 ("Navajos believe that individuals do not 'own' land, they merely enjoy 'use' rights.").
10. Hernando de Soto, *The Mystery of Capital: Why Capitalism Triumphs in the West and Fails Everywhere Else* (New York: Basic Books, 2000). *See also* Ezra Rosser, "Anticipating de Soto: Allotment of Indian Reservations and the Dangers of Land-Titling," in *Hernando de Soto and Property in a Market Economy,* ed. D. Benjamin Barros (Burlington, Vermont: Ashgate, 2010), 61–81 (using the history of allotment to critique the ambitions of land titling programs).
11. de Soto, *The Mystery of Capital,* supra note 10, at 45.
12. In part because the private sector market economy is often quite thin on reservations, it is common for tribes to act as market actors through tribally owned businesses or enterprises. Nicholas Christos Zaferatos, *Planning the American Indian Reservation: From Theory to Empowerment* (Syracuse, New York: Syracuse University Press, 2015), 152.
13. Demsetz, "Toward a Theory of Property Rights," *supra* note 7, at 350.
14. As Jessica Shoemaker explains: "Land tenure also impacts economic development in more foundational ways. Property systems fundamentally structure how markets and economies operate. Many economists and law and development scholars go so far as to argue that well-defined private property rights are *the* single most important precondition to successful economic development. In this view, property law's most important function is to facilitate desirable market transactions. By communicating quickly and transparently about who owns what, clear property rules can simplify bargaining and make transferring assets easier. In an economist's ideal world, these transactions ensure that resources move efficiently to their highest and best users and, by securing investments over time, encourage wise resource management." Jessica A. Shoemaker, "The Challenges of American Indian Land Tenure and the Vastness of Entrepreneurial Potential," in *Creating Private Sector Economies in Native America: Sustainable Development through Entrepreneurship,* eds. Robert J. Miller, Miriam Jorgensen and Daniel Stewart (New York: Cambridge University Press, 2019), 67–81, at 67–68.
15. Imre Sutton, *Indian Land Tenure: Bibliographical Essays and a Guide to the Literature* (New York: Clearwater Publishing Co., 1975), 1 (quoting Vine Deloria, "Introduction," in Kirke Kickingbird and Karen Ducheneaux, *One Hundred Million Acres*). *See also* Jessica A. Shoemaker, "No Sticks in My Bundle: Rethinking the Indian Land Tenure Problem," *Kansas Law Review* 63 (2014): 383–450, at 383 ("American Indian land tenure has long been the target of federal policies seeking to change, through property law reforms, indigenous peoples' relationships to each other, to the land and natural environment, and to surrounding non-Indian influences.").
16. For an overview of the land holding types in tribal areas, see David Listokin et al., *Housing and Economic Development in Indian Country: Challenge and Opportunity* (New Brunswick, New Jersey: Center for Urban Policy Research Press, 2006), 98–103.

17. Miriam R. Jorgensen, "Taking up the Challenge: Fundamental Principles of Economic Development in Indian Country," in *American Indian Studies: An Interdisciplinary Approach to Contemporary Issues*, ed. Dane Morrison (New York: Peter Lang, Inc., 1997), 125 ("[A] large majority were US government-inspired ... Almost all efforts posted poor track records.").

18. *American Indian Economic Development*, ed. Sam Stanley (Chicago:Mouton Publishers, 1978), 6.

19. In the interest of full disclosure, while in law school, I was a Harvard University Native American Program 1665 Fellow.

20. Stephen Cornell and Joseph P. Kalt, "Two Approaches to the Development of Native Nations: One Works, the Other Doesn't," in *Rebuilding Native Nations: Strategies for Governance and Development*, Miriam Jorgensen ed. (Tucson: University of Arizona Press, 2007), 3–33. The summary of Cornell and Kalt's nation-building approach in this section is taken from this chapter unless otherwise noted.

21. *Id.* at 7–8.

22. *Id.* at 12.

23. *Id.* at 13.

24. *Id.* at 17.

25. *Id.* at 18.

26. Charles F. Wilkinson, *Blood Struggle: The Rise of Modern Indian Nations* (New York: W. W. Norton and Company, 2006).

27. Cornell and Kalt, "Two Approaches to the Development of Native Nations," *supra* note 20, at 22 (emphasis in original).

28. *Id.* at 23 (emphasis in original).

29. *Id.* at 25.

30. *Id.*

31. Eric Lemont, "Developing Effective Processes of American Indian Constitutional and Governmental Reform: Lessons from the Cherokee Nation of Oklahoma, Hualapai Nation, Navajo Nation, and Northern Cheyenne Tribe," *American Indian Law Review* 26, no. 2 (2001/2002): 147–176, at 166–168.

32. *Id.* at 169–171.

33. *Id.* at 174.

34. Lerma, *Guided by the Mountains*, *supra* note 4, at 111.

35. *See, e.g.*, Gavin Clarkson, "Accredited Indians: Increasing the Flow of Private Equity into Indian Country as a Domestic Emerging Market," *University of Colorado Law Review* 80, no. 2 (2009): 285–326; Gavin Clarkson, "Tribal Bonds: Statutory Shackles and Regulatory Restraints on Tribal Economic Development," *North Carolina Law Review* 85 (2007): 1009–1085.

36. Angela Riley, "Good (Native) Governance," *Columbia Law Review* 107, no.5 (2007): 1049–1125.

37. For an overview of good governance, see Orly Lobel, "The Renew Deal: The Fall of Regulation and the Rise of Governance in Contemporary Legal Thought," *Minnesota Law Review* 89, no.2 (2004): 342–470.

38. Riley, "Good (Native) Governance," *supra* note 36, at 1051–1052.

39. *Id.* at 1054.

40. *Id.* at 1063.

41. *Id.* at 1064 ("Ineffective or bad governance, by contrast, produces suspicion and disrespect among citizens and outsiders alike. Not surprisingly, then, the presence of an

effective government is as critical to the success of an Indian nation as it is to any other.").

42. *Id.* at 1065.

43. *Id.* at 1054, 1062.

44. *See, e.g.,* Albert O. Hirschman, *Exit, Voice, and Loyalty: Responses to Decline in Firms, Organizations, and States* (Cambridge, Massachusetts: Harvard University Press, 1972).

45. Riley, "Good (Native) Governance," *supra* note 36, at 1083.

46. *Id.* at 1082.

47. *Id.* at 1083.

48. *Id.* at 1087.

49. *Id.* at 1087–1088.

50. *Id.* at 1093.

51. *Id.* at 1116.

52. *Id.* at 1051.

53. *Id.* at 1124.

54. For fuller treatment of this complicated dynamic, see Wenona Singel, "Indian Tribes and Human Rights Accountability," *San Diego Law Review* 49 (2012): 567–625.

55. Riley, "Good (Native) Governance," *supra* note 36, at 1121. For further exploration of this argument, see Kristen A. Carpenter and Angela R. Riley, "Indigenous Peoples and the Jurisgenerative Moment in Human Rights," *California Law Review* 102 (2014): 173–234.

56. Robert J. Miller, *Reservation Capitalism: Economic Development in Indian Country* (Denver, Colorado: Praeger, 2012). This section builds on an earlier book review of *Reservation Capitalism.* Ezra Rosser, "Creating Space for Reservation Growth," *Florida International University Law Review* 9 (2014): 351–359.

57. Miller, *Reservation Capitalism, supra* note 56, at 135.

58. *Id.* at 2.

59. *Id.* at 9-10. *See also* Terry L. Anderson, "The Property Rights Paradigm: An Introduction," in *Property Rights and Indian Economies,* ed. Terry L. Anderson (Lanham, Maryland: Rowman & Littlefield Publishers, 1992); Lloyd L. Lee, *Diné Identity in a Twenty-First-Century World* (Tucson: University of Arizona Press, 2020), 68 (identifying traditional Diné forms of ownership over land, personal items, and intellectual property).

60. Miller, *Reservation Capitalism, supra* note 56, at 9–24.

61. *Id.* at 47.

62. *Id.* at 135–137.

63. *Id.* at 139.

64. *Id.* at 142.

65. *Id.* at 139–140.

66. *Id.* at 143.

67. *Id.* at 144–146.

68. *Id.* at 155.

69. Douglass C. North, "The New Institutional Economics and Third World Development," in *The New Institutional Economics and Third World Development,* eds. John Harriss, Janet Hunter, and Colin M. Lewis (New York: Routledge, 1995), 17–26, at 18.

70. *Id.* at 23.

71. For more extensive exploration of NIE as it relates to tribal development, see Rosser, "This Land is My Land, This Land is Your Land," *supra* note 2, at 278–311.

72. Miller, *Reservation Capitalism, supra* note 56, at 164.

8 LOCALLY GROUNDED DEVELOPMENT

1. For a description of how chapter meetings work, see Sam Bingham and Janet Bingham, *Navajo Chapters*, rev. ed. (Tsaile, Arizona: Navajo Community College Press, 1987), 17–25.
2. See *Navajo Sovereignty: Understandings and Visions of the Diné People*, ed. Lloyd L. Lee (Tucson: University of Arizona Press, 2017), 3 ("Prior to colonization, Navajo authority and autonomy was located in the extended family networks, clans, and 'natural communities.'").
3. Michael Lerma, *Guided by the Mountains: Navajo Political Philosophy and Governance* (New York: Oxford University Press, 2017), 155.
4. This chapter's coverage of land privatization borrows from Ezra Rosser, "Right-Sizing Use Rights: Navajo Land, Bureaucracy, and Home," in *Creating Private Sector Economies in Native America: Sustainable Development through Entrepreneurship*, eds. Robert J. Miller, Miriam Jorgensen and Daniel Stewart (New York: Cambridge University Press, 2019), 82–96.
5. See Kristen A. Carpenter and Angela R. Riley, "Privatizing the Reservation?," *Stanford Law Review* 71 (2019): 791–878, at 794 fn. 5 (collecting cites of academics who support land privatization).
6. See Naomi Schaefer Riley, *The New Trail of Tears: How Washington Is Destroying American Indians* (New York: Encounter Books, 2016).
7. Matthew L. M. Fletcher, "Repeating the Mistakes of the Past in 'The New Trail of Tears'," *Los Angeles Review of Books*, Oct. 21, 2016. See Riley, *The New Trail of Tears*, *supra* note 6, at 14–15 ("The truth of the matter is that Dawes was right – *private property is an almost magical force*.") (emphasis in original).
8. Fletcher, "Repeating the Mistakes of the Past in 'The New Trail of Tears'," *supra* note 7.
9. Carpenter and Riley, "Privatizing the Reservation?," *supra* note 5, at 797.
10. *Id.* at 804.
11. Personally, I think it is an ahistorical and assimilative argument if taken seriously for all tribes, but the focus here is on the Navajo Nation. That is not to say that tribes cannot make productive use of land that they buy in fee and that is not converted into trust land.
12. See Ezra Rosser, "Anticipating de Soto: Allotment of Indian Reservations and the Dangers of Land-Titling," in *Hernando de Soto and Property in a Market Economy*, ed. D. Benjamin Barros (Burlington, Vermont: Ashgate, 2010), 61–81, at 61–75 (discussing the dangers of land titling in light of allotment).
13. See Judith V. Royster, "The Legacy of Allotment," *Arizona State Law Journal* 27 (1995): 1–78; Ann E. Tweedy, "UnjustifiableExpectations: Laying to Rest the Ghosts of Allotment Era Settlers," *Seattle University Law Review* 36 (2012): 129–188, at 133–137.
14. For an excellent overview of the complexity of Indian land tenure, which is partially a result of allotment, see Jessica A. Shoemaker, "Complexity's Shadow: American Indian Property, Sovereignty, and the Future," *Michigan Law Review* 115 (2017): 487–552. For more on the US Supreme Court's concerns about checkerboarding, see Ezra Rosser, "Protecting Non-Indians From Harm?: The Property Consequences of Indians," *Oregon Law Review* 87 (2008): 175–219.
15. See, e.g., Lawrence David Weiss, *Development of Capitalism in the Navajo Nation: A Political-Economic History* (Minneapolis, Minnesota: MEP Publications, 1984), 61 ("Given the inadequacy of reservation land for land-extensive stock-raising activity and given the significant population growth of the period, there was a great deal of pressure from the Navajo to expand the reservation. The lack of Anglo mineral claims, home-steaders, and corporate herders in the vicinity in the first few decades after the return

made such formal expansion possible."); Jessica A. Shoemaker, "No Sticks in My Bundle: Rethinking the Indian Land Tenure Problem," *Kansas Law Review* 63 (2014): 383–450, at 440 ("For example, the tribes of the arid southwest largely escaped allotment because, in that climate and landscape, federal officials acknowledged that 'tribes such as the Navajo had to live communally to survive,' and '[t]hese nomadic herdsmen who followed the grass and rain could not exist on 80 or even 320 acres.' Therefore, the Navajo today still operate with some of their own indigenous property systems and tenure rules on remaining reservation lands."); Caleb Michael Bush, "Land, Conflict and the 'Net of Incorporation': Capitalism's Uneven Expansion into the Navajo Indian Reservation, 1860–2000" (PhD diss., Binghamton University, State University of New York, 2005), 6 ("Ultimately, the barren quality was the reason why so much land was given over to the Navajos; such land was not much good for anything, it seemed, so why not give it to the Indians clamoring for more land?"); "Winning the Peace," in *Between Sacred Mountains: Navajo Stories and Lessons from the Land*, eds. Sam Bingham, et al. (Tucson: University of Arizona Press, 1982), 146 ("How did the Navajo win back in peacetime land that they lost in war? The won it with livestock. Sheep and cattle held land that guns and arrows could not.").

16. For a rich history of Navajo blood quantum requirements, see Paul Spruhan, "The Origins, Current Status, and Future Prospects of Blood Quantum as the Definition of Membership in the Navajo Nation," *Tribal Law Journal* 8 (2007): 1–17.

17. For a much more complete discussion of the meaning and significance of hozho and k'e, see Ray Austin, *Navajo Courts and Navajo Common Law: A Tradition of Tribal Self-Governance* (Minneapolis: University of Minnesota Press, 2009).

18. Robert J. Miller, "Sovereign Resilience: Reviving Private-Sector Economic Institutions in Indian Country," *Brigham Young University Law Review* 2018 (2019): 1331–1405, at 1391.

19. This section owes a particular debt of gratitude to Professor Michelle Hale for her dissertation and continued work on Navajo local governance. *See* Michelle Lynn Hale, *"Devolution and the Navajo Nation: Strategies for Local Empowerment in Three Navajo Communities" (PhD diss., University of Arizona, 2012).*

20. Navajo Nation Code, Title 26, Navajo Nation Local Governance Act, www.nndcd.org /uploads/FileLinks/aed50fb739694983b14b401d60210308/7Title26_LGA.pdf.

21. *Id*. at D-1.

22. *See* Hale, "Devolution and the Navajo Nation," *supra* note 19, at 55–56 ("One of the challenges that chapter officials face, however, is central government oversight. Many decisions require central government approval; approval takes time; and approval is not always forthcoming … From a chapter perspective, the system can often seem non-responsive and unnecessarily burdensome, and Window Rock can seem a very long way away."); Bingham and Bingham, *Navajo Chapters*, *supra* note 1, at 13–14 (emphasizing the participatory nature of chapter democracies and likening them to New England town meetings).

23. First Nations Development Institute, *Western Agency Chapters Technical Assistance Project: Strategies for Advancing Individual Farmers and Ranchers on the Navajo Western Agency* (Longmont, Colorado: First Nations Development Institute, 2012), 15.

24. *See* Lloyd L. Lee, "The Future of Navajo Nationalism," *Wicazo Sa Review* 22, no.1 (2007): 53–68, at 59 ("In 1998, the tribal council passed the Navajo Nation Local Governance Act. The purpose of the Act is to recognize governance at the [page break here] local level and allow chapters to make decisions over local matters. Although this attempt by the tribal council to 'give' chapter houses (local community settings) more local authority, the tribal council can still preempt chapter authority with a statute and/or a resolution.").

25. Hale, "Devolution and the Navajo Nation," *supra* note 19, at 90 ("The Navajo Nation has yet to see if the LGA will have large-scale, long-term success.").

26. Michael Parrish, *Local Governance and Reform: Local Empowerment* (Tsaile, Arizona: Diné Policy Institute, 2018), 12–13; Michelle L. Hale, "The Navajo Local Governance Act (LGA): A Help or Hindrance to Grassroots Self-Government?," *American Indian Culture and Research Journal* 42, no.1 (2018): 91–114, at 94–95, 100–101.

27. Hale, "Devolution and the Navajo Nation," *supra* note 19, at 103.

28. *See* Hale, "The Navajo Local Governance Act (LGA)," *supra* note 26, at 107 ("The community has difficulty attracting educated professionals – especially those who are Navajo citizens – to the reservation.").

29. Michelle Hale, "Empowered Sovereignty for Navajo Chapters Through Engagement in a Community-Planning Process," in *Navajo Sovereignty: Understandings and Visions of the Diné People*, ed. Lloyd L. Lee (Tucson: University of Arizona Press, 2017), 130–136, at 133.

30. Hale, "The Navajo Local Governance Act (LGA)," *supra* note 26, at 104.

31. Navajo Nation Office of the Auditor General LGA Certified Chapters webpage, www.navajoauditor.org/lgacertified_01.html. Note: some counts report forty-five certified chapters.

32. *Id.*

33. In the interest of full disclosure, late in her career the author's mother worked for a number of years late as a planner with the Tuba City satellite office.

34. Raymond Tsosie, Post LGA Update Report, Feb. 17, 2012, www.nndcd.org/uploads/FileLinks/aed50fb739694983b14b401d60210308/10PostLGAUpdateReport.pdf.

35. *See* Dana Powell, *Landscapes of Power: Politics of Energy in the Navajo Nation* (Durham, North Carolina: Duke University Press, 2018), 111 ("The process to gain LGA certification is long, uneven, difficult, and frustrating, with the end result of certification failing to deliver the full autonomy it appears to promise.").

36. Andrew Curley, Michael Parrish, and Majerle Lister, *Local Governance and Reform: Considering 20 Years of the Local Governance Act* (Tsaile, Arizona: Diné Policy Institute, 2016), 7.

37. As a Diné Policy Institute report notes, "Twenty years since the project of local empowerment began, the results have been disappointing. LGA Certification has not created the conditions for regional development. Local officials regularly complain about the oversight in Window Rock. And Window Rock complains about mismanagement at the chapter level." Andrew Curley and Michael Parrish, *Local Governance and Reform: A Conceptual Critique of Regionalization and the Title 26 Taskforce* (Tsaile, Arizona; Diné Policy Institute, 2016), 7.

38. Aubrey W. Williams, Jr., *Navajo Political Process* (Washington, D.C.: Smithsonian Institution Press, 1970), 2. For more on Hunter's motivation, see Bingham and Bingham, *Navajo Chapters*, *supra* note 22, at 2.

39. *See* Weiss, *Development of Capitalism in the Navajo Nation*, *supra* note 15, at 24–25 ("The chapter-house system was set up by a federal agent, and was utilized in the course of the last hundred years to promote various federal projects such as the sheep-reduction program and cooperative agricultural ventures. The centralized tribal council was initiated specifically by the BIA in order to give some legal veneer to the granting of oil and gas exploration and extraction leases."). *See also* Hale, "Devolution and the Navajo Nation," *supra* note 19, at 50–51 ("BIA superintendent John Hunter, who was based at the Leupp Agency, is generally credited for devising the chapter system in 1927. Hunter, a non-native, thought that a town hall style of local

government would help Navajo people within his agency to organize on local levels so they could weigh in on policy, receive information coming from Washington, and discuss issues pertinent to the area. Local government could make the job of the agency superintendent easier since there were dozens of small, local communities within one agency and few superintendents or their staff spoke Navajo. A 'chapter' would create a forum for local Navajos to gather, discuss and decide in their own language. The chapter system was established in 1927, using grazing districts as the basis for chapter boundaries. Reflecting this origin, in the early years they were more often referred to as Livestock Improvement Associations, but that designation changed over time.").

40. Hale, "The Navajo Local Governance Act (LGA)," *supra* note 26, at 92–93 ("Before European intrusion, leadership was local. Navajo people occupied vast territory but settled in small, localized, and often clan-based autonomous communities. Decision-making was local … The LGA attempts to honor that pre-treaty style of governance by centering the power locally."); Curley and Parrish, *Local Governance and Reform, supra* note 37, at 3 ("More than the central government, finalized in 1937, chapter house have reflected better traditional Navajo social and cultural boundaries, based on *k'é*."); Klara Kelley and Harris Francis, A *Diné History of Navajoland* (Tucson: University of Arizona Press, 2019), 21 ("The chapters formalized earlier ways of local governance, when families would meet as needed to make decisions or settle disputes, having a respected elder/leader to mediate, and making decisions by consensus.").

41. Bingham and Bingham, *Navajo Chapters, supra* note 1, at 1 ("There was no Tribal Council in the days before the Long Walk, and the leaders almost never got together.").

42. Hale, "Devolution and the Navajo Nation," *supra* note 19, at 93 ("The LGA was an attempt to return to traditional concepts of leadership. It is intended to reestablish local authority by decentralizing powers that can help local communities to 'do for themselves' through chapter government.").

43. For a discussion of Kayenta's amenities, educational facilities, and infrastructure, see *Kayenta Township Comprehensive Plan, Background and Current Conditions Volume* (Tucson: The Planning Center, 2011), http://kayentatownship-nsn.gov/Home/PDF/bg_final.pdf.

44. For an overview of the legislative acts related to Kayenta, see Kayenta Township website, "Township History" page, http://kayentatownship-nsn.gov/Home/index.php/2-uncate gorised/14-township-history.

45. *See* Hale, "The Navajo Local Governance Act (LGA)," *supra* note 26, at 98.

46. *See* Stephen Cornell et al., "Citizen Entrepreneurship: An Underutilized Development Resource," in *Rebuilding Native Nations: Strategies for Governance and Development*, ed. Miriam Jorgensen (Tucson: University of Arizona Press, 2007), 197–222, at 208 (noting that tourism provides Kayenta with "considerable economic potential").

47. Frank McNitt, *The Indian Traders* (Norman: University of Oklahoma Press, 1962), 271.

48. Cindy Yurth, "The Chapter with a Town: Kayenta Combines Beauty with Economic Muscle," *Navajo Times*, June 13, 2013.

49. The Opportunity Atlas website, www.opportunityatlas.org/ (Tract 04017942500, Kayenta, AZ, using 2015 dollars) (note, the Opportunity Atlas tract is based on census information which is not perfectly aligned with the township boundaries, but does approximate them).

50. Isaac Shapiro, Cecile Murray, and Barbara Sard, "Basic Facts on Concentrated Poverty," *Center on Budget and Policy Priorities*, Nov. 3, 2015, www.cbpp.org/sites/default/files/atoms/files/11-3-15hous2.pdf.

51. Associated Press, "Navajo Township is Rocking Tribal Establishment," *Deseret News*, Apr. 2, 2000, www.deseretnews.com/article/811993/Navajo-township-is-rocking-tribal-establishment.html.
52. Curley and Parrish, *Local Governance and Reform, supra* note 37, at 11.
53. *Id.* at 20.
54. *See* Curley, Parrish, and Lister, *Local Governance and Reform: Considering 20 Years of the Local Governance Act, supra* note 36, at 14 ("Several chapter communities that we spoke with created not-for-profit organizations to achieve their chapter house goals … These nongovernmental organizations (NGOs) are methods to achieve forms of community and economic development at a pace quicker than what the tribal government is capable of achieving with its central management at this point. With proper decentralization of administrative authority, spending and hiring authorities, and land-use planning, chapter officials believe that they can accomplish more.").
55. For a description of the pre-conquest form of Navajo sovereignty, see Mary Stephenson, *Navajo Ways in Government: A Political Process* (Menasha, Wisconsin: American Anthropological Association, 1963), 46 ("[T]he Navajo tribe, as it existed before the Conquest, had no centralized authority. It never convened as a group, but it was distinctly bounded by the limits of acceptance of a common culture, that is, a system of shared customs, beliefs, and values that was considered binding on the society.").
56. Andrew Curley arguably goes even further when highlighting the cultural mismatch between the tribe's current institutions and its structure historically: "Here the Navajo Nation is out of cultural compliance, if 'culture' can be unified into a general term. Historically the Navajo: 1) had disaggregate political units, 2) had leadership (i.e., the naataani) which didn't separate the roles of law-making and administration, 3) had no hierarchies— meaning had roles of responsibility, not authority and 4) had political institutions that didn't have coercive powers. If we wanted to move more toward a 'culture match' in the Kalt sense to the term, the Navajo Nation should abandon the Office of the President, which has been fraught with difficulties since it's inception, weaken the Council vis-à-vis the power of Chapter House governments and create regional decision-making units, similar to the function of agency meetings currently." Andrew Curley, "Constitutionalism" in *Navajo Nation Constitutional Feasibility and Government Reform Project* (Tsaile, Arizona: Diné Policy Institute, 2008), 12.
57. *See also* Hale, "The Navajo Local Governance Act (LGA)," *supra* note 26, at 111 ("The LGA may or may not be the change agent that enables local empowerment or achieves the scale or reforms sought by the Navajo people. However, it shows the Navajo people's willingness to try something different.").

9 RECLAIMING THE LAND

1. Navajo Land Department, *Navajo Nation Lands and Leases* (Mar. 15, 2015), www.dinehbikeyah.org/docs/title/NN_Lands_and_Leases-2016.pdf.
2. Significant portions of this chapter were previously published in Ezra Rosser, "Reclaiming the Navajo Range: Resolving the Conflict Between Grazing Rights and Development," *Connecticut Law Review* 51 (2019): 953–981 and Ezra Rosser, "Right-Sizing Use Rights: Navajo Land, Bureaucracy, and Home," in *Creating Private Sector Economies in Native America: Sustainable Development through Entrepreneurship*, eds. Robert J. Miller,

Miriam Jorgensen and Daniel Stewart (New York: Cambridge University Press, 2019), 82–96.

3. *See* Dana Powell, *Landscapes of Power: Politics of Energy in the Navajo Nation* (Durham, North Carolina: Duke University Press, 2018), 131 ("Grazing-permit holders, who represent only 5 percent of the 170,000 or so Navajos dwelling on the reservation, have tremendous power in land-use decisions. The laws governing customary land use require that the nation gain consent from a grazing-permit holder for any project within the permit's boundaries, much to the frustration of some agency directors who argue for stronger, more discernible 'boundaries' in land management.").

4. Klara B. Kelley and Peter M. Whiteley, *Navajoland: Family Settlement and Land Use* (Tsaile, Arizona: Navajo Community College Press, 1989), 84. *See also* Lawrence David Weiss, *Development of Capitalism in the Navajo Nation: A Political-Economic History* (Minneapolis, Minnesota: MEP Publications, 1984), 29 ("Land was not a commodity, but rather use was based on a system of traditional use-rights, where the ability to productively use land gave the user de facto control over it."); *Id.* at 32–33 ("Land for grazing and growing crops was not a commodity to be bought and sold. It was used by a family, to be used by others on the basis of reciprocal use agreements in times of visiting or stress, or it could be permanently used by another if the original owner permanently abandoned it for some reason."); Mary Stephenson, *Navajo Ways in Government: A Political Process* (Menasha, Wisconsin: American Anthropological Association, 1963), 30 ("The original settler and his family, who cleared and cultivated the land, are considered to have prior rights as long as the land is in use, but if it is left fallow for any great length of time, anyone may preempt it.").

5. Diné Policy Institute, *Land Reform in the Navajo Nation: Possibilities of Renewal for Our People* (Tsaile, Arizona: Diné Policy Institute, 2017), 8.

6. *Begay* v. *Keedah*, 6 Nav. R. 416, 421 (Nav.Sup.Ct.1991).

7. Homesite Lease Regulations 2016, Resolution of the Resources and Development Committee of the 23rd Navajo Nation Council – Second Year 2016, "An Action Relating to Resources and Development; Approving the Amendments to the Navajo Nation Homesite Lease Regulations," RDCO-74–16, Section One (E). Note: the Homesite Lease Regulations 2016 are available here:www.dinehbikeyah.org/docs/home site/Homesite_Lease_Regulations_2016.pdf.

8. Homesite Lease Regulations 2016, *supra* note 7, at § 2.01.

9. *See id.* at § 1.01.

10. *Id.* at § 6.01, 7.01.

11. *See* Andrew Curley, "The Navajo Nation's Coal Economy Was Built to Be Exploited," *High Country News*, June 28, 2017.

12. 2017 Homesite Lease NN200RL Flowchart. Note: the list of requirements that follows is also taken from this flowchart with some slight language modifications made for the purpose of readability.

13. Denee Bix, Letter to the Editor, "A Place to Call Home," *Navajo Times*, Oct. 20, 2016, https://navajotimes.com/opinion/letters/letters-land-kids-future/.

14. Homesite Lease Regulations 2016, *supra* note 7, at Exhibit F: Homesite Lease Application Fee; Penalties and Fines Fee Schedule.

15. Cindy Yurth, "Chapter Officials, Residents Worried About New Home Site Regs," *Navajo Times*, Aug. 10, 2017, https://navajotimes.com/reznews/chapter-officials-residents-worried-about-new-home-site-regs/.

16. *Id.*

17. Western Navajo Agency Council, "Demanding the Repeal of Amendments to the Navajo Nation Homesite Lease Regulations Approved by the Resources and Development Committee on October 4th, 2016 Via Resolution # RDCO-74-16; Calling Upon All Diné Chapters to Jointly Develop a Foundational Document Based on the Principles, Laws and Teachings Embedded in Diné Traditional Fundamental Law on the Use of Diné Bikéyah on Which All Navajo Nation Land Use Laws Must Be Based," Resolution No: WCAC18-03-NB8, Mar. 17, 2018. [Note: I serve on the board of a nonprofit, Indian Grassroots Support, whose Executive Director was consulted in connection with the resolution, but I was not involved in any way in this resolution or in its contents, though other board members did contribute.]

18. Cindy Yurth, "Halona on Homesite Regs: 'We're Going to Use K'e,'" *Navajo Times*, Aug. 24, 2017, https://navajotimes.com/reznews/halona-on-homesite-regs-were-going-to-use-ke/.

19. Adam Teller, Letter to the Editor, "Government Trying to Take People's Land," *Navajo Times*, Sep. 7, 2017, https://navajotimes.com/opinion/letters/letters-republic-does-not-deserve-spj-award/.

20. Diné Policy Institute, *Land Reform in the Navajo Nation*, supra note 5, at 6.

21. President Nixon, Special Message to the Congress on Indian Affairs (July 8, 1970) ("The time has come to break decisively with the past and to create the conditions for a new era in which the Indian future is determined by Indian acts and Indian decisions.").

22. Helping Expedite and Advance Responsible Tribal Home Ownership Act of 2012, Pub. L. No. 112-151, §§ 1–3, 126 Stat. 1150, 1150–54 (2012).

23. Donald L. Fixico, "American Indian Leadership in History to the Present," *Rikkyo American Studies* 29 (2007): 29–52, at 29 ("In modern times of the twentieth century, Peter MacDonald of the Navajo guided tribes throughout Indian County into the era of Self-Determination.").

24. *See also* Jessica A. Shoemaker, "Transforming Property: Reclaiming Indigenous Land Tenures," *California Law Review* 107, no. 5 (2019): 1531–1607, at 1589–1602 (arguing that tribes should foster flexibility and innovation in land governance, drawing in part on tribal traditions).

25. *See* Ruth Roessel and Broderick H. Johnson, *Navajo Livestock Reduction: A National Disgrace* (Chinle, Arizona: Navajo Community College Press, 1974), 45–49 (describing the "terrible sight" that was livestock reduction).

26. *See generally id.* (describing the impact of livestock reduction from a variety of different perspectives).

27. *See, e.g.*, Lynn Fuller, "Desertification on the Navajo Reservation: A Legal and Historical Analysis," *Stanford Environmental Law Journal* 8 (1989): 229–291, at 258 ("Navajo governmental authorities were politically unwilling or unable to enforce the grazing regulations.").

28. *See, e.g.*, Fuller, "Desertification on the Navajo Reservation," *supra* note 27, at 231–232 (discussing the extreme desertification of Navajo lands due to overgrazing by livestock and the impacts on the Navajo people).

29. *See id.* at 258 (explaining that "[e]conomic development efforts focused on exploiting non-renewable natural resources on the reservation" and that "[t]he tribal government in Window Rock did not take seriously the need for improving range productivity"). For a lengthy discussion of Navajo natural resource exploitation, see generally Ezra Rosser, "Ahistorical Indians and Reservation Resources," *Environmental Law* 40 (2010): 437–545.

30. *See Riggs* v. *Estate of Attakai*, 9 Navajo Rptr. 119, 121 (Navajo 2007) ("By placing the grazing permit with Sista Riggs, there is assurance that the land and herd will remain with the family, and that the grazing permit will remain intact.").

31. *See* Fuller, "Desertification on the Navajo Reservation," *supra* note 27, at 231, 280 (explaining that political pressures have resulted in ineffective and abused range-management controls).
32. *Id.* at 231.
33. *See* Julie Nania and Karen Cozzetto, *Considerations for Climate Change and Variability Adaptation on the Navajo Nation* (Boulder: University of Colorado Boulder, 2014), 99 (discussing the resistance by the Navajo to address feral animals, especially mustangs, that contribute to overgrazing of the range).
34. *See* Gary D. Libecap and Ronald N. Johnson, "Legislating Commons: The Navajo Tribal Council and the Navajo Range," *Economic Inquiry* 18 (1980): 69–86, at 69–70 ("Because of high enforcement costs [for] small herds and high political costs for elected officials, the Tribal Council since 1956 has *not* enforced grazing regulations.").
35. *See* Mark Schoepfle et al., "Navajo Attitudes Toward Development and Change: A Unified Ethnographic and Survey Approach to an Understanding of Their Future," *American Anthropologist* 86, no.4 (1984): 885–904, at 895, 901 (explaining that the survey found the Navajo people identified the loss of the grazing permit, and thus access to their land, as the most severe threat and that the Navajo will not support development if it interferes with tradition).
36. Navajo Nation Code Ann. tit. 3, § 781(A) (2010); *see also* Nania and Cozzetto, *Considerations for Climate Change and Variability Adaptation on the Navajo Nation, supra* note 33, at 101 ("In order to graze [livestock] on the range, a Navajo grazing permit is required.").
37. Navajo Nation Code Ann. tit. 3, § 706(D) (2010).
38. *Id.* at § 781(C).
39. Nania and Cozzetto, *Considerations for Climate Change and Variability Adaptation on the Navajo Nation, supra* note 33, at 101.
40. *Id.*
41. Navajo Nation Code Ann. tit. 3, § 171 (2010).
42. *Id.*
43. *See* 3 N.T.C. § 282 (1962) (citing the 1957 Navajo Reservation Grazing Handbook in the statutory history of the general regulations).
44. Navajo Nation Code Ann. tit. 3, § 703(C) (2010); *see also* 3 N.T.C. § 283 (1962) (citing pages 8 and 9 of the 1957 Navajo Reservation Grazing Handbook in the history for subsection (c), which states, "[t]he adjustment of livestock numbers to the carrying capacity of the range in such a manner that the livestock economy of the Navajo Tribe will be preserved").
45. Navajo Nation Code Ann. tit. 3, §§ 708(A)–(B) (2010).
46. Navajo Nation Code Ann. tit. 3, § 709 (2010).
47. *See* Estate of Navajo Joe, 4 Navajo Rptr. 99, 99 (Navajo 1983) ("[A] grazing permit is one of the most important items of property which a Navajo may own.").
48. 6 Navajo Rptr. 416, 421 (Navajo 1991); *see also In re* Quiet Title to Livestock Grazing Permit No. 8-487 Formerly Held by Martha Francis, No. SC-CV-41-09, slip op. at 6–7 (Navajo Dec. 29, 2011) (summarizing the five factors articulated by *Begay* v. *Keedah* when determining whether to award a grazing permit).
49. *See* Raymond Darrel Austin, *Navajo Courts and Navajo Common Law: A Tradition of Tribal Self-Governance* (Minneapolis: University of Minnesota Press, 2009), 190 (explaining that Navajo policy for land-use permits is to grant permits to "individuals who will make the most beneficial use of land," which "equates to the use it or lose it rule").

50. *See id.* (explaining the difference between Navajo land use policies and property law in the Anglo-American legal system).
51. *See Riggs* v. *Estate of Attakai*, 9 Navajo Rptr. 119, 120–121 (Navajo 2007) (emphasizing the importance of Navajo Nation policies regarding personal land use and prevention of fragmentation when awarding land use permits).
52. *Begay*, 6 Navajo Rptr. at 421.
53. *Riggs*, 9 Navajo Rptr. at 120–21.
54. Navajo Nation Code Ann. tit. 1, §§ 201-206 (2010).
55. For more on Navajo Fundamental Law, see Kenneth Bobroff, "Diné Bi Beenahaz'áanii: Codifying Indigenous Consuetudinary Law in the 21st Century," *Tribal Law Journal* 5, no.4 (2004–2005), which explains *k'é* as the Navajo clan system that maintains healthy bloodlines and avoids incest; *k'é* is considered the "foundation of all laws."
56. Riggs, 9 Navajo Rptr. at 120.
57. *In re* Quiet Title to Livestock Grazing Permit No. 8-487 Formerly Held by Martha Francis, No. SC-CV-41-09, slip op. at 7 (Navajo Dec. 29, 2011).
58. *See Riggs*, 9 Navajo Rptr. at 120 ("Navajo Fundamental Law … defines the role and authority of Diné women in [Navajo] society. Traditionally, women are central to the home and land base."). For more on gender-based governance in Indian communities generally, see Angela R. Riley, "(Tribal) Sovereignty and Illiberalism," *California Law Review* 95, no.3 (2007): 799–848, at 842–844.
59. *See* O. N. Hicks, *Sketch History of the Navajo Grazing Situation* (Window Rock, Arizona: Bureau of Indian Affairs, Navajo Area Office, Branch of Land Operations, 1966), 11 ("The Navajos are unlike all other southwestern tribes in their use of lands due to the strong feeling of individual ownership. Although admitting that the Navajo Tribe holds title to the land[,] their 'customary use rights' many times exceeds those of the Tribe when dealing with use and occupancy problems.").
60. David Listokin et al., *Housing and Economic Development in Indian Country: Challenge and Opportunity* (New Brunswick, New Jersey: Center for Urban Policy Research Press, Edward J. Bloustein School of Planning and Public Policy, Rutgers, 2006), 335 (internal citation omitted).
61. *See* Diné Policy Institute, *Land Reform in the Navajo Nation*, *supra* note 5, at 36; *see also id.* at 47 ("Grazing permittees are given the authority to decide whether development occurs within their area and community.").
62. *See* "Raw," *Oxford English Dictionary*, 3rd ed. (Oxford, England: Oxford University Press, 2008) (defining raw land as "undeveloped").
63. For the most influential article emphasizing exclusion, see Thomas W. Merrill, "Property and the Right to Exclude," *Nebraska Law Review* 77 (1998): 730–755, at 740–752. *See also* Larissa Katz, "Exclusion and Exclusivity in Property Law," *University of Toronto Law Journal* 58 (2008): 275–315, at 279–285 (2008) (providing a summary of the exclusion-based or boundary approach to property ownership).
64. *See* Ronald N. Johnson and Gary D. Libecap, "Agency Costs and the Assignment of Property Rights: The Case of Southwestern Indian Reservations," *Southern Economic Journal* 47, no.2 (1980): 332–347, at 333 (arguing that conferral of formal grazing rights created internal tribal conflicts that "retarded the development of formal property rights to range land on reservations").
65. *See* Schoepfle et al., "Navajo Attitudes Toward Development and Change," *supra* note 35, at 895 ("We see that the loss of the grazing permit, which confers rights to land and livestock, is the most severe threat, and this establishes the Navajo view that maintaining access to land is the most crucial factor in maintaining the viability of Navajo life.").

66. Michelle L. Hale, "The Navajo Local Governance Act (LGA): A Help or Hindrance to Grassroots Self-Government?" *American Indian Culture and Research Journal* 42, no. 1 (2018): 97.

67. Objections to development can come from other unlikely quarters as well, including from tribal members who are not directly involved in grazing but who want to protect their parents' interests. *See id.* at 901 ("[T]he more educated Navajos, though more willing to tolerate various adverse effects, prefer to maintain access to traditional land … Their purpose is *to keep traditional land holdings intact* … They thus are willing to participate in development, but are not happy about an outcome in which the traditional way of life for their parents is sacrificed.").

68. *See, e.g.*, Susan Carder, "Bashas' Diné Markets and the Navajo Nation: A Study of Cross-Cultural Trade," *American Indian Culture and Research Journal* 39, no.1 (2015): 47–64, at 54 ("The Navajo people are granted grazing permits for the land. The Navajo Nation holds the land in trust but the grazing permittees have *de facto* veto power over proposed use changes. For example, fifteen acres of land could have five individual grazing permittees. Arrangements would have to be made with each of the individuals before the land could be released back to the Navajo Nation for development."); Listokin et al., *Housing and Economic Development in Indian Country, supra* note 60, at 325 (highlighting "the de facto veto power of grazing permittees who tend to be conservative and block development proposals").

69. Carder, "Bashas' Diné Markets and the Navajo Nation," *supra* note 68, at 54.

70. Listokin et al., *Housing and Economic Development in Indian Country, supra* note 60, at 344 (internal citation omitted).

71. For discussion of the Navajo Nation's 2016 effort to reform the homesite lease approval process, see Rosser, "Right-Sizing Use Rights," *supra* note 2.

72. Navajo Nation Code Ann. tit. 26 (1998).

73. *See* Andrew Curley, Michael Parrish and Majerle Lister, *Local Governance and Reform: Considering 20 Years of the Local Governance Act* (Tsaile, Arizona: Diné Policy Institute, 2016), 18–21 (discussing structural flaws in the Local Governance Act).

74. For a recent study exploring governance reform at the chapter level, see Michael Parrish, *Local Governance and Reform: Local Empowerment* (Tsaile, Arizona: Diné Policy Institute, 2018), 23–28 (listing recommendations for governance reform as a result of the study).

75. Stephen Conn, "Mid-Passage—The Navajo Tribe and its First Legal Revolution," *American Indian Law Review* 6, no. 2 (1978): 329–370, at 344.

76. *See* Shoemaker, *Transforming Property, supra* note 24, at 63 ("To the extent a reservation community may choose to pursue the goal of revitalizing at least some traditional values around land and land tenure, many tribal governments are also focusing on nurturing those Indigenous traditions that have persisted.").

77. For more than a decade, academics have been debating just how important exclusion is to property law. Such debates show little sign of abating, and it is not worth rehashing the merits of each side here. *See* Rosser, "The Ambition and Transformative Potential of Progressive Property," *supra* note 29, at 115–126 (providing an overview of progressive property); Katrina M. Wyman, "The New Essentialism in Property," *Journal of Legal Analysis* 9, no.2 (2017): 183–246, at 192–203 (providing an overview of the new essentialism definition of property). But it can safely be said that exclusion is central to Anglo-American concepts of property, *see* Merrill, "Property and the Right to Exclude," *supra* note 63, at 740–752, even though not all scholars would agree that it is the core of property. *See, e.g.*, Gregory S. Alexander, "The Complex Core of Property," *Cornell*

Law Review 94 (2009): 1063–1071 (proposing a social-obligation theory of property and arguing that "the core [of property ownership] is more complex than exclusion alone").

78. Tellingly, though property can be held in a variety of forms, fee simple absolute enjoys pride of place in how Americans understand property. Though many Americans will be tenants for extended periods of their lives, words such as "ownership," "property rights," and "land rights" generally bring to mind the fee simple form of ownership rather than more complicated ownership forms in which title is split between different parties or varies across time. For more on the place of fee simple absolute in American property law, see Lee Anne Fennell, "Fee Simple Obsolete," *New York University Law Review* 91, no.6 (2016): 1457–1516, at 1466–1468; Katrina M. Wyman, "In Defense of the Fee Simple," *Notre Dame Law Review* 93, no.1 (2017): 1–50, at 6–12.

79. Arguably, the branch of property theory that emphasizes productive labor theory could provide a foundation for meaningful explorations of the nonuse/rights dynamic that is the focus of this chapter. There is a large amount of literature on productive labor theory, which emphasizes productive use of land, an obligation not to waste resources, and a requirement that others in the community have equal opportunity access to community resources, but contemporary property scholars treat it somewhat dismissively as a part of the now dis-favored natural rights approach to property law. *See* Eric R. Claeys, "Labor, Exclusion, and Flourishing in Property Law," *North Carolina Law Review* 95, No.2 (2017): 413–492, at 439–442 (highlighting the features of productive labor theory). Productive labor theory fits uncomfortably alongside a discussion of Navajo land reform given how John Locke's writings were used to justify dispossessing Indians who were seen as not making adequate use of the land. *See, e.g.,* Matthew Yglesias, "If Your House Is Built on Land Expropriated from its Indigenous Inhabitants – You Didn't Build That," *Slate* (Sept. 19, 2012), http://slate.com/business/2012/09/lockean-property-rights-and-native-americans.html (elaborating on the inconsistency between Lockean property theory and Native American dispossession).

80. For in-depth treatment of the law of abandonment, see Lior Jacob Strahilevitz, "The Right to Abandon," *University of Pennsylvania Law Review* 158 (2010): 355–420, at 390–404.

81. "Adverse Possession," *Black's Law Dictionary*, 10th ed. (Eagan, Minnesota: Thomson West, 2014).

82. Lee Anne Fennell, "Efficient Trespass: The Case for 'Bad Faith' Adverse Possession," *Northwestern University Law Review* 100 (2006): 1037–1096, at 1053 ("[C]ourts and commentators often regard the bad faith claimant as a thief.").

83. For the seminal article on how courts deal with "bad faith" adverse possessors, see Richard Helmholz, "Adverse Possession and Subjective Intent," *Washington University Law Quarterly* 61, no. 2 (1983): 331–358.

84. *See* "Lien," *Black's Law Dictionary*, 10th ed. (Eagan, Minnesota: Thomson West, 2014) (defining "lien" as a "legal right or interest that a creditor has in another's property, lasting … until a debt or duty that it secures is satisfied" and defining "tax lien" as a "lien on property, and all rights to property," imposed by the federal, state, or local government for nonpayment of taxes).

85. Of course, sometimes the state does not want to take on the obligations of ownership or does not want to lose part of its tax base, as it does when land moves from private hands to state hands. *See Pocono Springs Civic Ass'n v. MacKenzie*, 667 A.2d 233, 235 (Pa. Super. Ct. 1995) (describing how the landowners attempted to sell, gift, or abandon property to a city civic association to avoid paying delinquent property taxes, but the city declined to accept the property each time).

86. Marsha Weisiger, *Dreaming of Sheep in Navajo Country* (Seattle: University of Washington Press, 2009), 94 (footnote omitted).

87. Diné Policy Institute, *Land Reform in the Navajo Nation, supra* note 5, at 8. *See also* Kelley and Whiteley, *Navajoland, supra* note 4, at 84 ("Navajo individual tenure differed from the American capitalist form of private ownership in two ways, both holdovers from communal tenure. Anyone could take land from someone who claimed it but did not use it, and land in general could not be bought or sold." (citation omitted)).

88. *See* Katz, "Exclusion and Exclusivity in Property Law," *supra* note 63, at 289–290 (arguing that property rights can best be thought of in terms of owners' exclusive agenda-setting authority).

89. The problem of wild horses, not owned by tribal members, is not new nor is it unique to the Navajo reservation. The Meriam Report highlighted the problem in 1928: "*Worthless Horses.* Many reservations are now overrun with worthless horses. These consume much grass that could be utilized by cattle and sheep. Yet the Indians love horses and are often reluctant to get rid of them." Lewis Meriam et al., *The Problem of Indian Administration* (Baltimore: Johns Hopkins Press, 1928), 507.

90. *See, e.g.,* Lawrence C. Kelly, *The Navajo Indians and Federal Indian Policy: 1900–1935* (Tucson: University of Arizona Press, 1968), 196–197 ("After years of wrangling and strife the punitive provisions of the grazing regulations were suspended in 1948 and the burden of devising an adequate range-management program was placed entirely upon the Navajo Tribal Council. Not until 1956 did the Council come up with revised grazing regulations and enforcement continued to be difficult. Meanwhile, as a result of continuous overgrazing, it was estimated that 676,000 acres of land formerly used for grazing were not completely depleted and an additionally 5,500,000 acres had been severely damaged.").

91. *See* Robert J. Miller, "Sovereign Resilience: Reviving Private-Sector Economic Institutions in Indian Country," *Brigham Young University Law Review* 2018 (2019): 1331–1405, at 1374 ("Indian country seems to have a surplus of one infrastructure need: available land. Yet even here, Indian entrepreneurs often encounter serious problems in acquiring the infrastructure of sites to lease to operate businesses. Many reservations have lots of seemingly empty space, but preexisting grazing rights, for example, and other issues actually limit where businesses and storefront establishments can be established or built.").

92. For more on what land reform requires of tribes, see Jessica A. Shoemaker, "Complexity's Shadow: American Indian Property, Sovereignty, and the Future," *Michigan Law Review* 115, no.4 (2017): 487–552, at 549 ("The process of making Indian property law more adaptive – more in the spirit of tribal sovereignty, in line with self-determination goals, and consistent with an indigenous land ethic – must itself be implemented in an iterative (and adaptive) way. This requires participatory local processes to define the problem, set tribal community objectives, assess the land tenure baseline, and formulate models of reform that are iteratively tested as they are deployed.").

93. Charles F. Wilkinson, *American Indians, Time, and the Law* (New Haven, Connecticut: Yale University Press, 1987), 22.

94. Lloyd L. Lee, *Diné Identity in a Twenty-First-Century World* (Tucson: University of Arizona Press, 2020), 93.

95. *See* Ezra Rosser, "Displacing the Judiciary: Customary Law and the Threat of a Defensive Tribal Council," *American Indian Law Review* 34, no.2 (2011): 379–401.

10 CREATING SPACE FOR EXPERIMENTATION

1. *See generally* Ezra Rosser, "Ahistorical Indians and Reservation Resources," *Environmental Law* 40 (2010): 437–545 (discussing the Navajo Nation's proposed Desert Rock mine-mouth power plant).

2. *See* Robert J. Miller, *Reservation Capitalism: Economic Development in Indian Country* (Denver, Colorado: Praeger, 2012), 121.

3. Nancy Pindus et al., *Housing Needs of American Indians and Alaska Natives in Tribal Areas: A Report From the Assessment of American Indian, Alaska Native, and Native Hawaiian Housing Needs* (Washington, DC: US Department of Housing and Urban Development, 2017), xviii.

4. *Id.* at xix. As the GAO reported, "Historically, Native Americans in the United States have faced worse housing conditions than other socioeconomic groups." US Government Accountability Office, *Native American Housing: Additional Actions Needed to Better Support Tribal Efforts* (Washington, DC: US Government Accountability Office, GAO-14-255, 2014), 4.

5. David Listokin et al., *Housing and Economic Development in Indian Country: Challenge and Opportunity* (New Brunswick, New Jersey: Center for Urban Policy Research Press, 2006), 201.

6. RPI Consulting et al., *Phase II Housing Needs Assessment and Demographic Analysis* (Aug. 2011), 15, 18.

7. *Id.* at 15–16.

8. *Id.* at 16.

9. *Id.* at 15.

10. *Id.* at 16.

11. Shiloh Deitz and Katie Meehan, "Plumbing Poverty: Mapping Hot Spots of Racial and Geographic Inequality in US Household Water Insecurity," *Annals of the American Association of Geographers* 109, no.4, DOI: 10.1080/24694452.2018.1530587 (2018): 1092–1109, at 1093.

12. Sarah Tory, "The Woman Who Brings Drinking Water to Remote Navajo Homes," *High Country News*, Mar. 16, 2015.

13. Julie Nania and Karen Cozzetto et al., *Considerations for Climate Change and Variability Adaptation on the Navajo Nation* (Getches-Wilkinson Center for Natural Resourses, Energy, and the Environment, University of Colorado Law School, 2014), 54.

14. *Id.*

15. *See* Alejandra Reyes-Velarde, "California Will Have Water Consumption Limits for the First Time after 'Landmark' Legislation Passed," *Los Angeles Times*, June 1, 2018.

16. See Listokin et al., *Housing and Economic Development in Indian Country, supra* note 5, at 326 Table 11.1 Summary of Challenges to and Strategies for Economic Development in the Navajo Nation ("Relatively few Navajo homes (23 percent) have *telephone service*, and there is *minimal computer and Internet access*.").

17. For an overview of NAHASDA, see Pindus et al., *Housing Needs of American Indians and Alaska Natives in Tribal Areas, supra* note 3, at 95–134. *See also* Ezra Rosser, "Rural Housing and Code Enforcement: Navigating Between Values and Housing Types," *Georgetown Journal on Poverty Law and Policy* 13 (2006): 33–93, at 66–77.

18. G. Thomas Kingsley, *Housing Problems and Needs of American Indians and Alaska Natives* (Washington, DC: Urban Institute, 1996).

19. Eric Nalder et al., "Tribal Housing: From Deregulation to Disgrace," *Seattle Times*, Dec. 1–5, 1996.

20. *In the Matter of Navajo Housing Authority*, Department of Housing and Urban Development Office of Hearings and Appeals, 14-JM-0121-IH-002, Dec. 14, 2015, at 8. For an overview of other programs besides NAHASDA that serve Indian reservations, see Brian L. Pierson, "Developing Affordable Housing in Indian Country," *Journal of Affordable Housing and Community Development Law* 19, no. 3/4 (Spring/Summer 2010): 367–390, at 381–389.

21. National Congress of American Indians, *Policy Update 2016 Annual Convention and Marketplace* (Phoenix, Arizona: National Congress of American Indians, 2016), 56.

22. Congressional Research Service, The Native American Housing Assistance and Self-Determination Act (NAHASDA): Issues and Reauthorization Legislation in the 114th Congress (Jan. 2017), 1. For an overview of NAHASDA's provisions and amendments to NAHASDA through 2008, see Courtney Eagan-Smith, "A House with No Walls: The Federal Government's Role in Indian Housing," *Tulsa Law Review* 44, no.2 (2008): 447–466, at 452–459. See also David Listokin et al., *Mortgage Lending on Tribal Land: A Report From the Assessment of American Indian, Alaska Native, and Native Hawaiian Housing Needs* (Washington, DC: Urban Institute, Jan. 2017) (presenting loan programs serving Indian country and discussing the challenges facing those programs).

23. US Government Accountability Office, *Native American Housing, supra* note 4, at 8.

24. Congressional Research Service, *The Native American Housing Assistance and Self-Determination Act (NAHASDA), supra* note 22, at 10.

25. *See* Pindus et al., *Housing Needs of American Indians and Alaska Natives in Tribal Areas, supra* note 3, at xxiv ("One question raised before the enactment of NAHASDA was whether the tribes would be able to produce as much housing on their own as had occurred under the earlier HUD-directed system. These numbers give an answer clearly in the affirmative.").

26. US Government Accountability Office, *Native American Housing, supra* note 4, at 9.

27. Pindus et al., *Housing Needs of American Indians and Alaska Natives in Tribal Areas, supra* note 3, at xxvii.

28. *See* Virginia Davis, "A Discovery of Sorts: Reexamining the Origins of the Federal Indian Housing Obligation," *Harvard Blackletter Law Journal* 18 (2002): 211–239 (making just such an argument). *See also* Eagan-Smith, "A House with No Walls," *supra* note 22, at 448–451 (providing a history of federal housing assistance to tribes and discussing the legal basis for that assistance).

29. US Department of Housing and Urban Development, *Fiscal Year 2017 Congressional Justifications*, www.hud.gov/sites/documents/FY_2017_CJS_COMBINED.PDF, at 11-2.

30. Pindus et al., *Housing Needs of American Indians and Alaska Natives in Tribal Areas, supra* note 3, at xxiii.

31. *Id.*

32. US Commission on Civil Rights, *Broken Promises: Continuing Federal Funding Shortfall for Native Americans* (Washington, DC: US Commission on Civil Rights, Briefing Report, Dec. 2018), 142.

33. *Id.* at 145.

34. US Dep't of Housing and Urban Development, *Fiscal Year 2017 Congressional Justifications, supra* note 29, at 11-3. *See also* Pierson, "Developing Affordable Housing in Indian Country," *supra* note 20, at 369 ("The fundamental problem is that NAHASDA funding does not remotely meet tribes' housing needs."); Eagan-Smith, "A House with No Walls," *supra* note 22, at 461 ("Ultimately, it is not a problem in recognizing that there is a devastating need for adequate housing; it is a lack of funding. Even though NAHASDA did help give tribes access to funding that was more flexible and specifically

targeted at addressing the lack of adequate housing in Indian Country, without adequate funding there is only so much that the legislation, even at its best, can accomplish. Due to the inadequate funding, tribes are not able to significantly improve the overall living conditions and are barely able to maintain the housing that they are currently providing.").

35. US Commission on Civil Rights, *Broken Promises, supra* note 32, at 4.

36. For an early critique of devolution that highlighted many of the downsides of federal disengagement in the name of federalism and self-determination, see Jeff Corntassel and Richard C. Witmer II, *Forced Federalism: Contemporary Challenges to Indigenous Nationhood* (Norman: University of Oklahoma Press, 2008).

37. For in-depth analysis of federalism and welfare programs, see *Holes in the Safety Net: Federalism and Poverty,* ed.Ezra Rosser (Cambridge, England: Cambridge University Press, 2019).

38. *See* US Commission on Civil Rights, *Broken Promises, supra* note 32, at 152 ("Many tribal governments lack the administrative capacity to fully maximize the housing development opportunities available under the federal NAHASDA program.").

39. *See* Mary Manning, "Men Charged with Embezzling Money from Indian Housing Grants," *Las Vegas Sun,* May 27, 2009; Associated Press, "Former Navajo Housing Executive Director, Builder Indicted," *Indian Country News,* June 9, 2009.

40. *See* In the Matter of William H. Aubrey, AKA Bill Aubrey and Lodgebuilder, Inc., Docket Nos. 12-3853-DB(S), 12-3854-DB(S), Suspending Official's Determination, Aug. 14, 2002, *available at* www.hud.gov/sites/documents/WILLIAM_H_AUBREY82012.PDF.

41. Cindy Yurth, "Former NHA Head, Contractor Indicted," *Navajo Times,* May 29, 2009; Craig Harris and Dennis Wagner, "A Tale of Waste: The Navajo Nation Accepted More Than $1 Billion for Houses. So Where Did it All Go?," *Arizona Republic,* Dec. 14, 2016; Craig Harris and Dennis Wagner, "Who is Responsible: Battling Washington to try to help her tribe," *Arizona Republic,* Dec. 14, 2016.

42. *See* Admin, "Former NAIHC Chair Indicted on Housing Charges," The Circle: Native American News and Arts, July 23, 2009, http://thecirclenews.org/news/former-naihc-chair -indicted-on-housing-charges/.

43. *See* Dept. of Justice, US Attorney's Office, District of Nevada, "Press Release: Home Builder Convicted of Embezzling from Hud Grant Program," May 2, 2013, www .justice.gov/usao-nv/pr/home-builder-convicted-embezzling-hud-grant-program; Ken Ritter, "Nev. Homebuilder Convicted of Looting Navajo Funds," *Washington Examiner,* May 3, 2013.

44. Navajo Housing Authority, "NHA Statement on Chester Carl Verdict," *NHA Facebook Page,* May 3, 2013. *See also* Craig Harris and Dennis Wagner, "Who is Responsible," *supra* note 41 (describing the "mess" that Carl's successor CEO inherited after Carl's departure).

45. Harris and Wagner, "A Tale of Waste," *supra* note 41.

46. *See also* Cindy Yurth, "Barren Tolani Lake Chapter is Rich in History," *Navajo Times,* June 5, 2014.

47. The examples above are taken from Craig Harris and Dennis Wagner, "A Legacy of Waste: How 4 Navajo Housing Projects Broke Down," *Arizona Republic,* Dec. 14, 2016; Harris and Wagner, "Who is Responsible," *supra* note 41; Harris and Wagner, "A Tale of Waste," *supra* note 41. *See also* Associated Press, "Rundown Shiprock Homes to be Rebuilt," *Durango Herald,* Mar. 9, 2013.

48. Associated Press, "Rundown Shiprock Homes to be Rebuilt," *supra* note 47.

49. *See* Craig Harris and Dennis Wagner, "No Easy Answers: Why It's So Difficult to Build Homes on the Navajo Reservation," *Arizona Republic*, Dec. 14, 2016; Harris and Wagner, "Who is Responsible," *supra* note 41.

50. Harris and Wagner, "No Easy Answers," *supra* note 49.

51. Harris and Wagner, "A Legacy of Waste," *supra* note 47.

52. US Government Accountability Office, *Native American Housing*, *supra* note 4.

53. Associated Press, "Navajo Housing Authority to Forfeit $26M after Settlement," *Washington Times*, Oct. 5, 2017.

54. In the Matter of Navajo Housing Authority, Department of Housing and Urban Development Office of Hearings and Appeals, 14-JM-0121-IH-002, Dec. 14, 2015, at 29.

55. *See* Dennis Wagner and Craig Harris, "Navajo Nation to Remake Board after Republic Investigation," *Arizona Republic*, Feb. 14, 2017; Navajo Times, "Yazzie Agrees to Step Down as NHA CEO," *Navajo Times*, June 29, 2017.

56. Vida Volkert, "Whistleblower to Sue NHA for Wrongful Termination," *Gallup Independent*, Apr. 27, 2019.

57. Vida Volkert, "NHA Board Paid $114K in Stipends in 2 Months," *Gallup Independent*, Apr. 26, 2019.

58. *Id.*

59. *See* Dennis Wagner and Craig Harris, "McCain: Housing Reforms Necessary; Probe Confirms Misuse of Funds on Navajo Nation," *Farmington Daily Times*, June 3, 2017. Note, the report itself is no longer available on the Senate website.

60. *See* Vida Volkert, "Former NHA Board Member to Return $15,500: What about the Rest?," *Gallup Independent*, May 11, 2009.

61. For profiles of NHA board members, see NHA Board of Commissioners website, www .navajohousingauthority.org/board-of-commissioners/.

62. *See also* US Government Accountability Office, *Native American Housing*, *supra* note 4, at 25–26 (giving examples of internal conflicts between tribal governments and their TDHEs on other reservations).

63. Harris and Wagner, "Who is Responsible," *supra* note 41; US Government Accountability Office, *Native American Housing*, *supra* note 4, at 44.

64. *See Navajo Housing Authority v. Johns*, SC-CV-18-10 (Navajo Nation Supreme Court, Sept. 10, 2012) (overruling prior Navajo Supreme Court precedent that had weaken NHA's ability to claim sovereign immunity).

65. Sovereign immunity can also protect NHA when it mistreats suppliers or other contractors. *See* Paul E. Frye, "Lender Recourse in Indian Country: A Navajo Case Study," *New Mexico Law Review* 21 (1991): 275–326, at 323 (discussing *Howard Dana and Associates v. Navajo Housing Authority*, 1 Navajo Rptr. 325 (1978), a district court decision which faulted NHA and ordered damages be paid to a provider but which was overturned by the Navajo Supreme Court on sovereign immunity grounds in *Navajo Housing Auth. v. Howard Dana and Associates*, 5 Navajo Rptr. 157 (1987)).

66. Navajo Nation Division of Economic Development, *Navajo Nation Comprehensive Economic Development Strategy* (Window Rock, Arizona: Navajo Nation Division of Economic Development, Apr. 2018), 18.

67. *See* Navajo Nation Division of Economic Development, *Navajo Economic Data Bulletin* 002-0512 (Window Rock, Arizona: Navajo Nation, May 2012) (reporting that in 2011, border towns in Arizona and New Mexico collected $219 million in sales taxes, of which Farmington alone collected $133 million).

68. *Id.*

69. US Department of Interior, Bureau of Indian Affairs, Navajo Region, Western Navajo Agency webpage, www.bia.gov/regional-offices/navajo/western-navajo-agency.
70. Navajo Nation Division of Economic Development, *Navajo Nation Comprehensive Economic Development Strategy*, *supra* note 66, at 68–69.
71. *Id.* at 65.
72. Navajo Nation Shopping Centers, Incorporated, Locations webpage, www.nnscinc.com /locations.
73. For a particularly stunning book of photos of trading posts on and near the reservation, see Ed Grazda, *A Last Glance: Trading Posts of the Four Corners* (Brooklyn, New York: powerHouse Books, 2015). *See also* Willow Roberts Powers, *Navajo Trading: The End of an Era* (Albuquerque: University of New Mexico Press, 2001) (giving a history of trading posts and trade on the Navajo reservation).
74. *See* Trib Choudhary, 2005–2006 *Comprehensive Economic Development Strategy of the Navajo Nation* (Window Rock, Arizona: Navajo Nation Division of Economic Development, 2005), 17; Susan Carder, "Bashas' Diné Markets and the Navajo Nation: A Case Study of Cross-Cultural Trade," *American Indian Culture and Research Journal* 39, no.1 (2015): 47–63, at 57.
75. Choudhary, 2005–2006 *Comprehensive Economic Development Strategy of the Navajo Nation*, *supra* note 74, at 17.
76. Carder, "Bashas' Diné Markets and the Navajo Nation," *supra* note 74, at 53.
77. *Id.* at 55.
78. *Id.* at 55.
79. Navajo Nation Shopping Centers, Incorporated, About NNSCI webpage, www .nnscinc.com/about-nnsci.
80. *See* Carder, "Bashas' Diné Markets and the Navajo Nation," *supra* note 74, at 54.
81. According to an official history of Bashas' that is posted to the company website, Bashas' could enter the Navajo market when other grocery stores could not because of the flexibility and longer-term focus that comes from being a family-owned, privately held company as opposed to a company beholden to stockowners. *See* Rob Johnson, "A Family's Fortunes, Part IV," *Bashas' Family of Stores History*, www.bashas.com/bashas-family-of-stores/history/.
82. Carder, "Bashas' Diné Markets and the Navajo Nation," *supra* note 74, at 56.
83. *Id.* at 56–59.
84. *Id.* at 58.
85. *Id.* at 57.
86. *Atkinson Trading Co. v. Shirley*, 532 U.S. 645 (2001).
87. 532 U.S. at 651.
88. *Id.*
89. 532 U.S. at 659.
90. 532 U.S. at 657.
91. For an excellent history of Wal-Mart's origins and growth, see Charles Fishman, *The Wal-Mart Effect: How the World's Most Powerful Company Really Works – And How It is Transforming the American Economy* (New York: Penguin Books, 2006).
92. Compare Wal-Mart, Our Story webpage, https://corporate.walmart.com/our-story, with "List of Countries by GDP," Statistics Times, http://statisticstimes.com/economy/countries-by-gdp.php.
93. ROUND Great Seal of the Navajo Nation Sticker Decal, www.walmart.com/ip/ ROUND-Great-Seal-of-the-Navajo-Nation-Sticker-Decal-tribe-native-indian-logo-Size -4-x-4-inch/756754818.

94. Gavin Clarkson, "Tribal Finance and Economic Development: The Fight against Economic Leakage," in *American Indian Business: Principles and Practices*, eds. Deanna M. Kennedy et al. (Seattle: University of Washington Press, 2017), 83–98, at 83. Similarly, Navajo Nation Vice President Frank J. Dayish, Jr. told the Senate Committee on Indian Affairs in 2003, "We have heard that the most successful Walmart in the United States is in Gallup, New Mexico, which is just outside the Navajo Nation's border." Frank J. Dayish, Jr., Testimony to the Senate Committee on Indian Affairs, Hearings on S519, Apr. 30, 2003.

95. Dana E. Powell, *Landscapes of Power: Politics of Energy in the Navajo Nation* (Durham, North Carolina: Duke University Press, 2018), 95 (quoting Ben Shelly).

96. See Alastair Bitsoi, *Wal-Mart Position Paper: Wal-Mart is good for the Navajo Nation?* (Tsaile, Arizona: Diné Policy Institute, 2018); Moroni Benally, *Wal-Mart Position Paper: Wal-Mart is not good for the Navajo Nation?* (Tsaile, Arizona: Diné Policy Institute, 2018).

97. *See* Diné Policy Institute – Alumni Biographies: Alastair Bitsoi, http://hooghan .dinecollege.edu/institutes/DPI/alumni.php.

98. Navajo Nation Division of Economic Development, *Navajo Economic Data Bulletin 001-0212* (Feb. 2012).

99. BuildNavajo.org, Build Navajo Poster, http://buildnavajo.org/files/BuildNavajo_Posters .pdf.

100. Navajo Nation, Business Site Lease: Business Site Lease Application Requirements and Procedures Check List, www.navajobusiness.com/pdf/DngBus/Leasing/Bus%20Site% 20Lease.pdf.

101. Michael Parrish, *Local Governance and Reform: Local Empowerment* (Tsaile, Arizona: Diné Policy Institute, 2018), 20.

102. Resolution of the Economic Development Committee of the Navajo Nation Council, 21st Navajo Nation Council – Third Year 2009, *Relating to Economic Development; Approving the Navajo Nation Business Site Lease Management Plan and the Delegation of the Authority to Approve Business Site Leases to the Division of Economic*, EDCAU-39-09 (Aug. 5, 2009), 20-21, *available at* www.indiancountrygrassroots.org/BSL_AdminMgmnt_Plans.pdf.

103. *See* Diné Policy Institute, *Flea Markets on the Navajo Nation: A Report on the Informal Economy* (Tsaile, Arizona: Diné College, 2018).

104. *Id.* at 43.

105. Navajo Nation Project Development Department, Navajo Nation Industrial Development (2007), www.navajobusiness.com/pdf/DngBus/CommericalIndustrial/ IndParks/Industrialparks4.pdf.

106. *Id.*

107. Navajo Nation Project Development Department, Navajo Nation Industrial Site Lease Procedure, www.navajobusiness.com/pdf/DngBus/Leasing/IndstrlLsePrc1.pdf.

108. *Id.*

109. Navajo Nation Project Development Department, Navajo Nation Industrial Development, *supra* note 105.

110. *See, e.g.*, Navajo Nation Division of Economic Development, Available Business Sites Listing – Western RBDO Service Area, www.navajobusiness.com/sbdd/western/wester nlistings.html.

111. *See* Navajo Nation Division of Economic Development, Ft. Defiance RBDO Available Business Sites, www.navajobusiness.com/sbdd/ftdefiance/ftdefiancelistings.html.

112. *See* Navajo Nation Division of Economic Development, *Navajo Nation Comprehensive Economic Development Strategy*, *supra* note 66, at 49 (listing "No Zoning" as one of the weaknesses of the tribe in terms of economic development).

113. As David Listokin explains, "In considering impediments to economic development in the Navajo Nation, it is necessary to address the crucial problem of raw (i.e., unzoned) land. It is hard to achieve nonresidential development if land is not zoned for commercial and industrial purposes." Listokin et al., *Housing and Economic Development in Indian Country*, supra note 5, at 380.

114. Dennis Wagner and Craig Harris, "Navajo Refurbishments: $1 million per Home," *Arizona Republic*, Mar. 22, 2017.

115. The Navajo Nation government is not alone in making this basic bargain with its citizens. As Stephen Cornell and Joseph Kalt report, "In the standard approach [to tribal governance], tribal leadership is concerned much of the time with distributing resources: jobs, money, housing, services, favors, and so forth." Stephen Cornell and Joseph Kalt, "Two Approaches to Economic Development on American Indian Reservations: One Works, the Other Doesn't," in *Rebuilding Native Nations: Strategies for Governance and Development*, ed. Miriam Jorgensen (Tucson: University of Arizona Press, 2007), 3–33, at 13.

11 SOVEREIGN ASSERTIONS

1. Robert T. Anderson, "Indigenous Rights to Water and Environmental Protection," *Harvard Civil Rights-Civil Liberties Law Review* 53 (2018): 338–379, at 347.

2. Lloyd L. Lee, *Diné Identity in a Twenty-First-Century World* (Tucson: University of Arizona Press, 2020), 76.

3. Melanie K. Yazzie, "Unlimited Limitations: The Navajos' Winters Rights Deemed Worthless in the 2012 Navajo-Hopi Little Colorado River Settlement," *Wicazo Sa Review* 28, no.1 (Spring 2013): 26–37, at 34.

4. Andrew Curley, "Unsettling Indian Water Settlements: The Little Colorado River, the San Juan River, and Colonial Enclosures," *Antipode* (2019): 1–19, at 1.

5. *See* Leslie MacMillan, "A Difficult Choice on Water," *New York Times*, Apr. 5, 2012 (reporting on the meeting in Tuba City).

6. *See* Yazzie, "Unlimited Limitations," supra note 3, at 32.

7. Shaun McKinnon, "Arizona Navajo, Hopi Water Deal Stirs Controversy," *Arizona Republic*, May 13, 2012.

8. Andrew Curley, "'Our Winters' Rights': Challenging Colonial Water Laws," *Global Environmental Politics* 19, no. 3 (Aug. 2019): 57–76, at 67.

9. *Id.* at 66.

10. *Id.* at 71.

11. *Id.* at 72.

12. *See* Celene Hawkins, "Beyond Quantification: Implementing and Sustaining Tribal Water Settlements," *University of Denver Water Law Review* 16 (2013): 229–260, at 236–237 (listing the standard elements of Indian water rights settlements).

13. S 2109, 112th Congress, 2d Session, § 2 Findings (7), available at www.congress.gov/112/bills/s2109/BILLS-112s2109is.pdf.

14. *See* Congressional Research Service, *Indian Water Rights Settlements*, R44148 (Apr. 16, 2019), 2 (highlighting the advantages of negotiated settlements, including reduced expenses compared to litigation and the possibility for tribes to get water not just paper water).

15. 207 U.S. 564 (1908).

16. For a more complete telling of the story of *Winters*, see Judith V. Royster, "Water, Legal Rights, and Actual Consequences: The Story of *Winters v. United States*," in *Indian Law Stories*, eds. Carole Goldberg et al. (New York: Foundation Press, 2011), 81–107.

17. *See* Todd A. Fisher, "Winters of Our Discontent: Federal Reserved Water Rights in the Western States," *Cornell Law Review* 69, no.5 (1984): 1077–1093, at 1078–1080 (describing the prior appropriations regime).

18. 207 U.S. 564, 576 (1908).

19. *Id.*

20. *Id.* at 576–577.

21. 373 U.S. 546 (1963).

22. Robert T. Anderson, "Indian Water Rights, Practical Reasoning, and Negotiated Settlements," *California Law Review* 98 (2010): 1133–1163, at 1142.

23. 373 U.S. 546, 600 (1963).

24. *See also* Robert T. Anderson, "Water Rights, Water Quality, and Regulatory Jurisdiction in Indian Country," *Stanford Environmental Law Journal* 34, no.2 (2015): 195–245, at 209 ("In general, the PIA test evaluates tribal lands for their irrigation potential in an economically feasible manner to arrive at a final quantification for reservations with an agricultural purpose.").

25. April R. Summitt, *Contested Waters: An Environmental History of the Colorado River* (Boulder: University Press of Colorado, 2013), 153.

26. For an account of the how environmentalists, led by the Sierra Club, succeeded in blocking these dams, see Andrew Needham, *Power Lines: Phoenix and the Making of the Modern Southwest* (Princeton, New Jersey: Princeton University Press, 2014), 185–212.

27. *See* Central Arizona Project website, "About Us," www.cap-az.com/about-us.

28. *See* Central Arizona Project website, "Background and History," www.cap-az.com/about-us/background.

29. National Water Commission, *Water Policies for the Future: Final Report to the President and to the Congress of the United States* (Washington, DC: US Government Printing Office, 1973), 474–475.

30. *See* Benjamin Bahe Jones, "*The Paradox of Indigenous Sovereignty and American Democracy: Discourse of Exclusion in Navajo Water Rights*" (PhD diss., Northern Arizona University, 2011), 196 (arguing that "lack of a reliable and affordable potable water supply stifles economic development" on the reservation).

31. *See* Summitt, *Contested Waters*, *supra* note 25, at 149 ("As southwestern towns became vibrant urban centers in the twentieth century, native peoples of the river basin were subjugated, placed on otherwise unwanted land, and left to farm without necessary water supplies."); Monroe E. Price and Gary D. Weatherford, "Indian Water Rights in Theory and Practice: Navajo Experience in the Colorado River Basin," *Law and Contemporary Problems* 40, no.1 (Winter, 1976): 97–131, at 131 ("The stark truth of the matter is that, beginning at the turn of the century, the offices and powers of national government were marshalled to plan, construct, and finance non-Indian agricultural development in the West, and nothing comparable was done for the Native American.").

32. Yazzie, "Unlimited Limitations," *supra* note 3, at 33.

33. Summitt, *Contested Waters*, *supra* note 25, at 162.

34. Price and Weatherford, "Indian Water Rights in Theory and Practice," *supra* note 31, at 99.

35. Matt Jenkins, "Seeking the Water Jackpot," *High Country News*, Mar. 17, 2008.

36. *See also* Jones, "The Paradox of Indigenous Sovereignty and American Democracy," *supra* note 30, at 192 (calling the Navajo Nation the epicenter of the Colorado River basin).

37. Comptroller General of the United States, *Reserved Water Rights for Federal and Indian Reservations: A Growing Controversy in Need of Resolution*, CED-18-176 (Washington, DC: United States General Accounting Office, Nov. 16, 1978), 1, 6.

38. *See* Lyman Stone, "A Population History of Phoenix: How a Well-Positioned City Grew to a Rational Size," *Medium.com*, Aug. 9, 2016, https://medium.com/migration-issues /a-population-history-of-phoenix-76bd04467866.

39. Summitt, *Contested Waters*, *supra* note 25, at 150. *See also* Benedict J. Colombi, "Indigenous Peoples, Large Dams, and Capital-Intensive Energy Development: A View from the Lower Colorado River," in *Indians and Energy: Exploitation and Opportunity in the American Southwest*, eds. Susan L. Smith and Brian Frehner (Santa Fe, New Mexico: School for Advanced Research Press, 2010), 89–109, at 105 ("Rapid growth in the greater Southwest, in sum is using most if not all of the available water.").

40. Anderson, "Indian Water Rights, Practical Reasoning, and Negotiated Settlements," *supra* note 22, at 1136.

41. Robert T. Anderson, "Indian Water Rights and the Federal Trust Responsibility," *Natural Resources Journal* 46 (2006): 399–437, at 421–422.

42. Anderson, "Indigenous Rights to Water and Environmental Protection," *supra* note 1, at 350.

43. An additional factor contributing to tribes' hesitation regarding litigation identified by Professor Anderson is "the Supreme Court's abandonment of long accepted substantive and interpretive rules of Indian law." Anderson, "Indian Water Rights, Practical Reasoning, and Negotiated Settlements," *supra* note 22, at 1134.

44. Anderson, "Indigenous Rights to Water and Environmental Protection," *supra* note 1, at 379.

45. Anderson, "Indian Water Rights, Practical Reasoning, and Negotiated Settlements," *supra* note 22, at 1133.

46. Summitt, *Contested Waters*, *supra* note 25, at 159.

47. *See* Yazzie, "Unlimited Limitations," *supra* note 3, at 30–31 (noting that the agreement would set the tribal priority dates to 1968 for purposes of Colorado River water even though the Navajo reservation long predates that date).

48. Yazzie, "Unlimited Limitations," *supra* note 2, at 31.

49. Curley, "Our Winters' Rights," *supra* note 8, at 69.

50. 544 U.S. 197 (2005).

51. 544 U.S. 216–17.

52. Jones, "The Paradox of Indigenous Sovereignty and American Democracy," *supra* note 30, at 236.

53. Curley, "Our Winters' Rights," *supra* note 8, at 73.

54. Yazzie, "Unlimited Limitations," *supra* note 3, at 32.

55. *Id.* at 34.

56. Jones, "The Paradox of Indigenous Sovereignty and American Democracy," *supra* note 30, at 210.

57. *Id.* at 307.

58. *See* Fisher, "Winters of Our Discontent," *supra* note 17, at 1089–1091 (discussing the tension between state prior appropriation regimes and the *Winters* doctrine).

59. *Id.* at 304 ("Today, this maze of incomprehensible water discourse and the interrelated Native American issues prevent intelligent participation by the average Navajo citizen in discussions around water policies.").

60. Curley, "Unsettling Indian Water Settlements," *supra* note 4, at 6.
61. *Id*. at 8.
62. *Id*. at 11.
63. *Id*. at 16.
64. *See also* Note, "Indian Reserved Water Rights: The *Winters* of Our Discontent," *Yale Law Journal* 88, no. 8 (1979): 1689–1712, at 1711–1712 ("To the Indians, their water in the twentieth century resembles their land in the nineteenth. The inexorable pressures of white settlement restricted Indian access to much desirable land and ultimately confined the tribes to carved out reservations. Today, rapid economic and population growth grasps at Indian water.").
65. Mary Wallace, "The Supreme Court and Indian Water Rights," in *American Indian Policy in the Twentieth Century*, ed. Vine Deloria, Jr. (Norman: University of Oklahoma Press, 1985), 197–220, at 217.
66. *See* Jones, "The Paradox of Indigenous Sovereignty and American Democracy," *supra* note 30, at 197 ("the water discourse delimits Navajo geography and values; it also rendered invisible their impoverished development vis-à-vis their western state counterparts").
67. Curley, "Unsettling Indian Water Settlements," *supra* note 4, at 16.
68. This is not unique to the Navajo Nation's water rights: "Tribal reserved rights to water are almost always prior and paramount to state rights." Judith V. Royster, "Conjunctive Management of Reservation Water Resources: Legal Issues Facing Indian Tribes," *Idaho Law Review* 47 (2011): 255–272, at 268.
69. Professor Judith Royster, one of the foremost experts on Indian nations and natural resources, has argued in favor of a cooperative approach to water management in the west, one that understands water as part of a single system instead of broken up into isolated claims and uses. *See id*.
70. For a more optimistic take, see Reid Peyton Chambers, "Reflections on the Changes in Indian Law, Federal Indian Policies and Conditions on Indian Reservations since the Late 1960s," *Arizona State Law Journal* 46 (2015): 729–778, at 761 ("The end result of these judicial and congressional actions [between late 1960s and today] is that states today have assumed a much more significant role in major activities conducted by tribes on reservations, such as those related to tribal gaming and the determination and use of tribal reserved water rights, than was true or seemed likely in the early 1970s. But while there has been a very significant increase in interactions between states and tribes today, much more of this interaction has been positive and cooperative than was true in the 1970s.").
71. *See id*. at 14 ("In Indian water settlements, Arizona's Congressional representatives and senators have taken an adversarial role against Navajo water claims, even for communities they are supposed to represent."). *See also* Hawkins, "Beyond Quantification," *supra* note 12, at 235 (noting that "as a general rule, during the settlement negotiations, state representatives will try to protect existing non-Tribal uses of water (even if those existing uses hold junior priority dates and even if those existing uses deprive Tribes of important on-reservation water resources) and to quantify Tribal settlement rights in a way that provides certainty to other water users in the allocation and administration of water").
72. As a 1976 law review article noted in language that holds true a half century later, "In the case of the Indians' valuation of their water rights, there is the additional uncertainty of not knowing whether the outer logical boundaries of the Winters doctrine will really be possible of achievement." Price and Weatherford, "Indian Water Rights in Theory and Practice," *supra* note 31, at 108.

73. Stephen V. Quesenberry, Timothy C. Seward and Adam P. Bailey, "Tribal Strategies for Protecting and Preserving Groundwater," *William Mitchell Law Review* 41, no.2 (2015): 431–487, at 436.
74. 492 U.S. 408 (1989).
75. *See* James M. Grijalva, "The Origins of EPA's Indian Program," *Kansas Journal of Law and Public Policy* 15 (2006): 191–294 (giving a history of the EPA's relationship with tribes and defending the agency's recognition of tribal authority over the environment on and near reservations); Nicholas Christos Zaferatos, *Planning the American Indian Reservation: From Theory to Empowerment* (Syracuse, New York: Syracuse University Press, 2015), 58–59 (providing a summary of the EPA's Indian policy since 1984). *See also* Sibyl Diver, "Native Water Protection Flows Through Self-Determination: Understanding Tribal Water Quality Standards and 'Treatment as a State,'" *Journal of Contemporary Water Research and Education* 163 (April 2018): 6–30, at 14 ("For the EPA, applying a cooperative federalism model to tribal environmental management in Indian Country was 'born simply of practical necessity.' Because states lacked regulatory authority in Indian Country, the EPA was faced with a regulatory void for water quality. If state WQSs did not apply to tribal lands, what was the appropriate standard? This became an issue for the EPA, in part due to increased federal liability associated with the potential mismanagement of tribal trust lands. The EPA's alternative solution was to substitute tribes for states as its cooperative partner. The agency's new approach amounted to recognizing tribes (like states) as 'local governments' with site-specific knowledge of their territories, and governmental responsibility for protecting legitimate local interests.").
76. *See City of Albuquerque v. Browner*, 97 F.3d 415 (10th Cir. 2006). For more on the case and the issue of tribal water quality standards, see Janet K. Baker, "Tribal Water Quality Standards: Are There Any Limits?," *Duke Environmental Law and Policy Forum* 7, no.2 (1997): 367–391.
77. Diné Natural Resources Protection Act, 18 Navajo Nation Code § 1302(A).
78. Rebecca Tsosie, "Indigenous Peoples and the Ethics of Remediation: Redressing the Legacy of Radioactive Contamination for Native Peoples and Native Lands," *Santa Clara Journal of International Law* 13, no. 1 (2015): 203–272, at 255.
79. For a longer version of the litigation history than included in this chapter, see *id.* at 224–229.
80. Claire R. Newman, "Creating an Environmental No-Man's Land: The Tenth Circuit's Departure from Environmental and Indian Law Protecting a Tribal Community's Health and Environment," *Washington Journal of Environmental Law and Policy* 1, no.2 (2011): 352–411, at 357.
81. *Id.* at 367.
82. *Hydro Res., Inc. v. U.S. EPA* (HRI III), 608 F.3d 1131 (10th Cir. 2010) (en banc). For more on the case, see Andrew Brooks, "Tribal Sovereignty and Resource Destiny: Hydro Resources, Inc. v. U.S. EPA," *Denver University Law Review* 82 (2011): 423–442.
83. *Morris v. United States Nuclear Regulatory Comm'n*, 598 F.3d 677 (10th Cir. 2010).
84. *See* William Jenney, "Having Your Yellowcake and Eating It Too: The Environmental and Health Impacts of Uranium Mining on the Colorado Plateau," *Arizona Journal of Environmental Law and Policy* 7 (2017): 27–55, at 35–36 (describing in situ leaching).
85. 18 U.S.C. § 1151.
86. Tsosie, "Indigenous Peoples and the Ethics of Remediation," *supra* note 78, at 221.
87. Newman, "Creating an Environmental No-Man's Land," *supra* note 80, at 358.
88. Tsosie, "Indigenous Peoples and the Ethics of Remediation," *supra* note 78, at 205.

89. Rebecca Tsosie, "Indigenous Peoples and Epistemic Injustice: Science, Ethics, and Human Rights," *Washington Law Review* 87 (2012): 1133–1201, at 1174 (noting about HRI's proposed mine, "the costs of uranium mining will fall disproportionately upon the people who live on or near the lands that will be mined").

90. Tsosie, "Indigenous Peoples and the Ethics of Remediation," *supra* note 78, at 204.

91. Newman, "Creating an Environmental No-Man's Land," *supra* note 80, at 376.

92. Alastair Lee Bitsoi, "HRI Pleased with Church Rock Support for Mining," *Navajo Times*, Feb. 14, 2013.

93. Westwater Resources, West Largo webpage, www.westwaterresources.net/projects/uran ium/new-mexico/west-largo.

94. Jonathan Thompson, "A Gold King Mine Timeline," *High Country News*, May 2, 2016.

95. US Environmental Protection Agency, *Analysis of the Biological Data Collected from the Animas and San Juan Rivers Following the Gold King Mine Release*, EPA/830/R-18/ 003 (Washington, DC: US Environmental Protection Agency, November 2018), 1.

96. Dan Elliott and the Associated Press, "Three Years after Gold King Mine Spill, Victims Awaiting Payment from EPA," *Denver Post*, Aug. 3, 2018. For a detailed account of the disaster, see Clifford J. Villa, "Gold King Mine Spill: Environmental Law and Legal Protections for Environmental Responders," *Utah Law Review*, Vol. 2019, No. 1 (2019): 263–334, at 264–265, 288–298.

97. Richard Parker, "A River Runs Yellow," *The Atlantic*, Aug. 21, 2015.

98. Adam Wernick and Becky Fogel, "EPA Contractors Caused Gold-Mine Blowout that Turned a River Orange," *Public Radio International*, Aug. 27, 2015.

99. Lorena Iñiguez Elebee, "Gold King Mine's Toxic Spill," *Los Angeles Times*, Aug. 14, 2015.

100. *Compare* US Department of the Interior Bureau of Reclamation Technical Services Center, *Technical Evaluation of the Gold King Mine Incident* (Denver: US Department of the Interior, Oct. 2015) *with* US Environmental Protection Agency Office of Inspector General, *Gold King Mine Release: Inspector General Response to Congressional Requests*, Report No. 17-P-0250 (Washington, DC: EPA Office of Inspector General, June 12, 2017).

101. Timbre Shriver, "Holding the Harmful Harmless: Lessons from the Gold King Mine," *University of Colorado Law Review* 89 (2018): 1001–1031, at 1009. For a strong defense of the EPA leading up to and following the blowout, see Villa, "Gold King Mine Spill," *supra* note 96.

102. Associated Press, "Judge Won't Dismiss Gold King Mine Spill Lawsuit Against EPA," *Denver Post*, Mar. 1, 2019.

103. Michael Phillis, "Mining Cos. Must Face Claims Over Gold King Mine Spill," *Law360.com*, Mar. 27, 2019, www.law360.com/articles/1143174/mining-cos-must-face-claims-over-gold-king-mine-spill.

104. Villa, "Gold King Mine Spill," *supra* note 96, at 272.

105. Bruce Finley, "Inspector General Clears EPA in Investigation of Gold King Mine Disaster," *Denver Post*, June 12, 2017.

106. Donovan Quintero, "Gold King Mine Wastewater Contaminating the Rivers Once Again," *Navajo Times*, Mar. 16, 2019.

107. *See Report of the Special Rapporteur on the rights of indigenous peoples on her mission to the United States of America*, Human Rights Council, Thirty-sixth session, 11–29 September 2017, Agenda item 3, A/HRC/36/46/Add.1 (Aug. 9, 2017), 10 ("The fact that the mine had not been operational for nearly a century underscores the dangers of present-day extractive activities on future generations of indigenous peoples.").

108. Villa, "Gold King Mine Spill," *supra* note 96, at 272.

109. Diver, "Native Water Protection Flows Through Self-Determination," *supra* note 75, at 17.

110. *Id.* at 19.

111. *Id.* at 26.

112. Navajo Nation Human Rights Commission, *Assessing Race Relations between Navajos and Non-Navajos: A Review of Border Town Race Relations* (Window Rock, Arizona: Navajo Nation, 2010).

113. *Id.* at Executive Summary, xii–xvi.

114. *Id.* at xvii.

115. *Id.* at xix.

116. Kristen A. Carpenter and Angela R. Riley, "Indigenous Peoples and the Jurisgenerative Moment in Human Rights," *California Law Review* 102 (2014): 173–234, at 224.

117. New Mexico Advisory Committee to the US Commission on Civil Rights, *The Farmington Report: Civil Rights for Native Americans 30 Years Later* (2005), 1.

118. New Mexico Advisory Committee to the US Commission on Civil Rights, *The Farmington Report: A Conflict of Cultures* (1975), 1.

119. *Id.* at 89.

120. *Id.* at 132.

121. *Id.* at 146–150.

122. New Mexico Advisory Committee to the US Commission on Civil Rights, *The Farmington Report: Civil Rights for Native Americans 30 Years Later*, *supra* note 117, at 55.

123. *See* Navajo Nation Human Rights Commission website, http://www.nnhrc.navajo-nsn.gov/index.html. *See also* Noel Lyn Smith, "HRC targets predatory car sales," *Navajo Times*, Nov. 29, 2012 (reporting on the Commission's work to tackle questionable sales tactics used by border town car dealerships).

124. For a defense of cooperative agreements, see Matthew L. M. Fletcher, "Retiring the 'Deadliest Enemies' Model of Tribal-State Relations," *Tulsa Law Review* 43 (2007): 73–87. *See also* Paul Spruhan, "Standard Clauses in State-Tribal Agreements: The Navajo Nation Experience," *Tulsa Law Review* 47, no. 3 (2012): 503–513 (discussing the contract terms in the agreements that the Navajo Nation has reached with neighboring states).

125. For news coverage of the case, see Grant Schulte, "Nebraska Supreme Court Ends Beer Sales at Border of Dry Pine Ridge Indian Reservation in South Dakota," *Denver Post*, Sep. 29, 2017.

126. For a thoughtful discussion that rejects the stereotype of the drunk Indian while acknowledging the harms alcohol can have on tribal communities, see Robert J. Miller and Maril Hazlett, "The 'Drunken Indian': Myth Distilled into Reality Through Federal Indian Alcohol Policy," *Arizona State Law Journal* 28 (1996): 223–298.

127. Lyuba Zarsky, *Is Nothing Sacred?: Corporate Responsibility for the Protection of Native American Sacred Sites* (La Honda, California: Sacred Land Film Project, 2006), 8.

128. *See* Kennedy Warne, "Why Australia is Banning Climbers from this Iconic Natural Landmark," *National Geographic Magazine* (Apr./May 2018).

129. For an overview of the sacred site element of the Standing Rock protests, see Michael D. McNally, "Native American Religious Freedom as a Collective Right," *Brigham Young University Law Review* 2019 (2019): 205–291, at 206–208.

130. Ahmed Rashid, "After 1,700 Years, Buddhas Fall to Taliban Dynamite," *The Telegraph*, Mar. 12, 2001.

131. *See* Alex Tallchief Skibine, "Towards a Balanced Approach for the Protection of Native American Sacred Sites," *Michigan Journal of Race and Law* 17, no.2 (2012): 269–302, at 298 (discussing "the argument made by some that to the Indians, the whole earth is sacred and if we allow one claim, the floodgates will open and their will be no end to claims of sacredness"); Kristen A. Carpenter, Sonia K. Katyal and Angela R. Riley, "In Defense of Property," *Yale Law Journal* 118 (2019): 1022–1125, at 1027 (noting "the familiar fear that if the law were to protect Indian religious and cultural interests, Indians effectively would acquire 'ownership' of the public lands").

132. *See* Joshua A. Edwards, "Yellow Snow on Sacred Sites: A Failed Application of the Religious Freedom Restoration Act," *American Indian Law Review* 34, no.1 (2009–2010): 151–169, at 151 (comparing the lack of protection for Indian sacred sites with the protection that churches would receive).

133. The next three paragraphs are drawn in part from Ezra Rosser, "Ahistorical Indians and Reservation Resources," *Environmental Law* 40 (2010): 437–545, at 476–478.

134. Justin B. Richland, "Dignity as (Self-)Determination: Hopi Sovereignty in the Face of US Dispossessions," *Law and Social Inquiry* 41, no. 4 (Fall 2016): 917–938, at 919. For more on the role of the Peaks in the Hopi belief system, see Peter Nabokov, *Where the Lightning Strikes: The Lives of American Indian Sacred Places* (New York: Viking Press, 2006), 138–139.

135. Petition for a Writ of Certiorari, *Navajo Nation v. United States Forest Serv.*, 535 F.3d 1058 (2008), at 3–6, available at www.savethepeaks.org/Cert%20Petition%20final.pdf. *See also* Jonathan Knapp, "Making Snow in the Desert: Defining a Substantial Burden under RFRA," *Ecology Law Quarterly* 36 (2009): 259–316, at 295–296 (describing the importance of the Peaks in the beliefs of Navajos and Hopis).

136. Snowbowl is not the only ski resort in the west facing similar challenges ensuring enough snow, nor the only resort that has considered using recycled waste water to create snow. *See generally* Katie A. Duquette, "Don't Eat the Brown Snow! Utilizing Wastewater for Artificial Snow: A Slippery Slope Between Protecting Skiers and Encouraging Water Reuse," *Villanova Environmental Law Journal* 27, no.1 (2016): 123–148.

137. Skibine, "Towards a Balanced Approach for the Protection of Native American Sacred Sites," *supra* note 131, at 276.

138. This was not the first time that the Navajo Nation and the Hopi Tribe sued the federal government over permitting at Snowbowl; in the early 1980s, the tribes lost a suit to block an expansion of the ski resort. Nabokov, *Where the Lightning Strikes, supra* note 134, at 141–143.

139. Edwards, "Yellow Snow on Sacred Sites," *supra* note 132, at 153. *See also* Ruth Stoner Muzzin, "Seeing the Free Exercise Forest for the Trees: NEPA, RFRA, and Navajo Nation," *Hastings West-Northwest Journal of Environmental Law and Policy* 16 (2010): 277–303, at 280.

140. Though the toilet waste water complaint is straightforward, it might appear require little creativity to connect sewage with dead bodies, but according to the Navajo Nation President the connection is a significant one: "Practitioners of the Navajo religion are not concerned with what the scientists say about the quality of reclaimed wastewater. Some of this water has come into contact with death and sickness at, for example, hospitals and mortuaries. It does not matter what kind of treatment is provided, this water will compromise and contaminate the sacred Mountain that was established by the holy people."

Declaration of Joe Shirley, Jr, President of the Navajo Nation, *Navajo Nation v. U.S. Forest Serv.*, 408 F. Supp. 2d 866 (D. Ariz. 2006) (Nos. CV 05-1824-PCT-PCR, CV 05-1914-PCT-EHC, CV 05-1949-PCT-NVW, CV 05-1966-PCT-JAT), at p. 2, paragraph 9. The dissent seemed to agree, quoting Larry Foster, a Diné training to be a medicine man, at length for a description of the harm associated with sewage water, with Foster twice referring to "mortuaries or hospitals." *Navajo Nation v. United States Forest Serv.*, 535 F.3d at 1103. *See also* Richland, *supra* note 134, at 925 ("Environmental impacts aside, the ski resort operators were almost literally pissing on Hopi sacred ground.").

141. *Navajo Nation v. United States Forest Serv.*, 535 F.3d at 1067.
142. *Navajo Nation v. US Forest Service*, 479 F.3d 1024 (2007).
143. Richland, "Dignity as (Self-)Determination," *supra* note 134, at 933.
144. *Navajo Nation v. United States Forest Serv.*, 535 F.3d 1058, 1065 (2008).
145. *Id.* at 1070.
146. *Navajo Nation v. United States Forest Serv.*, 535 F.3d at 1070 (discussing amount of land impacted); *Id.* at 1089 (J. Fletcher dissenting) (critiquing "the majority's restrictive definition of 'substantial burden'"); Brief of Amici Curiae Religious Liberty Law Scholars in Support of Petition for a Writ of Certiorari, *Navajo Nation v. United States Forest Serv.*, 535 F.3d 1058 (2008), available at www.scotusblog.com/wp/wp-content/uploads/2009/05/08-846_cert_amicus_scholars.pdf at 4–7 (ditto).
147. *Navajo Nation v. United States Forest Serv.*, 535 F.3d at 1065.
148. *Navajo Nation v. United States Forest Serv.*, 535 F.3d at 1111 (J. Fletcher dissenting).
149. *Id.* at 1082.
150. *Id.* at 1113. Professor Kristen A. Carpenter, who has done a series of articles on the religious rights of non-Indian owners, tellingly begins one Article on sacred site jurisprudence by calling attention to the fact that "through varied means of acquisition, non-Indian governments, entities, and individuals have come to own Indian sacred sites." Kristen A. Carpenter, "Old Ground and New Directions at Sacred Sites on the Western Landscape," *Denver University Law Review* 83 (2006): 981–1002, at 983. *See also* Carpenter, Katyal and Riley, "In Defense of Property," *supra* note 131 (focused on protecting indigenous cultural rights through property interests); Kristen A. Carpenter, "A Property Rights Approach to Sacred Sites Cases: Asserting a Place for Indians as Nonowners," *UCLA Law Review* 52 (2005): 1061–1148.
151. *But see* Knapp, "Making Snow in the Desert," *supra* note 135, at 306–311 (critiquing Justice Fletcher's approach to the case).
152. *Navajo Nation v. United States Forest Serv.*, 2009 LEXIS 4206, 77 U.S.L.W. 3668 (US June 8, 2009). *See also* James M. Grijalva, *Closing the Circle: Environmental Justice in Indian Country* (Durham, North Carolina: Carolina Academic Press, 2008), 172 ("the Court's modern role is not to seek justice delayed for Indian people, but rather to ensure those who benefit from a nation built on land and natural resources acquired from Tribes by force, threats, artifice and fraud continue to do so").
153. The *amicus* certiorari petition brief submitted by the National Congress of the American Indian draws parallels between how Indians view the San Francisco Peaks and the importance for non-Indians of sacred sites around the world and asks: "If Mount Calvary, the Holy Mosque in Mecca, or the Wailing Wall were located on public lands in the United States, would they be denied protection under RFRA in the same manner as the San Francisco Peaks?" Brief of Amici Curiae National Congress of American Indians et al in support of petitioners, *Navajo Nation v. United States Forest Serv.*, 535

F.3d 1058 (2008), available at www.scotusblog.com/wp/wp-content/uploads/2009/05/08-846_cert_amicus_indians.pdf, at 17.

154. Leslie MacMillian, "Discolored Slopes Mar Debut of Snow-Making Effort," *New York Times Green Blog*, Jan. 11, 2013, https://green.blogs.nytimes.com/2013/01/11/discolored-slopes-mar-debut-of-snow-making-effort/.

155. Duquette, "Don't Eat the Brown Snow! Utilizing Wastewater for Artificial Snow," *supra* note 136, at 132.

156. *See* Emily Cowan, "US Tribe Fights Use of Treated Sewage to Make Snow on Holy Peaks," *The Guardian*, Feb. 15, 2018 (showing the warning sign).

157. Petition to the Inter-American Commission on Human Rights submitted by the Navajo Nation against the United States of America (Mar. 2, 2015): 4. Available at www.nnhrc.navajo-nsn.gov/docs/sacredsites/Navajo%20Nation%20Petition%20to%20IACHR%20March%202%202015.pdf.

158. Presidential Proclamation: Establishment of the Bears Ears National Monument, Dec. 28, 2016, https://obamawhitehouse.archives.gov/the-press-office/2016/12/28/proclamation-establishment-bears-ears-national-monument.

159. Robinson Meyer, "It's More Than Just a Monument," *The Atlantic*, Dec. 4, 2017.

160. Charles Wilkinson, "'At Bears Ears We Can Hear the Voices of Our Ancestors in Every Canyon and on Every Mesa Top': The Creation of the First Native National Monument," *Arizona State Law Journal* 50 (2018): 317–333, at 329.

161. *Id.* at 323–324; Sarah Krakoff, "Public Lands, Conservation, and the Possibility of Justice," *Harvard Civil Rights-Civil Liberties Law Review* 53 (2018): 213–258, at 242.

162. Krakoff, "Public Lands, Conservation, and the Possibility of Justice," *supra* note 161, at 243–244.

163. Wilkinson, "At Bears Ears We Can Hear the Voices of Our Ancestors in Every Canyon and on Every Mesa Top," *supra* note 160, at 324.

164. Krakoff, "Public Lands, Conservation, and the Possibility of Justice," *supra* note 161, at 244.

165. Bears Ears Inter-Tribal Coalitions, *Proposal to President Barack Obama for the Creation of Bears Ears National Monument* (2015), 1.

166. *Id.* at 21–34.

167. Krakoff, "Public Lands, Conservation, and the Possibility of Justice," *supra* note 161, at 250.

168. *Id.* at 255.

169. Presidential Proclamation: Modifying the Bears Ears National Monument, Dec. 4, 2017, www.whitehouse.gov/presidential-actions/presidential-proclamation-modifying-bears-ears-national-monument/.

170. *Id.*

171. Meyer, "It's More Than Just a Monument," *supra* note 159.

172. See US Department of the Interior, Bureau of Land Management, U.S. Department of Agriculture, US Forest Service, *Bears Ears National Monument: Proposed Monument Management Plans and Final Environmental Impact Statement Shash Jáa and Indian Creek Units* (Washington, DC: Bureau of Land Management, July 2019). See also EarthJustice, "Trump Administration Releases New Plan for What's Left of Bears Ears," July 26, 2019, https://earthjustice.org/news/press/2019/trump-administration-new-plan-for-bears-ears.

173. *See* Tony Semerad, "Federal Judge Declines to Dismiss Bears Ears Lawsuit," *The Salt Lake Tribune*, Oct. 4, 2019.

174. Wilkinson, "At Bears Ears We Can Hear the Voices of Our Ancestors in Every Canyon and on Every Mesa Top," *supra* note 160, at 333.

175. Krakoff, "Public Lands, Conservation, and the Possibility of Justice," *supra* note 161, at 258.

176. For an artist depiction of the proposed tramway, see Eric Betz, "Controversy at the Confluence," *Arizona Daily Sun*, Oct. 22, 2013.

177. Ron Dungan, "Is a Gondola Ride in the Grand Canyon's Future?," *Arizona Republic*, Apr. 18, 2017.

178. *Id.*

179. Cindy Yurth and Duane Beyal, "Targeting the Confluence," *Navajo Times*, June 14, 2012.

180. Lynda L. Butler, "Property as a Management Institution," *Brooklyn Law Review* 82 (2017): 1215–1274, at 1232.

181. As an Associated Press article reported, opponents called the proposed development "a monster." Felicia Fonseca, "Tribe Rejects Plan to Build Tram, Hotel in Grand Canyon," *Chicago Daily Herald*, Nov. 1, 2017.

182. 23rd Navajo Nation Council Office of the Speaker, "Navajo Nation Council Votes Down the Grand Canyon Escalade Project Bill," Press Release (Oct. 31, 2017). *See also* Editorial, "Navajo Do the Right Thing by the Grand Canyon," *Salt Lake Tribune*, Nov. 4, 2017.

183. Andrew Guilford, "Protecting the Sacred: Navajo Nation Buys Land at Revered Peak in Colorado," *Durango Herald*, Feb. 10, 2018.

184. Cindy Yurth, "Tribal Ranches: Too Much or Not Enough?," *Navajo Times*, Aug. 29, 2019.

185. *Id.*

12 CONCLUSION

1. *See* Lloyd L. Lee, *Diné Identity in a Twenty-First-Century World* (Tucson: University of Arizona Press, 2020), 95 ("Diné peoples and communities have had to adjust to many challenges, from relocation to livestock reduction to uranium mining to oppression, yet they have always sustained their identity."); *Id.* at 59 ("For hundreds of years, Diné people have sustained their way of life. They had to deal with many challenges, including Spanish encroachment, Mexican settlement, and an American invasion.").

2. Alexandra Sternlicht, "Navajo Nation Has Most Coronavirus Infections Per Capita in U.S., Beating New York, New Jersey," *Forbes*, May 19, 2020.

3. Simon Romero, "Checkpoints, Curfews, Airlifts: Virus Rips Through Navajo Nation," *New York Times*, Apr. 9, 2020.

4. *See* Scott Maier, "UCSF Health Care Workers to Serve in Navajo Nation," *UCSF News*, Apr. 22, 2020, https://www.ucsf.edu/news/2020/04/417236/ucsf-health-care-workers-serve-navajo-nation; Nathan Weiler, "UCSF Sends Second Wave of Health Care Workers to Navajo Nation," *UCSF News*, May 21, 2020, https://www.ucsf.edu/news/2020/05/417506/ucsf-sends-second-wave-health-workers-navajo-nation.

5. *See, e.g.*, Advertisement page A12, *Navajo Times*, May 28, 2020.

6. As Ethel Branch noted in an interview about her Navajo-focused COVID19 relief efforts, she "knew when it hit us, it would be really bad so we had to get prepared." Nina Lakhani, "'It Warms the Heart': Navajo Mount Grassroots Effort to Tackle Coronavirus," *The Guardian*, Apr. 2, 2020.

7. Kalen Goodluck, "COVID-19 Impacts Every Corner of the Navajo Nation," *High Country News*, May 19, 2020. For extended discussion of federal neglect of the funding needs of Indian tribes, see U S Commission on Civil Rights, *Broken Promises: Continuing Federal Funding Shortfall for Native Americans* (Washington, DC: US Commission on Civil Rights, Briefing Report Dec. 2018).

8. Zamir Brown, "The Navajo Nation Responds to COVID-19," *National Health Law Program*, Apr. 15, 2020, https://healthlaw.org/the-navajo-nation-responds-to-covid-19/.

9. Robert Klemko, "Coronavirus Has Been Devastating to the Navajo Nation, and Help for a Complex Fight Has Been Slow," *Washington Post*, May 16, 2020. COVID19 does not affect all groups equally. As experience with the virus grew, health researchers found comparative disadvantage means that "members of several racial, ethnic, and social and economic groups are at much higher risk of coronavirus infection and hospitalization and death from COVID-19 than others." Jake Miller, "Unequal Destroyer: COVID-19 Health Disparities and the Search for Solutions," *Harvard Medical School News and Research*, Sep. 23, 2020, https://hms.harvard.edu/news/unequal-destroyer. *See also* Samantha Artiga, "Growing Data Underscore that Communities of Color are Being Harder Hit by COVID-19," *Kaiser Family Foundation Policy Watch*, Apr. 21, 2020, https://www.kff.org/policy-watch/growing-data-underscore-communities-color-harder-hit-covid-19/.

10. Juana Summers, "Timeline: How Trump Has Downplayed The Coronavirus Pandemic," *National Public Radio*, Oct. 2, 2020, https://www.npr.org/sections/latest-updates-trump-covid-19-results/2020/10/02/919432383/how-trump-has-downplayed-the-coronavirus-pandemic.

11. Sahir Doshi et al., *The COVID-19 Response in Indian Country: A Federal Failure* (Washington, D.C.: Center for American Progress, June 18, 2020), https://www.americanprogress.org/issues/green/reports/2020/06/18/486480/covid-19-response-indian-country/. The delay was in part the result of the federal government's position that Alaska Native Corporations were eligible for CARES Act funding, a position that tribes challenged in court. *See* Mark Walker & Emily Cochrane, "Native American Tribes Sue Treasury Over Stimulus Aid as They Feud Over Funding," *New York Times*, May 1, 2020.

12. *See* Arlyssa Becenti, "Nez's Plan OK'd, with Changes," *Navajo Times*, June 25, 2020.

13. Percy Deal, "Letter-to-the-Editor: Stop the Relief Infighting," *Navajo Times*, June 11, 2020.

14. Press Release, "President Approves $475 million in CARES Act Funding to Provide Immediate COVID-19 Relief Funding for Water Projects, Power Line Projects, and More," *The Navajo Nation Office of the President and Vice President*, Aug. 18, 2020, www.navajo-nsn.gov/News%20Releases/OPVP/2020/Aug/FOR%20IMMEDIATE%20RELEASE%20-%20President%20approves%20475%20million%20in%20CARES%20Act%20funding%20to%20provide%20immediate%20COVID-19%20relief%20funding%20for%20water%20projects_power%20line%20projects_and%20more.pdf.

15. Jen Kirby, "US Native Tribes and Ireland's 170-year-old Connection is Renewed in the Pandemic," *Vox.com*, May 13, 2020, www.vox.com/2020/5/13/21251420/choctaw-ireland-navajo-hopi-gofundme-coronavirus.

16. Dana Hedgpeth, "The Irish are Repaying a Favor from 173 Years Ago in Native Americans' Fight Against Coronavirus," *Washington Post*, May 13, 2020.

17. Jason Swarner, "Mark Ruffalo, Jason Momoa, and Other Celebs Among Those Donating to Navajo Nation," *Copper Courier*, May 14, 2020, https://coppercourier.com/story/mark-ruffalo-jason-momoa-navajo-nation/.

18. Shira Feder, "One Navajo Woman has Raised Thousands of Dollars for the Navajo Nation's Fight Against the Coronavirus, as Officials Warn Reservations Could Be Hit

Hard by the Pandemic," *Insider.com*, Mar. 30, 2020, https://www.insider.com/former-navajo-attorney-general-raising-money-to-fight-covid-19-2020-3.

19. *See* Staff Reports, "COVID-19 Relief Fund Marks Three Months Providing Relief for Navajo, Hopi Families," *Gallup Sun*, June 19, 2020.

20. *See* Lakhani, *supra* note 6; Mara Santilli, "In Navajo Nation, Women Are on the Front Lines of COVID-19," *Marie Claire*, May 15, 2020.

21. *See, e.g.*, Rima Krisst, "Dueling Relief Groups at Odds," *Navajo Times*, June 4, 2020.

22. Rima Krisst, "Fauci: Navajo a Model for Containing Coronavirus," *Navajo Times*, Sept. 24, 2020.

23. David Wilkins, "Governance within the Navajo Nation: Have Democratic Traditions Taken Hold?," *Wicazo Sa Review* 17, no.1 (2002): 91–129, at 111. *See also* James Coates, "A Tribe at War," *Chicago Tribune*, Mar. 27, 1989.

24. *See* Elizabeth Reese, "The Other American Law," *Stanford Law Review* 73 (2021), 38–39 (pagination from draft of manuscript available at https://papers.ssrn.com/sol3/papers.cfm?abstract_id=3660166) (describing the turmoil).

25. Wilkins, "Governance within the Navajo Nation," *supra* note 23, at 113; Lloyd L. Lee, "The Future of Navajo Nationalism," *Wicazo Sa Review* 22, no.1 (2007): 53–68, at 58.

26. *See infra* Chapter 6.

27. *See* Associated Press, "Arizona Miners Rally at Capitol to Save Navajo Generating Station," *KNAU Arizona Public Radio*, June 6, 2018.

28. For more on tribal differences and the significance of those differences, see Saikrishna Prakash, "Against Tribal Fungibility," *Cornell Law Review* 89 (2004), 1069–1120.

29. This is an argument I explore in more detail elsewhere. *See* Ezra Rosser, "Ambiguity and the Academic: The Dangerous Attraction of Pan-Indian Legal Analysis," *Harvard Law Review Forum* 119 (2006): 141–147.

30. President Richard Nixon, Special Message on Indian Affairs to Congress (July 8, 1970).

31. This conclusion is not a new one but instead is something I have advocated for more than fifteen years. *See* Ezra Rosser, "The Trade-off Between Self-Determination and the Trust Doctrine: Tribal Government and the Possibility of Failure," *Arkansas Law Review* 58 (2005), 291–352.

32. For a great exploration of how US Supreme Court holdings limit the power of the Navajo Nation, see Sarah Krakoff, "A Narrative of Sovereignty: Illuminating the Paradox of the Domestic Dependent Nation," *Oregon Law Review* 83, no.4 (2005): 1109–1202.

33. Tellingly, although the United States has never officially apologized for its treatment of Diné, President Donald Trump in September 2020 signed an executive order that attacked trainings about American history that foreground matters of race. *See, e.g.*, The White House, Executive Order on Combating Race and Sex Stereotyping (Sep. 22, 2020), www.whitehouse.gov/presidential-actions/executive-order-combating-race-sex-stereotyping/ (declaring that federal funds cannot be used to teach "divisive concepts," including the idea that "the United States is fundamentally racist or sexist").

34. These fears are similar to the effect that termination arguably plays in the range of policies that Indian nations consider. As the leading Indian law textbook notes: "The termination policy adopted by the federal government following these events had a major impact on the attitudes of subsequent generations of Indian leadership. Though now formally repudiated by the federal government, the memory of congressional committees and bureaucrats in Washington 'terminating' the existence of hundreds of tribes across Indian country stands as a chilling reminder to Indian peoples that Congress can unilaterally decide to extinguish the special status and rights of tribes without Indian consent."

David H. Getches et al., *Cases and Materials on Federal Indian Law*, 7th ed. (St. Paul, Minnesota: West Publishing Company, 2017), 230.

35. As a coauthor of the leading poverty law textbook, I know quite well the limits and problems of the US approach to welfare. *See* Juliet Brodie, Clare Pastore, Ezra Rosser, and Jeffrey Selbin, *Poverty Law, Policy, and Practice*, 2nd ed. (Philadelphia, Pennsylvania: Wolters Kluwer, 2021). But even with their many faults, welfare programs continue to provide a limited safety net that should allow the Navajo Nation to take on some governance risks. *See also Holes in the Safety Net: Federalism and Poverty*, Ezra Rosser ed. (New York: Cambridge University Press, 2019) (highlighting ways that federalism leads to differences in welfare rights across states).

36. *See generally* Stephen Cornell and Joseph P. Kalt. "Two Approaches to Economic Development on American Indian Reservations: One Works, the Other Doesn't," in *Rebuilding Native Nations: Strategies for Governance and Development*, Miriam Jorgensen ed. (Tucson: University of Arizona Press, 2007), 3–33.

37. *See also* Michael Lerma, *Guided by the Mountains: Navajo Political Philosophy and Governance* (New York: Oxford University Press, 2017), 186 ("The Diné are in the best position to evaluate proposals for reform based on traditional Diné values.").

Acknowledgments

Every academic work is an act of love in one way or another. This book is itself the coming together of over a decade of work and study, so please forgive me for the fairly extensive nature of this thank you section. My work has benefited from the tremendous support of many faculty members, friends, and institutions. I will begin with my professors. It is nearly impossible for me to overstate my gratitude to Robert A. Williams, Jr. at the University of Arizona and Dean S. James Anaya at the University of Colorado. They continue to show me what one can accomplish as a law professor and were instrumental in helping me in my understanding of Indian issues and in advancing my career. This book similarly would not have been possible without the mentorship of Duncan Kennedy and Joseph Singer, both of Harvard Law School. Finally, my interest in the relationship between property/land use and economic development owes much to the inspired teaching of Daniel Ernst of Georgetown University Law Center and Shailaja Fennell of the University of Cambridge.

Over the years I have been teaching I have been the beneficiary of unbelievable institutional generosity and support. At Loyola University New Orleans, and with the support of Dean Brian Bromberger and Professors Mary Algero and Patrick Hugg, I refined my work on economic theory and Navajo economic development. Besides giving me the opportunity to come to love Kyoto, Japan, teaching at Ritsumeiken University provided me time and space needed to work on this project. I am now in my sixteenth year teaching at American University Washington College of Law and given that amount of time it is impossible to express my gratitude fully to everyone – from Maria who cleaned my office to Deans Claudio Grossman, Camille Nelson, and Robert Dinerstein – who helped make this book a reality. But this is an academic work so it is worth highlighting the phenomenal support of the librarians at Pence Law Library as well as the financial support of the Dean's Office.

And finally, my students: when I started teaching, I somewhat felt that teaching was what one does so that one can write but I have since discovered that teaching is amazingly rewarding and inspiring in its own right. Unlike at schools such as the University of Arizona or the University of New Mexico, very few Native students attend American University Washington College of Law, but I have still benefited from the passion, humor, and public interest commitments of countless students. I benefited from the inspiring example of a number of my former students who have gone on to work in Indian law: Adjua Adjei-Danso, Austin Badger, Connie Kim Briggs, Robert Conrad, Nick Cross, Leo Crippa, Colby Duren, Richael Faithful, Deanna Glickman, Mariah McKay, Abby Okrent, Jimmy Qaqundah, Nicholas Ravotti, Lillian Schwales, and Thomas Zlamal. Thanks also to the many research assistants who helped with this book: Shadia Ajam, Felicia Brown, Marissa Forte, Deanna Glickman, James Harrison, Drew Lavine, Elizabeth Leman, Spencer McGinty, Alia Mokaddem, Jesse Spiegel, Jacob Wohl, and Kailin Wu. A special thanks to Oliver Jury who read every chapter and whose editing made a tremendous difference. Thanks as well to the reviewers – some anonymous, some not – who took the time to consider this book. I did not follow all of the suggestions that I was given, if I had this would have been a very different book, but it is undoubtedly a better book because of the many great comments I received as part of the process of getting this to press.

This book is dedicated to my parents, James Rosser and Norma Cady. When I was younger, in many ways my goal was to be the opposite of them: to get as far away from the reservation as possible and to be able to worry less about money than them. But as I got older, I realized that children whose parents fight over who gets to spend more time with them in many ways are lucky children, even if frozen pizzas and macaroni and cheese were too much the staples. I also realized that I ended up following in their footsteps. My father and mother moved to the reservation almost as a matter of happenstance, they were not drawn there as some white people are because of romanticized notions of Indians but because it was only on the reservation that they found work. My father taught in public and BIA schools in Kayenta, Cove, and Red Valley, and my mother worked for Navajo Superfund, Navajo Department of Agriculture, Navajo EPA, and Navajo Community Economic Development. After briefly flirting with the idea of becoming a professional photographer, I moved into teaching Indian law and writing about tribal land use and economic development. Nobody wants to become their parents, but there are worse things. I am now a parent and better understand that a parent's love can never be repaid. But here I want to thank them for exposing me to the reservation as a child and for encouraging and supporting my explorations of Navajo issues as an adult.

This book is also dedicated to my dad's second wife, Zelma King. My understanding of, and commitment to, the Navajo Nation has benefited from the guidance and support of numerous Navajos and non-Navajos. My dad remarried late enough in my childhood that his wife, Zelma, was always more of a person than a direct relative to me, but I am very grateful for her continual help understanding everything from Navajo words to Navajo family structure. More importantly, Zelma provided my father a way to happily make the reservation home and I am very thankful that their home continues to be a home for me and my family whenever we come to visit. It is a long drive from Albuquerque airport to Kerr-McGee Road, but it is worth it.

Finally, as every academic knows, writing a book requires many things, but one of those things is time. Time away from family, time spent staring at a computer instead of helping to parent, and time spent mired in a combination of frustration and stress. I tried to find the right balance between time spent on this project and time with my wife and children, and partly for that reason this book took a long time to write. But I apologize and ask forgiveness for the times I struck the balance wrong or made the wrong choices. Elvia Maria Castro Galo de Rosser, Mateo Sebastian Rosser Castro, and Mario Andrés Rosser Castro, you are my life and I love you so much. Gracias por todo y te amo infinito.

Index

Made in United States
North Haven, CT
08 March 2022

16931593R00180